DAY BY DAY
VOLUME 2

Day by Day

VOLUME 2

>> The Bible Reading Fellowship

Text copyright © The Bible Reading Fellowship 1994

Published by
The Bible Reading Fellowship
Peter's Way
Sandy Lane West
Oxford OX4 5HG
ISBN 0 7459 2999 0
Albatross Books Pty Ltd
PO Box 320, Sutherland
NSW 2232, Australia
ISBN 0 7324 0910 1

First edition 1994

Acknowledgments

Good News Bible copyright © American Bible Society 1966, 1971 and 1976, published by the Bible Societies and Collins.

The Alternative Service Book 1980 copyright © The Central Board of Finance of the Church of England.

The Jerusalem Bible copyright © 1966, 1967 and 1968 by Darton, Longman & Todd Ltd and Doubleday & Company, Inc.

The New Jerusalem Bible copyright © 1985 by Darton, Longman & Todd Ltd and Doubleday & Company, Inc.

The *Revised Standard Version* of the Bible, copyright © 1946, 1952, 1971 by the Division of Christian Education of the National Council of the Churches of Christ in the USA.

The *New Revised Standard Version* of the Bible, copyright © 1989 by the Division of Christian Education of the National Council of the Churches of Christ in the USA.

The Holy Bible, *New International Version*, copyright © 1973, 1978, 1984 by International Bible Society. Used by permission of Hodder and Stoughton Limited.

Extracts from the Book of Common Prayer of 1662, the rights in which are invested in the Crown in perpetuity within the United Kingdom, are reproduced by permission of the Crown's patentee, Cambridge University Press.

The Holy Bible, *Living Bible Edition*, copyright © Tyndale House Publishers 1971, published by Kingsway.

Extracts from the *Authorized Version* of the Bible (The King James Bible), the rights of which are vested in the Crown, are reproduced by permission of the Crown's Patentee, Cambridge University Press.

New English Bible, © 1970 by permission of Oxford and Cambridge University Presses.

Revised English Bible © 1989 by permission of Oxford and Cambridge University Presses.

A catalogue record for this book is available from the British Library

Printed and bound in Slovenia

Contents

Introduction

This is a second volume of Bible readings and prayers to take you day by day through the year. The readings have been taken out of different issues of *New Daylight*, and you can start reading at any time and at any place in the book.

If you happen to start at the beginning, on New Year's Day, you will end up at the end of the year with Bible readings for the season of Christmas. If you want to start somewhere in the middle, and still read about Easter and Pentecost at the right time, you can work out where you are by looking at the dates of Easter and counting backwards or forwards from there.

In 1995 Easter Sunday will be on April 16; in 1996 on April 7; in 1997 on March 30; and in 1998 on April 12.

In between Christmas, Easter and Pentecost you will read more about the Christian story. A true story—told through the sacred history of the Jewish people, through events, prophecies, poetry and visions. A story that is also a love story, about the love of God for the whole world. Like all stories, it is told through words. Words that are what the Bible calls 'The word of God', and 'The word of life.'

'Let the word of God dwell in your richly' wrote the Apostle Paul to the Colossians (3:19), and the more richly we let that happen the richer our relationship with God will be.

That is the whole reason for reading. Not just to get information about the Christian faith, but to let the words lead us to the living God. So day by day the Bible reading and the comment will lead us into prayer.

My prayer and my hope is that as you read *Day by Day* you will be blessed through it and find that it really does enrich your spiritual life and your relationship with God.

Shelagh Brown
Editor, *New Daylight*

The life of faith

The life of faith starts with just one human being who hears the voice of God and obeys it. Obeys because he or she is drawn by the love of God and has seen something of the glory of God. That is where it starts for us and where it started for Abraham. God called him to go on a journey—and he calls all of us to do the same. But it isn't a solitary journey. It is a journey with God and into God.

So Abraham's journey seemed a good place to begin the New Year—and we shall travel along with him for four weeks. As we do, we can reflect on our own journey so far, and if we seem to have got a bit stuck we can make a fresh start. And we can discover how other people set out on their journey, and find out what happened to them along the way.

The great doctrines of the faith are all there in the story of Abraham. 'To him the unchanging God revealed himself, teaching most clearly lessons which are relevant today because they are timeless ... God's dealing with the patriarchs, and with Abraham especially, enable us to grasp the major themes of Scripture. Despite the lapse of time and the immense differences that separate the world of the patriarchs from our own, their god is our God, and he speaks to us today through his word to them' (Joyce G. Baldwin, *The Message of Genesis 12–52: from Abraham to Joseph*).

After our four weeks with Abraham we shall spend three weeks studying the letter of James. People sometimes think that Abraham and James contradict each other. Abraham seems to be all about faith and James seems to be all about works and actions. But there isn't really any conflict between James and the great Pauline doctrine of justification by faith. And the statements that James makes are totally in line with the teaching of Jesus. Jesus said, 'By their fruits you shall know them,' and James is saying, 'I'll show you what I am by what I do.'

Where the blessing begins

Now the Lord said to Abram, 'Go from your country and your kindred and your father's house to the land that I will show you. And I will make of you a great nation, and I will bless you, and make your name great, so that you will be a blessing. I will bless those who bless you, and him who curses you I will curse; and by you all the families of the earth shall bless themselves.'

The Bible is full of new beginnings and fresh starts. They happen at just the critical time—at the point of a person's or a nation's greatest need. At every new beginning a human being hears the voice of God and obeys it. If they disobey, there is no new start and no blessing. Abram hears and obeys, and the blessing of God starts to flow like a river—not just to him but to the whole of the world.

The word bless (or blessing) comes five times in this passage, and God is the one who blesses. When a person is blessed it means that those things happen to them which are conducive to their happiness. When Jesus began the Sermon on the Mount with the beatitudes, he was telling us how we can be really blessed and really happy. The promise that God made to Abram had three parts to it. He would make him a great nation, he would give him a great name, and he would give him such a relationship with himself that through it all the families of the earth would bless themselves. The relationship is crucial to the blessing— for Abraham and for us.

A prayer

Lord God, thank you for Abraham's relationship with you—and the blessing it brought to the world. Help me always to hear your voice—always to follow you—wherever you call me to go. Thank you for all the new beginnings and new starts that happen in my life. Not just in the big things, but in the small, ordinary, day-to-day things like painting the living room or just waking up in the morning to a new day. Be there for me, Lord, in my beginnings and in my endings. Bless me—and bless others through me.

SB

I will guide you . . .

So Abram went, as the Lord had told him; and Lot went with him. Abram was seventy-five years old when he departed from Haran. And Abram took Sarai his wife, and Lot his brother's son, and all their possessions which they had gathered, and the persons that they had gotten in Haran; and they set forth to go to the land of Canaan. When they had come to the land of Canaan, Abram passed through the land to the place at Shechem, to the oak of Moreh. At that time the Canaanites were in the land. Then the Lord appeared to Abram, and said, 'To your descendants I will give this land.' So he built there an altar to the Lord, who had appeared to him.

Abram did as he was told—and on his journey he came to the place in Canaan where there was a turpentine tree (a terebinth)—the famous 'oak of Moreh'. Moreh means 'oracle giver' and it was almost certainly a sacred tree. The Canaanites worshipped false gods— and took their guidance from them. A friend of mine from Africa, Jo, tells how his grandfather would throw down the bones of a chicken on to the floor of the tent when people from his village wanted guidance. It came through the way the bones arranged themselves— and Jo often saw them move after they had been thrown down. There was no doubt about it, so he found it bewildering when a sophisticated Christian minister arrived in his village and insisted it was simply imagination. Jo had seen these things happen, and he knew there was power there. He also knew that it was not the power of God.

It was God who was guiding Abram and in the face of the false gods the one, true God reiterated his promise to him:

'To your descendants I will give *this* land.' So Abram built an altar there—to the Lord of the whole earth—and worshipped the father of lights in the darkness of Canaan.

A thought

I will instruct you and teach you the way you should go; I will counsel you with my eye upon you.

Psalm 32:8

SB

11

A loss of faith

Now there was a famine in the land. So Abram went down to Egypt to sojourn there, for the famine was severe in the land. When he was about to enter Egypt, he said to Sarai his wife, 'I know that you are a woman beautiful to behold; and when the Egyptians see you, they will say, "This is his wife"; then they will kill me, but they will let you live. Say you are my sister, that it may go well with me because of you, and that my life may be spared on your account.' When Abram entered Egypt the Egyptians saw that the woman was very beautiful. And when the princes of Pharaoh saw her, they praised her to Pharaoh. And the woman was taken into Pharaoh's house. And for her sake he dealt well with Abram; and he had sheep, oxen, he-asses, menservants, maidservants, she-asses, and camels.

The fact that we have set out to follow Christ does not exempt us from suffering, and it didn't exempt Abram. He had obeyed the call of God to leave his country and his kindred and his father's house—and now his obedience had brought him to a land where there was a famine. Perhaps he asked 'Why?'—as we do, when we have set out in faith and things start to go wrong through no fault of our own. If we are being disobedient it is understandable. But if we are being obedient then it isn't—or at least not immediately. Not until we remember that the Son of God 'learned obedience through the things that he suffered' (Hebrews 5:8).

So it isn't surprising that we have to suffer. We don't like it, and neither did Abram. He was frightened. Frightened that the Egyptians would kill him and take Sarai. So he told her to say she was his sister. She was in fact his half-sister—but she was also his wife, and what he asked her to do was utterly wrong. Abraham, the great man of faith in the Old Testament, has lost this faith in the ability of God to look after him. I find that a real comfort for the times when my faith almost fails me...

A prayer

Lord Jesus Christ, help me to trust in you when the going gets tough and I start to lose faith in your promises. Help me to hold on to you . . . and to know that you will never let me go.

SB

Abram, why?

But the Lord afflicted Pharaoh and his house with great plagues because of Sarai, Abram's wife. So Pharaoh called Abram, and said, 'What is this you have done to me? Why did you not tell me that she was your wife? Why did you say, "She is my sister," so that I took her for my wife? Now then, here is your wife, take her, and be gone.' And Pharaoh gave men orders concerning him; and they set him on the way, with his wife and all that he had. So Abram went up from Egypt, he and his wife, and all that he had, and Lot with him, into the Negeb.

Sometimes people who don't believe in God behave much better than people who do—and that is what happens here. The great man of faith has lost his faith and is full of fear—and the Pharaoh shows that his standard of ethics is higher than Abram had thought it was. He tells Abram off—and behaves with great dignity and generosity.

He had given Abram 'sheep, oxen, male donkeys, male and female slaves, female donkeys, and camels' (12:16)—a big bride price for a beautiful bride. But he had to give her back to Abram—and he didn't ask for the bride price back. He told Abram to take Sarai and go—so the whole party set off back to the Negeb.

It was an astonishing episode, especially since Pharaoh's whole household had suffered because of Sarai—when the Lord afflicted them with great plagues.

Perhaps the Lord spoke to the Egyptian king in a dream to tell him the truth that Abram had so pathetically failed to tell him. They knew about dreams in those days, and believed in them (and in our day we are rediscovering their importance and power).

Reflect

What do you think of Abram's action? What do you think of Pharaoh's? And what do you think of God's? Do you realize that a wrong action on your part can involve other people in suffering? And can you think of any instances of this—in your own life, or in anyone else's?

Choosing

Now Abram was very rich in cattle, in silver, and in gold . . . And Lot, who went with Abram, also had flocks and herds and tents, so that the land could not support both of them dwelling together . . . and there was strife between the herdsmen of Abram's cattle and the herdsmen of Lot's cattle . . . Then Abram said to Lot, 'Let there be no strife between you and me, and between your herdsmen and my herdsmen; for we are kinsmen. Is not the whole land before you? Separate yourself from me. If you take the left hand, then I will go to the right; or if you take the right hand, then I will go to the left.' And Lot lifted up his eyes, and saw that the Jordan valley was well watered everywhere like the garden of the Lord . . . So Lot chose for himself all the Jordan valley . . .

Abram is behaving much better in today's passage. He is being generous to Lot, and letting him choose whichever part of the land he likes. And Lot looks round, and sees the richness and the beauty of the Jordan Valley, and chooses the whole of that. In the sub-tropical fertility of the valley he and his family will enjoy a prosperous lifestyle—so he goes down the hill to the rich plain 3,000 feet below. But it is a wicked place, with a reputation for evil, and Lot moves his tent as far as Sodom, and lives among the cities of the plain.

Sometimes, when I walk in the most beautiful parts of London, I enjoy the elegance of the houses—perfectly proportioned, with lovely curtains draped at the windows, with frilled and flounced pelmets—and outside stone-paved courtyards with urns of beautiful, colourful flowers—and perfectly painted front doors with polished brass letterboxes and handles. Then I start to wonder what goes on behind the doors—and what God sees in the hearts of the people who live there. Lot looked on the surface of things, but beauty outside can sometimes be the front of ugliness inside.

A prayer

Lord Jesus, help me to see to the heart of things—so that I see as you see—and choose the things that are right.

SB

Our inheritance

The Lord said to Abram, after Lot had separated from him, 'Lift up your eyes, and look from the place where you are, northward and southward and eastward and westward; for all the land which you see I will give to you and to your descendants for ever. I will make your descendants as the dust of the earth; so that if one can count the dust of the earth, your descendants also can be counted. Arise, walk through the length and the breadth of the land, for I will give it to you.' So Abram moved his tent, and came and dwelt by the oaks of Mamre, which are at Hebron; and there he built an altar to the Lord.

When Jesus told of his Father's care for us he said 'Seek first his kingdom and his righteousness, and all these things will be given to you as well' (Matthew 6:33), and he said it after telling people not to worry about what they wore or what they were to eat. The much-loved song based on that verse links it with Luke 11, and says 'Ask and it shall be given unto you, Seek and you shall find, Knock and the door shall be opened unto you, Allelu, Alleluia.'

But we don't always get what we ask for and pray so hard for. We don't always find what we are looking for. And the door that we long to be opened to us sometimes remains firmly shut. Then it isn't easy to keep faith. It isn't for us, and it cannot have been for Abram. God had promised to give him the land of Canaan—and now he sees Lot possessing one of the most fertile parts of it (even if it is full of wicked men)—while Abram is stuck on the stony heights. But God tells him to look all round him and promises again to give him *all* the land—and God tells him to walk through the whole of the land and to make a pilgrimage of faith. He was to check out his inheritance—and we can do the same.

A prayer

'I pray that . . . you may know what is the hope to which he has called you, what are the riches of his glorious inheritance among the saints . . .'

Ephesians 1:18

SB

Winners and losers

Then the king[s] of Sodom..., Gomorrah... Admah... Zeboiim and... Bela... went out, and they joined battle in the Valley of Siddim with [the kings of]... Elam... Goiim... Shinar and... Ellasar, four kings against five. Now the Valley of Siddim was full of bitumen pits; and as the kings of Sodom and Gomorrah fled, some fell into them, and the rest fled to the mountain. So the enemy took all the goods of Sodom and Gomorrah, and all their provisions, and went their way; they also took Lot, the son of Abram's brother, who dwelt in Sodom, and his goods, and departed... When Abram heard that his kinsman had been taken captive, he led forth his trained men, born in his house... and went in pursuit... And he divided his forces against them by night, he and his servants, and routed them... Then he brought back all the goods, and also brought back his kinsman Lot.

Some experts on the human condition divide the world up into two categories—winners and losers—and on that analysis Abram is a winner, and Lot a loser. The transactional analysts who make this division say there are three ways for a loser to turn into a winner: through the help of a transactional analyst; through falling in love; and through a religious conversion. In those situations we start to listen to a different voice from the destructive voice that told us we were no good— and the loser is transformed into a winner. The voice that Abram listened to was the voice of God—so he set off to rescue loser Lot—and he won. Winners make plans and carry them out, and they train for the tasks that they have to do. Winners win even when they are in prison—like Joseph in the Old Testament and Paul in the New. Winners win even when they lose their life. Like the martyrs—and like Jesus.

A prayer

Father God, I want to be a winner and not a loser. Help me to hear your voice and to obey it—in faith. Like Abraham—like Paul— and like your Son.

SB

16

Tension

For I received from the Lord what I also delivered to you, that the Lord Jesus on the night when he was betrayed took bread, and when he had given thanks, he broke it, and said, 'This is my body which is for you. Do this in remembrance of me.' In the same way also the cup, after supper, saying, 'This cup is the new covenant in my blood. Do this, as often as you drink it, in remembrance of me.' For as often as you eat this bread and drink the cup, you proclaim the Lord's death until he comes.

I have never ceased to be amazed at the original circumstances in which the Holy Communion, that central and most sacred act of Christian worship, was instituted. We might have expected it to have been the result of lengthy and detailed planning bolstered by committee work. But no, it was unexpected by the apostles. There was no advance publicity. The time and place were kept a close secret. Furthermore, we might have expected 'the atmosphere' of the occasion to be safeguarded, but it wasn't. Instead from start to finish there was tension, and the apostles disputing over the seating (reclining) arrangements. And then Jesus, the host of the occasion, not making an entry with ceremony but with a basin of water and a towel tied round 'his middle'. Worse to come, he started washing each one's feet in turn. They all kicked off their sandals. Not many feet are beautiful or capable of inspiring lofty thoughts. And then the shocking announcement that this was the *last* supper. And then the truly bewildering prediction that one of their own number would betray him to his enemies. Did some hands reach to see if swords were handy? There were two in that room!

Read the above verses again.

If you come to your Holy Communion today ill-prepared, tense, flustered or frightened about something, don't think the Lord's table is no place for you. It all began in an atmosphere like that. But Jesus was there.

DCF

Priest of God Most High

After his return from the defeat [of the kings], the king of Sodom went out to meet [Abram] at the Valley of Shaveh . . . And Melchizedek king of Salem brought out bread and wine; he was priest of God Most High. And he blessed him and said, 'Blessed be Abram by God Most High, maker of heaven and earth; and blessed be God Most High, who has delivered your enemies into your hand!'

This passage about Melchizedek is mysterious, and we must spend a day on it because of what the New Testament makes of it. The writer of the letter to the Hebrews says that the priesthood of Christ is like the priesthood of Melchizedek, who was both a priest and a king. His name means 'king of righteousness', and he is king of Salem, which means peace (and Jesus is the Prince of Peace). Melchizedek is a priest of the Most High God (so there were worshippers of the true God in existence at the time of Abram), and he brings out bread and wine and blesses Abram.

Scripture has nothing to say about Melchizedek's birth or his death—and the New Testament therefore sees him as having a priesthood without a beginning and without an end—and says that the priesthood of Christ is like that. Melchizedek's priesthood is greater than the Levitical priesthood; the New Testament writer of Hebrews works that out by arguing that Levi, who was the founding father of the Levitical priesthood, was a direct descendant of Abraham, and therefore in Abraham's loins when Melchizedek blessed him—and 'it is beyond dispute that the inferior is blessed by the superior' (Hebrews 7:7). The whole of that chapter, beginning with the last verse of chapter 6, is fascinating reading.

A prayer

Lord Jesus, this is a strange passage of Scripture. Help me to understand it—and help me to understand your eternal priesthood better because of it. Help me to reflect, now, on what it means—for me, and for your whole Church.

SB

Through faith

After these things the word of the Lord came to Abram in a vision, 'Fear not, Abram, I am your shield; your reward shall be very great.' But Abram said, 'O Lord God, what wilt thou give me, for I continue childless, and the heir of my house is Eliezer of Damascus?' And Abram said, 'Behold, thou hast given me no offspring; and a slave born in my house will be my heir.' And behold, the word of the Lord came to him, 'This man shall not be your heir; your own son shall be your heir.' And he brought him outside and said, 'Look toward heaven, and number the stars, if you are able to number them.' Then he said to him, 'So shall your descendants be.' And he believed the Lord; and he reckoned it to him as righteousness.

In his letter to the Romans Paul wrote the best commentary there has ever been on today's passage, so here it is—vital to an understanding of the doctrine of justification by faith.

'Hoping against hope, he believed that he would become "the father of many nations," according to what was said, "So numerous shall your descendants be." He did not weaken in faith when he considered his own body, which was already as good as dead (for he was about a hundred years old), or when he considered the barrenness of Sarah's womb. No distrust made him waver concerning the promise of God, but he grew strong in his faith as he gave glory to God, being fully convinced that God was able to do what he had promised. Therefore his faith "was reckoned to him as righteousness"' (Romans 4:18–22, NRSV).

A prayer

Lord God, help me to give glory to you . . . to reflect on the glorious things you have done . . . calling into existence the things that do not exist . . . creating the world out of nothing . . . making a barren woman the mother of a son . . . and thank you that as I give you the glory, and praise you for your glory, so my faith will grow . . . and my love . . . and my hope.

SB

The wrong voice

Now Sarai, Abram's wife, bore him no children. She had an Egyptian maid whose name was Hagar; and Sarai said to Abram, 'Behold now, the Lord has prevented me from bearing children; go in to my maid; it may be that I shall obtain children by her.' And Abram hearkened to the voice of Sarai. So, after Abram had dwelt ten years in the land of Canaan, Sarai, Abram's wife, took Hagar the Egyptian, her maid, and gave her to Abram her husband as a wife. And he went in to Hagar, and she conceived; and when she saw that she had conceived, she looked with contempt on her mistress.

Abram listened to Sarai's voice instead of God's—and as a result a river of hatred and conflict started to flow right down through the years to the tragic Arab–Israeli conflict of the present day. Perhaps Abram only gave in to Sarai just this once—but once was enough. Some men let their wives (or their mothers) nag them and boss them around all their lives, and it is a state of affairs that is a severe falling short of the mark of how things are meant to be (which is another way of saying that a man who lets his wife or his mother walk over him is sinning). And a woman can sin in the same way—if she allows her husband to treat her either as a plaything or a drudge or a fool. Each of them ought to obey God—and to be rooted and grounded in the love of God, growing day by day towards Christian maturity.

What Sarai and Abram and Hagar did was socially acceptable in that culture—but it was a failure of faith. Proverbs 13:12 says that 'Hope deferred makes the heart sick,' and perhaps Abram was heartsick with disappointment, and weary of waiting. So he gave in. But God didn't give up on him. A failure isn't the end of the line for God.

A prayer

Lord God, help me to wait . . . in hope and in patience.

SB

I am Almighty

When Abram was ninety-nine years old the Lord appeared to Abram, and said to him, 'I am God Almighty; walk before me, and be blameless. And I will make my covenant between me and you, and will multiply you exceedingly.' Then Abram fell on his face; and God said to him, 'Behold, my covenant is with you, and you shall be the father of a multitude of nations. No longer shall your name be Abram, but your name shall be Abraham.'

God is revealing his nature to Abram by telling him his name—El Shaddai, which means God Almighty. This name is used in passages which stress the power of God in contrast to human helplessness (Job calls on El Shaddai thirty-one times during his sufferings). 'It was the claim of El Shaddai to be powerful where man was weakest, and He exerts this claim supremely by promising to an obscure and numerically tiny family that they should one day possess and populate a land which, in their day, was inhabited and owned by people immeasurably their superiors in number and power' (J.A. Motyer, in a fascinating monograph, *The Revelation of the Divine Name,* Tyndale Press, 1959). God tells Abram his own name—and then he gives Abram a new name, which is also to give him a new nature. Abram means 'father exalted', but Abraham means 'father of many', and the promise is that Abraham will be the father of a multitude of nations. This is a reminder of the night when God said to him 'Look toward heaven and number the stars, if you are able to number them.' Then he said to him, 'So shall your descendants be' (15:5). The God who is almighty is the God of Abraham and all his descendants—and since Abraham is the father of all who have faith in God, that means you and me.

A meditation

Think of a situation in your life where you are deeply conscious of your weakness . . . and then spend two or three minutes holding it in the presence of El Shaddai . . . Almighty God.

SB

An outward sign

And God said to Abraham, 'As for you, you shall keep my covenant, you and your descendants after you throughout their generations. This is my covenant... Every male among you shall be circumcised. You shall be circumcised in the flesh of your foreskins, and it shall be a sign of the covenant between me and you. He that is eight days old among you shall be circumcised; every male throughout your generations...

The time had come now for the promise which God had made to Abraham in private to go public. A covenant was an agreement between a superior and an inferior party—and it was always the superior who 'made' the covenant and established it. It was a legal document—and the terms of it, laid down by the superior party, had to be kept by the inferior party. If the inferior did not keep the terms of the covenant then the superior would not give the benefits promised in the covenant. In those days a powerful king would promise to defend a weak king, in return for regular payments of goods, or the provision of fighting men when the powerful king needed them.

Abraham's side of keeping the covenant was that he and every male in his house, and throughout succeeding generations, should be circumcised. It was an outward sign that could be seen and (unlike the terrible act of female circumcision inflicted on 30 million women in the Middle East and Africa) it was not harmful but healthgiving, particularly for a wife. Cervical cancer is rare among Jewish wives, because of the absence of infection from a circumcised husband. In *None of these Diseases*, Dr S.I. McMillan says that an '8-day old baby has more available prothrombin (necessary for the normal clotting of blood) than on any other day in his entire life' and also 'the important blood-clotting element, vitamin K, is not formed in the normal amount until the fifth to the seventh day of life.' So (amazingly) 'the perfect day to perform a circumcision is the *eighth* day'.

A thought

The sign of circumcision is the sign of the promises of God, like the sign of the cross in baptism. The blessing flows from God to the people of God—and to receive the sign on one's body, in faith, is to receive the blessing in one's heart.

SB

At long last

And God said to Abraham, 'As for Sarai your wife, you shall not call her name Sarai, but Sarah shall be her name. I will bless her, and moreover I will give you a son by her; I will bless her, and she shall be a mother of nations . . .' Then Abraham fell on his face and laughed, and said to himself, 'Shall a child be born to a man who is a hundred years old? Shall Sarah, who is ninety years old, bear a child?' And Abraham said to God, 'O that Ishmael might live in thy sight!' God said, 'No, but Sarah your wife shall bear you a son, and you shall call his name Isaac . . . As for Ishmael, I have heard you; behold, I will bless him and . . . I will make him a great nation. But I will establish my covenant with Isaac, whom Sarah shall bear to you at this season next year.'

God gives Sarai a slightly changed name as a symbol of her share in the covenant he has made with Abraham. Both names mean 'princess'—and Sarah is going to be one. The blessing is to her as well as to Abraham, and she will be the mother of nations and of kings, through the baby son who is going to be born to her—to her, and not to anyone else. Ishmael will also be blessed (the promised blessing to Abraham flowing through both his sons)—but the greatest promise (and the promise impossible to fulfil except through the power of God) will flow through the son born when it is humanly speaking impossible. Abraham laughed at the sheer impossibility of it—but perhaps it was the laughter of delight. Of daring really to believe that the thing he had longed for through so many years was at last going to happen—the joy would well up inside him and become first of all a smile, and then the release of laughter. Now God had told him the time of the longed-for birth—and soon the long years of waiting and hoping would be over.

A prayer

Lord God, help me to believe your promises before they come true—and to act accordingly in the present.

SB

Betrayal

After saying this, Jesus exclaimed in deep agitation of spirit, 'In truth, in very truth I tell you, one of you is going to betray me.' The disciples looked at one another in bewilderment: whom could he be speaking of? One of them, the disciple he loved, was reclining close beside Jesus. So Simon Peter nodded to him and said, 'Ask who it is he means.' That disciple, as he reclined, leaned back close to Jesus and asked, 'Lord, who is it?' Jesus replied, 'It is the man to whom I give this piece of bread when I have dipped it in the dish.' Then, after dipping it in the dish, he took it out and gave it to Judas son of Simon Iscariot.

Last Sunday I made the point that Holy Communion was instituted in circumstances of acute tension. This Sunday we see that it was overshadowed by betrayal. "Who in the same night that he was betrayed" is repeated *at every Eucharist*. Judas is always there in the background. It was a personal betrayal. So it hurt as nothing else. Not until the Last Supper do we ever read of Jesus being in deep agitation of spirit as here.

He touched the depths when he handed Judas that piece of bread dipped in the dish. The action was the customary way of honouring a guest at a meal—to give him the first piece from the hand of the host. Judas took it but did not grasp his last chance to opt for loyalty. He rose, left the company and passed through the door out into the night. Was there tucked in the purse in his girdle thirty pieces of silver, the dirty money for which Jesus was sold to the priests bent on killing him? As he descended the stairs did he throw away, or spit out, the bread Jesus had given him? Or had he eaten it?

Anyway, he hurried off to the priests.

Did Jesus break down? I think not. No one in the room must know what was going on. Calmly he instituted the Holy Communion. All this 'in the same night when he was betrayed'.

Has any one of us ever attended the Holy Communion with a heavy heart? Someone we love is no longer by our side? They used to come, but not now. It would not be surprising if a tear fell on the broken bread when given. Betrayal? Let down? Desertion? What shall we call it? Today I bid you remember that Jesus was (and is) there.

DCF

Entertaining strangers

And the Lord appeared to [Abraham]. . . as he sat by the door of his tent in the heat of the day. He lifted up his eyes and looked, and behold, three men stood in front of him. When he saw them, he ran from the tent door to meet them, and bowed himself to the earth, and said, 'My lord, if I have found favour in your sight, do not pass by your servant. Let a little water be brought, and wash your feet, and rest yourselves under the tree, while I fetch a morsel of bread, that you may refresh yourselves . . .' So they said, 'Do as you have said.' And Abraham hastened into the tent to Sarah, and said, 'Make ready quickly three measures of fine meal, knead it, and make cakes.' And Abraham ran to the herd, and took a calf, tender and good, and gave it to the servant, who hastened to prepare it. Then he took curds, and milk, and the calf which he had prepared, and set it before them; and he stood by them under the tree while they ate.

This is a mysterious meeting—of three men who stand before Abraham, but it says that it was the Lord who appeared to him. Perhaps it was only afterwards that Abraham realized that it was the Lord— just as the disciples who walked with Jesus along the road to Emmaus only realized afterwards, and said to each other 'It is the Lord!' when he made himself known to them in the breaking of the bread, at the meal they had asked him to share with them. Abraham asks the three if he can get some bread for them to eat—and water to wash their feet in. Then Abraham sets the meal before them and stands by them while they eat it. The New Testament looks back to this event when it says 'Do not neglect to show hospitality to strangers, for by doing that some have entertained angels without knowing it' (Hebrews 13:2).

A prayer

Lord Jesus Christ—when you want to come to my home—as a stranger or a friend—let me never turn you away.

SB

Delayed answers

They said to him, 'Where is Sarah your wife?' And he said, 'She is in the tent.' The Lord said, 'I will surely return to you in the spring, and Sarah your wife shall have a son.' And Sarah was listening at the tent door behind him. Now Abraham and Sarah were old, advanced in age; it had ceased to be with Sarah after the manner of women.

As Sarah listened at the tent door she must have been astonished that the strangers knew her name. Then she hears amazing words—and it is the Lord who speaks them: 'I will surely return to you in the spring, and Sarah your wife shall have a son.' She laughs—as her husband had laughed when the Lord said the same thing to him—and the Lord then puts a question to Abraham to which the only answer can be 'No!' ... 'Is anything too hard for the Lord?' Perhaps Sarah didn't want to hope again because she couldn't bear to be disappointed again.

To think about

'Prayers that receive no immediate answer, though they are based on God's word, can be a source of considerable unease. Like Sarah, the praying person may conclude that God has either not heard the petition or is limited in his capabilities, whereas the explanation in this incident lay in quite another direction. Now that Sarah is past the usual age for childbearing, the son of her womb will be in an unusual sense the child of promise... The delay, far from indicating any limitation of God's power, showed rather God's total control over events. The prayer of Abraham and Sarah that they might have a son was entirely within the will of the Lord, because it was based on his direct and unmistakable promise. To wait for its fulfilment proved to be a trial almost beyond endurance, but to wait with contentment is an activity of faith which gives glory to God, not to be confused with passivity. Suddenly, when God's time comes, his purposes blossom like a long-awaited spring.'

Joyce Baldwin, The Message of Genesis 12–50
SB

The judge who does right

The Lord said, 'Shall I hide from Abraham what I am about to do, seeing that . . . all the nations of the earth shall bless themselves by him? No, for I have chosen him, that he may charge his chidren and his household after him to keep the way of the Lord by doing righteousness and justice . . . Then the Lord said, 'Because the outcry against Sodom and Gomorrah is great and their sin is very grave, I will go down to see whether they have done altogether according to the outcry which has come to me; and if not, I will know.' So the men turned from there, and went toward Sodom; but Abraham still stood before the Lord.

Our passage doesn't say here how the men of Sodom sinned. Tomorrow's passage will say—and anyway most of us will know what the particular sexual perversion was to which Sodom gave its name. Here the Lord is telling Abraham what he is going to do—so that Abraham will know what is righteous and what is wicked and then charge his children and his household to do righteousness and justice. We don't know who cried out against the wickedness of Sodom and Gomorrah—but the Lord heard their cry. And the story says that he went to check it out. In fact God knows all things—because he holds every thing and every person in existence by his word of power—and he is all-seeing and all-knowing. But Abraham needed to know how the Lord functioned in judgment—so there was this strange encounter. It leads to Abraham's famous prayer: 'Wilt thou indeed sweep away the righteous with the wicked? Suppose there are fifty righteous within the city; wilt thou then destroy the place and not spare it for the fifty righteous who are in it?' Abraham goes on dropping the number by fives, and stops at ten. And the assurance is the same as for fifty: 'For the sake of ten I will not destroy it.'

A question

What do you believe about God as judge?

SB

A horror story

This is a terrible tale that the Bible tells. The angels come to Sodom, where Lot is sitting in the gate. He persuades them to enter his house and spend the night there and, like Abraham, he washes their feet and makes a feast for them. Then the horror starts.

But before they lay down, the men of the city, the men of Sodom, both young and old, all the people to the last man, surrounded the house; and they called to Lot, 'Where are the men who came to you tonight? Bring them out to us, that we may know them.'

The demand to 'know' Lot's visitors was a demand to know them sexually. It is the word used for when Adam 'knew' his wife, Eve, and it is not at all the same as 'Getting to know you' in the innocent sense of the song in the musical comedy *The King and I*. But this horrible event gets worse. Lot wants to protect his visitors—so he makes an offer to the men that appals me every time I read it.

'Behold, I have two daughters who have not known man; let me bring them out to you, and do to them as you please; only do nothing to these men, for they have come under the shelter of my roof.'

It is a despicable suggestion, and the low value which Lot set upon his daughters is almost beyond belief. The strangers, who are angels, then step in to rescue Lot from the men, who are squashing him against the door and trying to break it down. They strike the men with blindness, and tell Lot that the Lord is about to destroy the city. Lot goes off to warn the two men who were due to marry his daughters—but their reaction (to use a modern phrase) is, 'You must be joking!'

A prayer

Lord God, I find it astonishing that the New Testament speaks of 'righteous Lot'. As I think about his appalling behaviour, help me to see and to understand that in your holy sight all unrighteousness and injustice is horrible, and that it all grieves you to the depths of your holy heart. Help me to see my own sin more clearly.

SB

A pathetic person

When morning dawned, the angels urged Lot, saying, 'Arise, take your wife and your two daughters who are here, lest you be consumed in the punishment of the city.' But he lingered; so the men seized him and his wife and his two daughters by the hand, the Lord being merciful to him, and they brought him forth and set him outside the city.

Abraham's prayer for Sodom and Gomorrah achieved what he really wanted, which was for the Lord to rescue Lot—and in the face of Lot's unbelievable indolence that is what the angels set about doing. 'Get up and go,' they said to him. But he lingered. Perhaps he had a nice house, and nice things in it, and didn't want to leave them all behind—and probably his wife and daughters didn't want to leave either, and didn't believe what he said was happening. The daughters' fiancés certainly hadn't believed it. Then, even when the angels forcibly removed Lot from the city, he still twittered pathetically on about it being too far to go up to the hills so please couldn't he stay in the valley in a little city nearby.

To think about

Remember the first choice of Lot—to live in the rich and fertile Jordan valley—near (and later in) a city renowned for its wickedness. Remember the words of St Paul: 'Don't let the world around you squeeze you into its own mould' (J.B. Phillips, Romans 12:2). Are there people, or programmes on television, or places that you go to, which take the edge off your Christian commitment and dull your desire for God? Do you compromise with sin—or do you confront it?

SB

Judgment on evil

Then the Lord rained on Sodom and Gomorrah brimstone and fire from the Lord out of heaven; and he overthrew those cities, and all the valley, and all the inhabitants of the cities, and what grew on the ground. But Lot's wife behind him looked back, and she became a pillar of salt. And Abraham went early in the morning to the place where he had stood before the Lord; and he looked down toward Sodom and Gomorrah and toward all the land of the valley, and beheld, and lo, the smoke of the land went up like the smoke of a furnace. So it was that, when God destroyed the cities of the valley, God remembered Abraham, and sent Lot out of the midst of the overthrow, when he overthrew the cities in which Lot dwelt.

The whole area of Sodom and Gomorrah was rendered infertile by the terrible cataclysm. The wicked cities of the plain were utterly destroyed in the terrible judgment of God. But Jesus said that if the men of Sodom had seen the works that he did, they would have repented. Commenting that those who had seen the miracles of Jesus and failed to receive him had less excuse than Sodom, Joyce Baldwin writes that 'In the gospel there is hope for even the most degraded. An up-to-date example which can be fully authenticated shows how the gospel brought new hope to some tribal groups in the island of Sarawak. So rotten were these people with alcoholism and disease that their government had given up on them, and was content to allow them to die out. Missionaries of the Borneo Evangelical Mission witnessed an amazing transformation of these hopeless tribes into a society of healthy, purposeful men and women of God' (*The Message of Genesis 12–50*).

A prayer

Lord Jesus Christ, I praise you that however degraded a sinner a man or a woman is, you can reach right down into the very depths of their sin, and raise them up, and forgive them, and give them a new and shining life—ablaze with the love and the holiness of God.

SB

Broken bread

And as they were eating, he took bread, and blessed, and broke it, and gave it to them, and said, 'Take; this is my body.' And he took a cup, and when he had given thanks he gave it to them, and they all drank of it. And he said to them, 'This is my blood of the covenant, which is poured out for many. Truly, I say to you, I shall not drink again of the fruit of the vine until that day when I drink it new in the kingdom of God.'

Last Sunday we read how Jesus took a piece of bread, dipped it in the dish and handed it to Judas. The action had a special purpose for him, but he failed to rise to it.

For the remaining eleven disciples after Judas' departure the action was different. Jesus took bread while they were eating, blessed and broke it. 'Take,' he said, 'this is my body.' So in their hands they saw a piece of *broken* bread. Thus each disciple in eating it partook of Christ's *broken* body. Then taking a cup of wine he gave thanks and passed it round, saying, 'This is my blood of the covenant which is poured out for many.'

These actions and words down the centuries have been thought over, worked out, discussed and (dare I say it?) argued about. Meant to be unifying they have (alas) even come to be divisive. We must be careful not to fall into that trap. In our reading today let us concentrate on the *broken* bread. When we come to the Lord's table our communion is with the Christ who was crucified—broken. The cross dominates the Lord's table. Jesus, the incarnate Christ, fought and won the battle there. And it was *for us*.

First of all then in our communion we must thank God for what Christ did. It is through this thanksgiving that the benefits of it will flow into us. Yet it is with the presence of the *risen Christ* in the sacrament that we communicate, the Christ whom God raised because he was willing to be broken for us. But Easter does not cancel out Good Friday. It celebrates it.

DCF

From faith to fear

From there Abraham journeyed toward the territory of the Negeb ... and he sojourned in Gerar. And Abraham said of Sarah his wife, 'She is my sister.' And Abimelech king of Gerar sent and took Sarah. But God came to Abimelech in a dream by night and said to him, 'Behold, you are a dead man, because of the woman whom you have taken; for she is a man's wife.' Now Abimelech had not approached her; so he said, 'Lord, wilt thou slay an innocent people? Did he not himself say to me, "She is my sister"? ...' Then God said to him in the dream, 'Yes, I know that you have done this in the integrity of your heart, and it was I who kept you from sinning against me ... Now then restore the man's wife, for he is a prophet, and he will pray for you, and you shall live ...'

Abraham had one or two serious lapses from faith into fear, and this is one of them. He did again what he had done in Egypt—told Sarah to say that she was his sister. So Abimelech took her into his harem—but didn't take her as a wife or a concubine because God stopped him. Again, Abimelech's behaviour is better than Abraham's—and God recognizes his integrity and innocence. If Abimelech restores Sarah to her husband, then Abraham will pray for him, because he is a prophet.

been Abimelech, would you have despised his prayers? Or would you have recognized that in spite of his human weakness this was a man of God—and a friend of God? Reflect that Jesus was (and is) the friend of sinners—and even forgiven sinners keep slipping into sin, and fall from faith into fear. Reflect on the words of Isaiah: 'a bruised reed shall he not break, and a smoking flax shall he not quench—until he brings forth a verdict of victory' (Isaiah 42:3). Then praise God for the glory and the wonder of his mercy.

SB

A meditation

Think about what Abraham did—and what Abimelech did—and get in touch with what you feel about both of them. Tell God what you feel—and then stay with your emotions for a few moments. Do you despise Abraham? If you had

Laughter at last

The Lord visited Sarah as he had said, and the Lord did to Sarah as he had promised. And Sarah conceived, and bore Abraham a son in his old age at the time of which God had spoken to him. Abraham called the name of his son who was born to him, whom Sarah bore him, Isaac. And Abraham circumcised his son Isaac when he was eight days old, as God had commanded him. Abraham was a hundred years old when his son Isaac was born to him. And Sarah said, 'God has made laughter for me; every one who hears will laugh over me.' And she said, ' Who would have said to Abraham that Sarah would suckle children? Yet I have borne him a son in his old age.'

'With God all things are possible' (Mark 10:27)—so long as they are within the will of God—and now God has kept the promise he had made to Abraham so many years before. Abraham's faith had been severely tested in the process (next week we shall be studying the book of James, and discovering what our response ought to be when we *are* being tested)—and his faith has now been vindicated. But perhaps Abraham's and Sarah's happiness and laughter at the birth of their promised son will evoke in some of us a certain wistfulness—for promises that we had believed God made to us. We prayed and hoped and trusted—but then our hope died, and perhaps the person whose healing we were praying for died as well. Teilhard de Chardin tells us that we have to pray our heart out— and then abandon the thing we are praying for utterly into the wounded hands of Christ. We cannot do the abandoning before we have agonized in prayer—but there can be a time to stop praying.

A prayer

Father God, thank you for that promise which you made to Abraham, and which you kept. Help us with the promises we believe you have made to us. Help us not to lose faith—but to trust you in the darkness of disappointment and misunderstanding.

SB

The test of faith

After these things God tested Abraham, and said to him, 'Abraham!' And he said, 'Here am I.' He said, 'Take your son, your only son Isaac, whom you love, and go to the land of Moriah, and offer him there as a burnt offering upon one of the mountains of which I shall tell you.' So Abraham rose early in the morning, saddled his ass, and took two of his young men with him, and his son Isaac; and he cut the wood for the burnt offering, and arose and went to the place of which God had told him. On the third day Abraham lifted up his eyes and saw the place afar off. Then Abraham said to his young men, 'Stay here with the ass; I and the lad will go yonder and worship, and come again to you.'

It was a terrible test that God put Abraham through—and Abraham would have been utterly alone in it. Can you imagine what Sarah would have said and done if he had told her what God had said? There must have been a terrible cry from the depth of Abraham's heart. If his beloved son Isaac had to die, his own heart would be broken—and if he had no son then he could have no descendants. Perhaps he held on to the promise that 'through Isaac shall your descendants be named'. The great chapter of faith in the Epistle to the Hebrews says that 'He considered the fact that God is able even to raise someone from the dead' (11:9)—and the words that he spoke to his servants show how great his faith was: 'I and the lad will go ... and worship, and come again to you.'

A meditation

Imagine what Abraham felt like as he walked with his son up the mountain . . . Isaac carrying the wood for the sacrifice . . . Then imagine the father heart of God when his son walked up the hill of Calvary, carrying the wood of the cross on which he would be sacrificed for the sins of the world . . .

SB

The passive victim

And Abraham took the wood of the burnt offering, and laid it on Isaac his son; and he took in his hand the fire and the knife. So they went both of them together. And Isaac said to his father Abraham, 'My father!' And he said, 'Here am I, my son.' And he said, 'Behold, the fire and the wood; but where is the lamb for a burnt offering?' Abraham said, 'God will provide himself the lamb for a burnt offering, my son.' So they went both of them together. When they came to the place of which God had told him, Abraham built an altar there, and laid the wood in order, and bound Isaac his son, and laid him on the altar, upon the wood. Then Abraham put forth his hand, and took the knife to slay his son. But the angel of the Lord called to him from heaven, and said, 'Abraham, Abraham!' And he said, 'Here am I.' He said, 'Do not lay your hand on the lad or do anything to him; for now I know that you fear God, seeing you have not withheld your son, your only son, from me.'

Isaac was very passive in this story. But he could have run away. He didn't have to stay there and be bound to the altar which Abraham had built—any more than Jesus had to move into his passion and passivity and allow them to nail him to the cross. Isaac asked where the lamb was for the sacrifice—and Abraham's answer was a prophetic truth that came to its fulfilment in Christ. 'God will provide himself a lamb...' When John the Baptist saw Jesus coming towards him he saw God's provision of the sacrifice: 'Behold, the lamb of God, who takes away the sin of the world' (John 1:29). The New Testament speaks of 'the obedience of faith' (Romans 1:5)—and (as we shall see in James) true faith always leads to action—sometimes even to death.

A meditation

Imagine Isaac on the altar as his father took the knife to slay him... Imagine Jesus on the cross... calling out 'My God, my God, why have you forsaken me?'...

SB

The lamb of God

And Abraham lifted up his eyes and looked, and behold, behind him was a ram, caught in a thicket by his horns; and Abraham went and took the ram, and offered it up as a burnt offering instead of his son. So Abraham called the name of that place The Lord will provide; as it is said to this day, 'On the mount of the Lord it shall be provided.' And the angel of the Lord called to Abraham a second time from heaven, and said, 'By myself I have sworn, says the Lord, because you have done this, and have not withheld your son, your only son, I will indeed bless you, and I will multiply your descendants as the stars of heaven and as the sand which is on the seashore.'

God does provide a lamb—as Abraham has believed in faith that he will. He unbinds Isaac from the altar and substitutes the ram in his place—and he offers it up as a burnt offering, instead of his son. The church has spoken down the centuries of the sacrifice of Christ on the cross as the substitutionary atonement—believing that he died in our place and on our behalf.

After all these things have happened, the day comes when Sarah dies—and Abraham buys a field to bury her in. Then, later on, he dies himself and is buried in the same field. He has been promised the whole land—but all he possesses of it at the end of his life is a burial ground. But that isn't the end of Abraham's story, or the end of the promise. The blessing is flowing right down to the present day—to all the people of God who are justified and counted righteous through their faith, and trust in God and in the sacrifice that God has made.

A prayer

Living God—the God of Jacob and Isaac and Abraham, and my God—help me to be faithful, as they were. Help me to trust you, whatever happens.

SB

The joy of testing

James, a servant of God and of the Lord Jesus Christ, To the twelve tribes scattered among the nations: Greetings. Consider it pure joy, my brothers, whenever you face trials of many kinds, because you know that the testing of your faith develops perseverance. Perseverance must finish its work so that you may be mature and complete, not lacking anything.

It isn't the first response for most of us— to say to ourselves, 'This is something I can really be joyful about,' when what is happening to us is the very opposite of joyful, and is perhaps causing us to cry out to God 'Why? Why is this happening to me?' The answer could simply be 'Because this is the sort of world we live in . . .' a world in which there are earthquakes and floods, and violent men who beat up people and rape women, and terrible viruses that take over the immune system of a newborn baby and wreck it. But James isn't answering the 'Why' question in this passage. He is telling us what our response ought to be when we are tested—and the original Greek word has the idea of testing and strengthening . . . like the young blackbird who is wobbling on top of my garden fence at this very moment, flapping its wings and then launching itself off the post on to the ground. The strengthening and testing is like the process which purifies gold, and gets rid of all its impurities. At the end of the process, if we let it do its work in us, we shall be perfect. That word describes a person who is fully grown and not a child any more, and it means that we are fit to do the work that God has created us to do.

A prayer

Lord Jesus Christ, teach me how to count it all joy when I meet trials and temptations. Help me to trust you when my sufferings—and the sufferings of other people—test my faith. Help me to hold on to the truth that 'all things work together for good to those who love God' (Romans 8:28).

SB

The same love

Your attitude should be the same as that of Christ Jesus: Who being in very nature God, did not consider equality with God something to be grasped, but made himself nothing, taking the very nature of a servant, being made in human likeness. And being found in appearance as a man, he humbled himself and became obedient to death—even death on a cross! Therefore God exalted him to the highest place and gave him the name that is above every name, that at the name of Jesus every knee should bow, in heaven and on earth and under the earth, and every tongue confess that Jesus Christ is Lord, to the glory of God the Father.

Always when I read this passage I am humbled. To think that my attitude should be the same as Christ's is something to really aim for, yet who of us could ever be open enough to God? Reading biographies of the saints I realize that it is possible to be so much in tune with God that Paul's great passage in Philippians begins to sing its message out of human beings.

A person in our own time respected by so many in the world is Mother Teresa. A new chaplain was appointed to her order, the Sisters of Jesus, in India. He asked to see the love of God in action.

At his first Communion service, the nuns filed to the front to take the elements. Among them he noticed Mother Teresa, frail and weak. As she cupped her hands in front of her, the priest placed the bread into her palms. Before she ate she simply looked in total adoration at this small piece of bread. Her head moved to one side and she shone with the deepest love. He said he would never forget that look.

Later the same day he asked to see round the wards and when he came to one in particular Mother Teresa stopped and said, 'This is my ward.' It was obviously for those who were closest to death. Just then a man cried out in terrible pain. Mother Teresa went across to him, so tenderly holding his hand, and again the chaplain saw her head move to one side as once more she shone with the same deepest love. The love that she received from Jesus in the communion was the same love that she gave to the dying man. With Jesus she found the glory of God the Father shining through her life.

GD

How to get it right

If any of you lacks wisdom, he should ask God, who gives generously to all without finding fault, and it will be given to him. But when he asks, he must believe and not doubt, because he who doubts is like a wave of the sea, blown and tossed by the wind. That man should not think he will receive anything from the Lord; he is a double-minded man, unstable in all he does.

What James says about asking for wisdom follows directly on from saying that Christians' response to the test of their faith should be joy. But if they don't know how to get it right then they are to ask God to give them wisdom. 'Now this thing has happened to me—how can I use it in the right way, so that I grow through it?' is the way to ask. Wisdom is about knowing the way really to live one's life. 'Blessed is the man who finds wisdom, and the man who gets understanding' it says in Proverbs (3:13). 'Her ways are ways of pleasantness, and all her paths are peace. She is a tree of life to those who lay hold of her; those who hold her fast are called happy. The Lord by wisdom founded the earth' (3:17–19).'

James says that the God who is the source of all wisdom will give it to us if we ask. But when we ask we mustn't doubt. God loves to give to us, and he is a generous giver. He gives a measure that is filled up and running over, like the measure that Jesus talked about in the Gospels. And when he gives us wisdom he is giving us nothing less than himself—to be with us in the suffering. It is Christ himself who is both 'the power of God and the wisdom of God' (1 Corinthians 1:24), and what we need in our trials isn't just a set of instructions on how to behave but a person to be with us in the depths of our being and the depths of our pain.

A prayer

*Lord Jesus Christ—give me wisdom—
and give me yourself.*

SB

A proper pride

The brother in humble circumstances ought to take pride in his high position. But the one who is rich should take pride in his low position, because he will pass away like a wild flower. For the sun rises with scorching heat and withers the plant; its blossom falls and its beauty is destroyed. In the same way, the rich man will fade away even while he goes about his business.

When James wrote his letter some people had virtually no status at all. Slaves and women and poor people were looked down on. But perhaps in their heart of hearts they knew that they were important and that they mattered—because there is something in all of us, put there by the God who imprinted our unique fingerprints on our hands, that cries out 'I am I—and I matter!' Jesus had said how much we matter—that one human soul is worth more than the whole world. Now that truth was being preached and taught, and now people who had had no status could boast in their high position. It needn't have been a cocky boasting (any more than it need be for us)—but a glorying and a wondering at the enormous love of God set on each individual, and the enormous importance of each human soul.

The rich man could boast too, in his low position. 'Humiliation' is how the RSV translates that, and it has to do with the state of humility, which is about the glory of creatureliness. The delight and the wonder of being a creature is that we have a Creator—and that our life and our being is utterly contingent on him. We have no life or being that does not derive and flow from our Creator. The rich man will pass away like a wild flower—and so shall we all. But Christians know that that isn't the end of the story.

A thought

You have been born anew, not of perishable seed but of imperishable, through the living and abiding word of God; for 'All flesh is like grass and all its glory like the flower of grass. The grass withers, and the flower falls, but the word of the Lord abides for ever.' That word is the good news which was preached to you.

1 Peter 1:23–25

SB

The crown of life

Blessed is the man who perseveres under trial, because when he has stood the test, he will receive the crown of life that God has promised to those who love him. When tempted, no-one should say, 'God is tempting me.' For God cannot be tempted by evil, nor does he tempt anyone; but each one is tempted when, by his own evil desire, he is dragged away and enticed. Then, after desire has conceived, it gives birth to sin; and sin, when it is full-grown, gives birth to death.

In the ancient world, a crown of gold or a linen band was the mark of royalty. At the end of a Christian's earthly life he or she will see their Father God face to face, and come into the heritage of a prince or princess—the sons and daughters of the King of kings. A crown of flowers was the mark of joy and happiness—worn at feasts and at weddings—and for the Christian, heaven is the marriage supper of the Lamb. The crown of laurel leaves was the crown that was bestowed on the victor at the Roman games—and in 2 Timothy 4:7 and 8 Paul says that there won't only be one victor, or one crown:

I have fought the good fight, I have finished the race, I have kept the faith. Henceforth there is laid up for me the crown of righteousness, which the Lord, the righteous judge, will award to me on that Day, and not only to me but also to all who have loved his appearing.

Some people would never think of blaming God for their temptations, but they would put them all down to Satan. James doesn't deny that there is a tempter outside us—but he is very clear that there is also a tempter inside us, and that without any outside influence at all we can produce a full-grown, death-dealing sin from our own desires.

A prayer

Lord Jesus Christ, help me to resist temptation, however it comes to me— from outside myself or inside. Help me to fight the good fight, and to keep the faith, and to think about the crown that one day you will give to me.

SB

The giver of life

Don't be deceived, my dear brothers. Every good and perfect gift is from above, coming down from the Father of the heavenly lights, who does not change like shifting shadows. He chose to give us birth through the word of truth, that we might be a kind of firstfruits of all he created. My dear brothers, take note of this: Everyone should be quick to listen, slow to speak and slow to become angry, for man's anger does not bring about the righteous life that God desires. Therefore, get rid of all moral filth and the evil that is so prevalent, and humbly accept the word planted in you, which can save you.

James isn't flying off at a tangent when he moves from temptation to God as giver. There is a flow to the argument. Far from being the source of temptation, God is the source of all good gifts. He made the sun and the stars. He is the source of all wisdom—and when a human being becomes a Christian it is because it is 'the God who said "Let light shine out of darkness," who has shone in our hearts to give the light of the knowledge of the glory of God in the face of Christ' (2 Corinthians 4:6). Jesus is the light of the world and the Word of God—and it is through the word of God that we become God's sons and daughters.

James tells us to listen to the voice of God with our ears pricked up—like the gorgeous Alsatian who lives in the stables next door to me, whom regular readers of *New Daylight* have met before. Whatever Zach is doing (I might be feeding him the delicious titbit I saved for him from my Sunday joint), the moment he hears the voice of his owner, whom he adores, he drops everything and rushes off to follow her.

A prayer

Lord God, help me to learn to listen to your voice—in the midst of all the clamour and busyness of my life. And when it comes to me—speaking your word—may I receive it into my heart, so that day by day your word takes root in me and grows, and so that day by day I know the power of your presence, making me whole and blessing me with salvation.

SB

Do it!

Do not merely listen to the word, and so deceive yourselves. Do what it says. Anyone who listens to the word but does not do what it says is like a man who looks at his face in a mirror and, after looking at himself, goes away and immediately forgets what he looks like. But the man who looks intently into the perfect law that gives freedom, and continues to do this, not forgetting what he has heard, but doing it—he will be blessed in what he does. If anyone considers himself religious and yet does not keep a tight rein on his tongue, he deceives himself and his religion is worthless. Religion that God our Father accepts as pure and faultless is this: to look after orphans and widows in their distress and to keep oneself from being polluted by the world.

James is still talking about listening to the word of God, and pressing his message home. Just to hear the word isn't enough. We have to do it. Those of us who have ever decided to reduce weight and get fit will know how the self-help books begin. 'Take your clothes off and take a good look at yourself in a mirror—sideways and frontwards.' In other words, look at yourself as you really are—and then do what the book says. It is no use just reading it. I know that all too well, since I have a well-read pile of such books on my bedroom table.

James tells us to do God's will, not just read about it, and it was passages like this which Luther didn't like. 'James drives us to law and works,' he wrote. But the blessing comes from *doing* the law—not just from reading about it.

A prayer

Lord Jesus Christ, help me to look at myself as I really am—and as you see me. Then show me yourself, so that I see as much of your glory as my eyes can bear. And then give me your Spirit, day by day, so that I live more and more like you, and love more and more like you.

SB

Wrong judgment

My brothers, as believers in our glorious Lord Jesus Christ, don't show favouritism. Suppose a man comes into your meeting wearing a gold ring and fine clothes, and a poor man in shabby clothes also comes in. If you show special attention to the man wearing fine clothes and say, 'Here's a good seat for you,' but say to the poor man, 'You stand there' or 'Sit on the floor by my feet,' have you not discriminated among yourselves and become judges with evil thoughts? Listen, my dear brothers: Has not God chosen those who are poor in the eyes of the world to be rich in faith and to inherit the kingdom he promised those who love him? But you have insulted the poor. Is it not the rich who are exploiting you? Are they not the ones who are dragging you into court? Are they not the ones who are slandering the noble name of him to whom you belong?

In my town two parishes were once one, with two churches—and the main church was where the posh people went, and the daughter church was where their servants went (and also the people who were poor and not posh). This unchristian practice went on until the Second World War. I knew one of the women who suffered from it. She was something of a saint and she went about doing good—not in the nasty way that makes the one being done good to long for the do-gooder to stop doing it and go away—but in the real sense. If someone was ill she would take them flowers; or clean their house for them; or do anything that was needed; just for love. But she had been prepared for confirmation at the un-posh church because she was lower-class and poor. And the people in the posh church would have sat in their pews Sunday after Sunday and sometimes listened to the Epistle of James. If it hadn't been well read they would probably have criticized the reader and complained to the Vicar—but they would not have seen themselves reflected in the mirror of the word.

A thought

Do I pay special attention to successful or clever people?

SB

Discernment

For as often as you eat this bread and drink the cup, you proclaim the Lord's death until he comes. Whoever, therefore, eats the bread or drinks the cup of the Lord in an unworthy manner will be guilty of profaning the body and blood of the Lord. Let a man examine himself, and so eat of the bread and drink of the cup. For any one who eats and drinks without discerning the body eats and drinks judgment upon himself.

I do not myself belong to the church tradition which celebrates the Holy Communion at infrequent intervals, but I understand and respect it. Far from underrating the sacrament it elevates it. Holy Communion Sunday is an occasion of importance. Church members are expected to be there and to prepare for it spiritually. The Anglican tradition is different. Since spiritual life is nourished at the Holy Communion it would seem tht frequent participation should be the norm. After all, the physical body could not be fed on meals once a quarter or three times a year! But there are dangers. We become used to it. We take it for granted. Mechanically we approach the communion rail. Automatically we stretch out our hands to receive the bread and the wine. We have done it all so many times before. The risk is even greater for the celebrant. He knows the service backwards. He could say it in his sleep. He may have to dash from one church to another to administer.

What is at stake here is failure to discern the Lord's body in the sacrament. It is the body that was crucified—broken—for us. And the actual partaking of the bread and the wine by the communicants is their proclamation, their preaching, of the crucifixion which the Church has to make until the Lord comes again. What they are saying in receiving is that the crucifixion is not only an event in the historical past but is God's action that gives eternal life to us now. It is interpreting and applying the cross of Christ.

It is better not to come to the Holy Communion than to come without discernment, for the risk is profaning the body and blood of the Lord. Harsh words? But I didn't write them. Read today's verses again. They hit me too.

DCF

45

The royal law

If you really keep the royal law found in Scripture, 'Love your neighbour as yourself,' you are doing right. But if you show favouritism, you sin and are convicted by the law as law-breakers. For whoever keeps the whole law and yet stumbles at just one point is guilty of breaking all of it. For he who said, 'Do not commit adultery,' also said, 'Do not murder.' If you do not commit adultery but do commit murder, you have become a law-breaker. Speak and act as those who are going to be judged by the law that gives freedom, because judgment without mercy will be shown to anyone who has not been merciful. Mercy triumphs over judgment!

Every Christian is a member of a royal priesthood—and this priesthood has a law. The royal law of love, James calls it. The Old Testament had told us to love our neighbour as ourselves, and so does the New. But the New Testament makes it quite clear who our neighbour is. The astonishing story of the Good Samaritan (it would have astonished its first hearers when Jesus told it because Samaritans were looked down on and priests and scribes were looked up to) shows us who Jesus sees as our neighbour, and shows us how people who keep this law actually treat their neighbours. It isn't loving to love a rich man and look down on a poor man. That is to break the royal law of love—and to break even one section of the law is to be a guilty person. That is true with human laws as well as God's laws—if we should ever be prosecuted for a parking offence, it won't help our case one jot to tell the magistrate that we haven't broken any of the laws relating to theft or murder or mugging. To break even one law is to

have earned and to deserve the penalty that goes with it—and the New Testament and the Old both say that 'the wages of sin is death'. What we earn and deserve through any sin is spiritual death, because all sins separate us from God.

To think about

Do I keep the royal priesthood's royal law of love?

SB

Show me!

What good is it, my brothers, if a man claims to have faith but has no deeds? Can such faith save him? Suppose a brother or sister is without clothes and daily food. If one of you says to him, 'Go, I wish you well; keep warm and well fed,' but does nothing about his physical needs, what good is it? In the same way, faith by itself, if it is not accompanied by action, is dead. But someone will say, 'You have faith; I have deeds.' Show me your faith without deeds, and I will show you my faith by what I do. You believe that there is one God. Good! Even the demons believe that—and shudder.

I am sitting in my garden as I write these notes, under a clear blue sky, and the late summer sunshine is ripening the heavy crop of blackberries on the bush which covers half my garden fence. Every year it gives a rich harvest to me and my friends—to make into bramble jelly, blackberry fool and blackberry and apple pie (which I like made with short pastry and served with double cream). The apples grow on a tree in the same border. But in a bucket by my back door there is a small blackberry bush with a big, dead branch on it—which will never bear a sweet, ripe blackberry.

A living faith isn't just about words, but about actions. Like Eliza Doolittle in a rage with Freddie in the musical *My Fair Lady*:

'Words, words, words, I'm so sick of words. I get words all day through, first from him, now from you. Is that all you blighters can do? Don't talk of stars, burning above. If you're in love—Show me!'

Words aren't enough. Belief in God isn't enough either. 'The demons be-lieve—and tremble', says James. If I just believe that my blackberries and apples are good for food it won't do me or my friends any good—only if I pick them and we eat them in a delicious pie.

Faith that works

You foolish man, do you want evidence that faith without deeds is useless? Was not our ancestor Abraham considered righteous for what he did when he offered his son Isaac on the altar? You see that his faith and his actions were working together, and his faith was made complete by what he did. And the scripture was fulfilled that says, 'Abraham believed God, and it was credited to him as righteousness,' and he was called God's friend. You see that a person is justified by what he does and not by faith alone. In the same way, was not even Rahab the prostitute considered righteous for what she did when she gave lodging to the spies and sent them off in a different direction? As the body without the spirit is dead, so faith without deeds is dead.

A week or two ago we looked at the agony of the day when Abraham went off into the wilderness to sacrifice his only son Isaac. He had believed God's promise that a son would be born to him and to Sarah. Then that belief was put to the most agonizing test of all—and it says that 'he reasoned that God could raise the dead' (Hebrews 11:19). It was faith that led to action. Just as the prostitute Rahab believed in the God of the Israelites and took action to shelter the two spies *because* she believed (see Joshua 2). Abraham's actions and hers flowed straight out of their faith, and showed to all the world that it was a living faith and not a barren one. Abraham and Rahab risked all that was most precious to them when the test of faith came to them—and (as it said in yesterday's passage) 'I by my works will show you my faith.' It was their actions that demonstrated their faith—just as my living blackberry bush shows me its life and its nature through its sweet, rich blackberries—and the dead blackberry branch, dry and full of prickles, shows me its deadness and its fruitlessness.

A question

Does my faith work?

SB

48

Tiny and powerful

Not many of you should presume to be teachers, my brothers, because you know that we who teach will be judged more strictly. We all stumble in many ways. If anyone is never at fault in what he says, he is a perfect man, able to keep his whole body in check. When we put bits into the mouths of horses to make them obey us, we can turn the whole animal. Or take ships as an example. Although they are so large and are driven by strong winds, they are steered by a very small rudder wherever the pilot wants to go. Likewise the tongue is a small part of the body, but it makes great boasts. Consider what a great forest is set on fire by a small spark.

A teacher's words are powerful, especially if the teacher is charismatic and popular. My own English teacher was a brilliant woman, who had once shared a flat with Dorothy Sayers (a cause of some pride to her pupils, and I suspect to her as well). She also had great charm, and when we were studying the works of George Meredith she told us that each one of us needed to have our own philosophy. I cannot remember how her statement connected with Meredith. But what she said sank in and had a powerful effect on me. I set out to find a philosophy of my own and read *The Riddle of the Universe* by Ernst Haenkl. It had a powerful effect on me. I became an atheist, and I remained one for several years—until reading the words of that great Christian teacher C.S. Lewis.

The power of a teacher lies in his words and his tongue. This summer I went sailing on the Norfolk Broads. A tiny turn on the rudder changed the whole direction of the boat—and a teacher's tongue can move a whole class of students.

A prayer

Lord Jesus, James says that we all make mistakes. Help me not to make serious ones—and may I never teach other people things that are seriously wrong.

SB

Destroying by fire

The tongue also is a fire, a world of evil among the parts of the body. It corrupts the whole person, sets the whole course of his life on fire, and is itself set on fire by hell. All kinds of animals, birds, reptiles and creatures of the sea are being tamed and have been tamed by man, but no man can tame the tongue. It is a restless evil, full of deadly poison. With the tongue we praise our Lord and Father, and with it we curse men, who have been made in God's likeness. Out of the same mouth come praise and cursing. My brothers, this should not be. Can both fresh water and salt water flow from the same spring? My brothers, can a fig-tree bear olives, or a grapevine bear figs? Neither can a salt spring produce fresh water.

James is getting swept along by his superb metaphor. A tiny fire can set a whole forest ablaze—most of us have seen the horror of a forest fire on television (and some of our Australian readers will have seen a live fire), with beautiful, living trees being destroyed in minutes—and terrified creatures racing for their lives from the flames.

In Britain today the courts are kicking against the high compensation awarded to people when the media have said or written something about them that isn't true—but perhaps the reason why juries have set such high figures is that they know how hard it is to wipe out a malicious word or kill a scandalous accusation once the thing has been said. People will say 'Well, I wonder— I expect there was something in it—after all, there is no smoke without fire.'

A prayer

Lord Jesus Christ, Word of the Father, James says that no human being can tame the tongue. So I ask you to tame mine— may I speak words of blessing that build people up and affirm them—and not words of destruction that burn them up. Let my words be like pure, unadulterated water that people can drink and enjoy.

SB

Works that are wise

Who is wise and understanding among you? Let him show it by his good life, by deeds done in the humility that comes from wisdom. But if you harbour bitter envy and selfish ambition in your hearts, do not boast about it or deny the truth. Such 'wisdom' does not come down from heaven but is earthly, unspiritual, of the devil. For where you have envy and selfish ambition, there you find disorder and every evil practice. But the wisdom that comes from heaven is first of all pure; then peace-loving, considerate, submissive, full of mercy and good fruit, impartial and sincere. Peacemakers who sow in peace raise a harvest of righteousness.

James is back to action. This time not showing our faith by our works, but showing our wisdom by our works. The way we behave will show to the world not just that we have a saving faith in the living God, in a relationship which means that we are the sons and daughters of God. The way we behave will also show the world how wise we are. We don't have to strut around in our cleverness—and anyway that sort of cleverness doesn't come from God. It is earthly and unspiritual and devilish—and the effect of it will be destructive. It is the sort of cleverness that likes to score off an opponent and put him or her down. But the wisdom that comes from God has a gentleness about it—a Christlikeness—which is tender and compassionate.

Sometimes the wisdom of God needs to deal with an opponent in a way that isn't tender and compassionate—but it still doesn't put the person down. It makes him think—and shows him his own soul. Think about the brilliant encounter that Jesus had with the Pharisees over paying taxes. When they brought the coin he told them to render to Caesar that which was Caesar's (because it had his image on it) and to God the things that were God's (and they knew that they were made in the image of God). That wisdom of God is there for us—in Christ. We only have to ask.

A prayer

Lord, give me wisdom, and let it show in my life, to the praise of your glory.

SB

It isn't fair!

The kingdom of heaven is like a landowner who went out early in the morning to hire men to work in his vineyard. He agreed to pay them a denarius for the day and sent them into his vineyard. About the third hour he went out and saw others standing ... He went out again about the sixth hour and the ninth hour and did the same thing. About the eleventh hour he went out and found still others standing around ... He said to them, 'You also go and work in my vineyard.' When evening came, the owner of the vineyard said to his foreman, 'Call the workers and pay them their wages ...' The workers who were hired about the eleventh hour came and each received a denarius. So when those came who were hired first, they expected to receive more. But each of them also received a denarius. When they received it, they began to grumble ... 'These men who were hired last worked only one hour,' they said, 'and you have made them equal to us who have borne the burden of the work and the heat of the day.'

'It isn't fair!' The child's cry that we never stop crying, even when we are very old. But what happened in the story *was* fair. The labourers got just what they had agreed with their employer. They got justice—but they didn't want the others to get mercy. 'It isn't fair'—for a dying thief to be promised paradise. 'It isn't fair'—for the women in the oldest profession in the world to go into the kingdom of heaven before the men who had made religion their profession. 'It isn't fair'—for the prodigal son to be given a party and the stay-at-home son nothing. Except that he wasn't given nothing. He was given the joy of his father's presence and his father's house all the days of his life—but he never saw the glory of them.

And what about the desolation of *not* working? Ask a man or woman who cannot get work what it feels like. Then think of the satisfaction of doing a good job for a lifetime—and of living a whole lifetime to the glory of God, and knowing the delight of that relationship, instead of the lostness of not knowing him until the very end.

SB

Doing it God's way

What causes fights and quarrels among you? Don't they come from your desires that battle within you? You want something but don't get it. You kill and covet, but you cannot have what you want. You quarrel and fight. You do not have, because you do not ask God. When you ask, you do not receive, because you ask with wrong motives, that you may spend what you get on your pleasures. You adulterous people, don't you know that friendship with the world is hatred towards God? Anyone who chooses to be a friend of the world becomes an enemy of God. Or do you think Scripture says without reason that the spirit he caused to live in us envies intensely?

A speaker I heard yesterday said that the choir of St Paul's Cathedral in London had won a Golden Disc for their astonishing recording of the Sinatra song 'I did it my way'. It wasn't that the recording itself was remarkable. It was as superb as that choir always is. But the subject astounded me, because it was the choir of a Christian cathedral. And the heart of Christian prayer is always 'Thy will be done'—not 'My will be done', followed by a triumphant song of praise about myself that 'I did it my way'.

James couldn't be clearer that demands for the satisfaction of our own passions are wrong and aren't answered—and the things we set our hearts on wrongly are the cause of all the wars and fightings in the world. When we desire passionately the things that we shouldn't have we are like an adulteress, and God gets jealous. When James is condemning friendship with the world he isn't talking about the sort of friendship that Jesus had with the publicans and sinners—that transformed their lives and turned some of them into saints. He is talking about 'human society in so far as it is organised on wrong principles and characterised by base desires, false values and egoism' (Revd Professor C.H. Dodd).

It is that egoism which sings triumphantly that 'I did it my way' instead of following the way of Jesus: 'Father, if it be possible, let this cup pass from me—nevertheless, not my will, but thine be done.'

SB

Draw near to God

But he gives more grace. That is why Scripture says: 'God opposes the proud but gives grace to the humble.' Submit yourselves, then, to God. Resist the devil, and he will flee from you. Come near to God and he will come near to you. Wash your hands, you sinners, and purify your hearts, you double-minded. Grieve, mourn and wail. Change your laughter to mourning and your joy to gloom. Humble yourselves before the Lord, and he will lift you up. Brothers, do not slander one another. Anyone who speaks against his brother or judges him speaks against the law and judges it. When you judge the law, you are not keeping it, but sitting in judgment on it. There is only one Lawgiver and Judge, the one who is able to save and destroy. But you—who are you to judge your neighbour?

Even if we have been unfaithful to God, and been friends with the world in the wrong way, that isn't the end of the story, or of our Christian lives. God will pour out his grace on us—the river of life that flows from the throne of God and gives life wherever it goes, washing away all pollution and degradation. The river of life is the Holy Spirit of God himself—and if we will come to him in obedience and faith, and wade into the river—and then start to swim in it—God will restore us and revive us.

James tells us to weep over our sins—and our most serious sin of all is a failure to love one another and to love God. But after the weeping then there is the wonder of joy and forgiveness. Christ loves us with an infinite and compassionate and tender love—and he longs to restore us, and for the love between us to start flowing again.

A prayer

Lord Jesus Christ, help me now to judge myself (and not my neighbour). Let the river of your grace wash over me and flood my heart with your love—and then flow out of me into the world that you love.

SB

We will . . . if God wills

Now listen, you who say, 'Today or tomorrow we will go to this city, spend a year there, carry on business and make money.' Why, you do not even know what will happen tomorrow. What is your life? You are a mist that appears for a little while and then vanishes. Instead, you ought to say, 'If it is the Lord's will, we will live and do this or that.' As it is, you boast and brag. All such boasting is evil. Anyone, then, who knows the good he ought to do and doesn't do it, sins.

James isn't condemning all forward planning—any more than Jesus was when he said in the Sermon on the Mount, 'Take no thought for the morrow.' Jesus was telling us not to fret about tomorrow's troubles. It's all right to decide on Friday what we want to eat on Sunday and go and buy it in the supermarket. For people in those days food and clothing weren't so certain (they aren't in other parts of our world in our day)—but they could look to God to provide for them.

What James is condemning isn't forward planning but arrogance. We can plan for the future within the will of God, but next week or next year we might be dead. Last week on my way to Oxford the prop shaft of my MGB sports car broke on the M25. I just had time, warned by an odd juddering, to move over from the fast lane into the slow lane, and then there was an enormous crack. My speed took me on to the hard shoulder but then I couldn't move. If I hadn't got there in time I suppose that I (and other people too) could have been dead, or at least badly injured—in one of those horrendous motorway pile-ups. I never got to my 10 o'clock meeting—and the whole event made me think quite solemn thoughts. James' remark seemed awesomely apt: 'If the Lord wills, we shall live, and we shall do this or that . . .'

A prayer

Lord, help me to plan ahead in the right way . . . knowing how uncertain my life is, and how fragile. Give me the wisdom to plan in accordance with your will . . . confident of your love, of your care, and of your infinite concern for me.

SB

Rich here, hungry there

Now listen, you rich people, weep and wail because of the misery that is coming upon you. Your wealth has rotted, and moths have eaten your clothes. Your gold and silver are corroded. Their corrosion will testify against you and eat your flesh like fire. You have hoarded wealth in the last days. Look! The wages you failed to pay the workmen who mowed your fields are crying out against you. The cries of the harvesters have reached the ears of the Lord Almighty. You have lived on earth in luxury and self-indulgence. You have fattened yourselves in the day of slaughter. You have condemned and murdered innocent men, who were not opposing you.

There is a great cry all through the Bible for social justice—and when it isn't done then God is very angry. We saw in Genesis this month (and probably knew anyway) that the great sin for which Sodom was infamous was sexual perversion. But it wasn't her only sin. Speaking through the prophet Ezekiel, God says: 'Now this was the sin of your sister Sodom: she and her daughters were arrogant, overfed and unconcerned; they did not help the poor and needy. They were haughty and did detestable things before me. Therefore I did away with them as you have seen' (Ezekiel 16:49, 50). When there was injustice, the cry of those who were sinned against reached the ears of God. James condemned the rich who didn't pay their reapers—and when they weren't paid it probably meant that they and their families didn't eat that day, because wages were so small. The poor who should have been paid were going hungry—and the rich who hadn't paid them were fattening themselves up, like a fatted calf being got ready for the day of slaughter.

A thought

Jesus said, 'But woe to you who are rich, for you have already received your comfort. Woe to you who are well fed now, for you will go hungry.'

Luke 6:24

SB

'He will come again'

Be patient, then, brothers, until the Lord's coming. See how the farmer waits for the land to yield its valuable crop and how patient he is for the autumn and spring rains. You too, be patient and stand firm, because the Lord's coming is near. Don't grumble against each other, brothers, or you will be judged. The Judge is standing at the door! Brothers, as an example of patience in the face of suffering, take the prophets who spoke in the name of the Lord. As you know, we consider blessed those who have persevered. You have heard of Job's perseverance and have seen what the Lord finally brought about. The Lord is full of compassion and mercy. Above all, my brothers, do not swear—not by heaven or by earth or by anything else. Let your 'Yes' be 'Yes', and your 'No', 'No', or you will be condemned.

The first Christians believed that the end of the world would be very soon. So soon that Paul had to write a letter to some of them in Thessalonica saying 'If a man will not work he shall not eat' (2 Thessalonians 3:10), because some people were sitting around waiting for the return of Jesus in glory—and living off their fellow Christians in the meantime. James is saying that the second coming of Christ will happen in the fullness of God's time. Just as a farmer has to wait patiently for his crop to be ready for the harvest, and is dependent on the spring rain to soften the soil for the planting, and the summer rain for the grain and the grapes to drink from the earth, so Christians have to wait in patience. Perhaps the picture is of the harvest to come of the souls of men and women when they are ready and ripe—and Christ who is the reaper wants the barns of heaven to be full.

A thought

'He will come again in glory to judge the living and the dead ...' What do you mean when you say those words? That last sentence of James is talking about oaths—but the implication is that every word which a Christian says should be true. So how does that apply to the words of the Creed?

SB

The power of prayer

Is any one of you in trouble? He should pray. Is anyone happy? Let him sing songs of praise. Is any one of you sick? He should call the elders of the church to pray over him and anoint him with oil in the name of the Lord. And the prayer offered in faith will make the sick person well; the Lord will raise him up. If he has sinned, he will be forgiven. Therefore confess your sins to each other and pray for each other so that you may be healed. The prayer of a righteous man is powerful and effective. Elijah was a man just like us. He prayed earnestly that it would not rain, and it did not rain on the land for three and a half years. Again he prayed, and the heavens gave rain, and the earth produced its crops. My brothers, if one of you should wander from the truth and someone should bring him back, remember this: Whoever turns a sinner from the error of his way will save him from death and cover over a multitude of sins.

James isn't talking about the gift of healing which some Christians are given by God. He is talking about what is ordinarily to happen when a church member is sick. I don't know how sick we have to be before we send (probably a common cold has to be put up with—as a way to give us an enforced rest because we have probably been overdoing it). But some of us never send at all. They did in the early Church and for several centuries after the start of it all. It wasn't until AD852 that the anointing with oil turned into the sacrament of extreme unction, anointing a person for his death. And that can sometimes have surprising effects. A Vicar I know gave extreme unction to an old lady in hospital. A week or so later he wondered why he hadn't been asked to take her funeral, so he rang the hospital. 'Oh, Mrs Smith has gone home,' they told him. So he went round to see her. 'Hello, Vicar,' she said as she opened the front door. 'Come in. You're the one who brought me back, aren't you?' Then she made him a cup of tea.

A thought

Pray... and sing!
Believe... and work!

SB

Two-way communications

God is the great communicator. He speaks to us and he listens to us—and we communicate with him in the same way. The difference is that we have to learn how to do it, and he does it perfectly. Once we know how it works we can encounter God through everything that exists and everything that happens to us—and the next seven weeks are about how God reveals himself and communicates with us.

We start with a week of Psalms about glory and living things from Douglas Cleverley Ford. The Psalms can teach us how to talk to God about everything—whether we are happy or sad, and whatever situation we are in. The Psalmist reflects on the nature and the glory of God and God's world, and on all our human joys and sorrows.

After that we look with David Winter at the way 'the Word became flesh and lived among us'. A skilled communicator himself, David Winter shows us how God communicates with us supremely by becoming one of us. We can know what God is like by looking at Jesus—and as we journey towards Easter Marcus Maxwell will help us to look at the life of Jesus in the Gospel of Matthew. His human life that ended in death—although that wasn't the end of the story. It is his death that we remember and 'show forth' in the Eucharist, and before we look at his life in Matthew's Gospel, Henry Wansbrough will give us some help on how to pray at the Eucharist, and also with different ways of praying (our side of the conversation and communication with God).

The hope of a glory

I consider that the sufferings of this present time are not worth comparing with the glory that is to be revealed to us. For the creation waits with eager longing for the revealing of the sons of God; for the creation was subjected to futility, not of its own will but by the will of him who subjected it in hope; because the creation itself will be set free from its bondage to decay and obtain the glorious liberty of the children of God. We know that the whole creation has been groaning in travail together until now; and not only the creation, but we ourselves, who have the first fruits of the Spirit, groan inwardly as we wait for adoption as sons, the redemption of our bodies. For in this hope we were saved. Now hope that is seen is not hope. For who hopes for what he sees? But if we hope for what we do not see, we wait for it with patience.

As we come today to Holy Communion we might find it helpful to think about suffering, in terms of what can lie on the other side of it. We could consider the men and women of the past who suffered for their faith, and of whom we can read in that marvellous chapter 11 of Hebrews. Chapter 12 goes on:

Therefore, since we are surrounded by so great a cloud of witnesses, let us also lay aside every weight, and sin which clings so closely, and let us run with perseverance the race that is set before us, looking to Jesus the pioneer and perfector of our faith, who for the joy that was set before him endured the cross, despising the shame, and is seated at the right hand of the throne of God.

Hebrews 12:1–2

Today, as you eat the bread and drink the wine of communion, will you remember the suffering of his death and passion—and also the great joy that came afterwards—for him and for us? Then think of what lies beyond our own sufferings, and rejoice in them, 'knowing that suffering produces endurance, and endurance produces character, and character produces hope . . .' (Romans 5:4). That is where today's reading finishes—with our hope for our own glorious redemption and liberty in which the whole of the creation will share.

SB

Properly rooted

And he shall be like a tree planted by the waterside: that will bring forth his fruit in due season. His leaf also shall not wither: and look, whatsoever he doeth, it shall prosper.

In spite of the beating it took in October 1987 in the great storm, the willow tree in my garden is still there, less a few branches and the foliage a bit thinner perhaps, but strong, upright and graceful.

I planted it (with more luck than judgment) in the right place when thirty years ago I carried it, then a sapling, from the nursery next door. We haven't a stream in our garden but parts of it are more damp than others, so my willow tree, rooted there, has never lacked moisture. Its leaves have never withered through drought.

Now your day today, and my day, is not going to be rooted in the right place unless we find some place in it for prayer as best we can. Otherwise in spite of all the rushing about we do (equally if our activities are restricted for some reason), we shall 'dry out'. By this I mean anxiety, fretfulness, maybe even bad temper, or depression will take over and we shall not be the strong, upright and graceful tree we could be. Prayer causes the day to be properly rooted.

So get down on your knees (arthritic sufferers excused) and start by thanking God for something. No excuses please! There is always something. That you can read this (with or without glasses) ...

that you have friends? (and perhaps a job?) ... that the birds still sing ...

Then confession. 'Lord I am sorry, I am not all I might be, I admit it; but you have promised to forgive me and help me to do better. I believe you.'

Then intercession, for other people who are in need, simply naming them, not telling God what to do! Then prayer for the day and what has to be done in it.

Simple? Yes, of course it is—and so was my planting of my willow tree in the proper place. But the result is striking. Prayer is the proper place to root each day.

A resolution

I will fix on a time and place for prayer each day, and stick to it.

DCF

We matter to God

For I will consider thy heavens, even the works of thy fingers: the moon and the stars, which thou hast ordained. What is man, that thou art mindful of him: and the son of man, that thou visitest him?

I haven't anything very important to do today. I shall not be flying to Hong Kong to arrange some big financial deal, nor pleading someone's cause in the Central Criminal Court, nor drafting some weighty memorandum for HM Government. Perhaps you will be occupied with activities of like importance with these. I don't know. But I shall dig my garden. That is all.

So what interest can the great God who made the heavens and the earth, the moon and the stars, possibly have in my little life? And how can I presume to bring my petty problems in prayer to the divine Creator and Sustainer of the Universe? From the standpoint of time and eternity all my affairs, yes especially mine, are but a drop in the ocean.

So what shall I do? Curl up and reckon I am of no more significance than a summer insect born at daybreak and destined to die at sundown, its little life over? Not if I take Psalm 8 to heart. 'What is man that thou art mindful of him (Did you notice that?—'mindful of him') and the son of man, that thou visitest him?...Thou makest him to have dominion of the works of thy hands and thou hast put all things in subjection under *his feet*.'

I matter to God. You matter to God.

So much is this the case that he is mindful of us and visited us notably in the coming of Christ to our world for our sakes.

So it is important how I go about today, even if I am only digging in the garden, and you too, occupied maybe on much more important affairs. And we can pray about them. God hears because we matter to him. Can we believe it? We ought to believe it. It helps us to lift up our heads and straighten our backs.

Prayer

Thank you, Lord, for letting me know you care for me.

DCF

A cheerful spirit

I have set the Lord continually before me: with him at my right hand I cannot be shaken. Therefore my heart exults and my spirit rejoices, my body too rests unafraid.

I like these two verses and the way the Psalm ends—

Thou wilt show me the path of life; in thy presence is the fullness of joy, in thy right hand pleasures for evermore.

Here is a cheerful person, and it's good to have such people around. Gloomy people create gloom and cheerful people create cheerfulness. And this writer's buoyant spirit was not superficial. It did not depend on a sense of well-being after a substantial meal, fine weather or the prospect of an evening's entertainment—none of which is to be despised. One the contrary he knew what it feels like to be afraid in life, even of life. Perhaps his heart had been torn by losing the love of someone, and all his future looked bleak. Possibly a job had fallen through. Could he trust anyone again? Could he even trust God? These are the hurting experiences, and the galling questions.

But he came through. He smiled again, he laughed again, he joked again. All because he got a grip again on the conviction that had all but slipped through his fingers that God cares, and is always at hand, and has pleasures to

give him even yet. God is no skinflint. This recognition lifted him up, not only one day, or two days, but right on beyond the last day of life altogether.

Prayer

Lord, I do not know what today will be like, what joys will come my way, what sorrows may hit me. I do not know how well I shall feel, what depressing news will be broadcast, what burdens I shall have to carry. But this I know: I know you care and I know I am in your presence— the Lord, with pleasures to give for evermore.

DCF

The glory of God

The heavens tell out the glory of God, the vault of heaven reveals his handiwork. One day speaks to another, night with night shares its knowledge, and this without speech or language or sound of any voice. Their music goes out through all the earth, their words reach to the end of the world.

When this note is read I would like to think the sun is shining, the sky a resplendent blue, with a gentle breeze from the south carrying warmth and freshness; but I can't arrange it! The weather may be wet, muggy and windy. That will be a pity because I would like to picture my reader drawn out of doors as if by a magnet, stretching arms and legs, throwing back the head and exclaiming out loud, whether anybody is at hand to hear or not, 'O what a *glorious day!*'

I wonder if our religion ever makes us erupt with such feelings? Not all the time, that is impossible, but sometimes? If not, there is something wrong with it. I once knew a lady who was a most dedicated Christian, earnest and worthy but oh so drab, not in her dress but in her demeanour. There seemed to be no glory in her faith, no buoyancy, no laughter, no slack, everything about her was taut and serious.

Psalm 19 reminds us of the glory of God; the heavens proclaim it, even the night sky with its myriads of myriads of stars cries out the message—God's work is glorious. So does every day, every night; the world over, the music of God's creation is heard from the North Pole to the Southern Seas.

Will I be revealing any glimpse of this glory as I go about today? Or will I be a drab, dull Christian, so that those who meet me will be tempted to exclaim, 'No thanks, I have enough troubles of my own'? What a pity! What a travesty of the light, even the light-heartedness, the Christian should show.

Prayer

Lord, give me grace to be cheerful today and reflect something of your glory, even if it rains.

DCF

Rejoicing

Have I not remembered thee in my bed: and thought upon thee when I was waking? Because thou hast been my helper: therefore under the shadow of thy wings will I rejoice.

Someone said to me recently, 'When I went to bed I thought over all that had happened during the day and I reckoned how fortunate I was about what had come my way and how happy it had made me.'

There is wisdom in running over the events of the day as in the presence of God before going to sleep. 'In every thing by prayer and supplication *with thanksgiving* let your requests be made known unto God', wrote Paul to the Christians in Philippi.

There is always something for which to be thankful, even if only for a bed on which to lie! And when the new day breaks and the eyes are opened, let the first thought be of God's continual care through the coming day as well as through the past night. Why? because God has been our helper, and will continue to be our helper. Knowing this we can face the dawn with confidence, and—who knows?—even sing, hum or whistle on the way to the bathroom: All will be well today. God will be with me.

Not that we can all be 'slap you on the back' types, though possibly such people have their place. Rejoicing 'in the Lord' in any case must not be forced. Perhaps it is most genuine when it is most modest. The hallmark is a look of contentment in eyes which does not quickly flare up into resentment. There is no more sure way of achieving this than by the habit of thanking God before falling off to sleep and remembering his continual presence on waking up.

A prayer

Lord, you are good and gracious and you know our frailties. I am sorry if sometimes I fall asleep resentful and wake up fearful. I am sorry if sometimes I am a gloomy person, withdrawn and complaining. Show me how to trust you, to rely on you, and to be thankful: I would like to be a joyful Christian.

DCF

We must sing

O sing unto the Lord a new song: sing unto the Lord, all the whole earth. Sing unto the Lord, and praise his Name: be telling of his salvation from day to day.

Wouldn't it be wonderful if instead of reading the words we all sang them! Think of it, hundreds and hundreds of people today right across the land and overseas all singing! Because the Psalms were written for singing. Some of them even have instructions attached about the tune. And they have become the songs of the Church. The Church has always been given to singing, to music and to bell-ringing.

People cannot, however, be made to sing. Singing has to come up from the heart. We need to have something to sing *about*. And anyone who has really heard the gospel of Jesus Christ, and trusted his/her life in consequence has precisely that. And how splendid if we know some hymns by heart, and not only the old ones but some of the modern ones as well. Sing them then, sing them out loud if you profess to be a Christian.

I like to sing in the garden when I am cutting the grass and somehow to sing outdoors amid the wonders of God's creation seems appropriate.

Let the heavens rejoice, and let the earth be glad: let the sea make a noise, and all that therein is. Let the field be joyful, and all that is in it:

then shall all the trees of the wood rejoice before the Lord.

Here is a picture of the whole creation praising God, and I joining in their company. Does this all sound comic? If you overheard me trying to sing now, though I was once a choirboy, you might think so. But I will hazard this guess, we shall do more to commend the gospel of our Lord by always being cheerful than by moralizing. Read verse 2 again, 'be telling of his salvation from day to day'. We do that when we have a song in our hearts and sometimes sing out loud with our throaty voices.

We praise thee, O God: we acknowledge thee to be the Lord. All the earth doth worship thee: the Father everlasting.

from the Te Deum

The light of life

In the beginning was the Word, and the Word was with God, and the Word was God. He was with God in the beginning. Through him all things were made; without him nothing was made that has been made. In him was life, and that life was the light of men. The light shines in the darkness, but the darkness has not understood it.

There came a man who was sent from God; his name was John. He came as a witness to testify concerning that light, so that through him all men might believe. He himself was not the light; he came only as a witness to the light. The true light that gives light to every man was coming into the world.

Matthew's Gospel begins in Bethlehem, Luke's in Jerusalem and Mark's by the river Jordan. But John's marvellous story of the life of Jesus begins in heaven: 'In the beginning was the Word'. The 'Word' is God's expression of himself. When we speak, we try to convey something of ourselves, even if it's no more than an urgent need for a cup of tea. Our words reveal to others what otherwise is kept inside our heads—they make our private ideas public! And so does God's 'Word'. In the beginning God 'expressed himself', made his private ideas public, in the creation of the universe. Now at this second turning point in history, with the coming into the world of Jesus, he has done it again. God has spoken to us (as the opening sentence to the Letter to Hebrews puts it) 'by his Son'. He has sent the perfect ambassador who will *in himself* perfectly convey God's message to the world.

A word that occurs over and over again in this Gospel makes its first appearance here: *light*. 'In him was light.' Years ago we took our children to the Dan yr Ogof caves in South Wales. In a huge underground vault the guide suddenly switched off all the lights, and the darkness almost hurt your eyes. It was really oppressive. And then, after a few seconds, he lit a match. It was like sun-rise!

Jesus comes into a dark world and he lights it up. As the prophet foretold, 'The sun of righteousness will rise, with healing in his wings.'

A prayer

Lord, help me to trust you in the darkness as well as in the light. But also give me day by day the light of Jesus to show me the way. Amen.

DW

One to one

He was in the world, and though the world was made through him, the world did not recognise him. He came to that which was his own, but his own did not receive him. Yet to all who received him, to those who believed in his name, he gave the right to become children of God— children born not of natural descent, nor of human decision or a husband's will, but born of God. The Word became flesh and made his dwelling among us. We have seen his glory, the glory of the One and Only [Son], who came from the Father, full of grace and truth.

Here is perhaps the single most vivid phrase in the whole Bible—and it certainly expresses the most extraordinary idea: 'The Word became flesh.' God's ideas, his purpose, his will had previously been communicated by his actions (in creation, for instance), in his words ('Let there be light') and in his influence on people ('He spoke by the prophets'). But now he has expressed himself in a person.

In my working life I have earned my living as a 'communicator'... to twenty children (as a teacher), to thousands of readers (as a writer) and even to millions of listeners (as a broadcaster). But if someone asked me who in the world *best* knows what I mean when I speak, it would be none of those, but my wife or my children. There is no substitute for one-to-one, inter-personal communication!

In the incarnation of Jesus, when the 'Word became flesh', God moved on from impersonal to personal communication. In Jesus, his Son, he showed us what he is like, spoke to us directly, as it

were. That's why most of us gain our best understanding of God by an encounter with Jesus. Of course, many failed to recognize him—'the world did not recognise him'. The 'world', in this Gospel, is society organized as though God doesn't exist—oblivious to his reality, his truth or his love. But the statement doesn't mean that *no one* recognized him. Look at the next sentence: 'Yet to all who received him, to those who believed in his name, he gave the right to become children of God'. Recognizing people is not a matter of skill, but of expectancy.

A prayer

Lord Jesus, forgive me when I have failed to recognize you, and help me to look expectantly for you, to believe in you and to receive you gratefully into my life.
Amen.

DW

Make way!

John testifies concerning him. He cries out, saying, 'This was he of whom I said, "He who comes after me has surpassed me because he was before me." ' From the fulness of his grace we have all received one blessing after another. For the law was given through Moses; grace and truth came through Jesus Christ. No-one has ever seen God, but God the One and Only [Son], who is at the Father's side, has made him known.

John the Baptist is a bit like the warm-up artist in a television show (if you'll pardon the comparison!). You never see him in the actual programme, because his work is done before it starts. But without him the studio audience would be totally unprepared and the show itself might never properly succeed.

John is *not* a minor figure in the New Testament story, but the last great prophet of the old one. And here he testifies that Jesus is the one of whom he had been speaking. Like all good preachers, he points away from himself to the Lord. As we read two days ago, he came to 'bear witness to the light'.

And now the light has come, in all its fulness, bringing 'one blessing after another'. Moses gave the Law to the human race, which, like the bathroom mirror, shows us the harsh truth about ourselves. By the standards of the Law we have failed—failed to love God with all our heart, mind, and soul and strength; failed to love our neighbour as ourselves.

But now that the light has come, there is fresh hope. The Law is harsh truth, which judges us. Jesus is the truth *and grace*, and he will show us a new way to God, not contrary to the Law of truth, but beyond and above it ... the way of grace. And *God himself has made this known*. The one who now stands by the river Jordan is the one who once was 'at the Father's side'.

So the coming of Jesus brings fresh hope to everyone who feels condemned by the requirement of the Law. It is, in other words, good news for failures ... the only sort of good news that's any use to most of us.

A prayer

Lord, as I look into the mirror of your Law I can only see my failure. Show me today in a fresh way the grace and truth that comes to us through Jesus. Amen.

DW

A voice . . .

Now this was John's testimony when the Jews of Jerusalem sent priests and Levites to ask him who he was. He did not fail to confess, but confessed freely, 'I am not the Christ.' They asked him, 'Then who are you? Are you Elijah?' He said, 'I am not.' 'Are you the Prophet?' He answered, 'No.' Finally they said, 'Who are you? Give us an answer to take back to those who sent us. What do you say about yourself?' John replied in the words of Isaiah the prophet, 'I am the voice of one calling in the desert, "Make straight the way for the Lord."'

John the Baptist drew huge crowds to hear him preach. He must have been an amazing sight, dressed in skins, wild-looking and unkempt. His message was uncompromising, too—repent, before it's too late! Not one calculated to win a lot of admirers.

The priests and Levites in Jerusalem were obviously a bit baffled by this strange man. He told them he wasn't the Messiah, of course—but was he, they wondered, the long-awaited returning Elijah? Or the great Prophet of the last days? No, he wasn't, he said. Then... who are you?

'I am a voice', he said. What a lovely, simple answer! The only important thing about me, he was claiming, is *what I say*. And what he said was in essence also sublimely simple: Get ready for the Lord's coming. In the marvellous imagery of second Isaiah, Flatten the hills, straighten the roads, build a highway—and watch him come!

But the astonishing thing was that the Lord they were to watch out for was *already there*. 'Among you stands one you do not know.' What an indictment of those religious leaders. Yet I suppose it could be said of me, often, that the Jesus I am looking for in different situations 'stands unrecognized'. Like the disciples on the road to Emmaus, my eyes are 'kept from recognizing him'. Sometimes we are praying for Jesus to come to us, and the thing above all that we need to grasp is that he is *already there*.

A prayer

Lord Jesus, help me today to recognize you, to see that in all the busyness of my life or the problems and anxieties of the day, you are already there. Amen.

DW

This is the one!

The next day John saw Jesus coming towards him and said, 'Look, the Lamb of God, who takes away the sin of the world! ...' Then John gave this testimony: 'I saw the Spirit come down from heaven as a dove and remain on him. I would not have known him, except that the one who sent me to baptise with water told me, "The man on whom you see the Spirit come down and remain is he who will baptise with the Holy Spirit." I have seen and I testify that this is the Son of God.'

We are nearly at the end of John the Baptist's part in this great drama of the coming of Jesus. In this passage, we are shown what *really* distinguished him from all the other people around at the time. *He knew who Jesus was.* Now I suppose Mary the mother of Jesus knew, or at least had a very strong idea, of the real identity of her son. But at this point in the story, the likelihood is that no one else in the whole world knew. Jesus had grown up through what have been called his 'hidden years', because we know virtually nothing about them, and to his neighbours and contemporaries he was simply 'the carpenter's son'.

But John the Baptist knew better, and he knew because he had been shown it. He had baptized hundreds, perhaps thousands of people, but on only one has he 'seen the Spirit come down and remain' (v. 33). And 'the one who had sent him to baptise'—God himself—had told him that the person to whom this happened would be the one who would 'baptise with the Holy Spirit.' It is the particular work of the Holy Spirit to make things plain, to reveal God's purpose, to open our eyes to things we should otherwise miss. Of course, it is not always obvious. I suspect it was not obvious to the other people standing by at the baptism of Jesus that the Holy Spirit had come down and remained on him. But it was seen by the one for whom it was intended.

Day by day the Holy Spirit of God is at work in us and around us, opening our eyes to see things we have missed before and showing us his purpose for us and those around us. *Our* part in this process is to be alert and open to the Spirit, as John was. Then we will see, and understand.

A prayer

Heavenly Father, keep me open and alert to what you are saying and doing, so that I may see and understand. Amen.

DW

See for yourself

The next day John was there again with two of his disciples. When he saw Jesus passing by, he said, 'Look, the Lamb of God!' When the two disciples heard him say this, they followed Jesus. Turning around, Jesus saw them following and asked, 'What do you want?' They said, 'Rabbi' (which means Teacher), 'where are you staying?' 'Come,' he replied, 'and you will see.'

There are two memorable sayings in this passage. The first has become well known to us in church art and in the liturgy: echoing 'The Lamb of God, who takes away the sin of the world'. Its familiarity may blind us to its astonishing claim. In the Law of Moses, the ritual involved in forgiveness required the sinner to lay his or her hand on the head of a lamb or goat, confess his sin and then offer the animal as a sacrifice. (Leviticus 4:27-29). In this way, ritually at least, the sins of the individual and of the community could be taken away. But now, says John, God has sent his own 'lamb' and he will take away 'the sin of the world'—a cosmic sacrifice for a cosmic fault. And that 'lamb' is Jesus. His death would be sufficient for all of the world's sin—past, present and future. He would 'take it away'.

The second saying is less dramatic, but also very revealing. It is the invitation Jesus gave to the two disciples of John—one of them was Andrew—when they asked where he was staying. 'Come and see,' he replied. In one sense it is an invitation no one ought to refuse. 'Just come and have a look', he says, 'See whether you like it, whether my lifestyle, my message, my friendship, really appeals to you. You don't have to stay, or commit yourself... just *come and see.*' Sometimes we are very anxious that those we pray for and care about should become totally committed to Christ. Very well. But first, let them 'taste and see how gracious the Lord is'. Give them a chance to 'come and see'. Few who have genuinely tasted have failed to stay.

A prayer

Lord Jesus, as you opened the door of your simple lodging by Galilee and invited those young seekers to come in, draw us and those we pray for gently into the place of blessing. Amen.

DW

Come and see Jesus

Andrew, Simon Peter's brother, was one of the two who heard what John had said and who had followed Jesus. The first thing Andrew did was to find his brother Simon and tell him, 'We have found the Messiah' (that is, the Christ). Then he brought Simon to Jesus. Jesus looked at him and said, 'You are Simon son of John. You will be called Cephas' (which, when translated, is Peter). The next day Jesus decided to leave for Galilee. Finding Philip, he said to him, 'Follow me.' Philip, like Andrew and Peter, was from the town of Bethsaida. Philip found Nathanael and told him, 'We have found the one Moses wrote about in the Law, and about whom the prophets also wrote—Jesus of Nazareth, the son of Joseph.' 'Nazareth! Can anything good come from there?' Nathanael asked. 'Come and see,' said Philip.

Jesus has begun to recruit his little band of disciples. Andrew was the first and he brought his brother, who was to be renamed Peter. Then he called Philip and Philip invited his friend Nathanael to come as well. It was a simple human process, yet something very deep was at work. I don't suppose Andrew or Philip saw at the time the enormous significance of what they had done. They just invited a brother and a friend to share an experience which they felt was rather special. But for the four of them things would never be the same again. Often in life apparently small events, casual meetings, become links in a life-changing experience, leading to a new career, perhaps, or a marriage, or a lasting friendship. A book or a talk can have the same effect—a huge impact from what we had thought was an unimportant event. I think it was like that for these four young men.

They could have declined the invitation. Nathanael, it seems, nearly did—'Can anything good come from Nazareth?' he asked scornfully. Wisely Philip didn't argue with him. He just repeated the invitation Jesus had given earlier—'Come and see.' Perhaps we make the whole business of sharing our faith in Jesus too complicated. Certainly nothing could be simpler or more straightforward than what we see here. Or, of course, more utterly effective.

A prayer

Lord, help me to share with others what you have shared with me, not by arguing or pleading, but by inviting them to come and see who you are and what you can do for them. Amen.

DW

The mind of Christ

For who among men knows the thoughts of a man except the man's spirit within him? In the same way no-one knows the thoughts of God except the Spirit of God. We have not received the spirit of the world but the Spirit who is from God, that we may understand what God has freely given us . . . The man without the Spirit does not accept the things that come from the Spirit of God, for they are foolishness to him, and he cannot understand them, because they are spiritually discerned. The spiritual man makes judgments about all things, but he himself is not subject to any man's judgment: 'For who has known the mind of the Lord that he may instruct him?' But we have the mind of Christ.

Today's reading provides the theme for the day. 'Who has known the mind of the Lord? . . . But we have *the mind of Christ.*' 'If I meet her today', my grandmother would say, 'I'll give her a piece of my mind'. As a child, I used to wonder what she meant. How could she give someone 'a piece of her mind'? And in any case, *which* piece? Wouldn't that leave her with less than she started with? What she meant, of course, was that she would like to convey to the other person exactly how she felt about something (usually, about something they had done that she didn't approve of!). And when the Bible speaks of Christians having 'the mind of Christ', or commands us to 'Let this mind be in you that was also in Christ Jesus', it is describing a process by which the way Jesus feels about something, or the way in which he sees it, becomes the way *we* feel about it or see it. It's almost a matter of thought transference: making his thoughts our thoughts. Now this may sound very mystical and mysterious, a process only open to exceptional saints.

Yet it's a process we're familiar with in ordinary life. When two people know each other very well, eventually they begin to share each other's thoughts. At the same moment *both* say, 'Let's make a cup of tea' or 'Should we phone Auntie?' They have truly begun to give each other (and receive from each other) a 'piece of their mind'! It's no more complicated than that in the spiritual realm. If we get to know the Lord very well and spend a good deal of time with him, then eventually we shall find ourselves feeling and thinking about things in the way he does. We shall have received 'a piece of his mind'.

A prayer

Heavenly Father, as I join with other Christians today in prayer and worship, draw me closer to your Son, so that I may think and feel as he does. Amen.

DW

The prayer of quiet

The lamp of God had not yet gone out, and Samuel was lying in Yahweh's sanctuary, where the ark of God was, when Yahweh called, 'Samuel! Samuel!' He answered, 'Here I am,' and, running to Eli, he said, 'Here I am, as you called me.' Eli said, 'I did not call. Go back and lie down.' So he went and lay down. And again Yahweh called, 'Samuel! Samuel!'

The first need for prayer is quiet. Quiet around us usually helps, as when the boy Samuel was at peace in the quiet of the sanctuary in the evening, though it is possible to pray amid the turmoil of the bus or tube. Some people train themselves to pray in such circumstances and manage to keep their quiet despite the noise.

Physical stillness is very important. Teresa of Avila, one of the greatest of all teachers of prayer, stressed that you must be comfortable to pray; there is no harm in praying on a bed, provided that you don't go to sleep! Lying flat on the ground is often safer.

But most important is interior stillness. For Samuel the lamp of God had not yet gone out. Some people like to concentrate in a darkened room on the flickering light of a candle. It can focus the mind on the silent, living, powerful presence of God. I am often driven to prayer by turmoil, disquiet, worry for the future, tragedy or failure in the past. Then especially I need the focus of light outside myself. I need deliberately to quieten myself and draw out my attention to the steady and reliable light which burns for ever. And, as I devote my attention to that light outside myself, I may hear a murmuring which could be no more than the sound of the wind. Samuel, Samuel.

No answer but 'Here I am, Lord.'

HW

The prayer of healing

Prayer needs to be a moment of healing. An athlete or a dancer is seldom without some sort of twinges; this sort of activity pushes the body to its limits—and yet it also brings a certain security of a well-tuned body. In prayer I can allow myself to feel the twinges, and can put them under the sun-lamp of God's healing, allowing God's warmth and light to play over the bruises and heal them as he wills. Paul compares his activity as a Christian to that of an athlete, training and straining forward to the prize. I buffet my body, he says. In trying to serve God we are always getting bruised, cut or hurt in some way. Again, it was Teresa of Avila who said, 'Lord, if you treat your friends like that, it is no wonder that you have so few of them.'

So prayer can be like the boxer withdrawing into his corner between rounds, or the soldier taking refuge in his dug-out to escape the shelling.

Two men went up to the Temple to pray, one a Pharisee, the other a tax collector. The Pharisee stood there and said this prayer to himself, 'I thank you, God, that I am not grasping, unjust, adulterous like everyone else, and particularly that I am not like this tax collector here.' ... The tax collector stood some distance away, not daring even to raise his eyes to heaven;

but he beat his breast and said, 'God, be merciful to me, a sinner.' This man, I tell you, went home again justified, the other did not.

One of the great comforts about prayer is that I need not even pretend to be invulnerable or successful. To the rest of the world I do perhaps feel the need to keep up appearances, put a brave face on it, not allow the chinks in my armour to be seen. When I come to pray I can forget all this. We know from the story of Adam and Eve that failure comes as no surprise to God; failure is built into our human nature. But even when I have failed, God still walks in the garden in the cool of the evening and calls to me. I have the alternative of trying to hide and feeling naked and defenceless like Adam, or coming out into the open and asking God to clothe and heal me.

A prayer

Have mercy on me, O God,
in your faithful love,
in your great tenderness
wipe away my offences;
wash me clean from my guilt,
purify me from my sin.

Psalm 51:1–2 (NJB)

HW

The prayer of thanks

Thanks can seem very artificial. A child is taught to say 'Thank you'—often a stilted, shy moment, as embarrassing to the donor as to the recipient. It is only when this little ceremony is over that the real thankfulness begins to be shown. Does the child rush around, showing the gift to everyone, demonstrating it, talking about it, asking about it (probably even breaking it!) within a short space of time? If so, then the gift is a success. If the gift is put quietly and reverently aside for another day—'for when Lucy grows up'—it may not have been quite so ideal! In the same way, the first thing to be done when children meet up after Christmas is to tell each other about their presents—and of course children often show in the raw the instincts that are covered up or dissipated by the restraints on adults.

...amid great rejoicing, [David] brought the ark of God up ... to the City of David ... And David danced whirling round before Yahweh with all his might, wearing a linen loincloth. Thus with war cries and blasts on the horn, David and the entire House of Israel brought up the ark of Yahweh ... Michal daughter of Saul was watching from the window and when she saw King David leaping and whirling round before Yahweh, the sight of him filled her with contempt.

The prayer of thanksgiving consists in being aware of the generosity of God, and sharing that joy with God and with our fellow human beings. Prayer is always directed to God, but this sort of prayer overflows into less 'holy' behaviour. When David leapt and danced before the presence of God symbolized by the ark, his regal wife, the daughter of the deposed king, disapproved: he was behaving like an uninhibited child. But that moment was her final rejection too, while David continued to enjoy God's favour. He was like the child who forgets everything in the delight of a present; he forgot his royal dignity in the delight of bringing the presence of God to his city, the sign of God's choice and favour. 'Religion' has a grim and solemn ring to it, but the love of God does not. I am a child of God, and have no need to inhibit my reactions of joy and thanksgiving at my awareness of his presents. Children make lists of birthday presents they want. It can do no harm sometimes to begin listing presents received from God (you can only begin; if you complete the list you have missed the point and gone wrong!). One way is to contrast with what might have been.

Pray

Give thanks to the Lord, for he is good.
His love has no end.

HW

77

The prayer of petition

For many people prayer means asking for things. It is always praying for something. Get into a desperate, cliff-hanging situation, and there is nothing to do but pray. Prayer becomes a sort of cupboard-love activity, a sort of supernatural rescue kit. There is no doubt that much more praying is done in schools and universities at examination time than at any other moment! However, in calmer moments we do recognize the short-sightedness of this activity; if the crisis is really great, we may even offer a prayer of thanksgiving if the rescue kit works. This prayer of asking is puzzling. A child asks its father for a present because the father needs to know what his child wants. If God knows everything, he knows already what we need and what we want. There is a further difficulty: if I pray for a fine day for a wedding, and the farmer next door prays for rain, are we to suppose that God weighs up the prayers, makes his decision, and changes the weather to suit? Or even that God knew beforehand, when planning the world's weather, that these petitions would be put to him?

David pleaded with Yahweh for the child; he kept a strict fast and went home and spent the night lying on the ground, covered with sacking ... On the seventh day the child died ... David ... realised that the child was dead ... David got off the ground, bathed and anointed himself and put on fresh clothes. Then he went into Yahweh's sanctuary and prostrated himself. On returning to his house, he asked to be served with food and ate it ... 'When the child was alive ... I fasted and wept because I kept thinking, "Who knows? Perhaps Yahweh will take pity on me and the child will live." But now that he is dead, why should I fast?'

I am not always given what I pray for. Jesus was not delivered from the death he feared, but the Letter to the Hebrews says that his prayer was heard. How can this be? Surely one of the purposes of the prayer of petition is to attune myself to God's fatherly will? I pray earnestly for my friend's recovery, but the friend dies. Is my prayer wasted? By the very act of praying I recognize that God is my loving Father, that he cares. I do not want to change his will. My prayer brings home to me that, however much it hurts at the time, what he wills is willed in love for me personally.

Reflect and pray

He offered up prayer and entreaty, with loud cries and with tears, to the one who had the power to save him from death, and his prayer was heard.

Hebrews 5:7

HW

Praying the Scriptures 1

Bible readers would hardly be Bible readers unless their reading issued in prayer. So in the School of Prayer it is undoubtfully helpful to include this particular matter. But one person's experience may be useful to others. How does reading the Scriptures lead me into prayer?

First, before embarking on the reading, comes a moment of prayer of recollection. I need to remind myself that the purpose of this reading is not study or simple recreation; it is not primarily even increased understanding of the things of God, but to bring me to awareness of God in my life now. God is there, within and around, if only I will open myself to him.

When I start to read, I find myself led to prayer in several ways:

1. The wonder of the preservation of the Scriptures at all. God has given us his word, handed down in the community, and treasured for so many centuries. A rough cross grasped in a martyr's hand is sanctified by the use made of it; just so, if the Bible were not God's word in the first place, it would have become a link with God through its use by God's people. At every stage it was treasured, handed on, recorded and meditated upon. I find it matters for prayer that so many Christians have found their way to God fortified by the Bible.

In the Revelation to John comes the vision of the saints and martyrs, waiting for the completion of their number.

> When he broke the fifth seal, I saw underneath the altar the souls of all the people who had been killed on account of the Word of God, for witnessing to it . . . Each of them was given a white robe, and they were told to be patient a little longer, until the roll was completed of their fellow-servants and brothers . . .

2. In reading the story of God's people before Christ, I am led to prayer by the thought of God's endless care and tenderness for his people, his humaneness (so to speak) in choosing an ordinary people, as unfaithful as ourselves, as primitive as their neighbours, as selfish and fallible as anyone. In a way, the point which leads most readily to prayer is how hard God had to work to achieve his aims! He led them on gradually, educating them as a Father educates his son, polishing them like a jewel, to be ready to give birth to his Son.

> When Israel was a child I loved him, and I called my son out of Egypt . . . I myself taught Ephraim to walk, I myself took them by the arm, but they did not know that I was the one caring for them, that I was leading them with human ties, with leading-strings of love.

HW

Praying the Scriptures 2

3. For the Christian, Jesus is the way to the Father, and learning to pray the Scriptures must be chiefly a matter of learning to pray in, with and through Christ in the Scriptures.

In reading the Gospel stories I may imagine myself beside him in the events described, witness with him, or with his disciples, the storm on the sea, the healings of the sick. A few verses often suffice to lead me to share this experience with the Lord. Or I may listen with them to the parables, hear the story of the lost sheep, or the judgment of the sheep and goats from the Good Shepherd himself. I may share his Passion— only too unfaithfully like Peter and the rest of the disciples, or at the foot of the cross, like Mary and the Beloved Disciple. At any moment of this, sharing to enter into conversation with the Lord is prayer itself. What does he say to me, knowing me through and through as he does? What do I say to him, who knows me so well? No pretence is needed or possible.

> During his stay in Jerusalem for the feast of Passover many believed in his name when they saw the signs that he did, but Jesus knew all people ... he never needed evidence about anyone; he could tell what someone had within.

4. One way of praying the Scriptures, taught to me years ago by an old monk (long since taken up into the prayer of heaven) is to be alert in reading to words and ideas which can spark off prayers on their own. Certain ideas are full of Christian values: 'faith', 'inheritance', 'hope', 'the glory of God', 'taking the form of a slave'. These words and phrases are so familiar that it is easy to pass them over without noticing. But they are full of meaning, and can become ever fuller if one notices them, arrests them in full flight and prays through them. It is easy to form a little quiverful of favourite phrases which lead to prayer. Any of these can become a sort of Christian mantra, repeated again and again, expressing a whole world of thought and prayer.

> ... you have been stamped with the seal of the Holy Spirit of the Promise, who is the pledge of our inheritance, for the freedom of the people whom God has taken for his own, for the praise of his glory.

It is always worth ending the prayer of reading with a moment's absolute quiet. I listen to God to see if there is any special message he wishes to leave in my mind, and special joy he wishes to give me.

HW

Getting up on Sunday morning

It is most important for the Christian life, to be sure that the calendar or diary you buy begins the week on a Sunday, not a Monday. Sunday is not just the tail end of the week, to be spent recovering from Saturday night and gearing up for the toil of Monday. It is not even a day of rest: the Jewish Sabbath, when God rested from his labour of creating, was Saturday.

For the Christian, the week begins on Sunday, because then is the celebration of the Lord's resurrection, the beginning of new life. So the first prayer on Sunday morning must always be about life. Open the curtains and look out of the window at the living trees and the grass and the sun—or the grey clouds bringing nourishing rain, and the human achievement in concrete buildings—or the shanty town of cardboard, pulsating with the myriad variations of life and temperament—and praise the Lord for his gifts.

This is only the beginning. Who would eat pizza if it was only the pastry-base? To be a Christian means to believe that everything important in life flows from the resurrection of Christ. The life that we see out of the window is only the pastry-base, enriched by and loaded with the Christian mystery.

Since you have been raised up to be with Christ, you must look for the things that are above, where Christ is, sitting at God's right hand. Let your thoughts be on the things above, not on the things that are on the earth, because you have died, and now the life you have is hidden with Christ in God. But when Christ is revealed—and he is your life—you, too, will be revealed with him in glory.

So my second prayer of the day on Sunday, following immediately on the first, must be about what makes life worth living in the long run, that my life is hidden with Christ in God. 'What profit would life have been to us, had Christ not come as our Redeemer? Most blessed of all nights, chosen by God to see Christ rising from the dead!' runs the ancient hymn of the resurrection on Easter night. My christening-day is far more important than my birthday. Quite apart from the quality of life, the life that began on the christening-day lasts far longer! Every Sunday is, so to speak, the birthday of that life, celebrating again the moment when that life began. So every prayer and every thought on Sunday has the resurrection as its background. The Eucharist is taken up into this.

HW

A noisy prayer

The idea that prayer must always be a quiet and private matter is relatively modern. Reading used always to be done aloud: the young St Augustine was astounded to see Bishop Ambrose of Milan reading without a sound proceeding from his lips. St Benedict needed to warn his monks not to make too much noise even when praying on their own. Then there were medieval stories of a juggler and an acrobat whose way of praying was to praise God by juggling and doing acrobatics in front of the altar.

The racket which signalled worship of the gods of Babylon—horn, pipe, lyre, zither, harp, bagpipe and every other kind of instrument—was described with relish by the author of Daniel, and only a slightly muted version appears in the Psalm of praise which closes the Psalter:

Praise him with fanfare of trumpet,
praise him with harp and lyre,
praise him with tambourines
    and dancing,
praise him with strings and pipes,
praise him with the clamour of
    cymbals,
praise him with triumphant
    cymbals.
Let everything that breathes praise
    Yahweh.

Prayer could be an effervescent and extrovert affair. There is no point in praising someone inaudibly: the praise must be heard, and the biblical instinct is to make sure of this with a clutch of noisy instruments.

HW

The Christian assembly

When we come to meet the people of God it is worth while to pause a moment and pray about them. As we assemble together to celebrate the Eucharist, the Supper of the Lord, we need to think who they are. People of God indeed! What a crew! A motley gathering from many walks of life, many ages, many professions and none, many temperaments, many achievements and none, many faults and never none. As people are assembling for the Eucharist it sometimes strikes me to ask mytself, 'Would you have chosen this lot for company?' But what about the company Jesus kept? A few fishermen, a customs-officer or two, constantly quarrelling, missing the point, needing the lesson to be endlessly repeated, sarcastic to their leader, squabbling about precedence behind each other's backs, and finally running away in a dead funk. And Peter! Enthusiastic, clumsy, impetuous, muscling in with helpful suggestions just where he was not wanted, unreliable, full of protestations not worth the breath that carried them. These were the foundation-stones of Christ's Church. They were joined by a motley crew of outcasts. Whatever my particular current pet hate, he or she was there! Jesus approached the genuine outcast, the moral and physical lepers, who revolted any decent people.

Even that lot looks quite good beside the people of Corinth who were such a constant headache to Paul: dockers, stevedores, prostitutes, philosophers, selfish rich people and the starving poor; some timidly scrupulous, some complacently sure of their opinions and conduct (which were wrong, into the bargain). That was the community so rich in the gifts of the Spirit: healing, teaching, speaking in tongues.

So whatever the Christian assembly I meet with is like, I can pray about the honour it is to be with them. After all, Christ chose each of them just as he chose me. Christ loves each of them as they are, just as he loves me as I am.

You are a chosen race, a kingdom of priests, a holy nation, a people to be a personal possession to sing the praises of God who called you out of the darkness into his wonderful light. Once you were a non-people and now you are the People of God; once you were outside his pity; now you have received pity.

It is not the achievements of the people of God or their holiness that should drive me to prayer, but the thought that God loves them. Am I any more perfect? Whatever the state of X or Y who are assembling to praise the Lord, they would not be assembling unless they were trying to praise the Lord at least as hard as I am.

'Lord, save your people' is the refrain of one of the litanies.

HW

This is the word of the Lord

The Bible reader should feel quite at home here, and well prepared to pray the readings. The word of the Lord has a quite special place in the Eucharist, and indeed in all its public readings.

First, the word of God was always a public proclamation, whether it was the word of the Law in the Pentateuch, or the word of the Prophets, or the word of Jesus himself. Even Paul's letters were intended to be read out in the assembly of the local church gathered together. It was not written to be read in private quiet; it was first announced by word of mouth in the heat of the moment, in response to some pressing need, and only later came to be written down for subsequent generations. So, even if we are used to reading the word of God in reflective solitude, the public reading is its prime position, and there we are the people of God. There we need to respond to God's message in a new and more immediate way.

I find it helps to imagine that I and the people around me are standing marooned on the baking sand amid the stark rocks of the desert of Sinai, or fearfully huddled in the starving and besieged Jerusalem which is being threatened by the Babylonian armies, or secretly gathered in the main room of Phoebe's small house in Corinth to hear the letter which has arrived from our brother Paul. What solution has the Lord to our problem? Perhaps the people of God are always threatened. Perhaps it is only then that we shed our complacency and turn to him. If we can see our need then, we will listen in prayer and respond with gratitude.

Secondly, there seems to be a feeling that the Eucharist simply does not take place without God's own teaching coming first. The Last Supper began with the recital of the great deeds of God at the exodus, the special acts by which God made them his special possession, his own people. The feeding of the 5,000 is a foretaste of the eucharistic meal—the Messiah gathered with his disciples—and that begins with teaching.

So as he stepped ashore he saw a large crowd; and he took pity on them because they were like sheep without a shepherd, and he set himself to teach them at some length.

In the discourse on the bread of life in John 6, the bread of life is presented first as the Wisdom of God to be believed, and only afterwards as the eucharistic bread to be eaten.

'It is my Father's will that whoever sees the Son and believes in him should have eternal life.'

In giving us his word, the Lord is preparing us for his Eucharist.

HW

Eucharist

'*Efcharisto*', says the little girl in Greece as you hand her a sweet: 'Thank you.' '*Efcharisto*', says the girl at the checkout counter casually as you hand her the money. The Eucharist is all about thanks (and modern Greeks pronounce the ancient *u* as *f*).

When Jesus sat at his last supper with his disciples for the Passover meal, the thanksgiving was about liberation. In response to a question from the youngest member of the party, the father of the household explained the meaning of the meal, and all its unusual elements, in terms of thanks for the deliverance from Egypt, and for all the mighty works God did for his people in the desert of Sinai. It was a recital of God's glorious interventions for his people. With pews, altars, pulpits, hymn books, stylized antiquated clothing, the appearance has moved on no little from a simple supper of nomads. But the great prayer of the Eucharist is still a hymn of thanks for the great deeds of God.

This thanks differs from the personal thanks I give when I get up, the care I have received in the 'accidents' of history. This is more an expression of thanks for the history of salvation, an external thanks for the external development of the people of God down the ages, an official act.

So the continuity and the tradition from the earliest times are important. As I stand at the altar, next to me in the circle may stand Abraham or David or John the Baptist. Next along perhaps comes one of those early martyrs, such as Felicity or Lucy or Clement. Then we might pair an interesting later couple (of very different mentality) like Teresa of Avila and John Wesley, then the Ugandan martyrs of the last century, both Protestant and Catholic (these, perhaps, less surprised to find themselves together). All these are my company in the prayer of thanks.

These also join in the prayer or petition for their successors who are now undergoing their period of testing, for the great Church in its present trials. In our easy church life, I had never realized the extent of this until I met, within the space of a few months, people who had worked beside Christian doctors and nurses shot in Zimbabwe, and able men whose Christianity had cost them careers behind the Iron Curtain and held them in menial, street-cleaning jobs. Our prayer is for the Church, known and unknown, and for the difficult decisions its leaders must take.

It ends with a prayer of confidence in God's glory. In Christ he can make it all his own: 'through him, with him, in him, in the unity of the Holy Spirit, all honour and glory is yours'.

HW

The bread of life

A meal is always a festive occasion. It may be the family meeting together. It may be friends joining up again. It may be a welcome to a passing acquaintance. It may be a sweetener in a business deal. But a meal without a smile, a meal without any joining of hearts, is a monster. In a society without police or hotels, this was even more the case: friends relied on friends to help them and provide safety on their journey. The horror of Judas' betrayal was that he had just shared the same dish, the expression of fraternity. In a world without telephones and little post, meeting together brought an added excitement.

When Paul comes to write to the Corinthians about the Eucharist, his main concern is unity in the Lord. The contrast is with what seems to have been actually happening: everyone brought their own provisions, the rich caroused and got drunk, while the poor were left hungry and ashamed. They then went on to share in the one loaf and the one cup. To Paul, this seemed a mockery: they were sharing in the body of Christ.

The most striking point is the sense in which Paul uses the expression 'body' of Christ.

The loaf of bread which we break, is it not a sharing in the body of Christ? And as there is one loaf, so we, although there are many of us, are one single body, for we all share in the one loaf.

He goes on to explain about the body of Christ: each member has a different function, but each has a vital part to play (and he nicely explains the decent conventions of clothing as lending honour to those parts which would otherwise lack honour!). Together, the various and varied members make up a body, Christ's body.

My instinct is to take Paul and shake him till he will explain himself: is the loaf the body? Is the sharing the loaf? Are we, the members, the body? Is Christ the body—or are we? Does the loaf make the body—or does the sharing? These questions are just as vexed as the set of questions which split Christians at the Reformation: In what sense is the bread Christ's body? In what sense is it bread?

Whatever the details, the essence of the Eucharist is sharing in Christ as one family at Christ's own meal. It is the expression and the nourishment of unity. Most important, it is the expression that our unity is in Christ. It is not because we particularly like each other, that we live near each other, or that we share the same interests or tendencies. But our unity is Christ, and as I look at another person across the church, our bond is Christ.

HW

The new covenant

The centre of the Eucharist is the words of institution. At every Christian Eucharist, whatever the brand or colour of Christianity, the action is justified by a recital of the little story of Jesus' actions. Already in Paul's time, this story was traditional. He handed it on to his converts to learn by heart. He himself had so learnt it; it is couched in terms significantly different from his own language. It is probably the most ancient Christian text we have. This would make it uniquely sacred, if there were no other reasons.

The tradition I received from the Lord and also handed on to you is that on the night he was betrayed, the Lord Jesus took some bread, and after he had given thanks, he broke it, and he said, 'This is my body, which is for you; do this in remembrance of me.' And in the same way, with the cup after supper, saying, 'This cup is the new covenant in my blood.'

Every schoolchild (certainly one who has read Mark Twain) knows that a special pact is sealed in blood. Blood is the sign of life. So to seal a pact in blood means to put one's life into it. The Israelites held that blood belongs to God because all life comes from him. So the pact God made with the Israelites was sealed in blood, the blood of the victims sacrificed. The blood was spattered, half on the altar (representing God) and half over the people, thus completing the union of God and his people.

The new pact Jesus made with his community was also sealed in blood, his own. So it is an alarming and courageous moment when I share in the blood of Christ at the Eucharist. I am committing myself to his covenant—each time afresh. I am sharing also in his own life, the divine life which he has in a unique way from God. Especially at the moment of his last supper Jesus was aware that his blood was to be shed in death. He saw himself as the Suffering Servant of the Lord, foretold in the Book of Isaiah, who by his suffering and death would atone for the sins of many. When I commit myself to that pact, I commit myself to sharing in the blood precisely at that moment of offering.

The Eucharist is not, then, to be lightly undertaken. One can see why Paul went on, 'Anyone who eats the bread or drinks the cup of the Lord unworthily is answerable for the body and blood of Christ' (11:27).

HW

Temptation

For the word of God is living and active. Sharper than any double-edged sword, it penetrates even to dividing soul and spirit, joints and marrow; it judges the thoughts and attitudes of the heart. Nothing in all creation is hidden from God's sight. Everything is uncovered and laid bare before the eyes of him to whom we must give account. Therefore, since we have a great high priest who has gone through the heavens, Jesus the Son of God, let us hold firmly to the faith we profess. For we do not have a high priest who is unable to sympathise with our weaknesses, but we have one who has been tempted in every way, just as we are—yet was without sin. Let us then approach the throne of grace with confidence, so that we may receive mercy and find grace to help us in our time of need.

God knows our hearts through and through. He knows our hopes and our dreams and our desires. He knows all the good things about us and all the bad things. The generous and loving side of us and the mean and nasty side. He sees it all and sooner or later we shall see it all. But it is all right to see it, because then we can set about praying in the right way. Jesus our high priest is right there at the throne of God interceding for us. He knows what it's like to be human and he knows what it's like to be us. So we can go to God and get help— whatever we have done and whatever our problem is.

A way to pray

Be aware of yourself in the presence of God, and let the word of God enter you, like a sword cutting into your heart and your mind. Reflect on what it says...
about loving your enemies...
about loving your neighbour...
about feeding the hungry...
about holiness and purity...
Ask the Spirit to show you yourself as you are. Then go back to the throne of the universe just as you are...
Know that Jesus is there,
our high priest...
Ask for grace, and receive
the help he gives you.

SB

Family tree

An account of the genealogy of Jesus the Messiah, the son of David, the son of Abraham. Abraham was the father of Isaac, and Isaac the father of Judah and his brothers . . . David was the father of Solomon by the wife of Uriah, and Solomon the father of Rehoboam . . . Jacob the father of Joseph the husband of Mary, of whom Jesus was born, who is called the Messiah. So all the generations from Abraham to David are fourteen generations; and from David to the deportation to Babylon, fourteen generations and from the deportation to Babylon to the Messiah, fourteen generations.

This is the bit we all skip when we read Matthew; the long list of who begat whom, as the Authorized Version puts it. Yet it is an important part of the Gospel. It fixes Jesus in time and space, and makes sure that we are dealing with a real person.

In some religions, it doesn't matter whether we take the origins of the faith seriously. They give a way of looking at the world, and a way of living, which are the important things. But not with Christianity. Matthew makes it clear that Jesus was real and belonged to a real nation, with a real history. Matthew reminds us that it is here in our world that Jesus meets us.

Many people today have a notion of a God who is probably 'up there somewhere'. The good news of the gospel tells us that he is not up there somewhere—he is down here, with us, where it counts.

Matthew works out the list of ancestors so that there are three groups of fourteen generations. Fourteen, being a multiple of seven (the Jewish number of completeness), probably is meant to show perfection. It's Matthew's way of saying that God acts in his own time, and then infallibly—and there's a lesson we need to learn!

A prayer

Father, thank you that in Jesus you were not shy of rolling up your sleeves and getting to grips with the world in which we live. Give us the grace to know your presence with us here and now.

MM

Power under threat

In the time of King Herod, after Jesus was born in Bethlehem of Judea, wise men from the East came to Jerusalem, asking, 'Where is the child who has been born king of the Jews? For we observed his star at its rising, and we have come to pay him homage.' When King Herod heard this, he was frightened, and all Jerusalem with him; and calling together all the chief priests and the scribes of the people, he inquired of them where the Messiah was to be born. They told him, 'In Bethlehem of Judea; for it has been written by the prophet...'

The wise men (not kings, but astrologer priests, the magi of Persia) were men of power. So was Herod. And each reacted differently to the coming of Jesus. The magi saw a greater power than theirs and came to bow before it. Herod saw a threat to his own power and was afraid.

Herod had a right to be frightened. If a new-born child was proclaimed Messiah, it could tumble Herod from his throne. His life would be turned upside down, and the delicate balance of power with Rome could topple into disaster.

Of course, he was wrong. Jesus had not come to rule from the throne of Jerusalem. And yet he was also right, for Jesus had come to challenge our world's ideas of power and authority. Jesus is a threat.

He is a threat to our way of viewing the world, he is a threat to our system of values and he is a threat to the way we live our lives. When Jesus comes, he demands that we let go of our lives and let him take charge. And we can respond in one or two ways. We can, like Herod, respond in fear and denial. Or, like the magi, we can pay him homage and offer him gifts; the gift of ourselves.

MM

A prayer

Lord, you threaten us with change, you demand to take over our lives. And often we respond with fear. Yet in return, you offer more than we can imagine. Give us grace to worship you.

Turn again!

In those days John the Baptist appeared in the wilderness of Judea, proclaiming, 'Repent, for the kingdom of heaven has come near.' This was the one of whom the prophet Isaiah spoke when he said, 'The voice of one crying out in the wilderness: "Prepare the way of the Lord, make his paths straight." ' Now John wore clothing of camel's hair with a leather belt around his waist, and his food was locusts and wild honey. Then the people of Jerusalem and all Judea were going out to him, and all the region along the Jordan, and they were baptized by him in the river Jordan, confessing their sins.

Back in the long-ago days of King Ahab, Israel had seemed peaceful and prosperous, part of a richly flowering civilization in the ancient Near East. Then a wild character came out of the hills to challenge Ahab and Israel. Elijah, dressed in camel hair, and living rough, called Israel to return to the God they had exchanged for prosperity. Elijah became one of the great heroes of Judaism, second only to Moses.

But that was then. Now a new figure, wild and rough, comes like Elijah to call the people to a new repentance. And suddenly the comfortable folk hero takes on a new dimension—was this what Elijah was like, this disturbing and disruptive prophet? Yes, he was.

When God acts, when the gospel is proclaimed, people are disturbed. We would like to have it differently. We would prefer to be able to see God at work, and to hear his word, without anything changing, without any challenge to our lives. But it cannot be. We can either be comfortable and complacent, or we can have God. So John the Baptist called for repentance, for the turn-around in life which marks the genuine encounter with God.

As I write, there is much debate about the Decade of Evangelism, with church leaders apologizing for any upset it may cause to people of other faiths. It is right to stress that we never set out simply to upset. But when the gospel is preached, there will be upset, as John the Baptist knew full well.

A prayer

Upset my life, Lord, so that you can set it up again in the way that gives glory to you.

MM

True food

[After his baptism by John the Baptist] Jesus was led up by the Spirit into the wilderness to be tempted by the devil. He fasted forty days and forty nights, and afterwards he was famished. The tempter came and said to him, 'If you are the Son of God, command these stones to become loaves of bread.' But he answered, 'It is written, "One does not live by bread alone, but by every word that comes from the mouth of God."'

Let's pause for the next three days, and look in detail at the story of the temptation in the wilderness. On one level, it is simply the story of how Jesus faced up to the human experience of temptation. He resisted through his trust in God and his knowledge of God's commands in the Bible (All of his answers to the devil come from the book of Deuteronomy.) And that's how we can beat temptation too.

One another level, the temptations are about the kind of Messiah he was to be. Would he win folk over by appealing to their stomachs, by spectacular miracles, or by leading armies to war? Or by obeying God?

But they are also examples of what temptations we all face. In the first one, Jesus is hungry. But he is hungry for a reason. He is fasting to clear his mind for prayer and meditation. If he eats, he will be putting his physical needs before his spiritual ones.

Human beings are creatures of two worlds. We are animals (95 per cent of our genetic make-up is identical to chimpanzees) but we are also spiritual. Alone of all creatures on earth, we have religion, prayer and worship. But it is easy to live all our lives on a purely physical level.

I don't mean thinking about nothing but food, sleep and sex. I mean not thinking about the purpose of life, about where we come from, where we go when we die, and whether it matters. I mean not reaching out in wonder and trembling for someone greater and more awesome than us. I mean ignoring the reality of God.

This is always the first temptation. If the devil can get us to ignore God, he need bother with no other sins at all.

A thought

How often do you spend time focused on God alone?

MM

True God

Then the devil took him to the holy city and placed him on the pinnacle of the temple, saying to him, 'If you are the Son of God, throw yourself down; for it is written, "He will command his angels concerning you," and "On their hands they will bear you up, so that you will not dash your foot against a stone."' Jesus said to him, 'Again it is written, "Do not put the Lord your God to the test."'

This is the most subtle of temptations. It looks very good and very pious. If I have true faith, surely I can move mountains. If I pray in absolute belief, surely what I pray for will come to pass? We hear a fair bit of preaching along these lines in some quarters: 'The only reason you weren't miraculously healed of your ingrowing toe-nail is your lack of true faith.'

But is it faith? Jesus rejected this approach, and he of all people can't be faulted when it comes to faith. But what is faith?

Surely faith is *trusting* in God. When we trust in someone, we put ourselves in their hands. We say to the surgeon, 'Carry on, you know what you are doing.' We say to our lover, 'I put my happiness in your hands, do what you want.' And we trust them to do their best for us. It is when love and trust break down that we begin to put them to the test. 'If I go home unexpectedly, who will she be with?' That is not love or trust.

To trust God, we say that he knows best. Yes, he commands his angels to watch over us—but when we spend all our time looking for angels out the corner of our eye, we no longer trust that they are there.

The devil's temptation to Jesus was not to trust God, but to demand proof of God's love. And how many proofs would be enough? 'Yes, he saved me in the fall at the temple, but will he save me now?' Once we cease to trust, no proof is enough.

A question

In what ways are you tempted to put God to the test? And why?

MM

True love

Again, the devil took him to a very high mountain and showed him all the kingdoms of the world and their splendour; and he said to him, 'All these I will give you, if you will fall down and worship me.' Jesus said to him, 'Away with you, Satan! for it is written, "Worship the Lord your God, and serve only him."' Then the devil left him, and suddenly the angels came and waited on him.

So far, we have seen in Jesus' temptations the errors we are often tempted to fall into. But surely we are rarely tempted to worship Satan? I don't suppose we are—consciously. And surely Jesus wasn't either. He was tempted to use power in the way of the world; the power of conquest and fear. To bring the nations under his iron heel, and rule from a throne of blood. With the power at his disposal, he'd have made Alexander the Great look like an amateur. But that would have been to worship Satan.

The devil conquers by force and fear. God conquers by love. And the great temptation was to fail to love. In the end, love is the only true conqueror. Rule by power breeds resistance and hatred. Conquered subjects always dream of freedom and yearn for the courage and strength to rebel. But the heart given in love stays freely, knowing that the door is always open to leave, but never wishing to escape.

When we love, we treat people as free and risk their rejection for the great prize of their own free gift of love. That is what God does. He offers his all and knows that we may reject it. Yet he also demands our all and knows that the only way he can get it is if we in turn give freely. He treats us as real people, and free people.

The great temptation is to replace love with force. We are tempted to manipulate people ('If you really loved me, you wouldn't do that . . .') And so we treat them as less truly human than ourselves. We conquer by fear and wonder why we are not fully loved. Jesus rejected that path. And so should we.

A thought

Whom do you love? And how often do you manipulate them?

MM

Nation of priests

The time is coming, says the Lord, when I will make a new covenant with Israel and Judah. It will not be like the covenant I made with their forefathers when I took them by the hand and led them out of Egypt. Although they broke my covenant, I was patient with them, says the Lord. But this is the covenant I will make with Israel after those days, says the Lord; I will set my law within them and write it on their hearts; I will become their God and they shall become my people. No longer need they teach one another to know the Lord; all of them, high and low alike, shall know me, says the Lord, for I will forgive their wrongdoing and remember their sin no more.

This is one of the great prophecies which help us to understand the Christian gospel. Jeremiah looks forward to a time when there will be a new covenant in which all of the people of God will have equal access to their Lord. In a sense, it is not a new covenant: it is still based on God's grace and love. But there will be no special categories of people who have a special standing with God, like priests and prophets. No one will need to be told about God, since all will know him for themselves.

We find this fulfilled in Jesus and the gift of the Holy Spirit. The Spirit was seen, in Old Testament times, as the mark of the prophet, inspired and instructed by God. In Christ, all are given the gift of the Spirit: all can have direct access to God, all can hear his voice.

Of course, that doesn't mean that all *will*—although we are given the enormous privilege of prayer and the ability to listen to God, we don't always take him up on it. Prayer is not something that we can use occasionally, as and when we need it. It is a life lived in the awareness of God. It is a habit of thought—to include conversation with God in our lives as naturally as breathing. And that takes practice and patience. Yet when we do practise, and develop the habit of prayer, we find that the living presence of God is a permanent part of our lives, and a constant companion.

MM

Manifesto

Blessed are the poor in spirit, for theirs is the kingdom of heaven. Blessed are those who mourn, for they shall be comforted. Blessed are the meek, for they will inherit the earth. Blessed are those who hunger and thirst for righteousness, for they will be filled. Blessed are the merciful, for they will receive mercy. Blessed are the pure in heart, for they will see God. Blessed are the peacemakers, for they will be called children of God. Blessed are those who are persecuted for righteousness' sake, for theirs is the kingdom of heaven.

We can meditate on the beatitudes for hours and never see everything they have to tell us. They are a puzzling, uplifting, challenging set of sayings. Do they offer rewards, give commands, or simply describe what it is to enter the kingdom of heaven? Perhaps all these things. But for me, they are a manifesto.

We write these notes a long time in advance of publication, which is why it is unsafe to mention topical items. They would soon be out of date. Yet as I write, the General Election is looming. Old hat by now, of course. But one thing that happens at elections is the publication of manifestos. Parties put down in black and white what their intentions are: 'Vote for us, and this is what you will get. (Perhaps!)'

In the beatitudes, Jesus gives a statement of what the kingdom of God is about. And it's revolutionary. It wouldn't get many votes in our elections (too soft on defence for instance). It presents a life that is based on God. Is he merciful? Comforting? Righteous? Then so are we.

It turns upside down the values of our world, discarding strength in favour of meekness, justice for forgiveness, war for peace. It is totally unrealistic. Follow that path, and they'll crucify you.

But perhaps it is all a matter of perspective. Perhaps it is the world that is unrealistic. Perhaps it is the world, with its stress on power, greed, strength and selfishness, however disguised, that is foolish. Foolish to imagine that such values could last into eternity, or endure for a second the scorching presence of the God of love.

A reflection

God chose what is foolish in the world to shame the wise; God chose what is weak in the world to shame the strong.

1 Corinthians 1:27

MM

New law, new life

You have heard that it was said, 'You shall not commit adultery.' But I say to you that everyone who looks at a woman with lust has already committed adultery with her in his heart. If your right eye causes you to sin, tear it out and throw it away; it is better for you to lose one of your members than for your whole body to be thrown into hell. And if your right hand causes you to sin, cut it off and throw it away; it is better for you to lose one of your members than for your whole body to go into hell.

'The Sermon on the Mount is what real Christianity is all about.' You've probably heard a saying rather like that, usually from a non-Christian. There's a lot of truth in it, but only when we understand what the Sermon is saying. And today's passage illustrates it well.

Firstly, it is about the authority of Jesus. 'But I say . . .' By these three words, he claims the authority to modify the Ten Commandments; the Law of God. He is someone even greater than Moses, who merely passed the Law on.

Secondly, it goes further than any law can. Laws can govern how we act. But Jesus is concerned with our thoughts and feelings. Of course, there is an obvious truth here, that actions spring from attitudes. Adultery doesn't happen if desire is under control. But it goes deeper than that. What power can change the human heart?

Certainly it requires something pretty drastic, as devastating as cutting off part of your body. Naturally Jesus didn't mean that literally. In the past, people have mutilated themselves in the quest for spiritual perfection, but that is wrong.

Not only does it destroy the God-created body, but it has no effect on the inner self.

Surely the only power to change our hearts is that of God—a power which comes from the life-changing meeting with God which we call conversion or repentance. All this means that the Sermon on the Mount is not a new set of even more difficult rules which replaces the Ten Commandments. It is a description of the kind of life which flows from a liberating meeting with Christ, in whom the love of God has come with power to change us in our deepest souls.

A prayer

Lord Jesus, I place myself under your authority, so that my life will come to fit the pattern of the kingdom of heaven.

MM

Chicken and egg

When you are praying, do not heap up empty phrases as the Gentiles do; for they think that they will be heard because of their many words. Do not be like them, for your Father knows what you need before you ask him. Pray then in this way: Our Father in heaven, hallowed by your name. Your will be done, on earth as it is in heaven. Give us this day our daily bread. And forgive us our debts, as we also have forgiven our debtors. And do not bring us to the time of trial, but rescue us from the evil one. For if you forgive others their trespasses, your heavenly Father will also forgive you; but if you do not forgive others, neither will your Father forgive your trespasses.

Many years ago, C.S. Lewis suggested that the reason why the creed says, 'I believe in the forgiveness of sins,' is not to remind us of God's forgiveness, which we surely accept. It is to remind us of our need to forgive. I don't know whether that is really why the sentence was first put in, but I'm sure it's why it ought to stay in. When we first read Jesus' words in the Lord's prayer and the verses following it, we surely get a cold shiver. Did he really mean that God won't forgive us unless we forgive others? Our minds flick over the things we have failed to forgive, the grudges we have harboured and the offences we are determined not to forgive.

But our ministers can come to the rescue. They will preach sermons on how our forgiveness flows from God's first forgiveness of us. We forgive because we are forgiven, and are forgiven because we forgive. A chicken and egg situation. It is true, of course. But it softens the impact of what Jesus no doubt intended as a shocking reminder.

Forgiveness is one of the hardest of Jesus' commands. After all, if it doesn't hurt, there is probably nothing much to forgive. But if we are to follow the pattern of the kingdom, we need to give forgiveness as much as we need it ourselves.

A way to pray

Say the Lord's prayer slowly and carefully. Think especially about forgiveness. Focus particularly on those who have hurt or upset you in the past week or so.

MM

True faith

Not everyone who says to me, 'Lord, Lord,' will enter the kingdom of heaven, but only the one who does the will of my Father in heaven. On that day many will say to me, 'Lord, Lord, did we not prophesy in your name, and cast out demons in your name, and do many deeds of power in your name?' Then I will declare to them, 'I never knew you; go away from me, you evil-doers.'

What seems at first a simple statement about true religion turns out to be rather more complicated. Of course we know that it is not enough simply to say, 'I'm a Christian.' There are many people in our country who would make that statement if they were pressed about their religion. Like the multitudes who put 'C. of E.' on their hospital records, but who never darken the doors of their parish church. And we know that real belief depends on more than merely having been baptized long ago.

But Jesus seems to go further. Surely someone who worked miracles in the name of Jesus would be someone who had genuine faith in Christ? Apparently not.

In the first century, there were many miracle workers, exorcists and magicians. They worked by calling on the name (that is, the authority and power) of gods and saints. In the New Testament, there are people who use the name of Jesus like that. But they were not necessarily Christians. They were people who used Jesus for their own ends.

Through history, many have done terrible things in the name of Christ (the Spanish Inquisition is only one example). Even today, though Christians are less ready to persecute, there are places where the church's authority is tied to unjust politics or economics. The name of Jesus becomes a source of power for worldly ends.

And in our own lives, don't we sometimes justify what we want by kidding ourselves that it is done 'for the Lord'?

True faith is about knowing God, learning *his* will, and putting it into practice.

A thought

Are you sometimes tempted to use Jesus for your own ends?

MM

Fit to serve

When Jesus entered Peter's house, he saw his mother-in-law lying in bed with a fever; he touched her hand, and the fever left her, and she got up and began to serve him. That evening they brought to him many who were possessed with demons; and he cast out the spirits with a word, and cured all who were sick. This was to fulfil what had been spoken through the prophet Isaiah, 'He took our infirmities and bore our diseases.'

I love one of Adrian Plass' little stories. It's about how he decided to improve his faith to the mountain-moving kind. So he started by trying to command a paper-clip to move. Nothing happened. Eventually, his wife asked, 'But why would God want you to move a paper-clip?'

Of course, it's just a funny story. Yet the point is rather like the healing of Peter's mother-in-law. She was healed and then began to serve Jesus.

God often does wonderful things for us. But he also does them for a purpose. He brings us salvation, lends us strength in our troubles, and yes, even sometimes he heals us. But he does it so that we can serve him.

A friend of mine was once seriously ill. He got worse and worse, and the doctors decided they could do no more. My friend prayed for days that God would heal him. Nothing happened. At last, he decided that, as is usually the case, God was not offering a miracle. And so his prayers changed. He asked God to show him how he could serve the Lord while he was ill, and for the little time he had left. By the evening he was well again.

Does this mean that God is selfish; only helping those who will help him? No. What it means is that we are created to serve God ('whose service is perfect freedom,' according to the Prayer Book). And only when we are serving God are we fully healed. Only by working for him are we truly saved.

After all, it makes sense. The Bible tells us we are made in the image of God, and in Jesus, God has shown himself to be the one who freely gives, and freely serves.

A prayer

Father, open my eyes to the opportunities for service which you give me. And in that service may I find my true and whole self.

MM

The greatest healing

Just then some people were carrying a paralysed man lying on a bed. When Jesus saw their faith, he said to the paralytic, 'Take heart, son; your sins are forgiven.' Then some of the scribes said to themselves, 'This man is blaspheming.' But Jesus , perceiving their thoughts, said, 'Why do you think evil in your hearts? For which is easier, to say, "Your sins are forgiven," or to say, "Stand up and walk"? But so that you may know that the Son of Man has authority on earth to forgive sins'—he then said to the paralytic—'Stand up, take your bed and go to your home.' And he stood up and went to his home. When the crowds saw it, they were filled with awe, and they glorified God, who had given such authority to human beings.

I was once called to the psychiatric ward at our local hospital. After a long talk with a patient, it turned out that he was unable to forgive himself for something he had done many years previously. It would be nice to say that I was able to declare God's forgiveness and heal him, but I was not. Yet the staff agreed that the first step in his healing must be forgiveness. To the patient, though, the sin seemed unforgivable. Few of us are crippled in mind or body by guilt. Yet in most of us there are burdens which we would all too willingly lay down. Often they are small things, which become symbols for sin. The great theologian St Augustine of Hippo was haunted by a boyhood prank of stealing apples. He knew he had done much worse, yet it became a sign of all his wrong-doing.

Like Augustine, we bear ridiculous burdens of guilt. And like the paralysed man, we need healing. The great news is that that is just what Jesus came to do.

Our part is to turn to him, and let him ease his shoulders under our burden.

A reflection

What things do you feel guilty about? Which things are really wrong, and which feelings are false? Tell them all to God, and picture him removing your burdens, and standing you straight again.

MM

Glory

We did not follow cleverly invented stories when we told you about the power and coming of our Lord Jesus Christ, but we were eye-witnesses of his majesty. For he received honour and glory from God the Father when the voice came to him from the Majestic Glory, saying, 'This is my Son, whom I love; with him I am well pleased.' We ourselves heard this voice that came from heaven when we were with him on the sacred mountain. And we have the word of the prophets made more certain, and you will do well to pay attention to it, as to a light shining in a dark place, until the day dawns and the morning star rises in your hearts.

When Peter, John and James were on a mountain near Jerusalem with Jesus they saw the divine glory shining out of him and he was transfigured before them. They saw Moses and Elijah standing there with him, and Peter wanted to build three shelters for them and Jesus—so the three of them could be with Peter, James and John. Moses represented the Law and Elijah represented the prophets. But Jesus was the Son. A voice came from heaven to say so. 'This is my Son, whom I love; with him I am well pleased. Listen to him!'

Which is what they are telling us to do—'Pay attention! Listen!': to the word of the prophets spoken perfectly in the Word made flesh, the light of the world shining in the darkness; to the one who is 'the bright Morning Star' and who said in the vision he gave to John of the glory of heaven, 'To him who overcomes and does my will to the end, I will give authority over the nations ... I will also give him the morning star.' (Revelation 22:16; 2:26, 28). So he will give us himself, and we shall shine like the stars and like the sun.

Meditate

Spend a few moments now thinking about the glory that shone out of Jesus— and that one day will shine out of us.

SB

Doubt

When John heard in prison what the Messiah was doing, he sent word by his disciples and said to him, 'Are you the one who is to come, or are we to wait for another?' Jesus answered them, 'Go and tell John what you hear and see: the blind receive their sight, the lame walk, the lepers are cleansed, the deaf hear, the dead are raised, and the poor have good news brought to them. And blessed is anyone who takes no offence at me.' ...
'Truly I tell you, among those born of woman, no one has arisen greater than John the Baptist; yet the least in the kingdom is greater than he ...'

It is easy to picture the despair of John the Baptist. He had been the fearless prophet of God, challenging rich and poor, weak and mighty, to repentance. Now he was locked away in a grim fortress by the barren Dead Sea, knowing that his time on earth was running out. And the Messiah he had proclaimed was not living up to expectations. Where was the wrath of God, the separation of wheat and chaff, the baptism in fire? So he sent disciples to Jesus to ask if he really had been right.

And don't we sometimes feel much like that? We can remember prayers answered, deeply felt worship, and great hopes. Then everything seems humdrum and ordinary. Prayer no longer flows easily. Everyday worries and demands take up our time, and God seems to fade into the background. Was it every really true?

Jesus' answer to John pointed beyond the prison walls. Look at all that God is doing! The words of the prophets are being fulfilled. How can you doubt?

And perhaps our vision sometimes narrows too far. As we become concerned with ourselves, we lose sight of what God is doing in the world, amongst our neighbours and in our church. We need to open our eyes and look around. God is at work. We can read about him in the papers and see him in our community. And yes, we too are part of what he is doing.

A prayer

Open our eyes, Lord, so that we can see you at work. Open our eyes to the ordinariness of our lives, and let us see the glory which is hidden within them.

MM

Unforgivable sin?

If I cast out demons by Beelzebul, by whom do your own exorcists cast them out? Therefore they will be your judges. But if it is by the Spirit of God that I cast out demons, then the kingdom of God has come to you. Or how can one enter a strong man's house and plunder his property, without first tying up the strong man? Then indeed the house can be plundered. Whoever is not with me is against me, and whoever does not gather with me scatters. Therefore I tell you, people will be forgiven for every sin and blasphemy, but blasphemy against the Spirit will not be forgiven. Whoever speaks a word against the Son of Man will be forgiven, but whoever speaks against the Holy Spirit will not be forgiven, either in this age or in the age to come.

Jesus has just performed a spectacular exorcism, but his enemies accused him of being in league with the devil. It was a foolish and obvious lie, and he easily refuted it. Then comes the strange saying about sin against the Holy Spirit.

Are we to suppose that we can say 'God' and 'Christ' as swear-words and be forgiven, but if we blaspheme in the Spirit's name we'll be damned forever? Hardly. To understand this saying, we need to realize what is going on in the story. The Spirit has obviously and clearly been at work. But to admit it would be to say that the kingdom of God was here—and in Jesus. So rather than accept Jesus, his enemies deny the work of God.

And since it is the Spirit who brings God's forgiveness, the very denial of his work is the denial of God's forgiveness. Blasphemy against the Spirit is the wilful denial of God, and a turning away from the forgiveness he offers. It is not that God refused to forgive a certain sin, but that a certain sin is the refusal of forgiveness.

A thought

Our relationship with God is affected by our attitude to other people. In the story, hatred led to a denial of God. Are there people whose good points we refuse to acknowledge because we don't like them?

MM

Safe with Jesus

Early in the morning [Jesus] came walking toward them on the sea. But when the disciples saw him walking on the sea, they were terrified, saying, 'It is a ghost!' And they cried out in fear. But immediately Jesus spoke to them and said, 'Take heart, it is I; do not be afraid.' Peter answered him, 'Lord, if it is you, command me to come to you on the water.' He said, 'Come.' So Peter got out of the boat, started walking on the water, and came toward Jesus. But when he noticed the strong wind, he became frightened, and beginning to sink, he cried out, 'Lord, save me!' Jesus immediately reached out his hand and caught him, saying to him, 'You of little faith, why did you doubt?'

The old stories are the best, and so are the old sermons. Here, in story form, Matthew gives us one of the oldest sermons. As long as we keep our eyes on Jesus, all will be well. But once we are afraid of the storms that surround us, and look away from the Lord, we sink.

All the Gospels have Jesus walking on the water, but only Matthew puts in the bit about Peter. And he does it simply to make this point. It is one of the most basic bits of teaching, and therefore one that needs repeating time and again. We're likely to say, 'Oh, but I know that!' And so we do. But putting it into practice is another matter. When we are tempted, when we are afraid, when we are troubled and upset, when we are regretful, guilty or lonely, we turn immediately to prayer and seek the Lord. Or do we? I suspect not. Even for Christians of much experience, prayer and practical trust in God tend to come as a last resort. Matthew wants to remind us of this one fundamental fact—that keeping our eyes on Jesus is the basic way of Christian life. It is not just for when we are sinking.

A reflection

When I used to do karate, most of the training was repetition of the most basic moves, so they became second nature. What are the basic moves of faith? And do you practise them enough for them to become second nature?

MM

Jesus first

Jesus . . . went away to the district of Tyre and Sidon. Just then a Canaanite woman from that region came out and started shouting, 'Have mercy on me, Lord, Son of David; my daughter is tormented by a demon.' But he did not answer her at all. And his disciples came and urged him, saying, 'Send her away, for she keeps shouting after us.' He answered, 'I was sent only to the lost sheep of the house of Israel.' But she came and knelt before him, saying, 'Lord, help me.' He answered, 'It is not fair to take the children's food and throw it to the dogs.' She said, 'Yes, Lord, yet even the dogs eat the crumbs that fall from their masters' table.' Then Jesus answered her, 'Woman, great is your faith! Let it be done for you as you wish.' And her daughter was healed instantly.

Jesus had come as the Jewish Messiah, and his mission was to God's chosen people. Later, it would widen, as Matthew's readers would know. But for now, this Gentile woman was asking for something which was not hers. She wanted a miracle. Jesus had not come to bring miracles, but the kingdom of God—and that could only be understood by the Jews. Miracles were only part of the picture, and could not be separated from the whole teaching of the kingdom.

The change came when the woman accepted that she was an outsider. Not one of the children, but an observer who knew that there was something special about the people of God. And that made Jesus more than just a wonder-worker. That was enough. Once she had caught a glimpse of that, the healing followed.

It wasn't enough just to want what Jesus could give. Jesus had to be accepted himself. And it still remains true. We may want many things from him—courage, self-control, strength. And we will get them, but only when we accept Jesus himself as the Lord.

A prayer

Father, take our eyes away from the fringe benefits of knowing you, and let us see you and love you for yourself.

MM

Who is Jesus?

Now when Jesus came into the district of Caesarea Philippi, he asked his disciples, 'Who do people say that the Son of Man is?' And they said, 'Some say John the Baptist, but others Elijah, and still others Jeremiah or one of the prophets.' He said to them, 'But who do you say that I am?' Simon Peter answered, 'You are the Messiah, the Son of the living God.' And Jesus answered him, 'Blessed are you, Simon son of Jonah! For flesh and blood has not revealed this to you, but my Father in heaven. And I tell you, you are Peter, and on this rock I will build my church, and the gates of Hades will not prevail against it. I will give you the keys of the kingdom of heaven, and whatever you bind on earth will be bound in heaven, and whatever you loose on earth will be loosed in heaven.' Then he sternly ordered the disciples not to tell anyone that he was the Messiah.

Christian faith is about our response to Jesus. It is more than simply an intellectual evaluation. It is a response of faith or unbelief, acceptance or rejection of the claim of Jesus to Lordship of our lives.

Peter's response was one of faith, and as the first to commit himself in faith, he became the foundation stone of the Church. Since then, the Church has grown by people recognizing Jesus as the Son of God, and committing themselves to him.

This is not purely a human activity. Faith is a gift of God, which he desires to give to everyone. So Peter's acceptance of Jesus was something God had given to him. And this is a great truth to bear in mind as we think of the Church's task of preaching the gospel.

As we present Jesus, God is at work, preparing people's minds and hearts, and paving the way for faith. He does not overrule their wills but where there is the slightest desire for faith, he is there to give it.

A way to pray

Think of someone you know who lacks faith. Make them the focus for your prayer, both that God will prepare the way for the gospel, and that you will be given the opportunity to present Jesus to them.

MM

Growing in faith

From that time on, Jesus began to show his disciples that he must go to Jerusalem and undergo great suffering at the hands of the elders and chief priests and scribes, and be killed, and on the third day be raised. And Peter took him aside and began to rebuke him, saying, 'God forbid it, Lord! This must never happen to you.' But he turned and said to Peter, 'Get behind me, Satan! You are a stumbling block to me; for you are setting your mind not on divine things but on human things.' Then Jesus told his disciples, 'If any want to become my followers, let them deny themselves and take up their cross and follow me.'

What a come-down. One minute Peter is given the keys of the kingdom of God, and the next he is being called Satan! The reason is not hard to find. Although Peter has taken the first step of faith, he is still not firmly following Jesus. He thinks he knows better than his master and is quite ready to put Jesus right.

But Jesus knows what God has called him to do, and Peter's advice is all too familiar, to turn away from God's path and follow the wisdom of the world. Jesus has faced this temptation in the wilderness, and will face it again in Gethsemane.

The lesson Peter has to learn is one which faces all of us; that the way of Jesus is the way of the cross.

Salvation comes through Jesus' death and resurrection, and this sets the pattern for Christian life. In our inner selves, there is much that needs to be put to death—anger, hatred, bitterness, envy and all the rest. And we are called to face the troubles of life with the love of Christ, and faith in him. It was not a lesson which Peter could learn easily, and it comes just as hard to us. But as we keep our eyes fixed on Jesus, day by day we see a little more clearly what he meant by the words which follow our passage and on which we now reflect.

A reflection

Those who want to save their life will lose it, and those who lose their life for my sake will find it. For what will it profit them if they gain the whole world but forfeit their life? Or what will they give in return for their life?

MM

From Death to Life

God communicates with us so that we shall know how much he loves us, and to draw us into a relationship of love with himself. Now, as we reflect on Easter, we see his glory and his love shining out in all its brilliance in the suffering of Christ.

We don't have to be good to be loved, and, even if we were, that wouldn't be why God loves us. The reason why he loves us is that it is his nature to love. It isn't our nature—and because he loves us he wants us to love him. So his plan of salvation is to make us 'partakers of the divine nature' and to give us a new heart. Then we shall love—God and our neighbour. Stumblingly at first, like babies learning to walk. But getting better at it all along the way—and with a powerful Helper inside us: the Holy Spirit, whose character and nature we shall look at in the section on Pentecost, which comes immediately after this section.

Now we look at the wonder of the love of God in the Easter story with Douglas Cleverley Ford and Marcus Maxwell—and then, starting on Easter Monday, we spend fourteen days reflecting on the glory of the resurrection in 1 Corinthians 15. In that great chapter of the Bible, so often read out at funerals, St Paul shows us how the next life is as closely connected with this one as the life of a plant is connected with the seed from which it grew. Intimately connected, but far more glorious.

Glory

And after six days Jesus took with him Peter and James and John his brother, and led them up a high mountain apart. And he was transfigured before them, and his face shone like the sun, and his garments became white as light. And behold, there appeared to them Moses and Elijah, talking with him. And Peter said to Jesus, 'Lord, it is well that we are here; if you wish, I will make three booths here, one for you and one for Moses and one for Elijah.' He was still speaking, when lo, a bright cloud overshadowed them, and a voice from the cloud said, 'This is my beloved Son, with whom I am well pleased; listen to him.' When the disciples heard this, they fell on their faces, and were filled with awe. But Jesus came and touched them, saying, 'Rise, and have no fear.' And when they lifted up their eyes, they saw no one but Jesus only.

Everything here is uncanny. Experiences of this order affect people in different ways. Some it stings into silence, others talk to counteract their fear. James and John said nothing. Peter on the other hand talked rubbish. Visions cannot be made permanent in booths or huts. He was still talking when the divine voice called from the bright cloud, 'This is my beloved Son . . . listen to him'. After which all three fell on their faces overcome with awe. Then the transfigured Jesus, with his face shining like the sun and his garments white as the light, compassionately aware how crushed they were, came and touched them. That touch reassured them that they were still in this world, but not half as much as when they opened their eyes and saw the familiar Jesus in the plain clothes of an ordinary Galilean man.

For all of us, if we are Christians, Jesus will have to be transfigured. He must be to us more than a wonderful teacher, a figure in history, he must be utterly different, he must be the Christ, the Son of the living God, not only a wonderful man.

Affirmation

Thou art the King of glory, O Christ. Thou art the everlasting Son of the Father.

DCF

Love and reason

Now when Jesus was at Bethany in the house of Simon the leper, a woman came up to him with an alabaster flask of very expensive ointment, and she poured it on his head, as he sat at table, But when the disciples saw it, they were indignant, saying, 'Why this waste? For this ointment might have been sold for a large sum, and given to the poor.' But Jesus, aware of this, said to them, 'Why do you trouble the woman? For she has done a beautiful thing to me. For you always have the poor with you, but you will not always have me. In pouring this ointment on my body she has done it to prepare me for burial. Truly, I say to you, wherever this gospel is preached in the whole world, what she has done will be told in memory of her.'

Then one of the twelve, who was called Judas Iscariot, went to the chief priests and said, 'What will you give me if I deliver him to you?' And they paid him thirty pieces of silver. And from that moment he sought an opportunity to betray him.

What were the guests talking about on this festive occasion? A ministry of healing? Relief activity on behalf of the poor? Perhaps they were planning a campaign. They certainly did not have Jesus' death and burial in mind. That is to say, all of them except two—one a woman, the other a man. Consider the woman first. With the possible exception of John she understood Jesus better than anyone else. She understood as a woman understands people. She read him through love. That alabaster box of expensive ointment poured over him symbolized her love. Through it she sensed his approaching end. Love has eyes like nothing else. Looking round the table she saw Judas Iscariot too. Did she also read him?

Judas was the man who knew about the impending death of his Master. He knew because he had already planned to betray him. He in fact left the supper table to make overtures to the high priest. Judas wrote off the woman's outpouring of devotion as unreasonable. Perhaps it was; but which brings us closer to the mind of Christ, love or reason?

DCF

The clear-out

When he entered Jerusalem, the whole city was in turmoil, asking, 'Who is this?' The crowds were saying, 'This is the prophet Jesus from Nazareth in Galilee.' Then Jesus entered the temple and drove out all who were selling and buying in the temple, and he overturned the tables of the money changers and the seats of those who sold doves. He said to them, 'It is written, "My house shall be a house of prayer"; but you are making it a den of robbers.'

'What's all the fuss about?' asked the people of Jerusalem, as Jesus rode in. 'It's a prophet,' came the reply. Anyone who knew their Bible would be aware that prophets did pretty strange things. They would be watching to see what Jesus did. And what he did was incredible. He attacked the holy place, the centre of Jewish worship. He disrupted the temple offerings and scattered the sacrificial doves. In short, he broke up the worship, if only for a short time.

There could be no doubt that this was a prophetic action, full of symbolism. But what did it mean? We're often told that Jesus was disgusted by the corruption of the dealers. But the money changers and sellers of animals were there quite legitimately, to enable the correct worship of God.

Probably, it was only later that people began to understand. Jesus was clearing out the old way of meeting God. There was about to become a new kind of worship, and a new path to God. Jesus himself was to be the one necessary sacrifice, and the one way to God. To make way for him, the old had to go.

The cleansing of the temple also becomes a symbolic action for us. When Jesus arrives, much has to go. Often we cling to attitudes and actions which do not fit in with him. But be warned. In the end, they have to go. There isn't room for both Jesus and our old lifestyle.

A way to pray

Isolate those things you do, or think, or feel, which are not in line with the way of Jesus. Bring them to him, and ask him to throw them out.

MM

The last judgment

When the Son of Man comes in his glory, and all the angels with him . . . All the nations will be gathered before him, and he will separate people one from another as a shepherd separates the sheep from the goats, and he will put the sheep at his right hand and the goats at the left. Then the king will say to those at his right hand, 'Come, you that are blessed by my Father, inherit the kingdom prepared for you from the foundation of the world; for I was hungry and you gave me food, I was thirsty and you gave me something to drink, I was a stranger and you welcomed me, I was naked and you gave me clothing, I was sick and you took care of me, I was in prison and you visited me.' Then the righteous will answer him, 'Lord, when was it that we saw you . . . ?' And the king will answer him, 'Truly I tell you, just as you did it to one of the least of these who are members of my family, you did it to me.' Then he will say to those at his left hand, 'You that are accursed, depart from me into the eternal fire prepared for the devil and his angels; for I was hungry and you gave me no food . . .' Then they also will answer, 'Lord, when was it that we saw you . . . ?' Then he will answer them, 'Truly I tell you, just as you did not do it to one of the least of these, you did not do it to me.' And these will go away into eternal punishment, but the righteous into eternal life.

Just two points. Jesus identifies himself with anyone in need ('members of my family' does not mean merely his disciples). In the Incarnation, God identifies himself with all people, in order to save them all. So judgment is on the basis of behaviour towards all people.

Does this mean the final judgment is on our deeds after all? Was St Paul, for instance wrong about salvation by faith? But remember that this Gospel is meant to be read by Christians, and the basis of the judgment is not obedience to the law, but action flowing from love and faith.

A thought

James tells us that faith without work is dead. What kind of action flows from your faith?

MM

Sacrament of division?

While they were eating, Jesus took a loaf of bread, and after blessing it he broke it, gave it to the disciples, and said, 'Take, eat, this is my body.' Then he took a cup, and after giving thanks he gave it to them, saying, 'Drink from it, all of you; for this is my blood of the covenant, which is poured out for many for the forgiveness of sins. I tell you, I will never again drink of this fruit of the vine until that day when I drink it new with you in my Father's kingdom.' When they had sung the hymn, they went out to the Mount of Olives.

It is one of the great tragedies of the Christian faith, and perhaps one of the devil's greatest triumphs, that the sacrament of the Lord's Supper should have become one of the greatest points of division in the Church. So much argument still goes into exactly what Jesus meant by 'This is my body.'

Perhaps we should draw encouragement from the words over the cup. Not 'Argue about this,' 'Theologize and philosophize about this,' but 'Drink this.' The Eucharist is something that Christians *do*. And for my money that should be enough.

Of course, we need to have some idea of what it is about, but Jesus provides that. It is about his sacrificial death on behalf of us. The talk of body and blood, especially blood of the covenant, points us to that. So whether you think of the Mass as a presentation of Christ's sacrifice to God, or the Lord's Supper as a memorial of his saving death, or the Eucharist as a celebration of new and eternal life through the cross, or whatever theory is in vogue at the moment, whether you see it as a part of the function of a priest or the activity of all God's people, remember this: Jesus, by our actions with bread and wine, draws us to the cross where salvation is his gift.

A thought

What is most important to you, as you share in the Eucharist? Thank God for that, and all the blessings he gives.

MM

Death of death

From noon on, darkness came over the whole land until three in the afternoon. And about three o'clock Jesus cried out with a loud voice, 'Eli, Eli, lama sabachthani?' that is, 'My God, my God, why have you forsaken me?' When some of the bystanders heard it , they said, 'This man is calling for Elijah.' At once, one of them ran and got a sponge, filled it with sour wine, put it on a stick, and gave it to him to drink. But the others said, 'Wait, let us see whether Elijah will come to save him.' Then Jesus cried again with a loud voice and breathed his last. At that moment the curtain of the temple was torn in two, from top to bottom. The earth shook, and the rocks were split. The tombs also were opened, and many bodies of the saints who had fallen asleep were raised. After his resurrection they came out of the tombs and entered the holy city and appeared to many.

Did some of the dead really come back to life when Jesus was raised? The episode seems almost embarrassing; a legend that detracts from the solemn story of the crucifixion. Certainly none of the other Gospels mentions it. Probably it is a later legend. But Matthew includes it for a special purpose.

The death of Jesus has two effects. Firstly the temple curtain, which separated off the inner room where the presence of God was thought to be most near, was torn. The sign is obvious. The death of Jesus has opened the way into the presence of God. The sign of the cleansing of the temple has been fulfilled. Now there is a new sacrifice, a new way to God, and a new type of worship, centred on Jesus.

Secondly the power of death has now been broken. Just as the tombs were wrecked and the dead raised, so death is no longer a barrier. Instead of leading to eternal separation from God, death itself has become the gateway to everlasting life.

A reflection

Death has been swallowed up in victory. Where, O death, is your victory? Where, O death, is your sting.

1 Corinthians 15:54–55

Courage at last

When it was evening, there came a rich man from Arimathea, named Joseph, who also was a disciple of Jesus. He went to Pilate and asked for the body of Jesus. Then Pilate ordered it to be given him. And Joseph took the body, and wrapped it in a clean linen shroud, and laid it in his own new tomb, which he had hewn in the rock; and he rolled a great stone to the door of the tomb, and departed.

Why did Joseph of Arimathea do this? Was it that he reckoned the possible lack of a proper burial for such an outstanding man as Jesus was shameful? He would put this right. He would make his own tomb nearby available. Or was there a deeper reason, a more personal ground for his action?

Joseph stared at that now limp body suspended on the cross festooned with nails. And what had he done to prevent this monstrous deed, he a member of the supreme Jewish Council? True, he had not given his consent when the vote was taken to hand Jesus over for crucifixion. That was something. But it was negative. He had done nothing positive. Truth to tell he had been a secret disciple of Jesus for some time but he never did tell this truth. He kept it to himself. And now as he stood there staring at the dead body of the man for whom he had done nothing, *he pulled himself together*. Taking his life in his hands he ran the risk of asking for the body from the governor himself, from Pilate, he Joseph, who could claim no blood relationship to Jesus. What right had he to ask? But he went.

Does it really matter what drives us to confess our Christian discipleship, so long as we do? Maybe it was not all that noble for Joseph not to confess to his faith till he was goaded by the ghastliness of that ugly crucifixion. But hasn't the cross of Christ made more people face the truth about themselves than any other part of the Christian proclamation?

A prayer

Lord, I think my name is Joseph of Arimathea, even though I am not rich, and possess no tomb ready for me hewn out of rock. But more than once I have funked owing up to being a Christian disciple. Lord, forgive me. I will do what I can to make amends.

DCF

Victory

The angel said to the women, 'Do not be afraid; I know that you are looking for Jesus who was crucified. He is not here; for he has been raised, as he said. Come, see the place where he lay. Then go quickly and tell his disciples, "He has been raised from the dead, and indeed he is going ahead of you to Galilee; there you will see him." This is my message for you.' ... Now the eleven disciples went to Galilee, to the mountain to which Jesus had directed them. When they saw him, they worshipped him; but some doubted. And Jesus came and said to them, 'All authority in heaven and on earth has been given to me. Go therefore and make disciples of all nations, baptizing them in the name of the Father and of the Son and of the Holy Spirit, and teaching them to obey everything that I have commanded you. And remember, I am with you always, to the end of the age.'

So they did. And he was. And he still is.

Jesus has conquered death, for himself and for those who put their faith in him. Because he is no longer tied by death or merely mortal life, he can still be met, by you and me, in the most unlikely places.

What does meeting Jesus mean? For the women who went to the tomb, it was the dawning of incredible joy. Where there had been despair, there was hope. In the face of the one certainty of human existence—death—there was now life. With Jesus, all the assumptions of the world are turned upside down, and the future becomes one of excitement and hope. And Jesus still brings that.

For the disciples, meeting Jesus was all this and more. It was a commissioning. Not only here, but in most of the stories of Jesus' resurrection appearances, those who meet him are given a job to do. We still are. We have met Jesus almost certainly because someone else heard his command and told us. This remains the task of Christians everywhere: 'Go, therefore, and make disciples ...'

A prayer

Father, we thank you for our own encounter with you in Jesus Christ. Open our eyes to the opportunities to tell others; so that they too may discover joy, hope and life.

MM

He's alive

Now I would remind you, brothers and sisters, of the good news that I proclaimed to you, which you in turn received, in which also you stand, through which also you are being saved, if you hold firmly to the message that I proclaimed to you—unless you have come to believe in vain. For I handed on to you as of first importance what I in turn had received: that Christ died for our sins in accordance with the scriptures, and that he was buried, and that he was raised on the third day in accordance with the scriptures, and that he appeared to Cephas, then to the twelve. Then he appeared to more than five hundred brothers and sisters at one time, most of whom are still alive, though some have died. Then he appeared to James, then to all the apostles.

This paragraph of Paul's letter is important, because it contains a very early summary of Christian belief. Paul had already preached the good news to them, and 'handed it on' to them. It had been handed on to him, probably by Ananias and the Christians at Damascus immediately after his own conversion. Those words 'handed on' mean that it was a precious truth of Christian tradition, and once it had been handed over it had to be held on to and guarded.

Christianity isn't good advice, thank God. It is good news. The original events happened so long ago that they don't seem like news any more—especially if we have been brought up to go to church and recite the creeds Sunday after Sunday. But for some of us the wonder of it really does dawn like glory in our souls, and then we can say with Charles Wesley, 'Amazing love! How can it be, that Thou, my God, shouldst die for me?' It was God-in-Christ who died, but the dying was followed by resurrection—and people saw the risen Christ. Yet the person they saw wasn't a resuscitated corpse. There was a mystery at the heart of all the resurrection appearances and a moment of recognition when the astonishing truth dawned on the people who witnessed it.

A spiritual exercise

Imagine you are at the crucifixion, and that you see Jesus nailed to the cross. You see him die, and watch him being taken down from the cross. Then imagine being there in the upper room with the disciples on the evening of the first Easter Day. Imagine Jesus standing in the midst of you—no longer dead, but alive.

SB

Grace that transforms

Last of all, as to one untimely born, he appeared also to me. For I am the least of the apostles, unfit to be called an apostle, because I persecuted the church of God. But by the grace of God I am what I am, and his grace toward me has not been in vain. On the contrary, I worked harder than any of them—though it was not I, but the grace of God that is with me. Whether then it was I or they, so we proclaim and so you have come to believe.

It must have been a very awesome moment for Saul when Jesus met him on the road to Damascus. Perhaps there had been a conflict going on in his heart as he persecuted the Christians, but all the time remembering being there at the death of Stephen, seeing that Stephen's face was like the face of an angel, and hearing him pray, 'Lord Jesus, receive my spirit,' and cry out 'Lord, do not hold this sin against them' (Acts 7:59–60, NRSV). Words so like the words that Jesus spoke when he was dying.

Then on the way to Damascus in pursuit of more Christians there was a bright light shining around Saul, and a voice speaking to him. 'Saul, Saul, why do you persecute me?' Saul asks who it is, but it is obvious that he knows. ' "Who are you, Lord?" The reply came, "I am Jesus, whom you are persecuting. But get up and enter the city and you will be told what you are to do" ' (Acts 9:4–5, NRSV).

It was a total turnaround for Saul, who became Paul—a new name for a transformed character. And although it happened once and uniquely for Saul, it has happened innumerable times (each one unique) for millions of converts to the Christian faith.

A prayer

Thank you so much, Lord, for your great apostle Paul. Thank you for his life and his energy. Thank you for his love for you and for your Church. Thank you that it was you and your grace working in him that made him what he was. Please work in me, to make me what you want me to be for you.

SB

Christ has . . . been raised!

Now if Christ is proclaimed as raised from the dead, how can some of you say there is no resurrection of the dead? If there is no resurrection of the dead, then Christ has not been raised; and if Christ has not been raised, then our proclamation has been in vain and your faith has been in vain. We are even found to be misrepresenting God, because we testified of God that he raised Christ—whom he did not raise if it is true that the dead are not raised.

Paul has given us his credentials. An encounter with the risen Christ, and the essential Christian creed is handed on to him and then handed on to others. The content of what he has preached and proclaimed is the forgiveness of sins and the resurrection of Christ. But if there isn't (and wasn't) a resurrection then Paul has been wasting his breath and his time. And he would be saying false things about God if it wasn't true that God raised Christ from the dead and that there will be a resurrection from the dead for all who believe.

We don't have to know how it happened, or what the resurrection body of Christ looked like. When his disciples saw the risen Christ they didn't always realize it was Christ. But then they did. Later on in this chapter Paul helps us to understand the nature of the resurrection body, but for now he is calling on his readers to believe what he says. He is spending the whole of his life and energy telling the world about it, so he certainly believes it. And the quality of his writing in the New Testament doesn't lead us to think he is confused in his thinking. In Paul we meet one of the most brilliant theological thinkers and writers there has ever been. And he tells us that Christ was raised from the dead and that he appeared to him.

A reflection

What does it mean to you to say, 'I believe in the resurrection of the dead'? Can Paul's words strengthen your belief and your hope? Spend some time reflecting on your faith in the resurrection and on the difference it makes to death.

SB

He is risen indeed!

For if the dead are not raised, then Christ has not been raised. If Christ has not been raised, your faith is futile and you are still in your sins. Then those also who have died in Christ have perished. If for this life only we have hoped in Christ, we are of all people most to be pitied. But in fact Christ has been raised from the dead, the first fruits of those who have died. For since death came through a human being, the resurrection of the dead has also come through a human being.

Imagine standing with the women outside the tomb on the first Easter morning. The stone is just where it was when the dead body of Jesus was put into the tomb. The body is still there, too. Someone helps them roll the stone away, and they do the work that they have come to do—anoint the body with their spices and ointments. Jesus is dead, and he is there in the tomb. You walk away with them, feeling desperately sad.

Then, a few years later, you hear Paul preaching. He is proclaiming with great passion that through the death of Christ your sins can be forgiven. The New Testament writers interpreted the life and death of Christ in terms of the Old Testament, so perhaps he quotes Isaiah: 'All we like sheep have gone astray; we have turned every one to his own way; and the Lord has laid on him the iniquity of us all' (Isaiah 53:6, RSV). 'That is what happened when Christ died,' he says, 'so now you can know that he carried your sins as well as the sins of all the rest of us.' You would be bound to ask, 'But how can I know that? Christ died the death of a common criminal. The Old Testament says that anyone who is put to death and hanged on a tree is cursed by God' (Deuteronomy 21:23). And you would be right. 'If Christ has not been raised, your faith is futile and you are still in your sins ... But in fact Christ has been raised from the dead, the first fruits of those who have died.'

First Christ. Then the rest of us.

A shout of triumph

Christ is risen!
He is risen indeed! Hallelujah!

SB

Then the main crop

...For as all die in Adam, so all will be made alive in Christ. But each in his own order: Christ the first fruits, then at his coming those who belong to Christ. Then comes the end, when he hands over the kingdom to God the Father, after he has destroyed every ruler and every authority and power. For he must reign until he has put all his enemies under his feet. The last enemy to be destroyed is death. For 'God has put all things in subjection under his feet.' But when it says, 'All things are put in subjection,' it is plain that this does not include the one who put all things in subjection under him. When all things are subjected to him, then the Son himself will also be subjected to the one who put all things in subjection under him, so that God may be all in all.

If you have ever grown your own potatoes you will know what a special feeling it is to dig up the first plant when it is ready and boil the first new potatoes of the season. There will be others in the crop, like the first ones. And because we know what the 'first fruits' are like we know what the rest will be like. The Israelites always gave the first pickings to God, in an offering to the priests, as a sign that everything came from God and belonged to God.

The whole human race is 'in Adam', which means that we are all sinful and all mortal. We live for a few years and then die. It happens to all of us, but to all who are in Christ it is a different story. All who are in Christ are made alive with eternal life, a relationship with God the Father that begins in this life and goes on for ever in the next one. Living a life in which 'there will be no more death' (Revelation 21:4).

A reflection

Think of the first new potatoes being dug out of the ground, then think of the main crop. Think of the resurrection of Christ. Then think of the resurrection of all who are in Christ. Then be quiet for a few more moments, and let the wonder of this creation speak to you about the wonder of the new one that will be there on the other side of the grave.

SB

Tell them the good news!

Otherwise, what will those people do who receive baptism on behalf of the dead? If the dead are not raised at all, why are people baptized on their behalf? And why are we putting ourselves in danger every hour? I die every day! That is as certain, brothers and sisters, as my boasting of you—a boast that I make in Christ Jesus our Lord. If with merely human hopes I fought with wild animals at Ephesus, what would I have gained by it? If the dead are not raised, 'Let us eat and drink, for tomorrow we die.' Do not be deceived: 'Bad company ruins good morals.' Come to a sober and right mind, and sin no more; for some people have no knowledge of God. I say this to your shame.

Today some friends are coming to lunch. We have just arranged it on the telephone, and I am planning the meal in one bit of my brain while I write these notes with the rest of it. Pasta with a sauce of sun-dried tomatoes, garlic and Greek yoghurt, with a green salad and a Bulgarian red wine. I love cooking, and eating and drinking—and so do they. But if all the good things of this life come to an end when we die then we had better make the most of them—even though there is a sadness at the heart of them.

But Paul knew that there is another life after this one, and because it mattered so much to him that other people should know it too—and share it—after his encounter with the risen Christ on the road to Damascus he spent the rest of his life telling the world the wonder of the good news. But he couldn't do it all himself, and the Corinthians (and presumably we too) should be ashamed that some people still have no knowledge of God.

A prayer

Lord Jesus Christ, thank you that this life isn't the end of the story when we know you. Help us to tell the greatest love story in the world to the people who don't know it, so that they might know God.

SB

A prayer on being in Christ

Since you have been raised up to be with Christ, you must look for the things that are above, where Christ is, sitting at God's right hand. Let your thoughts be on things above, not on the things that are on the earth, because you have died, and now the life you have is hidden with Christ in God. But when Christ is revealed—and he is your life—you, too, will be revealed with him in glory . . . You have stripped off your old behaviour with your old self, and you have put on a new self which will progress towards true knowledge the more it is renewed in the image of its Creator.

Lord, in your resurrection you have raised us up too. Since we were baptized into your death, we died with you. In so doing, we died to all that is temporary, provisional, fallible, corruptible in the world, the humdrum things of life. In our being joined to you in baptism, your history has become ours, so that we are joined to you even in your resurrection. The basis of my existence is no longer this everyday life of eating, working, relaxing, and sleeping. By your resurrection these have become provisional, and the dimension that matters is that of company with you before the Father. My base, my homeland, my citizenship, my roots, my family, my personality, are all now in heaven, wrapped up with you in God.

Yet I am still in exile from that homeland, waiting for this glory to be revealed, waiting for my whole being to be transformed by it. It is only too clear that I do not yet share in every way in your resurrection. My base and homeland may be in heaven, but my daily activity is on earth, with all its worries and temptations, its preoccupations, its stresses and its joys. Sometimes Scripture echoes this balance by saying that our full glory as risen brothers of Christ has only to be revealed, which suggests that it is already a reality, though in secret. Sometimes we are told that our bodies still need to be transformed, and we are still to expect that you will 'transfigure this wretched body of ours into the mould of' your glorious body.

If I already live with your risen life, I can live secure. To say that my homeland is in heaven is to say that any setback, any reversal or trouble here on earth, is of limited significance, provided that I hold firm to you. It is simply a matter of waiting and working till I come home to you at last.

HW

Seeds that 'die'

But someone will ask, 'How are the dead raised? With what kind of body do they come?' Fool! What you sow does not come to life unless it dies. And as for what you sow, you do not sow the body that is to be, but a bare seed, perhaps of wheat or of some other grain. But God gives it a body as he has chosen, and to each kind of seed its own body.

It wasn't a silly question. It was a sensible one, and one to which we all want to know the answer. That word 'fool' literally means someone without understanding. What Paul is saying is 'Open your eyes and look around!'

I hope that no one was offended last Friday when I talked about digging up the first crop of new potatoes and then wrote about the resurrection of Christ. I was in good company, though, because that is very much what Paul is doing—asking us to reflect on the world around us. What happens when we plant a seed? And what is the seed like when we plant it?

Last weekend a friend showed me a box full of tiny green seedlings. They were nicotiana, the white sweet-scented tobacco plant that grows more than a metre high and fills the night air with its fragrance. He was growing them for me, because the only tobacco plants we seem to be able to buy are the smaller plants in different colours. They look very tidy and compact but they hardly smell at all. This misses the whole point of planting them, outside a window, so that the wonderful smell will drift into the room. In the packet that my friend planted there were 2,000 tiny black seeds (we didn't count them, but that is what it said on the label!). So there will be plenty for both of us. Yet anyone looking at one of those tiny black seeds would never imagine the glory of the full-grown plant.

A reflection

Think of a tiny black nicotiana seed being sown—or some other seed that you know. Think of the full-grown plant. Then think of your own body being sown into the ground when you die—'in sure and certain hope of the resurrection to eternal life' (Funeral Service, ASB).

SB

The weight of glory

Not all flesh is alike, but there is one flesh for human beings, another for animals, another for birds, and another for fish. There are both heavenly bodies and earthly bodies, but the glory of the heavenly is one thing, and that of the earthly is another. There is one glory of the sun, and another glory of the moon, and another glory of the stars; indeed, star differs from star in glory.

If we plant lettuce seeds we shall get lettuces, not radishes. When the seed that is you is finally planted in the ground the glorified resurrection body that is you will not be the glorified resurrection body that is me. And when we meet our nearest and dearest on the other side we probably won't know them immediately, because of the sheer 'Weight of Glory'. In his marvellous article of that title, C.S. Lewis said: 'It is a serious thing to live in a society of possible gods and goddesses, to remember that the dullest and most uninteresting person you can talk to may one day be a creature which, if you saw it now, you would be strongly tempted to worship . . .' (C.S. Lewis, *Screwtape Proposes a Toast and Other Pieces*).

To think about

Then the new earth and sky, the same yet not the same as these, will rise in us as we have risen in Christ. And once again, after who knows what aeons of the silence and dark, the birds will sing out and the waters flow, and lights and shadows move across the hills and the faces of our friends laugh upon us with amazed recognition. Guesses, of course, only guesses. If they are not true, something better will be. For we know that we shall be made like Him, for we shall see Him as He is.

C.S. Lewis, Letters to Malcolm: Chiefly on Prayer

SB

From glory to glory

So it is with the resurrection of the dead. What is sown is perishable, what is raised is imperishable. It is sown in dishonour, it is raised in glory. It is sown in weakness, it is raised in power. It is sown a physical body, it is raised a spiritual body. If there is a physical body, there is also a spiritual body. Thus it is written, 'The first man, Adam, became a living being'; the last Adam became a life-giving spirit.

Paul is drawing the conclusion from his illustration—that everything has its own sort of body, and that every seed that is planted will grow up into its own sort of glory. And (to draw the conclusion from my illustration) the lettuce or the sweet-scented tobacco plant will have grown out of the seed that was planted, and will have an direct connection and an essential relationship with that seed.

The nature of the resurrection body is infinitely more glorious than the earthly body. Your body and mine are perishable, and one day we shall die. That is the nature of a human being. But when we are raised up in our resurrection bodies we shall never die. Our physical bodies are weak, but our resurrection bodies will be raised in power. They will be related to the human being who was us—but glorified.

A reflection

The New Testament promises us that our physical body shall be transmuted into a spiritualized body, like the body of the risen Christ, released from the domination of the material, the spatial and the temporal. Yet in some mysterious way it will be recognizable perhaps with its most significant features, as the nail-marks and the spear-wound on our Lord's resurrection body. We may think of the body as a life-long comrade, who will survive death and in some spiritualized form be our comrade still.

George Appleton, Journey for a Soul

SB

The next stage

But it is not the spiritual that is first, but the physical, and then the spiritual. The first man was from the earth, a man of dust; the second man is from heaven. As was the man of dust, so are those who are of the dust; and as is the man of heaven, so are those who are of heaven. Just as we have borne the image of the man of dust, we will also bear the image of the man of heaven.

Over the years I have set up a lot of home groups, and have discovered an interesting fact. This is that the groups which start with a simple meal invariably work far better than the ones that start without one and jump straight into the deep waters of spiritual conversation about the Christian faith and the Bible. It is as if we need to start with the natural, human things of our life, in the sharing of a meal—the thing that Jesus so often did with people. And then we can move on to the next stage.

As C.S. Lewis said, 'God likes matter: he made it.' And God made a material world with the possibility of a spiritual dimension and development. We can refuse that if we like, and a lot of people do. But God offers the possibility to everyone, and longs for them to accept it. We start with a relationship with our human parents, but we can go on to a relationship with God as our heavenly parent. It is like a second birth, and Jesus explained it to Nicodemus:

Very truly, I tell you no one can enter the kingdom of God without being born of water and Spirit.

What is born of the flesh is flesh, and what is born of the Spirit is spirit. Do not be astonished that I said to you, 'You must be born from above.' The wind blows where it chooses, and you hear the sound of it, but you do not know where it comes from or where it goes. So it is with everyone who is born of the Spirit.

John 3:5–8 (NRSV).

Reflect

Think about your own human parents, or adoptive parents, and your relationship with them. Think about your relationship with God as your heavenly Father. Then spend some time in quiet, reflective prayer.

SB

We shall all be changed

What I am saying, brothers and sisters, is this: flesh and blood cannot inherit the kingdom of God, nor does the perishable inherit the imperishable. Listen, I will tell you a mystery! We will not all die, but we will all be changed, in a moment, in the twinkling of an eye, at the last trumpet. For the trumpet will sound, and the dead will be raised imperishable, and we will be changed. For this perishable body must put on imperishability, and this mortal body must put on immortality.

Part of what Paul is writing about here is the doctrine of the second coming of Christ. It isn't talked about much these days, and a lot of Christian believers wouldn't count it as a vital part of their faith. We say we believe it every Sunday if we say the creed, but the wonderful words are mysterious: 'He will come again in glory to judge the living and the dead, and his kingdom will have no end.'

Trumpets in the Bible very often have to do with judgment, and to believe that one day there will be a righteous judgment by Christ of the whole world can comfort us when terrible things happen all around us—so long as we know we are forgiven for our own evil, and are living a new life of love in the power of Christ.

But in whatever way the end comes we can know for certain that these bodies of flesh and blood that are you and me will not go on for ever. Not because they aren't wonderfully created by God, but because they cannot inherit and possess immortality. For that, they need to be changed—and the New Testament says that one day they will be.

A reflection

' "No eye has seen, no ear has heard, no mind has conceived what God has prepared for those who love him"—but God has revealed it to us by his Spirit' (1 Corinthians 2:9–10, NIV). Spend some time reflecting on these words— and pray that God will reveal to you something of the glory that lies ahead.

SB

A whole new story

When this perishable body puts on imperishability, and this mortal body puts on immortality, then the saying that is written will be fulfilled: 'Death has been swallowed up in victory.' 'Where, O death, is your victory? Where, O death, is your sting?' The sting of death is sin, and the power of sin is the law. But thanks be to God, who gives us the victory through our Lord Jesus Christ. Therefore, my beloved, be steadfast, immovable, always excelling in the work of the Lord, because you know that in the Lord your labour is not in vain.

People sometimes refer to church services for births, marriages and deaths as 'rites of passage'—each one a passage into a different stage of life. Out of the womb into birth. Then, perhaps, the new birth of Christianity. For some, there is the passage from the single life to being married that the wedding service celebrates. And for everyone there is the passage through death. But for the believer that is a passage with a door at the end of it.

David Watson, the evangelist who died of cancer at the age of 51, said that death is the friend who opens the door—a friend, because on the other side of the door we shall see Christ. Because of that, nothing is meaningless and nothing is wasted.

To think about

'There was a real railway accident,' said Aslan softly. 'Your father and mother and all of you are—as you used to call it in the Shadowlands—dead. The term is over: the holidays have begun. The dream is ended: this is the morning.' And as He spoke He no longer looked to them like a lion; but the things that began to happen after that were so great and beautiful that I cannot write them. And for us this is the end of all the stories, and we can most truly say that they all lived happily ever after. But for them it was only the beginning of the real story. All their life in this world and all their adventures in Narnia had only been the cover and the title page: now at last they were beginning Chapter One of the Great Story which no one on earth has read: which goes on for ever: in which every chapter is better than the one before.

C.S. Lewis, The Last Battle

The greatness of God and the glory of Christ

Before we look at the coming of the Holy Spirit at Pentecost, we shall consider the greatness of God and the glory of Christ. We shall do that first as we spend seven days with Douglas Cleverley Ford reflecting on some Psalms in which the writer delights in the God whom he worships—and through his delight evokes a sense of delight in us.

Then, with Marcus Maxwell, we consider the stunning statements which Paul's letter to the Colossians makes about the nature and the glory of God the Son, who died on the cross on Good Friday, and whom God the Father raised from the dead on Easter Day. We shall see what the implications and the blessings are for us who believe in that God and follow that Christ, and we shall see how an apostle struggles and prays for the believers in the Colossian church.

Through that we shall learn more about how to pray ourselves, and how to love, and realize the truth of the astonishing statement that Paul makes about Christ and about all of us who have received him:

For in him the whole fullness of deity dwells bodily, and you have come to fullness of life in him.

Colossians 2:10 (RSV)

A way to pray

The prayer that we are looking at today is so superb that we can't do better than to make it our own and use it throughout the year. But it helps to reflect on each phrase in this prayer, so that is what we shall do today—very briefly because of lack of space.

For this reason I kneel before the Father, from whom his whole family in heaven and on earth derives its name.

(3:14–15)

We can call God Father, or 'Abba', Daddy... and all the people in this world and in the next who call him Father are our brothers and sisters.

I pray that out of his glorious riches he may strengthen you with power through his Spirit in your inner being, so that Christ may dwell in your hearts through faith.

(3:16–17)

We can have an incredibly glorious power within us... but it's the power of a *person* in us, the risen Christ, living in us in his Spirit.

And I pray that you, being rooted and established in love, may have power, together with all the saints, to grasp how wide and long and high and deep is the love of Christ,

and to know this love that surpasses knowledge—that you may be filled to the measure of all the fulness of God.

(3:17–19)

Deeply rooted in love we can have the power to know love—a love that's beyond words and knowledge, but one that we can know and experience—and then be filled with the love of God and with God himself right up to overflowing...

Now to him who is able to do immeasurably more than all we ask or imagine, according to his power that is at work within us, to him be glory in the church and in Christ Jesus throughout all generations, for ever and ever!

(3:20–21)

No wonder there's such a shout of glory from Paul—and from us—because the possibilities and the promises are beyond all our imaginings. Read the prayer through now from the beginning, out loud. Name some people before God, then pray the prayer for them and include yourself in it as well.

SB

Our stronghold

Walk about Zion, go round about her, number her towers, consider well her ramparts, go through her citadels; that you may tell the next generation that this is God, our God for ever and ever. He will be our guide for ever.

Picture the inhabitants of a city, long-besieged, streaming out when the siege was lifted, to look at what was still standing. Look at the towers! that they haven't been destroyed! See how the ramparts have stood up to the battering! What a story we have to tell our children! Zion, God's dwelling place, may be attacked *but it cannot be obliterated*. Yes, this is the God we acclaim, and will do for ever and ever.

No, we can't pin-point the historical occasion, but does this matter? Our Zion, our Jerusalem, is the Church of God. It is not perfect. It never has been perfect. There are some disgraceful periods in its long history. But it is God's dwelling place, no, not his only dwelling place, but his special one. And remember this. God does not only choose perfect places in which to dwell, otherwise he would never look at your heart or mine.

There may be a fashion these days to despise the church. Don't go in for it. God has chosen it; this is all that matters. It is not perfect but it can boast many saints, and look what art, music and learning it has inspired! What is more, it has withstood all the decrying, disdaining and destruction aimed at it. Why? Because the Spirit of the living God has made it his humble dwelling place, and no one can destroy him.

A prayer

Lord, I thank you for the Church, warts and all—You founded it, the apostles built it up, and it has withstood a thousand knocks. Through the Church, Lord, directly or indirectly, I came to know you, and trust you, and be guided by you. Give me grace to do so today.

DCF

The mighty God

Bless the Lord, O my soul! O Lord my God, thou art very great! . . . Thou didst set the earth on its foundations, so that it should never be shaken. Thou didst cover it with the deep as with a garment; the waters stood above the mountains. At thy rebuke they fled; at the sound of thy thunder they took to flight. The mountains rose, the valleys sank down to the place which thou didst appoint for them. Thou didst set a bound which they should not pass, so that they might not again cover the earth.

Is our God too small? This Psalm points to the great God who made the world. It carries our thoughts back to God as Creator, reflecting his mighty works as set out in Genesis, chapter 1. When I kneel down to pray today, and you kneel down, this is the God before whom we are coming—the great and the mighty one.

This means we must approach with reverence. We cannot tell God what he should do for us, or for *his* world, or for *his people*. And if we complain about our lot in life in his presence—and better that than not praying at all—we shall have to 'eat humble pie' in the end. 'O Lord, I am sorry. You are great and I am small and of no reputation!'

Yet the mighty God hears our prayers; we, they, are not too small for his attention. Have you ever boasted of a friend in high places? Someone who could do for you what no ordinary person without influence could do? *But he can.* And the mighty God is like that. A friend in high places! What a description of God! But if we really believe it we shall manage today with far more confidence.

A faith for today

Lord, you are very great and you do wonderful things. You alone are God. And yet you have a great love and concern for every creature in your world; and that includes me.

DCF

God the provider

Thou dost cause the grass to grow for the cattle, and plants for man to cultivate, that he may bring forth food from the earth, and wine to gladden the heart of man, oil to make his face shine, and bread to strengthen man's heart. The trees of the Lord are watered abundantly, the cedars of Lebanon which he planted. In them the birds build their nests; the stork has her home in the fir trees. The high mountains are for the wild goats; the rocks are a refuge for the badgers. Thou has made the moon to mark the seasons; the sun knows its time for setting . . . Man goes forth to his work and to his labour until the evening.

I have come to the country late in life; almost all my working life has been in central London. Now I am retired and I love my garden. I thank God for it. And shall I ever forget that first April when the various shades of green as the new foliage opened out almost took my breath away.

The trouble about living in built-up areas is that we can miss the beauty of nature. We half think that our food comes from man-made factories. But the truth is, the towns live because of the country. Everything we have derives from the good earth which God has given us. Yes, that is our faith. God is the provider and not only of the bare necessities of life, but of beauty too.

Read again today's verses. Note what are mentioned. Grass, cattle, trees, birds, wild goats, badgers... Also food to strengthen us, and wine to cheer us up. And the moon and the sun. How we should lift up our hearts in thanks and praise for all of this. Could we, perhaps, say our prayers sometimes out of doors?

An act of praise

Bless the Lord, O my soul, and forget not all his benefits.

DCF

Our ultimate security

I lift up my eyes to the hills. From whence does my help come? My help comes from the Lord, who made heaven and earth.

Imagine an inhabitant of Jerusalem (the writer of this Psalm) sitting on one of the hills surrounding the city and taking in the impressive panorama before him. There was the city itself perched on its hill protected by walls. What a sight!, and how proud he was of it!

And how envious were the surrounding nations! And how often they made military expeditions to capture it for themselves! And this man, squatting there, began to ask himself what protection the city had from its enemies! Did its security perhaps lie in its extraordinary geographical situation? Jerusalem was not easy to capture. Maybe not, but its ultimate security did not rest in its peculiar location but in God's protection, the God who made heaven and earth. He had chosen Jerusalem.

When you have looked out on your own life with anxiety about the future, have you never answered your own question by telling yourself how well insured you are, how you have a pension scheme, and how there is National Health Security? What is more, you have a medical check-up and everything seems to be in order. What is there to worry about? Let there be no doubt, all these are a defence against calamity and we need them.

In the last resort, however, God is our real helper. So let us re-word the psalm for our situation.

'I will lift up my eyes to all my securities, insurance policies, and provisions for my future. Does not protection come from these? No, in the last resort it comes from the Lord, my Lord, who has made heaven and earth.'

Something to sing

Glorious things of thee are spoken,
Zion, city of our God;
He whose word cannot be broken
Formed thee for his own abode.
On the Rock of ages founded,
What can shake thy sure repose?
With salvation's walls surrounded,
Thou may'st smile at all thy foes.

J. Newton

DCF

Joyful laughter

When the Lord turned again the captivity of Sion: then were we like unto them that dream. Then was our mouth filled with laughter: and our tongue with joy. Then said they among the heathen: The Lord hath done great things for them. Yea, the Lord hath done great things for us already: whereof we rejoice.

Picture a great crowd of people in an internment camp. They have been shut in for years. Old people have died there, been buried and mourned. Children have been born there and never known anything else but life behind bars; and prison food and prison beds and prison rules and regulations governing everything anyone wanted to do. No future. The internees had almost forgotten what laughter was like, genuine laughter and not wry laughter.

And then it happened. They could scarcely believe it. Notices plastered everywhere that on such and such a day the gates would be opened and they would be free. They could go home. Picture the scene. First open-mouthed astonishment. Then disbelief. Gradually belief growing. Then shouting, whistling, dancing and almost uncontrolled laughter. Incredible? Very well, read what happened in the prisoner-of-war camps in Germany at the cessation of hostilities in 1945.

Perhaps it is a 'bit much' to expect us as Christians to laugh and dance and sing like these freed internees, but if we haven't inside us a little merriment on account of our religion we have never reached the heart of the matter; because we have been set free by Christ for time and eternity. That is why he came, to set us free. Do let us have some laughter in our lives in consequence, joyful laughter, grateful laughter.

Thanksgiving

Now thank we all our God,
With hearts and hands and voices,
Who wondrous things hath done,
In whom this world rejoices...

M Rinkart

DCF

137

Willing response

I will teach you, and guide you in the way you should go. I will keep you under my eye. Do not behave like horse or mule, unreasoning creatures, whose course must be checked with bit and bridle. Many are the torments of the ungodly; but unfailing love enfolds him who trusts in the Lord. Rejoice in the Lord and be glad, you righteous men, and sing aloud, all men of upright heart.

We don't like the phrase, 'torments of the ungodly', but think of it this way. Here is a man who has played the fool with his health. Overeating, over-drinking, chain smoking—not to mention some secret recourse to drugs in order to pep himself up. He has to pay for this. Duodenal ulcers, alcoholism, lung cancer. The consequent pain can be tormenting. How can he be guided in the right way? If he is an unreasoning creature, and the likelihood is that he will become so as a result of these follies, he will have to be checked with stiff regulations, even some form of hospitalization. He will only go straight if he is held in like a horse or mule with a bit and bridle.

A far more sensible way to go about life is to listen to the words of wisdom which God has given us in the Scriptures and to give a willing, not a compulsory response. We must understand that God guides us and teaches us in the way we should go *because he loves us* and longs for our welfare. He has no pleasure in punishment. He wants willing and loving obedience from men and women with a song in their hearts. One ounce of it is worth more than a ton of compulsion.

Prayer

Teach me, O Lord, the way of thy statutes:
and I shall keep it unto the end.
Give me understanding,
and I shall keep thy law:
yea, I shall keep it with my whole heart.
Make me to go in the path of thy
commandments: for therein is my desire.
Incline my heart unto thy testimonies:
and not to covetousness.

Psalm 119:33–36 (BCP)

DCF

You are like God

Then the Pharisees went and took counsel how to entangle him in his talk . . . 'Tell us, then, what you think. Is it lawful to pay taxes to Caesar, or not?' But Jesus, aware of their malice, said, 'Why put me to the test, you hypocrites? Show me the money for the tax.' And they brought him a coin. And Jesus said to them, 'Whose likeness and inscription is this?' They said, 'Caesar's.' Then he said to them, 'Render therefore to Caesar the things that are Caesar's, and to God the things that are God's.'

Imagine yourself as a Pharisee. You are a passionate Jew and you hate it that the Romans occupy your land. You also hate it that an unlearned Jew (he isn't trained in the law as you are) is attracting large crowds by his preaching and teaching.

So you try to trip him up—and whether he says 'yes' or 'no' to your question you have caught him. Or you think you have. The Jews will be angry with him if he says that they should pay taxes to Rome. The Romans will be angry if he says they shouldn't.

But then this infuriating and un-trained man makes you get a coin and asks you whose image is on it. You have to admit that it is Caesar's. So he says that you should give to Caesar what is Caesar's—and you can tell it belongs to Caesar because his image is on it.

But you are also to give to God what belongs to God—and as a man trained in the holy Scriptures you know what that means. God created you in his image, so you belong to God.

Reflect

Reflect for a few moments on whether you are avoiding the issue of personal self-surrender by being religious and concerning yourself with outward ceremonial, or even with political and social affairs, in a way that makes them more important than your relationship to God.

As you come today to Holy Communion, will you give yourself in love to the God who gives himself to you and gave himself for you?

SB

Like a mighty army...

In our prayers for you we always thank God, the Father of our Lord Jesus Christ, for we have heard of your faith in Christ Jesus and of the love that you have for all the saints, because of the hope laid up for you in heaven. You have heard of this hope before in the word of truth, the gospel that has come to you. Just as it is bearing fruit and growing in the whole world, so it has been bearing fruit among yourselves from the day you heard it and truly comprehended the grace of God.

Paul almost always begins his letters with encouragement. He will have hard things to say, but he wants to make it clear that his concern is really for the good of the Christians at Colossae. In passing, we should note his attitude for ourselves. When we discover someone's bad points (and we soon do if we pay any attention to them!), we easily forget their good ones. Paul is writing to correct a heresy, but he doesn't forget that the strange ideas of the Colossians spring out of a real faith and a genuine desire to know God.

The other encouraging thing he mentions is that the Colossians belong to a fellowship which is spreading throughout the whole world. It is easy, when we belong to a small, fairly isolated church, to forget the size and scope of the whole Church. The Colossians felt free to go their own way, perhaps because they had forgotten that they were only a part of the whole.

Today, Christians in Europe feel that they are a small minority. So few people seem interested in the Church or in God. Yet that is not the whole picture. The Church throughout the world is growing at a rate never seen before. New churches spring up every minute. And we are part of that great Church, and have a role to play in it as we support it through our prayers and our giving.

A way to pray

Pray for the Church all over the world, for its growth and witness, the work of its leaders and the unity of its people. Thank God for the part you have to play, and for the encouragement of belonging to such an exciting period of Church growth.

MM

The faithful servant

You learned [the gospel] from Epaphras, our beloved fellow servant. He is a faithful minister of Christ on your behalf, and he has made known to us your love in the Spirit . . . Epaphras, who is one of you, a servant of Christ Jesus, greets you. He is always wrestling in his prayers on your behalf, so that you may stand mature and fully assured in everything that God wills. For I testify for him that he has worked hard for you and for those in Laodicea and Hierapolis.

There is a lot of truth in the old cliché that familiarity breeds contempt. Epaphras can hardly have been a fool (after all, he founded the Colossian church) but he was making no headway against the false teaching that had sprung up in his congregation. Instead, he had to get Paul to sort it out, and twice in this short letter, Paul reminds the Colossians of what a good job Epaphras has done. He was a successful evangelist, a hard worker and a man who cared deeply for the people in his church. Yet they wouldn't listen to him. Why? We are not told, but somehow I think I hear mutters of, 'Oh, it's only Epaphras, what does he know?' And while Paul was probably a much greater thinker, I suspect that what was needed was not so much a better theologian as simply a fresh voice.

In most of our churches today, there are people like Epaphras. Some are ordained, some are not. But they are the people who wrestle in prayer for the church, who strive to keep it true to the gospel, who uncomfortably prick our conscience and remind us of our calling to spread the word about Jesus. And all too often they are taken for granted, or dismissed as too religious or too simple in their faith. But they are the people we should cherish and thank God for, if we are lucky enough to have one or two.

Pray

Thank you, Father, for the people who shoulder our burdens in prayer, for the ones who struggle to serve you and your Church, and are too easily taken for granted. Open our eyes to see the work they do for you, and give us the grace to share in the work.

MM

True wisdom

For this reason, since the day we heard it, we have not ceased praying for you and asking that you may be filled with the knowledge of God's will in all spiritual wisdom and understanding, so that you may lead lives worthy of the Lord, fully pleasing to him, as you bear fruit in every good work and as you grow in the knowledge of God. May you be made strong with all the strength that comes from his glorious power, and may you be prepared to endure everything with patience, while joyfully giving thanks to the Father . . .

Isn't it fun to be in the know; to be someone who knows what is going on while others are still baffled? And don't we feel left out when we see someone else being confided in when we are on the fringe of the action? We see the 'insiders' in action in our church sometimes—the ones who mutter importantly with the minister about some obscure details just before the service begins.

It's even worse when some people claim to be insiders with God; to have some sort of special claim on his attention. At various times, there have been groups like that in the Church, some official (like the priesthood) and some simply members of strange sects with the true wisdom of God at their fingertips! The Colossians fell into the second category.

It is fairly clear that some of the Colossian Christians claimed to have a special type of 'wisdom' which put them in closer touch with the heavenly world, and from which other Christians could be disqualified. But Paul would have

none of that. As far as he was concerned, the true knowledge of God came through prayer and a life lived in obedience to God, not through any secret and mysterious rituals. And that was what he prayed the Colossians would get for themselves.

Pray

Take Paul's prayer and say it for yourself. Meditate on each quality that you pray for, and on where it is needed in your life. Where do you need the ability to recognize God's will, to draw on his power and so on? Make them special topics for prayer.

MM

Life in two worlds

...giving thanks to the Father, who has enabled you to share in the inheritance of the saints in the light. He has rescued us from the power of darkness and transferred us into the kingdom of his beloved Son, in whom we have redemption, the forgiveness of sins.

It is easy to skip over these few verses without noticing how strange they are. They don't say that God *will* rescue us, but that he *has* rescued us. On the face of it, it might seem more sensible to say that we live in a wicked and tortured world, but that we have something better to look forward to. After all, we still sin, we still suffer, and we still see evil around us. But the fact remains that we have already been rescued.

And indeed, we do have something better to look forward to. The 'inheritance of the saints', the promise of heaven—what Paul calls the kingdom of God—lies ahead. But what he calls the kingdom of Christ is already here. Jesus has already brought us under his wing. As his followers, we may still sin, but we have forgiveness ready to call upon. Those who have put their trust in Christ will still be a part of the sinful world, but they have resources far beyond most people's imagining—the strength that comes from God, which we read about yesterday. This is something we need to keep in mind, because it helps us to understand the ups and downs of the Christian life, and gives us the hope we often need to carry on.

As people who live in the world, we still suffer from its imperfections and injustices. But as people who belong to Jesus, we can call on the help of God to see us through. More than that, we look forward to the final righting of all wrongs, and the final triumph of God. As we live out our lives here and now, we are called to live by the light of God's coming kingdom, secure in the knowledge that Jesus is our Lord, and that he has set us free from the hopelessness of separation from God.

Pray

Father, thank you that we can call on your help, and know your forgiveness for our failure.

MM

Lord of creation

He is the image of the invisible God, the firstborn of all creation; for in him all things in heaven and on earth were created, things visible and invisible, whether thrones or dominions or rulers or powers—all things have been created through him and for him. He himself is before all things, and in him all things hold together.

Do you ever feel that your life is getting out of control? Perhaps your job pushes you around, or just as your money seems under control, another bill arrives. Or it could be more serious things, like a sense of hopelessness in coping with the threats of the world—war and famine sweep the world, and what can I do?

In ancient times, that sort of feeling was as common as today. People spent a lot of time and effort trying to find out what fate had in store for them. Astrology was a growth industry. Various cults claimed to put their members in touch with supernatural forces (thrones, dominions, rulers and powers) which controlled the world. Others taught that fate could not be avoided, so all one could do was face it with dignity. But whatever a person's attitude, nearly all agreed that our life was not in our hands.

In one sense, Paul agrees; a Christian's life is not in his or her hands. It is in Christ's. But this is not blind fate. Jesus Christ is the creative power of God embodied in a human being. And he is a living person, who can be known and loved. To be in his care is not to be tossed about by the blind winds of fate or chance, but to be loved and looked after. Whatever may seem to threaten or control us in this life need not make us afraid, for Jesus is more powerful than whatever threatens us.

Of course, there is evil in the world, and Christians are not immune to suffering. But nothing that comes our way is beyond Christ's ability to see us through.

Meditate

I am convinced that neither death, nor life, nor angels, nor rulers, nor things present, nor things to come, nor powers, nor height, nor depth, nor anything else in all creation, will be able to separate us from the love of God in Christ Jesus our Lord.

Romans 8:38–39

MM

Lord of the church

He is the head of the body, the church; he is the beginning, the firstborn from the dead, so that he might come to have first place in everything. For in him all the fullness of God was pleased to dwell, and through him God was pleased to reconcile to himself all things, whether on earth or in heaven, by making peace through the blood of his cross.

The Christian Church exists because of Jesus Christ. In him God came to be one of us, and on the cross died for us. He rose from the dead, and that resurrection launched the Church, as the disciples went out to spread the good news that God had made peace with his rebellious creation. Christ, Paul says, is the head of the Church.

In Greek, 'head' didn't just mean 'boss'. It more often meant 'source' or 'origin'—the point from which life and energy flow. Jesus is the source of the Church's life, the one who gives it power and purpose. The Church exists because of him and to serve him.

By this point you may well wonder why I am virtually repeating what the passage has already said. I think it is worth repeating—not just once but many times. In the Church, it is easy to let things get between us and our Lord. There are so many aspects of Church life which can bog us down. For some it is simply the mechanics of belonging to a local church. The business of attending worship, of organizing meetings, sidesmen's rotas and fund-raising can become, without our quite realizing it, the main point of the church. For others, it can be loyalty to a particular tradition, such as the desire to preserve the pure evangelical gospel, or true catholic order.

In Colossae, a desire for a particular kind of spiritual experience had become the most important thing. For them and us Paul gives a timely reminder; Christ is the source of all our spiritual life. Anything that gets between us and him, no matter how good it may seem, can only lead to spiritual deadness.

Meditate

Jesus alone is the focus of our life as the Church—what things are we tempted to focus on instead?

The marriage

Then I saw a new heaven and a new earth; for the first heaven and the first earth had passed away, and the sea was no more. And I saw the holy city, new Jerusalem, coming down out of heaven from God, prepared as a bride adorned for her husband; and I heard a loud voice from the throne saying, 'Behold, the dwelling of God is with men. He will dwell with them, and they shall be his people, and God himself will be with them; he will wipe away every tear from their eyes, and death shall be no more, neither shall there be mourning nor crying nor pain any more, for the former things have passed away.' And he who sat upon the throne said, 'Behold, I make all things new.'

Communion is about the deep intimacy of a shared life. So is a good marriage. Before you come today to Communion, will you reflect on today's reading? The vision which God gives to John of the glories of heaven shows a holy city prepared as a bride adorned for her husband—and early on in the vision an angel has spoken to John about a marriage.

Hallelujah! For the Lord our God the Almighty reigns. Let us rejoice and exult and give him the glory, for the marriage of the Lamb has come, and his Bride has made herself ready; it was granted her to be clothed with fine linen, bright and pure'—for the fine linen is the righteous deeds of the saints. And the angel said to me, 'Write this: "Blessed are those who are invited to the marriage supper of the Lamb."'

Revelation 19:6–9

As you come to the communion table today, will you look ahead to a wedding reception and a marriage, in which the whole Church (and you as one of its members) is joined to Christ in an eternal union of total blessedness and happiness: Will you pray for the Church's bridal dress—her righteous deeds of love and mercy and justice to a suffering, weeping world?

SB

Beyond forgiveness

And you who were once estranged and hostile in mind, doing evil deeds, he has now reconciled in his fleshly body through death, so as to present you holy and blameless and irreproachable before him—provided that you continue securely established and steadfast in the faith, without shifting from the hope promised by the gospel that you heard, which has been proclaimed to every creature under heaven. I, Paul, became a servant of this gospel.

Last week we saw that to be a Christian is to have God's forgiveness at hand when we let him down. I suppose that could lead people to think that it doesn't matter what they do; after all, God is ready and willing to forgive. But it does matter, because God is not merely concerned to forgive us. He wants us to be reconciled to him.

Forgiveness, you might say, is only the first part of the story. If I offended you, you can (and should!) forgive me, whether I am sorry or not. But we can only make up and be friends again if I accept the forgiveness, and admit that I was wrong. This is what Jesus came for—to open the way for us to make up with God. And that is why Paul adds a word of warning, 'provided that you continue ... in the faith.'

We can never take God for granted, because taking anyone for granted is the first stage in forgetting about them altogether. (Haven't we all lost friends by simply not bothering with them—not bothering to write, to get in touch, until all contact has faded away?) God has called us to be his friends, so that we can share with him 'the hope promised by the gospel'; the hope of heaven. Of course, Paul doesn't want us to live in fear of making mistakes. We do wrong every day. And God is willing to forgive us every day. But what we must never do is get into the habit of thought which takes our sins lightly.

Meditate

All this is from God, who reconciled us to himself through Christ, and has given us the ministry of reconciliation.

2 Corinthians 5:18

MM

The suffering God

I am now rejoicing in my sufferings for your sake, and in my flesh I am completing what is lacking in Christ's afflictions for the sake of his body, that is, the church. I became its servant according to God's commission that was given to me for you, to make the word of God fully known, the mystery that has been hidden throughout the ages and generations but has now been revealed to his saints. To them God chose to make known how great among the Gentiles are the riches of the glory of this mystery, which is Christ in you, the hope of glory.

One of the most difficult problems which faces all Christians at one time or another is the problem of suffering. Why does God allow suffering if he is so good? It is more than a theoretical question. One of my most painful memories is of a call to the children's emergency department of our local hospital. A baby had died suddenly and the young mother wanted to see the chaplain to ask just one question: 'Is there a reason for this?'

The honest answer is that if there is, we are not told of it. But that does not mean that we are left without comfort. In his own sufferings as a missionary, Paul had come to realize that he was not alone. He was a part of the body of Christ, and when his body suffered, Jesus suffered too. That is what Paul means by saying that he is somehow making up a shortfall in Jesus' sufferings. It isn't that the suffering of the cross was not enough to bring about salvation, but simply that as long as his people (and indeed his world) suffer, then God in Christ suffers too.

So when we are faced with the problem of pain, we are offered no neat intellectual answers. Instead, we know that we suffer in the company of God who knows what suffering is.

The other gods were strong,
but Thou wast weak.
They rode, but Thou didst stumble
to a throne.
But to our wounds,
God's wounds alone can speak
And not a God has wounds
but Thou alone.

Edward Shillito

MM

Divine love

For I want you to know how much I am struggling for you, and for those in Laodicea, and for all who have not seen me face to face. I want their hearts to be encouraged and united in love, so that they may have all the riches of assured understanding and have the knowledge of God's mystery, that is, Christ himself, in whom are hidden all the treasures of wisdom and knowledge. I am saying this so that no one may deceive you with plausible arguments. For though I am absent in body, yet I am with you in spirit, and I rejoice to see your morale and the firmness of your faith in Christ.

As we have seen, the false teaching at Colassae claimed to give its members secret wisdom and knowledge which was hidden from the outsiders who did not know the full teachings of God. That is why Paul uses the language of mystery, wisdom and knowledge here. The true wisdom of God is available to anyone who puts their faith in Christ, and the key to unlock it is the love which comes from God.

It is easy to love our friends, and to fall in love with an attractive man or woman. It is hard not to love our children. But God's love reaches out to those who are not particularly attractive, or friendly; to those who reject and hurt the one who loves. We see this in Jesus, dying to save those who crucified him, and here in Paul.

Paul is willing to pour out his greatest effort for people he has never met, eager for them to know Jesus and to grow in faith even when he thinks their beliefs are dangerously mistaken. Although their teaching undermines the lordship of Christ, he is ready to praise their faith and unity.

How different it is with debates in our churches! This is one of the tests of true love, the love that comes from knowing God: that we have good and generous words for our opponents, and will strive with might and main to do what is best even for those who have no time for us.

Reflect

Who do you most disagree with? What do you do to show your love for them?

MM

Working at faith

As you therefore have received Christ Jesus the Lord, continue to live your lives in him, rooted and built up in him and established in the faith, just as you were taught, abounding in thanksgiving. See to it that no one takes you captive through philosophy and empty deceit, according to human tradition, according to the elemental spirits of the universe, and not according to Christ. For in him the whole fullness of deity dwells bodily, and you have come to fullness in him, who is the head of every ruler and authority.

What would you say to someone who complained that, after scattering a packet of seeds out of their window, their garden was still untidy? It sounds ridiculous, doesn't it? A good garden only comes about through hard work. It's the same for everything else, whether our work, our hobbies or our homes. Everything, that is, except our faith. Somehow, we seem to think that we will develop a deep and abiding faith with no effort at all. And if it is suggested that we ought to study what we believe, put in a bit more Bible reading, maybe read a book or two, we have an answer for that: 'I like to have a simple faith, Vicar. I'll leave all that complicated stuff to you professionals!'

Paul knew better. 'Live your lives . . . See to it . . .', are commands to actually *do* something. To be rooted and built up in Christ means to work at our relationship with him. It means learning to speak to him in prayer even when we don't feel like it. It means taking time to listen for his word in the Scriptures. And it means learning enough about our faith to recognize what is likely to be true and what is wrong.

It is only out of that sort of effort that a simple faith can grow, for a simple faith is not a childish understanding, but a childlike trust in one we have come to know well, and recognize as deserving our trust.

Reflect

How much effort do you put into your work, hobbies and home? How much do you put into knowing Christ? And just how much do you rate your faith?

MM

The victory

In him also you were circumcised with a spiritual circumcision, by putting off the body of the flesh in the circumcision of Christ; when you were buried with him in baptism, you were also raised with him through faith in the power of God, who raised him from the dead. And when you were dead in trespasses and the uncircumcision of your flesh, God made you alive together with him, when he forgave us all our trespasses, erasing the record that stood against us with its legal demands. He set this aside, nailing it to the cross. He disarmed the rulers and authorities and made a public example of them, triumphing over them in it.

If we thought yesterday of the need to work at our Christian lives, we must not make the mistake of thinking that our efforts are what make our relationship with God. They are the way of expressing and getting the most out of a relationship which has been given to us by Jesus.

Jesus died, was buried and rose again to open up the way to our new life with God. When we accept that life by putting our faith in God, Jesus' death becomes our death—death to the old sinful life—and his resurrection becomes our new life with him. All this is symbolized in baptism. Just as baptism is done to us (no one baptizes himself) so the new life is *given* to us by God.

Today's reading piles up images to stress this point. The Colossians thought they needed all kinds of spiritual exercises and rituals to get close to heaven. Paul tells them that heaven has been handed to them on a plate. They have been brought into the people of God (circumcision), died to their old life (baptism), been given new life, been forgiven, all charges have been dropped and the powers that terrorized them are captive slaves in the triumphal procession of Christ. They have the victory. Now they (and we) must live out that victory in the real world.

Pray

Lord you have done so much for me. Give me grace to do my little for you.

MM

Visions to order

Therefore do not let anyone condemn you in matters of food and drink or of observing festivals, new moons or sabbaths. These are only a shadow of what is to come, but the substance belongs to Christ. Do not let anyone disqualify you, insisting on self-abasement and worship of angels, dwelling on visions, puffed up without cause by a human way of thinking, and not holding fast to the head, from whom the whole body, nourished and held together by its ligaments and sinews, grows with a growth that is from God.

Here we begin to get a clear picture of what was happening at Colossae. The inner circle, who claimed to know the hidden wisdom of God, were strict in observing special religious festivals, probably with fasting (self-abasement can mean physical self-denial), and through these they expected to get wonderful visions of the angels at worship. For a time they could escape from the hum-drum life of earth into an experience of heaven itself.

Paul's comment is scathing: 'These have indeed an appearance of wisdom in promoting self-imposed piety, humility, and severe treatment of the body, but they are of no value in checking self-indulgence' (v. 23). Of course not; they *were* self-indulgent. Paul had nothing against visions. He had more than his fair share of them. But great spiritual experiences are the gift of God, they are not something we can seek after as a matter of course. When we do that, we are unlikely to succeed, and we lose sight of the real task of being a Christian here and now.

I remember my first encounter with Pentecostal Christians. For weeks I was desperate to speak in tongues. Eventually I realized that I didn't want it so as to improve my prayers, or my knowledge of God. It was simply something I wanted to experiment with, and impress people with, rather like trying a new drug. God's message to me then was the same as Paul's to the Colossians; even if it looks very spiritual, it can still cut us off from Jesus.

Reflect

Is any part of your Christian life done mainly for show?

MM

It's up to you

'You have heard that it was said to the men of old, "You shall not kill; and whoever kills shall be liable to judgment." But I say to you that every one who is angry with his brother shall be liable to judgment; whoever insults his brother shall be liable to the council, and whoever says, "You fool!" shall be liable to the hell of fire. So if you are offering your gift at the altar, and there remember that your brother has something against you, leave your gift there before the altar and go; first be reconciled to your brother, and then come and offer your gift. Make friends quickly with your accuser, while you are going with him to court, lest your accuser hand you over to the judge, and the judge to the guard, and you be put in prison; truly, I say to you, you will never get out till you have paid the last penny.'

When you come to Holy Communion today, you might be confident in your heart that neither your brother nor your sister has anything against you. But have you anything against them? When someone talked to me recently of someone else's sin they said, 'It's up to them to make the first move...' But we're supposed to love people with the love of God—and he made the first move towards us. Later on in this chapter Jesus says, 'Love your enemies and pray for those who persecute you, so that you may be sons of your Father who is in heaven.'

Has someone wronged you and not done anything to put it right? If so, what will you do to put it right and to be reconciled to them? As you take the bread, and as you drink the wine, will you remember what God did for you?

But God shows his love for us in that while we were yet sinners Christ died for us. Since, therefore, we are now justified by his blood, much more shall we be saved by him from the wrath of God. For if while we were enemies we were reconciled to God by the death of his Son, much more, now that we are reconciled, shall we be saved by his life. Not only so, but we also rejoice in God through our Lord Jesus Christ, through whom we have now received our reconciliation.

Romans 5:8–11

SB

Heavenly-minded

So if you have been raised with Christ, seek the things that are above, where Christ is, seated at the right hand of God. Set your minds on things that are above, not on things that are on earth, for you have died, and your life is hidden with Christ in God. When Christ who is your life is revealed, then you also will be revealed with him in glory. Put to death, therefore, whatever in you is earthly: fornication, impurity, passion, evil desire, and greed (which is idolatry).

At first, this seems a strange thing for Paul to say. After all, the trouble with the Colossians was that they were concentrating altogether too much on heaven. But the big difference is that in all their rituals and self-denial, the Colossians were trying to reach into heaven. For Paul, he was already there, because he was united with Jesus. As long as he was with Jesus, he was in heaven. His job was not to escape from the world into an experience of heaven, but to bring heaven into this world.

That meant a change in the way he lived his life. There is no room in heaven for sinful things, and so for someone who has been given new life by Christ, who already shares his special relationship with God, there should be no room in their life for sin. So the real sign of someone who has met Jesus, and been given a glimpse of heaven, is not visions and secret knowledge, or belonging to some mysterious inner ring, but a life which is patterned on that of Jesus himself.

Of course, it's not all that straightforward. We are not truly in heaven yet, and we are far from perfect. It is a struggle to rid ourselves of our sinful ways. But it should remain true to say that those who have really set their minds on heavenly things—on knowing God—can be recognized by the changes in their lives.

Pray

Lord, give me the grace to set my mind on you, and to live my life for you, so that by the changes in my life, others may see Jesus Christ.

MM

The wrath of God

On account of these [sins] the wrath of God is coming on those who are disobedient. These are the ways you also once followed, when you were living that life. But now you must get rid of all such things—anger, wrath, malice, slander, and abusive language from your mouth. Do not lie to one another, seeing that you have stripped off the old self with its practices and have clothed yourselves with the new self, which is being renewed in knowledge according to the image of its creator. In that renewal there is no longer Greek and Jew, circumcised and uncircumcised, barbarian, Scythian, slave and free; but Christ is all and is in all!

Almost every New Testament book mentions God's judgment, or wrath, on sinners. Yet it remains something that we prefer not to think about, and certainly not to preach about. That may not be a bad thing. I suspect that more people are attracted into the kingdom than scared into it. But on the other hand, it is something that we can't afford to ignore, either.

A lot of our distress at the thought of judgment is due to a strange image of God as a kindly old chap who wouldn't hurt a fly, and certainly would never do anything harsh to us. But the biblical picture is very different. God is love itself—but he is also a consuming fire. He is the essence of moral purity and holiness. Anything that is evil or perverted has as much chance of surviving an encounter with him as a matchbox on a bonfire. It is God's sheer inability to compromise with evil which makes salvation necessary. If we are to be brought back to God, we have to be remade and renewed; our old sinful self must be stripped off and replaced with the slowly growing image of Jesus himself.

God's judgment and love are opposite sides of the coin. God's love demands the very best for us—nothing less than absolute perfection and bliss will do as our final destiny. But if we reject the best, there is nothing else at all.

Reflect

What does the idea of the purity of God say to you?

MM

Dressing up

As God's chosen ones, holy and beloved, clothe yourselves with compassion, kindness, humility, meekness, and patience. Bear with one another and, if anyone has a complaint against another, forgive each other; just as the Lord had forgiven you, so you also must forgive. Above all, clothe yourselves with love, which binds everything together in perfect harmony.

Our three-year-old son has a favourite set of clothes—a Superman costume. When he is wearing it, he becomes someone else, and often doesn't answer to his own name. At other times, we see small children dressing up in their parents' clothes. And again, they become, in their imaginations, someone else; and their behaviour changes. Dressing up is all part of the process of learning which children go through. It helps them to model themselves on their parents or their heroes, and provided they have the right heroes (and parents), it helps them to grow up properly.

It is the pattern of Jesus which we are meant to grow up into. So we are called to dress up as Jesus, knowing that it is not always our true self, but that is what we want to become. When we are angry, we can ask ourselves, 'What would Jesus do now?' When we are hurt, we can ask the same question. And then, painful though it may be, we should do not what we would like, but what we think Jesus would do.

At first, that may seem hypocritical. After all, we know that the picture we're presenting isn't the true one. If we act lovingly when we really want to scream and shout at someone, or speak words of forgiveness when we're really crying out for revenge, isn't it play-acting?

Yes, it is, one one level—like the children playing at grown-ups. But like them, we know that we will one day be grown up. For now, we need the practice. What is more, we usually find that our feelings follow our actions. When we make a habit of behaving like Jesus, we find that it is much easier to think like him as well.

Pray

Father, help me to dress up in the way you want me to grow up.

MM

Under new management

Let the peace of Christ rule in your hearts, to which indeed you were called in the one body. And be thankful. Let the word of Christ dwell in you richly; teach and admonish one another in all wisdom; and with gratitude in your hearts sing psalms, hymns, and spiritual songs to God. And whatever you do, in word or deed, do everything in the name of the Lord Jesus, giving thanks to God the Father through him.

Yesterday we thought about the possibility of acting our way into our roles as Christians. Of course, that can't be the whole story. If there is no spiritual reality behind our efforts to behave in a Christ-like way, then we are indeed just play acting. But Paul adds something more— 'Let the peace of Christ rule ... Let the word of Christ dwell ...' Behind our efforts to live in the way in which God calls us, is the spiritual reality that God himself is helping us along. Through his word to us, and through the peace-giving presence of his Spirit, he is working to transform us into the kind of people he has always intended us to be.

Even then, though, he asks for our cooperation. We can shut him out (for a while, anyway) and turn our backs on him. But that is foolish. The proper thing to do is to open ourselves up to him, to invite him into our lives at the deepest level, and to let him take over. The business of being a Christian, you might say, is to let God establish a new management in our lives, and to try to go along with what the new boss wants.

Paul gives us some pointers as to how to do this; it is done in worship. It is when we get together to listen to God and to sing his praises that we are most able to let go of our selves and let God in. And when that happens, we will be on the way to being able to do everything in the name of the Lord.

Meditate

Look at the areas of your life which are (or seem to be) least open to God. Where do you keep control from him? Bring them to him in prayer.

MM

Rules for the household

Wives, be subject to your husbands, as is fitting the Lord. Husbands, love your wives and never treat them harshly. Children, obey your parents in everything, for this is your acceptable duty in the Lord. Fathers, do not provoke your children, or they may lose heart. Slaves, obey your earthly masters in everything, not only while being watched and in order to please them, but wholeheartedly, fearing the Lord. Whatever your task, put yourselves into it, as done for the Lord, and not for your masters . . . Masters, treat your slaves justly and fairly, for you know that you also have a Master in heaven.

Traditionally, this passage has been seen as a sort of rule-book for the ideal Christian family. It has governed the church's teaching on marriage, and has been used to defend the practice of slavery. But I am not sure that any of this is what Paul had in mind.

A look at 1 Corinthians 7 shows us that Paul did not see marriage as a matter of dominant husbands and submissive wives, but as an equal partnership, and that slaves were encouraged to become free if it lay in their power. His letter to Philemon shows that Christian slaves of Christian masters were to be treated as brothers and sisters in Christ. So this simple list is much less than Paul's view of an ideal Christian household.

In this letter, Paul has argued that true Christian discipleship is not about escaping from the world, but about serving God in it. Here he describes a typical pagan household, and shows how even within the boundaries of a non-Christian family, individual believers can live out their faith. Each example shows how a Christian should behave in a pagan setting. In a Christian family, things would be rather different. Over the next few days we shall look in more detail about how this advice may affect us.

Reflect

Being a Christian means living the faith in a less than ideal setting.

MM

Happy families?

Wives, be subject to your husbands, as is fitting in the Lord. Husbands, love your wives and never treat them harshly.

As a rule, in Paul's time, it was expected that the man was clearly the head of the household. The ideal wife was submissive to him. In practice, of course, it was probably rather different, but certainly few women headed households or owned much property. The New Testament itself shows us some interesting exceptions; but here Paul's question was, how can a Christian wife demonstrate her faith amongst an unbelieving family? The answer was, by fitting in with what was normally expected. Being a Christian is not necessarily about rebellion. The pagan husband was unlikely to be converted to a faith which he experienced as destructive of his family.

In a similar way, a man who was a believer should not abuse his position of authority. It is tempting to use whatever power we have to its limits. But this is not the pattern we learn from Jesus, who left his power behind to submit to death for us.

Today's reading raises a more interesting point about the way we use the Bible. For centuries these verses (and the similar ones in Ephesians) have formed the way the Church has viewed marriage. Yet there are other New Testament passages (by Paul, too!) which point in another direction. Galatians 3:28 tells us that for Christians there is no distinction between male and female, while 1 Corinthians 7:4 sees the husband as belonging to the wife as much as the other way round. As we saw yesterday, it is possible to live a Christian life in many different types of society, but at the same time, we must allow the Bible to challenge the way we do things. By ignoring the passages about equality, Christians have been untrue to the full message of the gospel.

So the moral is clear: we cannot afford to read the Bible only to confirm our own views. We need to let it speak to us and change the way we live our lives.

Think

Are there parts of the Bible that disturb our view of our faith and life? How do we deal with them, and could it be that God has a challenge for us in those areas?

MM

Join in with the angels

The Lord has established his throne in the heavens,
and his kingdom rules over all.
Bless the Lord, O you his angels,
you mighty ones who do his word,
hearkening to the voice of his word!
Bless the Lord, all his hosts,
his ministers, that do his will!
Bless the Lord, all his works,
in all places of his dominion.
Bless the Lord, O my soul!

Soon after the start of all four Eucharistic prayers in the Alternative Service Book of the Church of England (and in the Eucharistic prayers of most other churches as well) we join in with the angels and praise the name of God:

'Therefore with angels and archangels, and with all the company of heaven, we proclaim your great and glorious name, for ever praising you and saying: Holy, holy, holy Lord, God of power and might, heaven and earth of full of your glory. Hosanna in the highest.'

Perhaps you are one of those modern Christians who believe in an empty heaven, with no angels or archangels there glorifying God for the greatness of all his works. If you are, then you had better stop reading! One of the feasts of the Church is of St Michael and All Angels, and the Bible speaks of glorious beings whom God created to do his will. But they didn't have to do it. They had choices, just as we have, and some of them rebelled. So they were cast out of the presence of God and fell out of the light into the darkness. Lucifer, the light-bearer, was the most glorious of them, but now through his pride he is known as the Prince of Darkness. Our salvation doesn't depend on our belief in angels. But a belief in them may well increase our awareness of the glory of God.

When you come to the prayer in the Communion Service that speaks of them, will you pray to be made aware of the glorious company of heaven, who praise God with you?

SB

Children in church

Children, obey your parents in everything, for this is your acceptable duty in the Lord. Fathers, do not provoke your children, or they may lose heart.

'I do wish the children would be quieter, so we could concentrate on our worship!' 'When we were little we sat quietly in church and didn't disturb people!' Comments like these are the terror of parents who struggle into church with their children, making a real effort to come and worship, only to feel that because their children make a noise (and often not much), they are not welcome. Yet today's reading seems to be on the side of the complainers. Children should be obedient to in all things—there's more than a hint of 'be seen and not heard' here. Of course, once again we are looking at what was normally expected of children in the ancient world. They had no rights, and were on the same level as slaves until they grew up. In a situation like that, Christian children could serve Christ only by model obedience. (And Christian fathers were warned not to push their power too far!)

But the very fact of this command to children undermines the traditional view of Paul's day. What we fail to notice is that it assumes that children would be part of the worshipping church when the letter was read out. What is more, it assumes that they had responsibilities—they were *worth* speaking to, because they were part of the Church, and

were called to follow Jesus as much as the adults.

I don't think that many people today would want children to be as lacking in rights as they were in Paul's time. But in other ways we lag behind Paul. We are still tempted to see church as an adult occupation, forgetting that children have as much right to be there as adults, and as much right to have the worship geared for them as do adults.

Reflect

'Unless you turn and become like children, you will never enter the kingdom of heaven' (Matthew 19:4). What does this say to our attitude to children, and their place in the Church?

MM

Everyone counts

Slaves, obey your earthly masters in everything, not only while being watched and in order to please them, but wholeheartedly, fearing the Lord. Whatever your task, put yourselves into it, as done for the Lord and not for your masters, since you know that from the Lord you will receive the inheritance as your reward; you serve the Lord Christ. For the wrongdoer will be paid back for whatever wrong has been done, and there is no partiality. Masters, treat your slaves justly and fairly, for you know that you also have a Master in heaven.

When we read Paul today, it seems strange that he never says that slavery was a bad thing. There are probably several reasons for this, but the main reason is that it almost certainly never crossed his mind. It never crossed anyone's mind in those days. Slavery was simply a fact of life that was hardly ever commented on (even by slaves!). Yet Paul's attitude to slaves was startling. For one thing, he assumes that in the Church, slaves are the equal of anyone else. That means that he saw them as people with rights and responsibilities, which was a far cry from the usual notion of a slave as a 'living tool', with no rights to speak of, and no responsibilities.

This is a strong reminder to us that there can be no one who doesn't count. We are tempted to write off people who are too old, too poor, too eccentric for our tastes. But in the Church, there must be no distinction. Just as Jesus died for everyone, so we are called to value everyone—and for that very reason. Who are we to write off anyone that Jesus thought it worth dying for?

Another thought that comes out of the passage is that we tend to think of some work as 'religious' and the rest as 'secular'. But God, who created the whole world, is interested in all that we do. We are called to be honest, trust-worthy, hard-working and loving in all of our life, not just in 'churchy' things.

A way to pray

What people, and what tasks, do you despise? Make them a focus for prayer, and ask God's help to change your attitude.

MM

Using power

Husbands, love your wives and never treat them harshly . . . Fathers, do not provoke your children, or they may lose heart . . . Masters, treat your slaves justly and fairly, for you know that you also have a Master in heaven.

We have noticed how the 'household rules' in Colossians have been used to teach wives to be submissive, children to be quiet and slaves to be obedient. In other words, they have been used to put down the ones who had little power of their own. But they have much less often been used to soften the actions of those with power. Yet in these verses, we see just that. Paul is concerned that those who have power in the household should not abuse it. Under ancient Roman law the man who headed the household had the right to kill his children and his slaves if they displeased him, and sometimes this could apply to his wife as well. By Paul's time, that had mostly changed, but the way of thinking that led to that law was still there. Paul knew that this was not a Christian approach. Power is given to help and to heal, not to destroy or terrorize.

All the same, it seems almost a rule of human nature that we push our powers as far as they will go. It applies not only in families but almost everywhere. Don't we all know churches where the minister will never really let anyone else into the jobs he does? Or governments that refuse to step down, even when they lose elections? And don't we sometimes do things, not because we should, but simply because we can—even if they hurt other people?

In Jesus, we are given a different pattern. He became poor and powerless to save us. He preached good news to the poor and the outcast. The essence of knowing God is not to seek power for ourselves, but to live in obedience to him. And the example he gives in Jesus is to see what power we have (great or small) as a gift from him, to be used in his service.

Reflect

What powers do you have?
(The answer may surprise you.)
How do you use them?

MM

News to tell

Devote yourselves to prayer, keeping alert in it with thanksgiving. At the same time pray for us as well, that God will open to us a door for the word, that we may declare the mystery of Christ, for which I am in prison, so that I may reveal it clearly, as I should. Conduct yourselves wisely towards outsiders, making the most of the time. Let your speech always be gracious, seasoned with salt, so that you may know how you ought to answer everyone.

In the Decade of Evangelism, it is worth taking stock of our attitude to people outside the Church. Do we live a double life, faith shining on Sundays, rather quiet about church on weekdays? Do we feel secretly superior to all those poor souls who haven't any notion of what life is all about? I'm sure these are exaggerations, but I know quite a few who suffer from mild forms of similar attitudes. None of them does justice to our faith or to Christ. In Jesus, we have found a friend, a saviour and a God who deserves our love and our trust. We have found someone who is Good News. And good news is always worth sharing. Here Paul gives us some pointers to sharing the gospel.

We begin with prayer. Unless we pray, both for opportunities and for a desire to share the news, we will get nowhere. Paul was one of the greatest evangelists ever, but he was always asking people to pray for him. He knew that in the end, it is God who brings the gospel, God who opens doors, and God who changes people's hearts and minds. We are merely the messengers, whom God sends to people at the right time—provided we are willing to be used.

We also need the right approach. We must be willing to speak, politely and considerately, warmly and welcomingly, to everyone. When someone sees that we are interested in them, they will be much more interested in what we have to say, and in what makes us tick—God.

A prayer

Lord, make me excited enough about you to see you as worth sharing, and loving enough to want to share you.

MM

The beloved brothers

Tychicus will tell you all the news about me; he is a beloved brother, a faithful minister, and a fellow servant in the Lord. I have sent him to you for this very purpose, so that you may know how we are and that he may encourage your hearts; he is coming with Onesimus, the faithful and beloved brother, who is one of you. They will tell you about everything here.

Paul seems to have sent this letter to Colossae by two of his helpers. Tychicus was in charge, but with him was Onesimus—and Onesimus was a walking sermon. This is almost certainly the Onesimus whom we read about in the letter to Philemon. A runaway slave, he had taken refuge with Paul, who had converted him and sent him back to his Christian master with a short letter which re-introduced Onesimus; no longer a slave, but a brother in Christ. Meeting Onesimus was meeting the changing power of Christ in action. Here was a person who had felt badly done to, oppressed, without purpose. Then Paul had introduced him to Jesus. Now he was a valued helper in Paul's work, with self-respect and a place in the Church. His former master was now his brother in the faith. In short, Onesimus had found his place.

Our modern world is a far cry from the society of ancient Rome. Our letters are sped across the world by aircraft and satellite communications. Work that was done by the human muscle of slaves is carried out by vast and complex machinery. Yet all this has only served to bring home to us the realization of the same problem that Onesimus had. So many people still feel out of place. We live in a time when the problem of pointlessness strikes at the heart of individual lives and whole societies. We have still not invented any reason for our lives. Like Onesimus, we still need to find that reason—and like him we can find it in God. It is the God who made us for himself who alone can fulfil our deepest needs.

Pray

For all who feel displaced, pointless and despairing. And give thanks that in Jesus Christ we have found an answer for ourselves, and for any who are willing to accept it.

MM

Teamwork

Aristarchus my fellow prisoner greets you, as does Mark the cousin of Barnabas, concerning whom you have received instructions—if he comes to you, welcome him. And Jesus who is called Justus greets you. These are the only ones of the circumcision among my co-workers for the kingdom of God, and they have been a comfort to me ... Luke, the beloved physician, and Demas greet you. Give my greetings to the brothers and sisters in Laodicea, and to Nympha and the church in her house. And when this letter has been read among you, have it read in the church of the Laodiceans; and see that you read also the letter from Laodicea. And say to Archippus, 'See that you complete the task that you have received in the Lord.' I, Paul, write this greeting with my own hand. Remember my chains. Grace be with you.

It is easy to imagine Paul and a few other apostles as lone missionaries who single-handedly brought the gospel out of Palestine and into the wider Roman Empire. But the endings of his letters show that nothing could be further from the truth. Paul was the leader of a team of missionaries. The membership of his group changed, with new helpers joining, and others leaving for various reasons. Acts 13:13 shows John Mark, the cousin of Barnabas, getting fed up with missionary work—though here he is back again, the disagreement with Paul (see Acts 15:36–39) mended.

Christian ministry, of whatever kind, is rarely the work of one person. In Paul's image of the Church as the body of Christ (see Colossians 1:18) we get a picture of Jesus working in the world through his people as a whole, rather than just through particular people. This means that all of us, no matter what official titles we may have, are part of that work.

To think about

What do you see as your role in the Church? If it is simply joining in Sunday worship, expand it by learning about other activities in your church and making them specific topics of prayer.

MM

Pentecost: the presence of God with us

Pentecost is the story of how God, who had revealed himself to the Jewish people, was continually reaching out to the people in the rest of the world. Pentecost was the fulfilling of the Old Testament promise of the giving of the Spirit:

I will pour out my Spirit on all people. Your sons and your daughters will prophesy, your old men will dream dreams, your young men will see visions. Even on my servants, both men and women, I will pour out my Spirit in those days.

Joel 2:28–29 (NIV)

So in the next seven weeks we shall look at the events of Pentecost, and how the good news about God started to spread through the whole of the known world. For two weeks Gerard W. Hughes connects what happened then with what is happening day by day in our own lives and in the world of the 1990s. After that (for three weeks, with Rosemary Green) we look at the amazing acts of the apostles in Acts 8–18.

But then we shall look at the book of Jonah—the Old Testament prophet who didn't want to tell the good news about his glorious God to people of whom he didn't approve. That comes immediately after the story of the spread of the Church to remind us of our tendency to want to keep the good news to ourselves. But God wants us to share it and to tell it to people. Not forcing it down their throats, but ready to talk to them about it if they ask us. The Apostle Peter told us the way to do it: 'Always be prepared to give an answer to everyone who asks you to give the reason for the hope that you have. But do this with gentleness and respect...'

Day of Pentecost

Only a lovely person can fill us with love. Only a joyful person can fill us with joy. Only a peaceful person can fill us with peace. And only a Christ-like person can change us into the likeness of Christ. Such a person is the Holy Spirit. Yet the Day of Pentecost leaves many Christians, not ready and eager to receive a fresh touch from this life-giving Spirit, but rather fearful. As one woman put it to her vicar, 'I hope nothing supernatural is going to happen in this church'!

Resisting the Holy Spirit in this way saddens and stifles him. As St Paul reminds us, it puts out the Spirit's fire (1 Thessalonians 5:19).

Far from putting out the Spirit's fire, on the Day of Pentecost the disciples displayed a very different attitude. They were prepared in heart and mind to receive the promised baptism of the Holy Spirit:

When the day of Pentecost came, they were all together in one place. Suddenly a sound like the blowing of a violent wind came from heaven and filled the whole house where they were sitting. They saw what seemed to be tongues of fire that separated and came to rest on each of them. All of them were filled with the Holy Spirit and began to speak in other tongues as the Spirit enabled them.

Like pieces of fabric being dipped into a vat of dye so that every fibre soaks up the colour of the dye, the disciples seemed to be soaking up the character of the Holy Spirit and in doing so were absorbing the very life of Jesus himself.

Jesus longs to penetrate every cell and fibre of our being in this way—not once, but many times. The question is, this Pentecost Sunday, is that what we want? Or, from fear or apathy, ignorance or disobedience, will we grieve and suppress the Spirit's offered life?

A prayer

Come down, O Love divine,
Seek Thou this soul of mine,
And visit it
with Thine own ardour glowing;
O Comforter, draw near,
Within my heart appear,
And kindle it,
Thy holy flame bestowing.

Bianco da Sienta, tr. Richard Littledale

JH

God in us and for us

'When the Advocate comes, whom I shall send to you from the Father, the Spirit of truth who comes from the Father, he will be my witness. And you too will be my witnesses.'

In contrast to the Holy Spirit, our Advocate, Scripture speaks of the evil spirit as 'the accuser', 'the father of lies'. In conscientious people who want to know and serve God, the evil spirit's action is always to discourage, to accuse, and to paralyse with guilt feelings.

When we are so afflicted, we should turn to the Spirit of truth within us and then look at our feelings of discouragement, failure or guilt. If we have failed through our own sin, stupidity or idleness, and hurt others, then we must acknowledge our guilt before God, who is always merciful and welcoming. The devil works on us through lies, leading us to put our trust not in God's mercy, but in 'the shrine of our own achievement', so that when we fail we feel utterly helpless and hopeless. The deceit lies in the assumption that it is our achievements which count, so that we convince ourselves that our failures are the most important factors in our lives, more important than God's goodness and mercy. Jesus said to the rich young man, 'Why do you call me good? No one is good but God alone' (Mark 10:18, RSV). And it is our trust in that goodness which saves us—'Your faith has saved you; go in peace' (Luke 7:50, RSV).

When we are attentive to the Spirit dwelling within us and obey the Spirit's promptings, then there will be within us an increase of 'love, joy, peace, patience, kindness, goodness, trustfulness, gentleness and self-control' (Galatians 5:22–23, JB). Life will also become much more interesting, for we are no longer imprisoned within the shrine of our own achievements or failures and, taking ourselves less seriously, we shall find we can laugh more easily, especially at ourselves. These attitudes will grow in us through our attentiveness to the promptings of the Spirit within us rather than through our own efforts.

A prayer

God, enlighten our minds and hearts so that in every situation we can recognize you, Spirit of truth, enfolding us in your goodness. Amen.

GWH

The God we get wrong

'And when he [the Holy Spirit] comes, he will show the world how wrong it was, about sin, and about who was in the right, and about judgement.'

It is a frightening and sobering truth that when God manifests himself to the world in Jesus, he is rejected by the very people who are the official preservers of Israel's faith, and crucified in the name of law. It is frightening, because the same pattern continues. We cannot stand too much reality, as T.S. Eliot wrote, and have to defend ourselves against it.

> **. . .for my thoughts are not your thoughts, my ways not your ways—it is Yahweh who speaks.**
>
> Isaiah 55:8 (JB)

Jesus reveals a God who upsets the prevailing notions of what God is like. He declares that the sabbath is made for human beings, not human beings for the sabbath, a God who welcomes and serves all, wicked and good alike, a God who welcomes sinners and dines with them, who recognizes true faith in the pagan woman, and true virtues in the Samaritan, whom the Jews considered the scum of the earth. He is a God who will not judge us on our religious beliefs and practices, but on the way we relate to one another and respond to one another's needs (Matthew 25). He is a God who does not seek vengeance on his enemies, but blesses and loves them, and tells us to do the same (Luke 6:27–

35). He is a God who does not dominate, but serves, and so Jesus instructs his followers, 'You know that among the pagans their so-called rulers lord it over them, and their great men make their authority felt. This is not to happen among you. No; anyone who wants to become great among you must be your servant, and anyone who wants to be first among you must be slave to all' (Mark 10:42–44, JB).

Such teaching undermines the power foundations of our religious and secular society. The violent reaction of the powerful to Jesus' message manifests their sinfulness and false judgment.

A prayer

God, may your Spirit of love and truth so permeate us that we oppose all that is false in ourselves, our Church and nation. Amen.

GWH

God with us

'Since the God who made the world and everything in it is himself Lord of heaven and earth, he does not make his home in shrines made by human hands . . . He is not far from any of us, since it is in him we live, and move, and exist.'

This is a quotation from Paul's sermon to the Athenians. St Augustine said of God, 'He is nearer to us than we are ourselves.' St Catherine of Genoa expressed this truth in a startling sentence: 'My God is me; nor do I recognize any other me except my God himself.'

At first, most of us think of God as being outside us, separate, remote, and he can remain so for us. Our notion of God comes to us through our parents, teachers, preachers, from our experience of church services, from the prayers we hear and from books. We can inherit very horrifying ideas of a God whose primary interest is in our sins, and whose main occupation is in inflicting punishments suited to our crimes. Or we can inherit a very domesticated God, who approves of us, our family, church and nation, whose ways are our ways and whose thoughts are our thoughts, so that he is always on our side, even when we are exploiting, oppressing, or even killing others: 'pro Deo et Patria'.

Only God can teach us who God is. We live in the mystery of God, ourselves most mysterious beings. If some intelligent minds in outer space were to hear a description of human beings, they would probably conclude that we can-

not exist! We consist of billions of cells, wonderfully intelligent and coordinated, but consisting mostly of empty space. There is nothing solid about us. We talk of atoms as the ultimate constituents of matter, but they are also largely empty space, energy charges. Every particle of us is connected with every other particle in the universe, and we find ourselves in so far as we live in love and respect and reverence of all creation.

We are all intimately connected with one another. God tells us, 'Love your neighbour as yourself.' The Holy Spirit in whom we live is the Spirit of unity.

A prayer

God, in whom we live and move and have our being, grant us the wisdom to know the true harmony of things, and the joy that comes from living in that harmony.
Amen.

GWH

Creator and lover

The most distant parts of the earth have seen the saving power of our God. Acclaim Yahweh, all the earth, burst into shouts of joy!

Christian faith is not primarily a belief in propositions about God, Jesus Christ and the Church. The New Testament word for faith is *pistis*, meaning trust, and the object of our trust is God. We cannot see God, nor touch him: we can only know him in and through his creation. Creation itself is a sacrament of God, that is, a sign—and an effective sign—of God's presence within us and among us. Faith is an attitude of trust in life, which enables us to see and experience life as God's gift.

The Book of Wisdom says of God, 'Yes, you love all that exists, you hold nothing of what you have made in abhorrence, for had you hated anything, you would not have formed it... You spare all things because all things are yours, Lord, lover of life, you whose imperishable spirit is in all' (Wisdom 11:25–27, JB). That is why the Psalmist sings, 'Acclaim Yahweh, all the earth, burst into shouts of joy!'

As we begin to see life in this way, it begins to change for us. We become less fearful, more appreciative of the wonder of life, enabling us to feel more at ease with ourselves, with others, and with all creation. Even when things go wrong for us, faith assures us that our situation, however bleak it may appear, cannot be hopeless because God is there.

A way to pray

A very simple way of nurturing our faith in God is to spend a few minutes at the end of the day reflecting on those moments that we enjoyed, for which we are grateful. Recall them, relish them. They come to you from God with love, gestures of his care for you. Most people on doing this exercise, are surprised at the number of good moments they can recall, moments which would have been obliterated in memory by the less pleasant memories of the day. Thank God for those good moments. If this exercise is done once, it makes little difference to our lives, but if it is done regularly, it can transform our outlook and we may find our hearts saying, 'Shout to the Lord, all the earth'!

GWH

Tears of joy and sorrow

'I tell you most solemnly, you will be weeping and wailing while the world will rejoice; you will be sorrowful, but your sorrow will turn to joy.'

Some enthusiastic Christian preachers tell their hearers that if they would only turn to Jesus, all their troubles will be over, including their financial ones. 'Invest a dollar with Jesus and you will get tenfold, or a hundredfold, return. If you don't, your faith is weak!' This is not the message of the Hebrew prophets. 'Woe is me, my mother, for you have borne me to be a man of strife and of dissension for all the land ... Why is my suffering continual, my wound incurable, refusing to be healed?' (Jeremiah 15:10, 18, JB). Jesus tells his disciples, 'You will be weeping and wailing while the world will rejoice.'

In John's Gospel, Jesus appears to the frightened disciples on Easter Sunday evening; he shows them his wounded hands and side, and says, 'Peace be to you.' Then he says, 'As the Father sent me, I am now sending you.' The Acts of the Apostles describes what happened in this sending: the imprisonments, beatings, rejections, and the death of Stephen.

The peace and joy which the Spirit brings is not peace and joy as the world understands it. For the world, peace means not being disturbed and being left free to enjoy ourselves in our own way, irrespective of what this may be doing to other people, other nations, or to the environment. God's peace is different: it is peace for all peoples, for all creation, what St Augustine called 'the tranquillity of right order'. It is a revolutionary peace, which threatens all those individuals, groups and nations whose power enables them to enjoy peace at the expense of other people's misery.

Those who follow Christ and live in the power of his Spirit will always disturb the society in which they live, uncovering its injustices and opposing them. They will then be opposed, denounced and persecuted, just as Jesus was. Yet despite the pain and conflict that the true followers of Christ experience, they will also know that this is where they want to be. They can do no other.

A prayer

God, open our minds to understand your peace, and our hearts to receive it, so that we may find you, even in the tears of things. Amen.

GWH

Not my will, but yours . . .

'...anything you ask for from the Father he will grant in my name.'

For most of us, this promise of Jesus proves untrue most of the time, until we notice the qualification 'in my name'. The request has to be made in Jesus' name.

In many of our requests in prayer, although we may invoke Christ, we are praying that my kingdom, or our group's, or church's or nation's kingdom shall be realized.

Whenever we pray in Jesus' name we are praying that God's will, not our own, should be done. That is the essence of all Christian prayer, and that is the prayer which is always answered. Once we come to realize this, we may find ourselves less keen on praying than before!

All prayer is risky. It is an abandonment of our kingdom, our own control over things. Hurling ourselves instead into the hands of the living God, whose ways are not our ways and whose thoughts are not our thoughts.

If that were all we knew about God, our reluctance to pray would be wise. But the God to whom we surrender ourselves in prayer is the God who loves us more than we can love ourselves. From him we come, to him we go, and in every circumstance of our lives he is drawing us to himself. The sacrament of baptism celebrates our awareness of this truth. There is no situation, however painful to us, where he is not present,

whether the pain is inflicted by others or even by ourselves.

It is right that we should pray to be delivered from painful situations, and for others to be delivered from them, but the core of our prayer in Christ's name is that, whatever the situation, we should (like Jesus on the cross) be able to say, 'Into thy hands I commend my spirit', and this prayer will always be answered.

A prayer

God, deepen our trust in you, present in every circumstance of our lives, so that we may live always in your peace. Amen.

GWH

The mystery of God

'Go, therefore, make disciples of all the nations; baptise them in the name of the Father and of the Son and of the Holy Spirit . . . And know that I am with you always; yes, to the end of time.'

Once a year the Church celebrates Trinity Sunday, which comes a week after Pentecost Sunday. As Christians we believe that there are three Persons in one God, and God is mystery. Being a mystery does not mean being totally unintelligible. It means that the more we understand, the more we realize there is to understand. We can grow in the knowledge of God, but we can never adequately grasp God with our finite minds. But God has revealed himself to us in creation, and uniquely in Jesus. We are made in God's image, called to share in his life. We can learn more of God, we are also learning more about ourselves. That is why St Augustine used to pray, 'That I may know Thee, that I may know myself.'

We are made in God's image, and baptized into the life of God, Father, Son and Holy Spirit. The doctrine of the Trinity is telling us something about the nature of our life now.

God's life is a communion between three Persons, who so relate that no one Person has anything which does not equally belong to the other two. That is why theologians say that personality in God means relationship. We can think of ourselves (falsely) as persons who relate to other persons and things.

The doctrine of the Trinity is telling us that we become persons through the way we relate, and that we only become persons in so far as we do relate. This is a profoundly important and puts a large question mark over much of our striving in secular and religious life with its current emphasis on me, my development, my improvement. The doctrine of the Trinity is telling us that we can only find our true selves in so far as we live not for ourselves, but for others. Jesus said, 'Unless you lose your life you cannot find it.' He also summed up his life before his death by taking a piece of bread, breaking it, and giving it to his disciples, saying, 'This is me, given for you.'

A prayer

God, draw us more closely into the mystery of your life, so that living in your power we may serve rather than be served. Amen.

GWH

God in the present moment

'And eternal life is this: to know you, the only true God, and Jesus Christ whom you have sent.'

We tend to think of eternal life as meaning life which has no end, and that we shall know only after death. In St John's Gospel, eternal life is not promised in the future: it is promised now.

When we speak of God as 'eternal God', it does not mean that God has a life which goes on and on, but that God lives always in the now. Time does not exist in itself; it is the measurement of change. If we were not conscious of change, we should have no concept of time. That is why, when we are absorbed in some activity, we say 'time flies', and when we are bored and longing for some activity to be over, we say 'time drags'.

Jesus lived in time, died at a particular time, but the risen Christ is beyond time, is always present in the now. That is why we can contemplate him in the Gospels, imagine the scene which, historically, is past, and yet meet the Christ of the Gospels now. The Spirit who lived in Jesus and raised him from the dead, now lives in us, in our circumstances, in our temperament, in our abilities and disabilities. The more we can live in this consciousness, the more we are living in eternal life.

One way of developing this consciousness is to practise living in the present. As soon as we try to do this, we realize just how we spend most of our time—either anticipating the future or dwelling in the past, neither of which now exist. So it is not surprising that we find life empty!

A French spiritual writer, Pierre de Caussade, has written a book called *The Sacrament of the Present Moment*. Where is God, and where do I find him? I find him wherever I am at the moment, 'nearer to me than I am to myself' as St Augustine said. He also wrote, and it follows from this, *age quod agis*, 'do whatever you are doing', so that if you are washing dishes, wash dishes, and don't be planning what you are going to do when they are finished.

A prayer

God in all things, God of the now, calm our minds and hearts, so that we can find you in the sacrament of the present moment. Amen.

GWH

God so loved the world . . .

'I have glorified you on earth and finished the work that you gave me to do.'

The most striking characteristic of Jesus' life is his relationship to God, whom he calls 'Abba', a child's name for Father. The Gospels give only one sentence spoken by Jesus in his first thirty years: his reply to his mother after he had been lost for three days and was found in the temple—'Did you not know that I must be busy with my Father's affairs?' The same theme runs through all his teaching, culminating in his agony, 'Father, if you are willing, take this cup away from me. Nevertheless, let your will be done, not mine' (Luke 22:42, JB).

At the Last Supper, Jesus prayed that we should all be one as he and the Father are one. As God is the God of all creation, his prayer is that we should all be at one with one another and with all creation.

We pray for the unity of Christ's Church, and it is right that we should do so and it gives us plenty to pray about! But even if our prayers were to be answered and all Christians were united in the one Church, that would account for only a small percentage of the human race.

God's gifts are never given only for the good of a particular individual, group or nation. St Thomas Aquinas says that it is the nature of goodness that it is always overflowing, it always goes beyond itself. God's gifts are always given for the sake of the whole world, not just for an individual. Similarly, God's gifts to any group, or church, or nation are given for the good of all peoples of all nations. That is why, when the Holy Spirit is given to the apostles, they are sent to preach the good news to the whole world, and why Israel is called 'Light of the nations'.

This raises important questions about our lives as Christians. If the Spirit of God is within us and amongst us, then our attention must be directed not primarily to our own maintenance, security or comfort, but to mission; and mission directs our attention to any area of human need, not just to the needs of our Church or nation.

A prayer

Spirit of God, transform our hearts with your compassion for all creation, so that we reverence every human being and treat your creation with care. Amen.

GWH

Our Christ-like God

'Holy Father, keep those you have given me true to your name, so that they may be one like us.'

When we look back at the history of Christianity and of our own lives, we can appreciate the urgency of Jesus' prayer.

Recently, I saw a beautiful wooden statue, a representation of Christ, Lord of all creation. He was seated on a throne, clothed in royal garments with a crown on his head, but he was holding his head in his hands, with a despairing look on his face, as though exclaiming, 'O my people, what have you done to me?'

In all religion the constant temptation is to construct a God in our own image and likeness, a plasticine God, who assumes our shape and form, assures us of the rightness of our ways and the wrongness of everyone who disagrees with us. As I write this, there is a brutal war being waged in former Yugoslavia between Serbs, who are Orthodox Christians, Croats, who are Catholic, and Muslims. And we have seen the tragic end of the Waco community in Texas under the fanatical leadership of David Koresh, who believed himself to be the Messiah.

God is the God of all creation, who loves all that he has created, and whose living Spirit is in all. How do we know whether in our lives and in our prayers it is God whom we are worshipping and not some idol of our own making? The test is not in the beautiful experiences we may have in prayer, nor in the hours we may spend in prayer, nor in the church to which we may belong. Nor is it in the way we relate to our own immediate circle of family and friends, although these good relations are an important indication of our relationship with God. The test is in how we relate to those who are outside our own immediate circle, class, race, nation and religion.

If we are true to God's name, then every human being, including our enemies, is our brother and sister.

A prayer

God, keep us true to your name. As individuals, as Church and as nation, give us eyes to see the effect of our actions on the lives of others, and save us from every form of idolatry and oppression. Amen.

GWH

Reconciling all things...

'With me in them and you in me, may they be so completely one that the world will realise that it was you who sent me and that I have loved them as much as you loved me.'

The Holy Spirit is the Spirit of unity. The Book of Wisdom says that there is in Wisdom 'a spirit intelligent, holy, unique, manifold, subtle, active, incisive, unsullied, lucid, invulnerable, benevolent, sharp, irresistible, beneficent, loving to man, steadfast, dependable, unperturbed, almighty, all-surveying, penetrating all intelligent, pure and most subtle spirits; for Wisdom is quicker to move than any motion; she is so pure, she pervades and permeates all things' (Wisdom 7:22–24, JB).

Some modern physicists, in describing the nature of matter, speak of it in language not unlike the Book of Wisdom. They write of the interdependence of all things in the universe. One has expressed it, 'When a baby throws its rattle out of the cradle, the planets rock'! At one time, scientists thought that our material world was made up of solid building blocks called 'atoms'. Now they have discovered that there are no ultimate building blocks, but only energy charges; none of which have an independent existence, but all exist in relationship to the whole. There is a mysterious communication system within the universe faster than the speed of light, and it pervades and permeates all things!

We are part of that mysterious unity. Jesus knew this unity within himself, and he knew that love was at the heart of it. So he prays 'that the world will realise that it was you who sent me and that I have loved them as much as you loved me'. Unity among Christians is not something we have to create, but something we have to discover, for it exists already. The unity is not just for the sake of Christians, but 'that the world may realise that it was you who sent me'.

Reflection

We are called into a unity of all creation, 'because God wanted all perfection to be found in him and all things to be reconciled through him and for him, everything in heaven and everything on earth, when he made peace by his death on the cross' (Colossians 1:19–20, JB).

GWH

You, not me, God

'I tell you most solemnly, when you were young you put on your own belt and walked where you liked; but when you grow old you will stretch out your hands, and somebody else will put a belt round you and take you where you would rather not go . . . Follow me.'

Babies appear to have only one focus of interest: their own well-being—that they should be fed, cleaned, held, kept warm and comfortable. As we develop and become more aware of an external world, our focus is still primarily on our own needs, but we become more subtle at having them answered and start on the games people play. We may then grow up to be a highly successful business tycoon, or a political or military leader, blighting the lives of thousands.

Failure can be a great blessing—*if* we can learn from it. The first lesson we can learn is that our life is impoverished when centred on me, for me is a gaoler who bars me from relating to others as persons, and restricts me to treating others as objects.

Me-centredness is an attractive trait in small children, but repulsive and dangerous in adults. When we are pulled off our me-pedestals, or fall from them, we can begin to realize that we are called to something much greater than our own aggrandizement. When our attention is no longer concentrated on me, we can begin to notice a wider and more interesting and wonderful world. Jesus said, 'Unless you lose your life,

you cannot find it.' If I concentrate my attention and energies on me, I cannot discover the joy of relatedness, of inter-dependence, of being part of something much greater.

Jesus tells Peter that in his old age his plans will fail and he will be called to glory! In the seventeenth century, St Philip Neri, looking back on his life, said that in his youth he was full of activity. Then God gave him the gift of stillness. In his old age God had given him the gift of laughter. As we emerge from the cocoon of our own self-importance, we learn to laugh more easily, a gift of the Holy Spirit.

A prayer

Spirit of God, release us from the narrow prison of our own self-importance into the vision of glory to which you are calling us. Amen.

GWH

Hope in the darkness

There were many other things that Jesus did; if all were written down, the world itself, I suppose, would not hold all the books that would have to be written.

This is a strange ending to St John's Gospel and prompts the question: Why, then, did they restrict themselves to four short Gospels? There are many other things that Jesus has been doing since John finished his Gospel and if we were all to spend the rest of our lives writing about them, we should only be touching the surface of the subject, for 'All that came to be had life in him' (John 1:3, JB).

Scripture is given to us not primarily to tell us about events in ancient history, but through those events to help us recognize God at work in us and among us now. If our view of the world is derived mostly from the media, we can feel overwhelmed by the world's pain, human cruelty and depravity. God seems to be absent. Northern Ireland is presented as full of ruthless terrorists, former Yugoslavia as a land of barbaric savagery, Israel as a land of bitter hatred between Jew and Arab, our own inner cities as seething with an immoral underclass of thieves, drug pushers and muggers.

A friend of mine is a religious sister who has lived for some years in an inner-city area in Britain with a notorious reputation. She says that she has learned more about Christianity from the tenants in that area than in any other place. I spent some time living in a housing estate in Northern Ireland. I was overwhelmed by the friendliness, warmth and openness I met from Protestants and Catholics, including many who were prisoners in the Maze prison. In 1987 I walked through what was then Yugoslavia, en route for Jerusalem, and met with nothing but kindness from the people I met, Serbs and Croats. When I reached Israel, the first family I met was Jewish, who took me into their home, and the Arabs I met welcomed me—although I was a total stranger. I know this is only part of the reality, but it is the part we need to notice, for Christ is in all peoples, giving us hope when everything seems hopeless, working on all of us through our own failures, stupidities and sinfulness.

A prayer

Holy Spirit, give us eyes to recognize you and ears to hear you in the confusion of our times, so that we may always live trusting in your power at work in our weakness. Amen.

GWH

Bread for the world

When the people heard this, they were cut to the heart and said to Peter and the other apostles, 'Brothers, what shall we do?' Peter replied, 'Repent and be baptised, every one of you, in the name of Jesus Christ for the forgiveness of your sins. And you will receive the gift of the Holy Spirit. The promise is for you and your children and for all who are far off—for all whom the Lord our God will call.' With many other words he warned them; and he pleaded with them, 'Save yourselves from this corrupt generation.' Those who accepted his message were baptised, and about three thousand were added to their number that day. They devoted themselves to the apostles' teaching and to the fellowship, to the breaking of bread and to prayer. Everyone was filled with awe, and many wonders and miraculous signs were done by the apostles. All the believers were together and had everything in common. Selling their possessions and goods, they gave to anyone as he had need. Every day they continued to meet together in the temple courts. They broke bread in their homes and ate together with glad and sincere hearts, praising God and enjoying the favour of all the people. And the Lord added to their number daily those who were being saved.

On Sundays we almost always concentrate on prayer or on Holy Communion. Today's passage is about those things, and about all the other things we need in order to live the Christian life, to grow in maturity and to spread the good news. It starts with a call to repentance and the promise of forgiveness. Then baptism— the outward and visible sign of the inward, invisible grace that has come to us—in a washing away of our sins, a new birth, and the gift of the Spirit. It was a corrupt generation then and it is now. But then that generation saw a group of people who were different. Who devoted themselves to living the Christian life— to the apostles' teaching, to the fellowship, to the breaking of bread, and to prayer. The world outside looked at them and they enjoyed 'the favour of all the people. And the Lord added to their number daily those who were being saved.'

That is the pattern for our Christian living, and the way to be the light of the world and the light of the nations. It is very dark out there—and the world God created and loves is a very unhappy world. Real happiness is real blessedness—and the way to be blissfully happy is the way of Christ.

SB

The word spreads

A great persecution broke out against the church at Jerusalem, and all except the apostles were scattered throughout Judea and Samaria. Godly men buried Stephen and mourned deeply for him. But Saul began to destroy the church. Going from house to house, he dragged off men and women and put them in prison. Those who had been scattered preached the word wherever they went. Philip went down to a city in Samaria and proclaimed Christ there. When the crowds heard Philip and saw the miraculous signs that he did, they all paid close attention to what he said. With shrieks, evil spirits came out of many, and many paralytics and cripples were healed. So there was great joy in that city.

Stephen had been martyred. A young Pharisee, Saul, was systematically persecuting the Christians. But these apparently disastrous events became God's opportunity for the gospel to spread further afield. It is typical of him to take a bad situation and turn it upside down for good.

The church leaders stayed in Jerusalem while the ordinary Christians scattered. Persecution did not shut their mouths; wherever they went the 'preached the word'. They chatted about Jesus on the street, in shops, in the inns. We need that freedom today. The clergy mainly meet churchgoers; it is lay people who meet non-believers in their daily lives. Neighbours, colleagues, friends, casual acquaintances; all need to be told about Christ.

Philip had been chosen for practical service. (Acts 6:2–5) When he went to Samaria he found that the Spirit gave him unexpected gifts, not only of preaching, but of healing and power over evil spirits. In these days of modern medicine and psychology we might believe those last gifts to be irrelevant. But evil spirits are real (I have seen them active in many people), and the Holy Spirit is powerful enough to work apart from twentieth century science as well as through it.

Something to do

List the places where your life day by day intersects with other people. Then start to pray for some of those individuals in their need to know Christ.

RG

The person God uses

An angel of the Lord said to Philip, 'Go south to the road—the desert road—that goes down from Jerusalem to Gaza.' So he started out, and on his way he met an Ethiopian eunuch, an important official in charge of all the treasury of Candace, queen of the Ethiopians. This man had gone to Jerusalem to worship, and on his way home was sitting in his chariot reading the book of Isaiah the prophet. The Spirit told Philip, 'Go to that chariot and stay near it.' Then Philip ran up to the chariot and heard the man reading Isaiah the prophet. 'Do you understand what you are reading?' Philip asked. 'How can I,' he said, 'unless someone explains it to me?' So he invited Philip to come up and sit with him.

Philip was immersed in a highly successful evangelistic campaign in Samaria. How astonishing—divine instructions to travel fifty miles into the desert! Notice some of the characteristics of this servant of God.

◇ *His ability to recognize God's directions.* An angel was unmistakable; the Spirit's communication was more subtle. When we make a habit of asking God for guidance in everyday matters we learn to perceive his nudges.

◇ *His obedience.* We do not read 'I can't leave Samaria—I'm indispensable!' or, 'The man won't want me.' Philip did not argue with God's messengers. He did what he was told. I have learnt that God's purposes for us are unfailingly loving and wise; so disobedience—or procrastination— is folly.

◇ *His enthusiasm.* He ran—in the desert heat! Would you rather be enthusiastic or apathetic for Jesus?

◇ *His courage and his sensitivity.* When he reached the chariot he asked an open, unthreatening question. His bold initiative and his gentle manner together made him acceptable to the stranger. A few of us need to cultivate boldness in expressing our faith.

A project and a prayer

Write down all you can discover about the Ethiopian. Then pray: Lord, please help me to listen to your voice, and to grow in obedience; in joyful enthusiasm; in boldness; in sensitivity.

RG

The way we speak

The eunuch was reading this passage of Scripture: 'He was led like a sheep to the slaughter, and as a lamb before the shearer is silent, so he did not open his mouth. In his humiliation he was deprived of justice. Who can speak of his descendants? For his life was taken from the earth.' The eunuch asked Philip, 'Tell me, please, who is the prophet talking about, himself or someone else?' Then Philip began with that very passage of Scripture and told him the good news about Jesus. As they travelled along the road, they came to some water and the eunuch said, 'Look, here is water. Why shouldn't I be baptised?' And he ordered the chariot to stop. Then both Philip and the eunuch went down into the water and Philip baptised him. When they came up out of the water, the Spirit of the Lord suddenly took Philip away, and the eunuch did not see him again, but went on his way rejoicing.

The Ethiopian treasurer started in the right place in his search to know God, with worship and in Scripture, but he was puzzled. In his reply Philip models three important principles in sharing our faith.

1. 'He began with that very passage of Scripture.' He started from the seeker's position and moved on from there.

2. 'He told him the good news about Jesus.' He did not merely talk about his Christian activity; he explained the heart of our faith, Jesus.

3. He made clear the need for commitment to Christ. Whether we are baptized as infants or as adults we all need to be definite about our personal response to Jesus.

Afterwards the Ethiopian drove south, with joy in his heart. Philip travelled north, still talking about Jesus wherever he went.

A challenging assignment

Read Isaiah 53 and note the pointers to Jesus' life, death and resurrection. Could you start with that passage of Scripture and explain the good news about Jesus? Find a Christian friend to try this; then ask God for an opportunity to share your faith with a non-believer.

RG

A vital meeting

Saul was still breathing out murderous threats against the Lord's disciples . . . As he neared Damascus on his journey, suddenly a light from heaven flashed around him. He fell to the ground and heard a voice say to him, 'Saul, Saul, why do you persecute me?' 'Who are you, Lord?' Saul asked. 'I am Jesus, whom you are persecuting,' he replied. 'Now get up and go into the city, and you will be told what you must do.' The men travelling with Saul stood there speechless; they heard the sound but did not see anyone. Saul got up from the ground, but when he opened his eyes he could see nothing. So they led him by the hand into Damascus. For three days he was blind, and did not eat or drink anything.

Saul was a top dog; a highly educated Jew, from David's tribe, a Pharisee, a Roman citizen, faultless in his legalism, determined to eradicate the Christians. But he met the risen Jesus and was transformed. Temporarily blinded, this powerful man was led in weakness into Damascus. But his spiritual eyes were opened as he recognized Jesus and yielded to him; then a new power grew in Saul. Soon he 'grew more and more powerful and baffled the Jews living in Damascus by proving that Jesus is the Christ' (Acts 9:20–22).

Is Saul's experience unique? 'That would not happen today!' we think. I heard recently about a nominal church member; a successful business executive, under great stress, his marriage collapsing. He visited Christian friends in the country. Unable to relax, he walked alone in the rain. When he returned he was trembling. He told them with awe, 'God spoke to me.' They listened quietly. 'Don't you understand?

This was the God of the Bible. *He spoke to me!*' Whatever God said to him, an utterly changed man went home.

Each individual has a personal encounter with the living God. That is the heart of Christian experience. There are no rules about *how* God meets us; the infinite God meets unique individuals in an infinite variety of ways. The essential thing is that each one meets the living Christ through his Spirit. That is the new birth of which Jesus spoke to Nicodemus.

A question

How has God spoken to you?

RG

A reluctant visitor

In Damascus there was a disciple named Ananias. The Lord called to him in a vision, 'Ananias!' 'Yes, Lord,' he answered. The Lord told him, 'Go to the house of Judas on Straight Street and ask for a man from Tarsus named Saul, for he is praying. In a vision he has seen a man named Ananias come and place his hands on him to restore his sight.' 'Lord,' Ananias answered, 'I have heard many reports about this man and all the harm he has done to your saints in Jerusalem. And he has come here with authority from the chief priests to arrest all who call on your name.' But the Lord said to Ananias, 'Go! This man is my chosen instrument to carry my name before the Gentiles and their kings and before the people of Israel. I will show him how much he must suffer for my name.' Then Ananias went to the house and entered it. Placing his hands on Saul, he said, 'Brother Saul, the Lord—Jesus, who appeared to you on the road as you were coming here—has sent me so that you may see again and be filled with the Holy Spirit.' Immediately something like scales fell from Saul's eyes, and he could see again. He got up and was baptised, and after taking some food, he regained his strength.

Read the passage again, imagining yourself in Ananias' shoes. How did he feel when the Lord spoke to him? How readily did he obey? After he obeyed, what was it like for him at the end of the story?

Now think of Ananias supposedly writing his diary at the end of the day. 'What an amazing day! This morning Jesus came to me in a vision. I was terrified when he told me to go and find Saul the Pharisee! We have heard about Saul's atrocities against the Christians in Jerusalem. He was the last person I wanted to meet. But the Lord's words were very clear and reassuring, and I could not go on arguing.'

A project

Now continue writing the 'diary', in your imagination or on paper. Then reflect about the insights it gives you about the Lord and his relationship with us.

RG

Transparent before God

At Caesarea there was a man named Cornelius, a centurion in what was known as the Italian Regiment. He and all his family were devout and God-fearing; he gave generously to those in need and prayed to God regularly. One day at about three in the afternoon he had a vision. He distinctly saw an angel of God, who came to him and said, 'Cornelius!' Cornelius stared at him in fear. 'What is it, Lord?' he asked. The angel answered, 'Your prayers and gifts to the poor have come up as a remembrance before God. Now send men to Joppa to bring back a man named Simon who is called Peter. He is staying with Simon the tanner, whose house is by the sea.' When the angel who spoke to him had gone, Cornelius called two of his servants and one of his soldiers who was a devout man. He told them everything that had happened and sent them to Joppa.

People who looked at Cornelius could see his actions; the spiritual leadership of his family, his regular prayer and his generosity to the poor. God saw his heart and knew that he could use him to open a new chapter in the life of the Church. The Jewish Christians had to see that their faith was for the Gentiles too. When Cornelius saw the angel, he was frightened but, unlike Ananias yesterday, he did not argue. He risked appearing foolish in front of the men he sent to Joppa. What if he had made a mistake? But God was as specific in his message to Cornelius as he was to Ananias. Cornelius listened, and did what he was told. Trust and obedience go hand in hand.

A thought to consider

'Man looks at the outward appearance, but the Lord looks at the heart' (1 Samuel 16:7). Does your visible behaviour before people agree with your invisible character before God? Do you consider one more important than the other? Jesus' example to us is found in John 5:30. 'I seek not to please myself but him who sent me.' If our prime aim is to please God, the rest will follow.

RG

Move with the Spirit

... Right then three men who had been sent to me from Caesarea stopped at the house where I was staying. The Spirit told me to have no hesitation about going with them. These six brothers also went with me, and we entered the man's house. He told us how he had seen an angel appear in his house and say, 'Send to Joppa for Simon who is called Peter. He will bring you a message through which you and all your household will be saved.' As I began to speak, the Holy Spirit came on them as he had come on us at the beginning. Then I remembered what the Lord had said, 'John baptised with water, but you will be baptised with the Holy Spirit.' So if God gave them the same gift as he gave us, who believed in the Lord Jesus Christ, who was I to think that I could oppose God?

The living God is always pouring out his love and himself into improper places and improper people—and the rigidly religious find it disturbing and upsetting. They would prefer God to behave like a tidy canal, staying within the banks which they have dug, and directed where they have chosen. But instead the river of life flows just where it chooses. It floods its banks in glorious abandon and abundance, and the desolate deserts of the earth start to blossom and bear fruit. Isaiah prophesies that one day, 'The earth shall be filled with the knowledge of the Lord as the waters cover the sea' (11:9), and in 49:6 of the same book God speaking through Isaiah says, 'It is too light a thing that you should be my servant to raise up the tribes of Jacob ... I will give you as a light to the nations, that my salvation may reach to the end of the earth' (49:6). Now it was happening. God was giving himself to Gentiles as well as to Jews—and not doing it in the proper order! Pouring out himself in the baptism of the Spirit *before* they had gone through the procedures—and doing it even as Peter was in the process of preaching. First the baptism of the Holy Spirit—and then the baptism of water. You can read all about it in Acts 10.

SB

A surprise command

While Peter was wondering about the meaning of the vision, the men sent by Cornelius found out where Simon's house was and stopped at the gate. They called out, asking if Simon who was known as Peter was staying there. While Peter was still thinking about the vision, the Spirit said to him, 'Simon, three men are looking for you. So get up and go downstairs. Do not hesitate to go with them, for I have sent them.' Peter went down and said to the men, 'I'm the one you're looking for. Why have you come?' the men replied, 'We have come from Cornelius the centurion. He is a righteous and God-fearing man, who is respected by all the Jewish people. A holy angel told him to have you come to his house so that he could hear what you have to say.' Then Peter invited the men into the house to be his guests.

God's timing is amazing! The men left Cornelius' house one afternoon. At lunchtime the next day Peter, in his house in Joppa thirty miles down the coast, had an unexpected experience. As he was praying out on the flat roof of his house, he saw a vision of a sheetful of animals, some ceremonially clean, some unclean. A voice from heaven told him to eat, but he remonstrated; then the voice said, 'Do not call anything unclean that God has made clean.' After the conversation was repeated twice Peter finally paid attention, although he was still puzzled about the vision's relevance.

That is when the visitors arrived. At last Peter was seriously considering what God was showing him. As he listened to the messengers, he quickly understood at least part of the vision, for he invited them—Gentiles—to be his guests, to share his lunch and even to stay overnight.

What do *you* learn from this story? I notice the stages in Peter's listening to God. First he was resistant to something new; then he pondered it; then he acted. We rarely like change, but God often takes us by surprise, for his plans are bigger than ours. But I have realized that he never makes a mistake, so arguments, disobedience and procrastination are all futile.

RG

The heart of the gospel

Peter began to speak: 'I now realise . . . that God does not show favouritism but accepts men from every nation who fear him and do what is right. This is the message God sent to the people of Israel, telling the good news of peace through Jesus Christ, who is Lord of all. You know what has happened . . . how God anointed Jesus of Nazareth with the Holy Spirit and power, and how he went around doing good and healing all who were under the power of the devil, because God was with him. We are witnesses of everything he did in the country of the Jews and in Jerusalem. They killed him by hanging him on a tree, but God raised him from the dead on the third day and caused him to be seen . . . He commanded us to preach to the people to testify that he is the one whom God appointed as judge of the living and the dead. All the prophets testify about him that everyone who believes in him receives forgiveness of sins through his name.'

After yesterday's reading Peter welcomed the strangers into his home; next day he and a group of Christians from Joppa travelled with them back to Caesarea, where they found a large group of Cornelius' friends and relations in his house, and the centurion explained why he had asked Peter to come. Peter then talked to them about Jesus, in a sermon that contains all the main elements of the gospel.

◇ God has no favourites.

◇ The heart of the gospel is Jesus.

◇ He came as a man, 'Jesus of Nazareth'.

◇ He taught, he healed, he overcame the devil.

◇ He died on the cross and he rose from the dead.

◇ He forgives sins

◇ He is Lord of all and judge of all people.

Everyone who is a witness to the resurrection through an encounter with the living Christ has a responsibility to share this good news with others.

An idea

Have you ever thought of inviting your friends, neighbours or relations into your home, to meet someone who would tell them the good news about Jesus?

RG

New believers

While Peter was still speaking these words, the Holy Spirit came on all who heard the message. The circumcised believers who had come with Peter were astonished that the gift of the Holy Spirit had been poured out even on the Gentiles. For they heard them speaking in tongues and praising God. Then Peter said, 'Can anyone keep these people from being baptised with water? They have received the Holy Spirit just as we have.' So he ordered that they be baptised in the name of Jesus Christ. Then they asked Peter to stay with them for a few days.

The Holy Spirit and baptism; here are the two keys to real Christianity. It does not matter which happens first, but both are vital. The gift of the Holy Spirit is God's part; he gives us new life as we open ourselves to his indwelling. The baptism is our part, as we declare our intention of wanting to follow Christ and to belong to his Church. You may wonder where infant baptism fits in. It is a marvellous sign of God's initiative, with a declaration of faith made by the family that needs to be underlined by personal response in adulthood.

Peter's hospitality to Cornelius' emissaries and the start of his sermon show that he already understood the vision of the unclean animals, that the Gentiles were to be welcomed into the Church. But the Jewish Christians who were with him needed to be convinced as well. When Cornelius and his friends started to speak in tongues Peter's companions recognized the same mark of the Holy Spirit that God had given the apostles on the Day of Pentecost (Acts 2:4). Tongues—the ability to pray or to speak a message from God in an unknown language—is one of the gifts that the Spirit gives to many Christians to enrich their communication with God. But it is not the indispensable sign of the Spirit's activity in a person, as some Christians want us to believe.

A prayer

Lord, please show me if I am hindering the full flow of your Spirit in my life. I want to experience the joy and certainty that I see in these early Christians, and I am willing for you to change me.

RG

A new church

Those who had been scattered by the persecution in connection with Stephen travelled . . . telling the message only to Jews. Some of them, however . . . went to Antioch and began to speak to Greeks also, telling them the good news about the Lord Jesus. The Lord's hand was with them, and a great number of people believed and turned to the Lord . . . For a whole year Barnabas and Saul met with the church and taught great numbers of people. The disciples were first called Christians at Antioch. During this time some prophets came down from Jerusalem to Antioch. One of them, named Agabus, stood up and through the Spirit predicted that a severe famine would spread over the entire Roman world . . . The disciples, each according to his ability, decided to provide help for the brothers living in Judea.

How would you describe the church at Antioch? These are the traits I find.

◇ It was founded by enthusiastic lay people.

◇ It was innovative, primarily made up of Greeks.

◇ It grew fast.

◇ It welcomed steady teaching.

◇ The members were known as the 'Christ-men'.

◇ It responded generously.

◇ It was not dependent on the presence of its leaders.

Check each of these comments in the passage, and then think about your own church.

◇ Are the lay people enthusiastic?

◇ Is it willing to make changes?

◇ Is it growing?

◇ Is the teaching consistent?

◇ Can its members be described as Christlike?

◇ Is it open to hearing from God?

◇ Is it generous?

◇ Is it dependent on its full-time minister?

A prayer

Lord, sometimes I complain about my church, because I do not like the way it is. But sometimes I am complacent about it, because I do not like to face change. Show me how you want me to pray for it and to work for it, because I recognize that it is your church, not mine.

RG

An encourager

When [Paul] came to Jerusalem, he tried to join the disciples, but they were all afraid of him, not believing that he really was a disciple. But Barnabas took him and brought him to the apostles. He told them how Saul on his journey had seen the Lord and that the Lord had spoken to him, and how in Damascus he had preached fearlessly in the name of Jesus . . .

News [of growth of the church at Antioch] reached the ears of the church at Jerusalem, and they sent Barnabas to Antioch. When he arrived he saw the evidence of the grace of God, he was glad and encouraged them all to remain true to the Lord with all their hearts. He was a good man, full of the Holy Spirit and faith, and a great number of people were brought to the Lord. Then Barnabas went to Tarsus to look for Saul, and when he found him, he brought him to Antioch. So for a whole year Barnabas and Saul met with the church and taught great numbers of people.

We first meet Barnabas, a Levite from Cyprus, giving the apostles the proceeds from selling a field in Acts 4:36. His real name was Joseph; Barnabas, meaning Son of Encouragement, was a nick-name, and we find him living up to his reputation in various ways.

He was generous. He sponsored Saul when the apostles mistrusted him. He was sent by the apostles in Jerusalem to encourage the fast-growing church in Antioch. When he found that the task was too big for him alone he searched for Saul to join him. That was an encouragement for Saul as well as for the church. He was faithful in teaching and discipling the Christians. Later on he withstood Paul to give his young cousin Mark a second chance (15:36–39). Mark gave up on his first journey with Paul and Barnabas. Paul refused to take him again, but Barnabas the Encourager was willing to take the risk.

A way to pray

'He was a good man, full of the Holy Spirit and faith.' That is the secret of Barnabas' character. I pray that the Spirit may fill and refill me, to make me an encourager instead of a criticizer.

RG

Lessons in prayer

Peter was kept in prison, but the church was earnestly praying to God for him . . . [Then an angel came one night and released him miraculously] . . . He went to the house of Mary the mother of John, also called Mark, where many people had gathered and were praying. Peter knocked at the outer entrance, and a servant girl named Rhoda came to answer the door. When she recognised him she ran back without opening it and exclaimed 'Peter is at the door!' 'You're out of your mind,' they told her. When she kept insisting that it was so, they said, 'It must be his angel.' But Peter kept knocking, and when they opened the door and saw him, they were astonished.

'The church was earnestly praying to God for him.' Much is packed into this one sentence.

1. *The church.* Many people had collected at Mary's house. Jesus said that 'where two or three come together, there am I with them' (Matthew 18:19–20). While he is always with us, there is a special strength when Christians are together.

2. *Earnestly.* This word implies a deep desire, with persistence and determination.

3. *Was praying.* They were interceding, not to a God unwilling to answer their prayer but to one who loves to hear his children.

4. *For him.* They were specific in their prayers, not just 'God bless Peter.'

Their prayer was answered. An angel came and released Peter! But sadly, they were not really expecting it. How had they prayed? Perhaps, 'Lord, please keep him safe. May he witness to the guards . . .' These are good prayers. But we come to an infinite God with whom *all* things are possible, and his view on the situation may differ from ours. Often our prayers seem to be unanswered. Maybe we are praying only from our own perspective, not from his; or maybe we are looking for the answer in the wrong direction; maybe we do not really believe God. It is a good idea when we pray to ask the Holy Spirit to guide us; part of his job is to teach us how to pray (see Romans 8:26).

A way to pray

If you had been in Mary's house, how would you have prayed? Now choose one difficult situation known to you, and ask God how he wants you to pray.

RG

The sword of the Spirit

Jesus was led up by the Spirit into the wilderness to be tempted by the devil. And he fasted forty days and forty nights, and afterward he was hungry. And the tempter came and said to him, 'If you are the Son of God, command these stones to become loaves of bread.' But he answered, 'It is written, "Man shall not live by bread alone, but by every word that proceeds from the mouth of God."'

Then the devil took him to the holy city, and set him on the pinnacle of the temple, and said to him, 'If you are the Son of God, throw yourself down; for it is written, "He will give his angels charge of you," and "On their hands they will bear you up, lest you strike your foot against a stone."' Jesus said to him, 'Again it is written, "You shall not tempt the Lord your God."'

Again, the devil took him to a very high mountain and showed him all the kingdoms of the world and the glory of them; and he said to him, 'All these I will give you, if you will fall down and worship me.' Then Jesus said to him, 'Begone, Satan! for it is written, "You shall worship the Lord your God and him only shall you serve."' Then the devil left him, and behold, angels came and ministered to him.

If we want to know how to pray when we are tempted, this passage tells us. Jesus fought the temptations of Satan with Scripture (and Satan fought him back with Scripture—so we need to be wary), and the New Testament describes Scripture as 'the sword of the Spirit'.

I know of a Christian couple who fell in love. She was divorced already, but he was married. They broke up his marriage and started to live together—writing to their friends that they knew their relationship was of God. But it can't have been. The forgiveness they can know is of God. The pleasure and delight in their new marriage and in each other's company is of God (because all real pleasure comes from God). But the marriage break-up wasn't of God. They could have fought off temptation (and it is a tough, hard battle) with the seventh commandment: 'You shall not commit adultery.'

SB

Christ the victor

They travelled . . . to Paphos. There they met a Jewish sorcerer and false prophet named Bar-Jesus, who was an attendant of the proconsul, Sergius Paulus. The proconsul, and intelligent man, sent for Barnabas and Saul because he wanted to hear the word of God. But Elymas the sorcerer (for that is what the name means) opposed them and tried to turn the proconsul from the faith. Then Saul, who was also called Paul, filled with the Holy Spirit, looked at Elymas and said, 'You are a child of the devil and an enemy of everything that is right! You are full of all kinds of deceit and trickery. Will you never stop perverting the right ways of the Lord? Now the hand of the Lord is against you. You are going to be blind, and for a time you will be unable to see the light of the sun.' Immediately mist and darkness came over him, and he groped about, seeking someone to lead him by the hand. When the proconsul saw what had happened, he believed, for he was amazed at the teaching about the Lord.

We meet two very different men. Sergius Paulus was an intelligent man with power and authority, the governor of the province. Elymas was one of his servants. But a bigger contrast lies in their attitude to God. Sergius Paulus wanted to discover the truth about God. Elymas already knew where his spiritual loyalties lay. He drew on demonic powers for his witchcraft; it is not surprising that he was opposed to the proconsul's search for God.

But the tables were turned. Empowered by the Spirit, Paul could look straight at Elymas. I was scared the first time I met a woman who was possessed by evil spirits; she seemed to be evil personified. Trembling I wondered whether Jesus was stronger. Then I saw his victory in action and I knew he was. I learnt more about the power of Christ through my encounters with that woman than I have through any other means. It was similar for Sergius Paulus. He saw the power of God demonstrated, and that brought him to faith in Christ.

A prayer

Lord, please stretch me beyond my intellectual belief, to know your power.

RG

God's guidance

Paul and his companions travelled throughout the region of Phrygia and Galatia, having been kept by the Holy Spirit from preaching the word in the province of Asia. When they came to the border of Mysia, they tried to enter Bithynia, but the Spirit of Jesus would not allow them to. So they passed by Mysia and went down to Troas. During the night Paul had a vision of a man of Macedonia standing over him and begging him, 'Come over to Macedonia and help us.' After Paul had seen the vision, we got ready at once to leave for Macedonia, concluding that God had called us to preach the gospel to them.

Certainty about God's guidance often seems to be one of the hardest aspects of the Christian life. Even Paul did not find it easy. He persevered in his travels in mid-Turkey (Phrygia and Galatia), having been prevented from travelling further north. But he reached Troas, a port in the north-west corner of the country. There God spoke to him; it may have been a vision as he was awake, praying; it may have been a dream in his sleep. But Paul was clear that he was being called by God further afield, across to northern Greece. Another new chapter in the spread of the gospel was starting.

As I thought about this story I remembered the summer when two of our children's exam results were not as good as expected. We were all disappointed, but in both cases God used those results to alter their planned courses of action. Ten years later, it is clear that they might have missed God's best for them. Our 'worm's-eye view' is limited. God's 'bird's-eye view' is far more sure, even if it is painful or incomprehensible to us at the time.

A way of living

Are you perplexed to know what to do? Seek God, and trust that he has a good and wise purpose for you. If we are humble and flexible, we can step out in what we believe to be the right direction, but allow him to alter our course if he sees something better. 'Whether you turn to the right or to the left, your ears will hear a voice behind you, saying, "This is the way walk in it"' (Isaiah 30:21).

RG

Know and tell

When they had passed through Amphipolis and Apollonia, they came to Thessalonica, where there was a Jewish synagogue. As his custom was, Paul went into the synagogue, and on three Sabbath days he reasoned with them from the Scriptures, explaining and proving that the Christ had to suffer and rise from the dead. 'This Jesus I am proclaiming to you is the Christ,' he said. Some of the Jews were persecuted and joined Paul and Silas, as did a large number of God-fearing Greeks and not a few prominent women. But the Jews were jealous; so they rounded up some bad characters from the market-place, formed a mob and started a riot in the city.

Paul obeyed the vision without delay and crossed from Turkey to Greece, sailing down the coast, visiting the ports and travelling a few miles inland to the big city of Philippi. Each place he visited was different, but his strategy was similar. He went first to the synagogue, where he found both those who were Jews by birth and those who had joined their faith. He built on the foundation of their knowledge of the Old Testament,; he used those Scriptures to open their eyes, and to explain in a reasoned way that Jesus was the Christ, the Messiah to whom the Old Testament points. At the heart of his preaching were the cross and the resurrection, twin pillars of our faith.

What strikes you as important about this passage? I notice two things. The first is the importance of the Bible as the foundation of our understanding of our faith. The second is the need for apologetics—the ability to explain our faith to others in a reasoned way. We are not all as gifted in this as Paul was; but we live in an age of widespread ignorance about Jesus Christ, when people are turning to many other faiths or to none. So we should be solid in our own understanding and able to teach others.

A suggestion for study

Read two Christian books during the coming weeks; one to instruct your mind, one to warm your heart.

RG

The Bible in action

As soon as it was night, the brothers sent Paul and Silas away to Berea. On arriving there, they went to the Jewish synagogue. Now the Bereans were of more noble character than the Thessalonians, for they received the message with great earnestness and examined the Scriptures every day to see if what Paul said was true. Many of the Jews believed, as did also a number of prominent Greek women and many Greek men.

Jealous Jews in Thessalonica stirred up noisy opposition against the Christians, who thought it wise to send Paul and Silas fifty miles on to the next port. But the missionaries were undeterred, and they did not change their strategy, but went first to the synagogue, where they found a congregation full of people eager to know the truth and to learn from God. So what did the Bereans do? 'They examined the Scriptures every day.' That is a good example to us, who are often weak on our Bible study. Read 2 Timothy 3:16 to see what Paul wrote later about the source of Scripture, and that it is foundational for the way we think and the way we live.

A word of warning comes to us from Jesus, speaking to the orthodox Jews of his day. 'You diligently study the Scriptures because you think that by them you possess eternal life. These are the Scriptures that testify about me, yet you refuse to come to me to have life.' Yes, careful study of the Bible is necessary. It is God's revelation of himself to us; it points us to Jesus. But head-knowledge is insufficient; we need a commitment to Christ that leads to a personal relationship with him.

Some questions

What do I really believe about the source and reliability of the Bible? Do I allow my Bible reading to influence the way I think about the world, as well as about my own personal life? Have I started a personal relationship with Jesus? How is it growing?

RG

A dedicated couple

Paul left Athens and went to Corinth. There he met a Jew named Aquila, a native of Pontus, who had recently come from Italy with his wife Priscilla . . . Paul went to see them, and because he was a tent maker as they were, he stayed and worked with them . . . every Sabbath he reasoned in the Synagogue, trying to persuade Jews and Greeks . . . Paul stayed on in Corinth for some time. Then he left the brothers and sailed for Syria, accompanied by Priscilla and Aquila . . . They arrived at Ephesus, where Paul left Priscilla and Aquila . . . A Jew named Apollos, a native of Alexandria, came to Ephesus. He was a learned man, with a thorough knowledge of the Scriptures. He had been instructed in the way of the Lord, and he spoke with great fervour and taught about Jesus accurately, though he knew only the baptism of John. He began to speak boldly in the synagogue. When Priscilla and Aquila heard him, they invited him to their home and explained to him the way of God more adequately.

Aquila and Priscilla are a fascinating couple, their marriage is marked by:

◇ their partnership—Aquila and Priscilla, Priscilla and Aquila, always working together;

◇ their industry—he was a leatherworker;

◇ their hospitality—first to Paul, later to Apollos;

◇ their knowledge of the faith and their teaching gifts;

◇ their adaptability—they moved from Rome to Corinth to Ephesus;

◇ the leadership—1 Corinthians 16:9 speaks of 'the church that meets at their home';

◇ their courage—'they risked their lives for me,' says Paul in Romans 16:3.

An exercise

If you are married, compare your marriage with each of these comments. Are you challenged to pray for, and work for, any changes? If you are not married, think about one Christian couple whom you know. As you compare them with Aquila and Priscilla, you may be tempted to criticize! Don't! Instead, turn your thoughts into constructive prayer for them.

RG

Don't be afraid

One night the Lord spoke to Paul in a vision: 'Do not be afraid; keep on speaking, do not be silent. For I am with you, and no-one is going to attack you or harm you, because I have many people in this city.' So Paul stayed for a year and a half, teaching them the word of God.

I am very encouraged to find God saying so often, throughout the Bible, 'Do not be afraid.' The frequency of his assurance tells me two things. First, he knows how prone we are to fear. Second, he is always ready to meet us with that fear; he constantly encourages and rarely rebukes us for it.

Think of Paul's situation. Wherever he had gone he had met opposition: beating and imprisonment in Philippi (16:23); mob riot in Thessalonica (17:5); eviction from Berea (17:13, 14). Even the intrepid Paul may have felt fearful as he wondered what would happen in Corinth. But the Lord understood; he always does. 'Paul don't be afraid. I am here, and I have got good plans for you and for this city.' I once used a concordance to look up many of the Lord's 'Fear nots' in the Old Testament, and I found two strands coming regularly.

◇ Fear not, for I am with you (e.g. Isaiah 41:10).

◇ Fear not, because I have got it all under control (e.g. 2 Chronicles 20:15).

He says: 'Trust me for my presence. Trust me for my power.' His word in Scripture is reliable, and his Spirit will underline that word when we particularly need it; he may even give us a picture ('vision') or a clear word while we pray. This direct communication from God to us happens in the twentieth century as it did in the first.

A prayer

Just as I am, though tossed about,
With many a conflict, many a doubt.
Fighting and fears, within, without,
O Lamb of God, I come.

Charlotte Elliott

RG

Listen to Jesus

When [Jesus] came in sight of the city, he wept over it and said, 'If only you had known, on this great day, the way that leads to peace! But no; it is hidden from your sight. For a time will come upon you, when your enemies will set up siege-works against you; they will encircle you and hem you in at every point; they will bring you to the ground, you and your children within your walls, and not leave you one stone standing on another, because you did not recognize God's moment when it came.'

Then he went into the temple and began driving out the traders, with these words: 'Scripture says, "My house shall be a house of prayer"; but you have made it a robbers' cave.'

Last Sunday we saw Jesus using Scripture as the sword of the Spirit in his battle against temptation. This Sunday we see him using Scripture to rebuke people who are getting things wrong and to tell them what the will of God really is.

The religious authorities had allowed people to trade in the temple and to rob the poor. What used to happen was that people would bring their own lambs and pigeons to be sacrificed, and the authorized traders would look at them and say they weren't perfect. So the people would have to buy a 'perfect' animal at a high price from the stalls in the temple and be robbed.

That wasn't how God meant it to be. The will of God for his house was that it should be a house of prayer. Jesus was so angry at what was happening that he overturned the stalls and drove the thieving traders out of the temple.

The will of God for his Church and for his people is that we should pray. Religious people don't always like what Jesus says to them, and non-church people don't always like what the Church says to them.

A friend of mine was a glass blower in a big factory. His wife came to church, but he never did. Not to the services. Yet every week he would clean out the cloakrooms and the lavatories. 'Bill, why don't you come to church?' I asked him once. 'I don't like it,' he said bluntly, 'and it's not for the likes of me.'

'But what about Jesus?' I asked. 'Oh, that's different,' said Bill, giving a large smile of approval. 'He's all right. Jesus is a great bloke!'

Perhaps a bit more Jesus and a bit less religion would fill our empty churches.

SB

He didn't want . . .

Now the word of the Lord came to Jonah the son of Amittai, saying, 'Arise, go to Nineveh, that great city, and cry against it; for their wickedness has come up before me.' But Jonah rose to flee to Tarshish from the presence of the Lord. He went down to Joppa and found a ship going to Tarshish; so he paid the fare, and went on board, to go with them to Tarshish, away from the presence of the Lord.

But the Lord hurled a great wind upon the sea, and there was a mighty tempest on the sea, so that the ship threatened to break up. Then the mariners were afraid, and each cried to his god; and they threw the wares that were in the ship into the sea, to lighten it for them. But Jonah had gone down into the inner part of the ship and had laid down, and was fast asleep.

God loves people far more than some people want him to. God *is* love—and it is his nature to love. The New Testament shows us that love shining at its brightest in Jesus—the light of the world.

But the people of the Old Testament also knew that God is love. They knew that God's heart yearned after the whole world because their prophets told them so.

'It is too light a thing that you should be my servant to raise up the tribes of Jacob and to restore the preserved of Israel', God says through Isaiah: 'I will give you as a light to the nations, that my salvation may reach to the end of the earth' (Isaiah 49:6).

But Jonah didn't even want the salvation of God to reach Nineveh. He knew what God was like, and he didn't approve of the width of his mercy. So when God told him to go to Nineveh he bought himself a ticket to take himself to Tarshish—in the totally opposite direction.

Jonah is an endearingly human prophet—and as we smile and shake our heads at his cussedness perhaps we shall be able to laugh a bit shamefacedly at our own.

To think about

He drew a circle to keep me out,
Heretic, rebel, a thing to flout.
But love and I had the wit to win,
We drew a circle that took him in.

Anon

SB

What is wrong?

So the captain came and said to him, 'What do you mean, you sleeper? Arise, call upon your god! Perhaps the god will give a thought to us, that we do not perish.'

And they said to one another, 'Come, let us cast lots, that we may know on whose account this evil has come upon us.' So they cast lots, and the lot fell upon Jonah. Then they said to him, 'Tell us, on whose account this evil has come upon us? What is your occupation? And whence do you come? What is your country? And of what people are you?' And he said to them, 'I am a Hebrew; and I fear the Lord, the God of heaven, who made the sea and the dry land.' Then the men were exceedingly afraid, and said to him, 'What is this that you have done!' For the men knew that he was fleeing from the presence of the Lord, because he had told them.

There is nowhere we can go away from the presence of God. That can be glorious or terrible, and for Jonah it must have been terrible. He thought he had got away with it—but then the captain wakes him up out of a deep sleep and tells him to call on his God. He repeats the command that God had given to Jonah in the first place: 'Arise, cry ...'

But Jonah hadn't wanted to do it then to Nineveh and he would hardly want to do it now to God—any more than a young person who has run away from home would want to call home on the telephone.

What Jonah wanted was to be out of touch with God. But it was no use. The sailors discover that God has sent the storm on account of Jonah, and they ask him questions. He answers them, after a fashion, though he must have been a bit ashamed.

But the real question—'What is wrong between you and your God?'—they never ask him.

A meditation

Sit still for a few minutes with your eyes shut. In the silence, be aware of the presence of God. Then search your heart, and ask the Spirit of God to search it. Are you running away from God in any area of your life? Is there something or some person or some relationship that you don't want to think about? If so, what is wrong between you and your God?

SB

Thrown out

Then they said to him, 'What shall we do to you, that the sea may quiet down for us?' For the sea grew more and more tempestuous. He said to them, 'Take me up and throw me into the sea; then the sea will quiet down for you; for I know it is because of me that this great tempest has come upon you.' Nevertheless the men rowed hard to bring the ship back to land, but they could not, for the sea grew more and more tempestuous against them. Therefore they cried to the Lord, 'We beseech thee, O Lord, let us not perish for this man's life, and lay not on us innocent blood; for thou, O Lord, hast done as it pleased thee.' So they took up Jonah and threw him into the sea; and the sea ceased from its raging. Then the men feared the Lord exceedingly, and they offered a sacrifice to the Lord and made vows. And the Lord appointed a great fish to swallow up Jonah; and Jonah was in the belly of the fish three days and three nights.

The sailors are suffering on account of Jonah's disobedience. They are innocent victims. Perhaps the hardest question of all that we have to wrestle with is why God allows the innocent to suffer on account of the guilty and doesn't intervene: a baby with Aids because its mother (for whatever agonizing reasons in her past) is a drug addict; a haemophiliac with Aids because blood banks and governments were so slow to make the necessary tests because of the cost and political pressures.

Jonah gets thrown into the deep, and in the tale that we are reading the storm stops then. But that only happens sometimes for us. Sometimes the cancer goes away. Sometimes the rejection of our love changes into acceptance. But only sometimes. Most of the time it is otherwise. Then the only thing that can ever comfort us in our pain (though it doesn't take it away) is to know that God is suffering with us.

Reflect

He was despised and rejected by men; a man of sorrows, and acquainted with grief; and as one from whom men hide their faces he was despised, and we esteemed him not. Surely he has borne our griefs and carried our sorrows.

Isaiah 53:3–4

SB

I cried

Then Jonah prayed to the Lord his God from the belly of the fish, saying, 'I called to the Lord, out of my distress, and he answered me; out of the belly of Sheol I cried, and thou didst hear my voice. For thou didst cast me into the deep, into the heart of the seas, and the flood was round about me; all thy waves and thy billows passed over me. Then I said, "I am cast out from thy presence; how shall I again look upon thy holy temple?" The waters closed in over me, the deep was round about me; weeds were wrapped about my head at the roots of the mountains...'

Jonah is a perverse prophet, but he can still teach us about the ways of God with his people, with his prophets, and with his Son. Jesus made a connection between himself and Jonah—so we are not being far-fetched when we do. What Jonah did in the depths, and what Jesus did, we can do.

Jonah cried out from the belly of the fish: 'I am cast out from thy presence...' Jesus cried out from the cross: 'My God, my God, why have you forsaken me?'— the only time in the Gospels where he doesn't call God 'Father'. But both Jonah and Jesus were in the depths of desolation, and you can't see in the darkness.

Jonah wasn't cast out from the presence of God, even though he thought he was. God was there in the darkness, fully aware of Jonah and of his own plan for Jonah. And Jesus wasn't forsaken by God. 'God was in Christ,' wrote the Apostle Paul, 'reconciling the world to himself' (2 Corinthians 5:19). So in our desolation, as we cry out from our depths, we can know that God is with us—even if it doesn't feel as if he is.

A cry from the heart

If thou, O God, the Christ didst leave,
In him, not thee, I do believe;
To Jesus, dying all alone,
To his dark cross, not thy bright throne,
My hopeless hands will cleave.

But if it was thy love that died,
Thy voice that in the darkness cried,
The print of nails I long to see
In thy hands, God, who fashioned me.
Show me thy pierced side.

Edward Shillito

SB

I've got it right, God!

'I went down to the land whose bars closed upon me for ever; yet thou didst bring up my life from the Pit, O Lord my God. When my soul fainted within me, I remembered the Lord; and my prayer came to thee, into thy holy temple. Those who pay regard to vain idols forsake their true loyalty. But I with the voice of thanksgiving will sacrifice to thee; what I have vowed I will pay. Deliverance belongs to the Lord!'

And the Lord spoke to the fish, and it vomited out Jonah upon the dry land.

Jonah is a bit like the nine lepers out of the ten who were healed. Only the tenth one—a Samaritan—went back to Jesus to thank him and to praise God. Then Jesus told him that he was really healed and made whole.

Jonah has been delivered from the deep but not yet delivered from himself. He is decidedly smug.

'Those who pay regard to vain idols forsake their true loyalty,' he prays, 'But *I* (virtuous, righteous I—an early version of the Pharisee's prayer: I thank you that I am not like other men, extortioners, unjust, adulterers, or even like this tax collector . . .'): I will sacrifice to thee . . .'

'I've got it right, God!' 'Deliverance belongs to the Lord!'

And then, as Golka delightfully puts it in his commentary, 'the big fish throws up!'. Jonah, the indigestible prophet, is quite unceremoniously vomited 'upon the dry land . . . whose Creator he had earlier confessed his God Yahweh to be.'

A prayer

Lord God, you who made the sea and the land, and all the animal creatures and all the human creatures—and me—show me if I am being smug when I pray, and help me to stop it.

SB

A second chance

Then the word of the Lord came to Jonah the second time, saying, 'Arise, go to Nineveh, that great city, and proclaim to it the message that I tell you.' So Jonah arose and went to Nineveh, according to the word of the Lord. Now Nineveh was an exceedingly great city, three days' journey in breadth. Jonah began to go into the city, going a day's journey. And he cried, 'Yet forty days, and Nineveh shall be overthrown!'

A second chance for Jonah and a second chance for Nineveh.

I wonder what you or I would feel like if we were just as certain as Jonah that God had told us to cry out the same message against the wickedness in our great cities—London, New York, Johannesburg... To tell them that their wickedness had come up before God. The wickedness of violence and rape, drunken driving, dishonest trading, sexual immorality—and homelessness, injustice, racial and sexual inequality.

What if we could tell them with certainty (because God had told us so) that because of these things they would be overthrown in just over a month—riddled with corruption like a wooden building riddled with death-watch beetles. The building collapses and the city falls through its rottenness—and there is a tiny bit inside us which says, 'It serves them right... the things they did were evil and hurtful.'

We are on the side of the righteous because we hate the sin and corruption (even our own, which we are fighting against in the power of God)—and God is angry with the wickedness too.

But the trouble is that we know (and Jonah knew) that on the other side of the coin of the wrath of God is the love of God, and because he loves sinners he can't be relied upon to blot them out of existence, Jonah mistrusts God's intentions.

To think about

God so loved the world that he gave his only Son, that whoever believes in him should not perish but have eternal life. For God sent the Son into the world, not to condemn the world, but that the world might be saved through him.'

John 3:16–17

SB

A flood of joy

When the Lord restored the fortunes of Zion
we were like those who dream.
Then our mouth was filled with laughter,
and our tongue with shouts of joy;
then they said among the nations,
'The Lord has done great things for them.'
The Lord has done great things for us;
we are glad.
Restore our fortunes, O Lord,
like the watercourses in the Negeb!

This is one of my very favourite Psalms, so although many churches omit the Psalms from their Communion services I chose it for our reading today.

As you come to Communion, will you think about the wonderful feeling that the Psalm sings about? Of being set free from imprisonment in a foreign land and brought home again. Like Terry Waite, John Macarthy and Brian Keenan.

It's like a dream, and you are so full of delight that your mouth is filled with laughter and you are singing for joy. Or at least, you are when you feel well enough, and when it has finally dawned on you that you really are home again and that you aren't dreaming.

The 'Easter Hymn' in Mascagni's opera *Cavalleria Rusticana* says:

O rejoice, for the Lord has arisen!
He has broken the gates of the prison.
He has arisen in glory, in his glory to save:
He has broken the power, the power
of the grave.

Christ has set us free from the fear of death and the prison of death. He has also set us free from the power and captivity of sin, and given us a new life and a new power to fight against sin and to overcome it.

As you come to Communion, will you remember all these things? And as you remember, thankfully, pray (if you need to) for a similar deliverance in some area of your life where things seem to be going wrong for you, or perhaps for someone else.

Imagine the instantaneous restoration of dry river beds in the Negeb, suddenly flooded with the rain from heaven. And pray, 'Restore our fortunes like that, O Lord ...'

SB

Turn around and change

And the people of Nineveh believed God; they proclaimed a fast, and put on sackcloth, from the greatest of them to the least of them. Then tidings reached the king of Nineveh, and he arose from his throne, removed his robe, and covered himself with sackcloth, and sat in ashes. And he made proclamation and published through Nineveh, 'By the decree of the king and his nobles: Let neither man nor beast, herd nor flock, taste anything; let them not feed, or drink water, but let man and beast be covered with sackcloth, and let them cry mightily to God; yea, let every one turn from his evil way and from the violence which is in his hands. Who knows, God may yet repent and turn from his fierce anger, so that we perish not?'

The worst has happened—from Jonah's point of view. They have immediately believed his message, and from the king downwards they are all sitting in sackcloth, not eating or drinking, and turning away from their violence and their evil ways. They are crying out to God and repenting (theologically the word repent means to turn around from the wrong direction and go in the right one), and they are wondering hopefully whether God might not do the same, and turn away from his fierce anger and spare them.

The whole idea of God 'repenting' is a tricky one—because there isn't any question of God turning from a wrong direction to go in a right one. But theologians seem to think that human behaviour as it were 'triggers' the action of God. We read that God 'opposes the proud but gives grace to the humble' (1 Peter 5:5) and it must be that if we have a proud, haughty spirit then the loving will of God is bound to resist it and oppose it,

for our own good. And just as water always descends to the lowest place, so the grace of God is drawn to a person with a gentle, humble spirit.

Reflect

For thus says the high and lofty One who inhabits eternity, whose name is Holy: 'I dwell in the high and holy place, and also with him who is of a contrite and humble spirit, to revive the spirit of the humble and to revive the heart of the contrite.'

Isaiah 57:15

SB

I knew what would happen!

When God saw what they did, how they turned from their evil way, God repented of the evil which he had said he would do to them; and he did not do it.

But it displeased Jonah exceedingly, and he was angry. And he prayed to the Lord and said, 'I pray thee, Lord, is not this what I said when I was yet in my country? That is why I made haste to flee to Tarshish; for I knew that thou art a gracious God and merciful, slow to anger, and abounding in steadfast love, and repentest of evil. Therefore now, O Lord, take my life from me, I beseech thee, for it is better for me to die than to live.' And the Lord said, 'Do you do well to be angry?' Then Jonah went out of the city and sat to the east of the city, and made a booth for himself there. He sat under it in the shade, till he should see what would become of the city.

Nineveh has repented, and so has God, and Jonah is furious. This is what he knew would happen, and it is why he didn't want to come in the first place.

Jonah says how wonderful our God is, in one of the most marvellous descriptions of the nature of God that there has ever been. But he says it in a great rage, and instead of being a paean of praise it is an accusation: 'I knew that thou art a gracious God and merciful, slow to anger, and abounding in steadfast love, and repentest of evil.'

Jonah is so angry about it that he wants to die. In view of this appalling forgiveness of God death is preferable. He won't answer when God asks him if it's good for him to be angry. He just goes out of the city to sit and watch what will happen—perhaps hopeful that God will wipe it out for its wickedness after all.

To think about

Would I prefer God to be a bit less merciful and forgiving to other people? Would I like it if the divine mercy was not offered to terrorists, rapists and child-abusers? Can I manage to pray for people who do those things—that they might know 'the love and forgiveness of God'. Do I think that the Sermon on the Mount is rather extreme? When Jesus says 'Love your enemies and pray for those who persecute you . . .'

SB

Persuading a prophet

And the Lord appointed a plant, and made it come up over Jonah, that it might be a shade over his head, to save him from his discomfort. So Jonah was exceedingly glad because of the plant. But when dawn came up the next day, God appointed a worm which attacked the plant, so that it withered. When the sun rose, God appointed a sultry east wind, and the sun beat upon the head of Jonah so that he was faint; and he asked that he might die, and said, 'It is better for me to die than to live.'

We don't know much of what is going on inside Nineveh, except that they are in the process of repenting. But we have a fairly clear idea of what is going on inside Jonah, because God is in the process of teaching him a lesson. Not in any nasty sense, as if God says '*I'll* teach him . . .!' But because God is enormously merciful he desires that we should both know what the quality of mercy is and be merciful ourselves.

To teach him his lesson God makes a plant grow so that Jonah can sit in its shade out of the heat of the day, and 'provide a "cooling–off period" for an irate prophet!' (Golka) Jonah then feels quite different. In verse 4:1 the original says that he 'evils a great evil'. Now, in verse 6, he 'joys a great joy.' But unlike the sailors back at the beginning who 'feared a great fear to the Lord' and became God-centred, Jonah doesn't shift from his self-centredness.

Jonah's joy doesn't last, because the source of it withers up. God sends a worm and makes it wither, and then a sultry east wind. The merciful shade and coolness under the green leaves has gone, and Jonah goes back to wanting to die.

Consider

Though the fig tree do not blossom,
nor fruit be on the vines,
the produce of the olive fail
and the fields yield no food,
the flock be cut off from the fold
and there be no herd in the stalls,
yet I will rejoice in the Lord,
I will joy in the God of my salvation.

Habakkuk 3:17–18

SB

The divine pity

But God said to Jonah, 'Do you do well to be angry for the plant?' And he said, 'I do well to be angry, angry enough to die.' And the Lord said, 'You pity the plant, for which you did not labour, nor did you make it grow, which came into being in a night, and perished in a night. And should not I pity Nineveh, that great city, in which there are more than a hundred and twenty thousand persons who do not know their right hand from their left, and also much cattle?'

God has got Jonah in a corner. 'Do you do well to be angry for the plant?' The furious answer, like a stubborn child, is 'Yes—angry enough to die for it.' So then God draws out the lesson. Jonah pities a plant, which grew up in one night and died the next. He isn't even the plant's creator. Shouldn't God pity Nineveh, with all its people? There is no anwer from Jonah. Perhaps, at last, he has understood. And perhaps we have.

The book was probably written to show the Jews that the Gentiles are also God's creatures, and that love and pity are for them as well. Jews read the book out at their great festival of *Yom Kippur*, the Day of Atonement.

But let's turn the spotlight that has been on Jonah on to us. Do we have pity for the great cities of the earth? Do we weep over them, as Jesus wept over Jerusalem, because we love them? God's command to Jonah to cry against Nineveh came out of his infinite pity and infinite love. Does God call any of us to cry out against our cities?

Dr Campbell Morgan wrote: 'Why cry out against Nineveh's wickedness?

Because it is damning Nineveh; because God would save Nineveh; because God's act of desctruction is forever a strange act. The act that comes out of His heart is the act of construction, salvation and love. Therefore cry out against the wickedness that blights and spoils . . .'

For action and information

'. . . seek the welfare of the city where I have sent you into exile, and pray to the Lord on its behalf, for in its welfare you will find your welfare.'

Jeremiah 29:7

'Blessed are the merciful, for they shall obtain mercy.'

Matthew 5:7

SB

At a time of crisis . . .

On the third day a wedding took place at Cana in Galilee. Jesus' mother was there, and Jesus and his disciples had also been invited to the wedding. When the wine was gone, Jesus' mother said to him, 'They have no more wine.' 'Dear woman, why do you involve me?' Jesus replied, 'My time has not yet come.' His mother said to the servants, 'Do whatever he tells you.'

There was a wedding at Cana, a tiny place a few miles from Nazareth (which was also in those days a tiny place). Jesus and his disciples had been invited and his mother was also there.

Weddings in ancient Israel were lengthy affairs—not just a few hours, but several days of wining and dining. At this wedding the unthinkable happened: the wine ran out. Now you can have quite a good wedding party without the bride and groom, but not without wine. It was not just inconvenient—the hosts would be the laughing stock of the district. It may seem surprising that at this moment of domestic crisis Mary should have turned to her son. After all, you get wine from vineyards, not from prophets. 'They've no more wine', she told him. The reply from Jesus was not rude, but it appeared to suggest she was rushing things for him a bit: 'My time has not yet come.' But Mary just said to the servants, 'Do whatever he tells you.'

'Why are you trying to involve me?' Jesus had asked her. I imagine her answer would have been, because no one else can do anything about it. Presumably there was no money, or time, or both, to get a fresh supply of wine. There was no one else—except this young man on whom God's Spirit had so recently come to rest. 'Do whatever he tells you' sounds like good advice. We're often told that we shouldn't just call on God's help in times of crisis—'lifeboat prayers', as they're sometimes called. But there's also a sense in which our dependence on him is never greater than when we absolutely *know* that the situation is beyond us. Perhaps it's then that we need to hear Mary's words again: Whatever he says to you, do it.

A prayer

Lord Jesus, when we are really in a corner, absolutely desperate and don't know what to do, help us to hear what you are saying to us, and to do it. Amen.

DW

A great wine

Nearby stood six stone water jars, the kind used by the Jews for ceremonial washing, each holding from twenty to thirty gallons. Jesus said to the servants, 'Fill the jars with water'; so they filled them to the brim. Then he told them, 'Now draw some out and take it to the master of the banquet.' They did so, and the master of the banquet tasted the water that had been turned into wine. He did not realise where it had come from, though the servants who had drawn the water knew. Then he called the bridegroom aside and said, 'Everyone brings out the choice wine first and then the cheaper wine after the guests have had too much to drink; but you have saved the best till now.' This, the first of his miraculous signs, Jesus performed in Cana of Galilee. He thus revealed his glory, and his disciples put their faith in him.

Today we complete the story of the wedding at Cana, the first of the great 'signs', as St John calls them. The details are fascinating, of course. I love the moment when the master of ceremonies tastes the 'new' wine and says, 'You've saved the best till now'. As someone has said, when Jesus makes wine it isn't 'plonk'! But undoubtedly, as with all of these 'signs' in the Fourth Gospel, there is more to the story than the apparent 'facts'. Jesus takes the plain water—water used by the Jews for ceremonial washings—and turns it into the rich, red wine of the kingdom of God. He takes the insipid 'old' religion and transforms it into the vivid new one— new wine in new wineskins, as he put it elsewhere. He takes the grapes of God's vineyard, Israel (a common Old Testament picture) and wrings from them the splendid full-bodied wine of the New covenant. It's possible to go on and on with comparisons like that, and in a way that's what we're meant to do with these stories.

For most of us, and above all else, this is a 'sign' of transformation: water is transformed into wine. And there is no better sign of what the coming of Jesus means, then, or now. He doesn't leave things alone. He changes them ... and he always changes them for the better.

A prayer

Lord Jesus, often my life seems flat and stale, like insipid water. As I seek to 'do what you say to me', by your loving power fill my life with the rich, rewarding flavour of the new wine of your kingdom. Amen.

DW

The God who acts

God didn't absent himself from the world after he had set the stars spinning in space and created life. God in Christ is holding all things together (and that means you and me as well as the whole world) and 'sustaining the universe with his powerful word' (Hebrews 1:3). And God still acts in his world—without impinging on its freedom. (For a brilliant explanaton of how that happens read John Polkinghorne's *Science and Providence*.)

One way in which God acts in the world is through people—and the Acts of the Apostles is Luke's account of how he acted through those first Christians in the infant Church. And he is still acting today through people who let him into their lives. It's not a take-over. We don't lose our humanity or abandon our brains and our thinking. We live a life in union and communion with God—filled with the Spirit—and in that creative union we live a new life and learn how to love. All the wisdom and the power of God is available to us through the presence of God-with-us in the Spirit.

In the first three weeks of this section we look at more of the Acts of the early Church—and Rosemary Green connects then with now. In the last three weeks Marcus Maxwell leads us through the life of Elijah, the great Old Testament prophet. It is an immensely encouraging life, because we see how human Elijah was. He did great things for God, but after the height of success he was plunged into the depths of despair and wanted to die. We see God's tenderness and care for him—and read how God met with him and spoke to him. Not dramatically in the wind, the earthquake or the fire, but in the gentle whisper of a still, small voice.

Just as I am

Now there was a man of the Pharisees, named Nicodemus, a ruler of the Jews. This man came to Jesus by night and said to him, 'Rabbi, we know that you are a teacher come from God; for no one can do these signs that you do, unless God is with him.' Jesus answered him, 'Truly, truly, I say to you, unless one is born anew, he cannot see the kingdom of God.' Nicodemus said to him, 'How can a man be born when he is old?' Can he enter a second time into his mother's womb and be born?' Jesus answered, 'Truly, truly, I say to you, unless one is born of water and the Spirit, he cannot enter the kingdom of God.'

This story about Jesus and Nicodemus can be a strength to us whether we are a very private sort of person or a person who likes to make very clear statements about our Christianity. If we like clear statements, here is one of them. 'Unless a man is born again, he cannot see the kingdom of God.' A man cannot enter a second time into his mother's womb (and nor can a woman), but both he and she can enter into a relationship with God as their Father which they have never known before. They can call God their 'Abba', the little child's word for father, and it comes about through the forgiveness of their sins and the love of God.

But there is relief here for the private, reserved person, shy of talking publicly about their faith. Nicodemus came to Jesus by night—and Jesus accepted his need for secrecy and told him all he needed to know.

Joseph of Arimathea was another secret disciple. But when the time was right he became very brave and went very public: 'Joseph of Arimathea, who was a disciple of Jesus, but secretly, for fear of the Jews, asked Pilate that he might take away the body of Jesus, and Pilate gave him leave. So he came and took away his body' (John 19:38).

As you are given the body of Christ today at the Eucharist, remember that he comes to you just as you are, and accepts you just as you are. And as he comes to you, and to all of us, and accepts each one of us just as we are, then over the years we shall become all that we have it within us to be—to the glory of God.

I used to have a poster on my wall, which requested that you 'Accept me as I am, so that I might learn what I can become.' And that is just what Jesus does.

SB

A right start

While Apollos was at Corinth, Paul took the road through the interior and arrived at Ephesus. There he found some disciples and asked them, 'Did you receive the Holy Spirit when you believed?' They answered, 'No, we have not even heard that there is a Holy Spirit.' So Paul asked, 'Then what baptism did you receive?' 'John's baptism,' they replied. Paul said, 'John's baptism was a baptism of repentance. He told the people to believe in the one coming after him, that is, in Jesus.' On hearing this, they were baptised into the name of the Lord Jesus. When Paul placed his hands on them, the Holy Spirit came on them and they spoke in tongues and prophesied. There were about twelve men in all.

'Did you receive the Holy Spirit...?' 'No, we have not even heard...' That conversation might happen in many churches nowadays. Perhaps we have just heard of the Holy Spirit, on Whit Sunday, but we perceive him as a shadowy and irrelevant member of the Trinity. Look at the stages of Christian initiation for these Ephesians. First, they had to repent. Repentance means a 180 degree turn away from the intention of sinning. Secondly, they committed themselves to follow Jesus. I like the phrase 'baptised into'; it makes me think of baptism by immersion, when the candidates go right into the water, a symbol of their desire to be fully cleansed and wholehearted for Christ. Then, when Paul put his hands on them, there was immediate, powerful evidence of the Spirit's activity in their lives. There is often confusion over this. The outward signs (baptism and confirmation) and the inward realities (repentance, commitment to Jesus and being filled by the Holy Spirit) fit together, but they are often not simultaneous. Baptized as a baby; I was sincere but ignorant when I was confirmed at 14; four years later I really started to follow Christ. Another 24 years on I opened myself more fully to the Spirit's life-changing power. What matters most is that now, at 60, I continue to let him change me and invigorate me.

To think over

How far does my inward, spiritual experience match the words expressed outwardly at my baptism and confirmation?

RG

Models for evangelism

Paul entered the synagogue amd spoke boldly there for three months, arguing persuasively about the kingdom of God. But some of them became obstinate; they refused to believe and publicly maligned the Way. So Paul left them. He took the disciples with him and had discussions daily in the lecture hall of Tyrannus. This went on for two years, so that all the Jews and Greeks who lived in the province of Asia heard the word of the Lord. God did extraordinary miracles through Paul, so that even hand-kerchiefs and aprons that touched him were taken to the sick, and their illnesses were cured and the evil spirits left them.

Paul's consuming desire was for Jesus to be understood and known. His methods give us some models for our own Decade of Evangelism. **1. In the synagogue.** He went first to the people who expected the Messiah, and used all his knowledge as a Jew to 'argue persuasively' about God's kingdom. Yet acceptance of God's truth is not only a matter of the mind but also of the will and the heart. A conscience pricked by truth plus reluctance to change can lead to obstinate refusal, and 'I can't believe' becomes a disguise for 'I won't believe'. **2. In the public lecture hall.** Paul frequented the place where open-minded, thinking people gathered. He was flexible in his teaching methods, and he used lectures and debates to teach God's truth. He did not go alone, but took with him 'the disciples', converts from the synagogue. I think they shared in the discussions and talked with individuals, enabling the truth about Christ to spread from this centre of trade, learning and culture through a wide area. God uses experienced, professionally trained preachers and also untrained, 'ordinary' Christians to share his work. **3. Through astonishing miracles.** Rational argument was appropriate for the synagogue and for Tyrannus college. But God is bigger than any concepts of him, and now he healed—even drove out evil sprits—in a way that Luke, familiar as he was with miraculous healing, rated as 'extraordinary'.

A prayer

God, please show me how you want me to help other people understand and know you.

RG

Realities of evil

Some Jews who went around driving out evil spirits tried to invoke the name of the Lord Jesus over those who were demon-possessed. They would say, 'In the name of Jesus, whom Paul preaches, I command you to come out.' Seven sons of Sceva, a Jewish chief priest, were doing this. One day the evil spirit answered them, 'Jesus I know, and I know about Paul, but who are you?' Then the man who had the evil spirit jumped on them and overpowered them all. He gave them such a beating that they ran out of the house naked and bleeding. When this became known to the Jews and Greeks living in Ephesus, they were all seized with fear, and the name of the Lord Jesus was held in high honour. Many of those who believed now came and openly confessed their evil deeds. A number who had practised sorcery brought their scrolls together and burned them publicly. When they calculated the value of the scrolls, the total came to fifty thousand drachmas. In this way the word of the Lord spread widely and grew in power.

At first reading we might think this passage irrelevant for the twentieth century. But here are some of the things that my own experience has shown me are right up to date. (1) Evil spirits are real and can infect people's lives. (2) We counteract them, not merely by saying Jesus' name but by being empowered by Jesus' Spirit. Sceva's sons were copying Paul's methods but they did not share the source of his power. (3) An evil spirit may give supernatural physical strength. I have seen a young woman of slight build needing four people to constrain her when evil was active in her. (4) When people saw the effect of evil and Paul's power they honoured Jesus. I have learnt more about Christ's power through encounters with evil than through any other means. (5) They confessed their occult involvement and destroyed any associated object, even if it cost money. Things tainted by non-Christian worship block many Christian lives. The best motto is 'When in doubt, throw it out.'

A prayer

Lord, please show me if I have, knowingly or unknowingly, been influenced by any unholy spirit.

RG

A leader's example

From Miletus, Paul sent to Ephesus for the elders of the church. When they arrived, he said to them: 'You know how I lived the whole time I was with you, from the first day I came into the province of Asia. I served the Lord with great humility and with tears, although I was severely tested by the plots of the Jews. You know that I have not hesitated to preach anything that would be helpful to you but have taught you publicly and from house to house. I have declared to both Jews and Greeks that they must turn to God in repentance and have faith in our Lord Jesus ... I have not coveted anyone's gold or silver or clothing. You yourselves know that these hands of mine have supplied my own needs and the needs of my companions. In everything I did, I showed you that by this kind of hard work we must help the weak, remembering the words the Lord Jesus himself said: "It is more blessed to give than to receive." '

Paul was determined to reach Jerusalem quickly, so he sent for the Ephesian church leaders to meet him at the port. His farewell speech to them is a rich resource for Christian leaders. We notice his humility; the vulnerability and compassion seen in his tears; his steadfastness against attack. He was not selective in the subject matter of his preaching ('anything that would be helpful to you') nor biased towards his audience (Jews and Greeks alike heard the same challenging message of repentance from sin and faith in Christ). He spoke in public places (remember the lecture hall of Tyrannus) and also visited in homes. He was not afraid of hard physical work, supporting himself and others in a simple, non-covetous lifestyle. How do you (if you have any leadership responsibilities) or those over you compare with Paul in his attitude and behaviour?

To think about

'It is more blessed to give than to receive.' Can I give to others as freely as Paul did? Am I also willing to receive, not greedily, but so that others have the joy of giving?

RG

A leader's responsibilities

'Keep watch over yourselves and all the flock of which the Holy Spirit has made you overseers. Be shepherds of the church of God, which he bought with his own blood. I know that after I leave, savage wolves will come in among you and will not spare the flock. Even from your own number men will arise and distort the truth in order to draw away disciples after them. So be on your guard! Remember that for three years I never stopped warning each of you day and night with tears. Now I commit you to God and to the word of his grace, which can build you up and give you an inheritance among all those who are sanctified . . .' When he had said this, he knelt down with all of them and prayed. They all wept as they embraced him and kissed him.

As Paul continues speaking to the Ephesian elders I find five principles for Christian leaders. **1. Keep watch.** The theme of Christian leaders as shepherds recurs frequently in the Bible, and God vehemently rebukes those who do not follow Christ's example of loving, intimate care. Paul had to warn them that even some Christians would split the church by distorting the truth and by their own egotistical need to be followed. Watch out for modern 'wolves'! **2. Teach the word.** The best safeguard against false teaching is to be built up by 'the word of his grace' in the Bible. Clergy have a responsibility to see their congregations deeply rooted in Scripture. **3. Trust God.** 'I commit you to God.' I like that word 'commit'. It speaks of definite action, being put—or putting ourselves—into reliable hands. Are you carrying an anxiety or a fear? Remember that God's hands are utterly reliable. **4. Pray anywhere.** The Ephesians had come to see Paul near the ship; they were probably outside in the harbour. But they were not ashamed to kneel down, whoever was watching. I remember a similar scene at Durban airport, with ten of us linked together, visibly praying before saying goodbye to departing friends. **5. Be vulnerable.** Is there greater strength in a leader who can shed tears publicly or in one who always shows a stiff upper lip?

Pray

Pray for the leaders of your church—that they might grow more and more like Paul: watchful, teaching, trusting, prayerful and vulnerable.

RG

Single-mindedness

'And now, compelled by the Spirit, I am going to Jerusalem, not knowing what will happen to me there. I only know that in every city the Holy Spirit warns me that prison and hardships are facing me. However, I consider my life worth nothing to me, if only I may finish the task the Lord Jesus has given me—the task of testifying to the gospel of God's grace.'

Paul's mind was clear; first Jerusalem (the headquarters both of Judaism and of the Church), then Rome (the heart of the civilized world). When he left Ephesus he decided to go to Jerusalem, saying 'After I have been there, I must visit Rome also' (19:21). Although he had stayed in Greece for several months his purpose had not wavered. The Holy Spirit warned him in many ways about the immense difficulties ahead of him; through his own prayer, through the Christians in Tyre and the prophet Agabus in Caesarea (21:11). His friends were deeply concerned for his safety, and pleaded with him not to go to Jerusalem (21:12). But his motivation was so strong that nothing would deter him. To many people he looks like a fool; but he was a fool *for Christ's sake*. He knew that the Spirit was pushing him ('compelling' is a strong word) and he had only one concern; obedience to the mission given to him by his Master, to witness to the truth of the gospel.

Think and pray

How far can you identify with Paul in his dedication, in his zeal to spread the gospel, in his certainty about the task Jesus had given him?

Thanks be to thee,
O Lord Jesus Christ,
for all the benefits
which thou hast given us,
for all the insults
thou hast borne for us.
O most merciful Redeemer,
Friend and Brother,
may we know thee more clearly,
love thee more dearly,
and follow thee more nearly,
day by day.

Richard of Chichester

RG

The light of love

'... As Moses lifted up the serpent in the wilderness, so must the Son of man be lifted up, that whoever believes in him may have eternal life.' For God so loved the world that he gave his only Son, that whoever believes in him should not perish but have eternal life.

... For every one who does evil hates the light, and does not come to the light, lest his deeds should be exposed. But he who does what is true comes to the light, that it may be clearly seen that his deeds have been wrought in God.

When you look up to the Communion table today and see the bread and wine laid out, will you look back to the first Good Friday, when the Son of Man who is also the Son of God was lifted up on a cross so that everyone who looks upon him can know the forgiveness of their sins. Let a deep thankfulness to God well up inside you if you know that your sins are forgiven. If you don't, then realize that there is no sin so unspeakable that it can't be spoken of to the Saviour of the world. He knows all about it anyway—and wants to have it out in the open. The sinner simply has to tell him about it—and then turn away from it, through the power of the Holy Spirit. Enormous sins and seemingly small sins all have to be told to him.

But remember that God didn't send his Son into the world to condemn it. He sent him to save it. Remember that you come into the presence of the one who is the light of the world. When you come into the light so that your sins are revealed, you will be forgiven. So don't hide away in the darkness. Come into the light of the love that streams from the cross.

Eternal Light! Eternal Light!
How pure the soul must be,
When, placed within Thy searching sight,
It shrinks not, but with calm delight
Can live and look on Thee.

Oh, how shall I, whose native sphere
Is dark, whose mind is dim,
Before the Ineffable appear,
And on my naked spirit bear
The uncreated beam?

There is a way for man to rise
To that sublime abode;
An Offering and a Sacrifice,
A Holy Spirit's energies,
An Advocate with God.

T. Binney

SB

225

Concern for the news

When we arrived at Jerusalem, the brothers received us warmly. The next day Paul and the rest of us went to see James, and all the elders were present. Paul greeted them and reported in detail what God had done among the Gentiles through his ministry. When they heard this, they praised God.

Does a missionary ever come to speak at your church? How do you receive him or her? Are you interested to hear the news of difficulties and encouragements? Or does it all seem rather far away and irrelevant? My son is a missionary in Pakistan. He has talked sadly of the members of his supporting churches who have asked 'What do you do in India?' His carefully written prayer letters have apparently been ignored, an experience shared by many of his fellow missionaries. When a member of your church leaves to go and work in a tough place, do you pray, write letters, show interest in what the other person is doing? When your vicar goes away on a conference do you want to hear about it on his return? The church leaders in Jerusalem set us a good example for such situations. Paul had plenty to say about the places he had visited, the people he had met and the ways he had seen God work. They listened to it all for a long time! They rejoiced over the news and they praised God together. I am ashamed to think of occasions when I have failed to listen to others, more concerned with my own affairs than with theirs. I remember many times when my husband returned home excited from overseas trips, and I hurt him by my lack of interest and my refusal to share his joy. I thank God for overcoming my indifference and I pray that I will become even more ready to listen and to try to understand what life is like for those in situations very different from my own.

To think over

Paul said 'Rejoice with those who rejoice; mourn with those who mourn' (Romans 12:15). Do I?

RG

Do old rules matter?

Then they [the church leaders] said to Paul: 'You see, brother, how many thousands of Jews have believed, and all of them are zealous for the law. They have been informed that you teach all the Jews who live among the Gentiles to turn away from Moses, telling them not to circumcise their children or live according to our customs. What shall we do? They will certainly hear that you have come, so do what we tell you. There are four men with us who have made a vow. Take these men, join in their purification rites and pay their expenses, so that they can have their heads shaved. Then everybody will know that there is no truth in these reports about you, but that you yourself are living in obedience to the law. As for the Gentile believers, we have written to them our decision that they should abstain from food sacrificed to idols, from blood, from the meat of strangled animals and from sexual immorality.'

The apostles were delighted to hear about the tremendous growth of the Church among the Gentiles. An earlier decision of the synod in Jerusalem had ruled that Gentile Christians need not be circumcised and that they should keep the minimum number of Jewish laws (15:20). But many Hebrew believers were still bound by the old laws; they were disturbed by rumours about Paul's new attitudes and were afraid he had discarded his Jewishness. The church leaders, wanting to allay their fears, asked Paul to join in the purification rites and even to pay for others to do so. I see Paul's willingness to comply as another mark of his dedication before God to serve other people and not hinder their faith.

Suggestions for prayer

Thank God *that we are not bound by all the Jewish laws.* **Pray** *for the grace to obey God's laws and to live a holy life.* **Pray** *for Jews who have become Christians.* **Pray** *that we do not inhibit growth in our own churches by being stuck with our traditions and bound by our own fear of change.*

RG

Religious prejudice

When the seven days were nearly over, some Jews from the province of Asia saw Paul at the temple. They stirred up the whole crowd and seized him, shouting, 'Men of Israel, help us! This is the man who teaches all men everywhere against our people and our law and this place. And besides, he has brought Greeks into the temple area and defiled this holy place.' (They had previously seen Trophimus the Ephesian in the city with Paul and assumed that Paul had brought him into the temple area.) The whole city was aroused, and the people came running from all directions. Seizing Paul, they dragged him from the temple . . . While they were trying to kill him, news reached the commander of the Roman troops . . . He at once took some officers and soldiers and ran down to the crowd. When the rioters saw the commander and his soldiers, they stopped beating Paul.

What provoked the crowd's violent reaction? It seems that they ignored Paul's shaved head, an obvious mark of his ceremonial vow. There were two main causes. First was the deep underlying prejudice against the Gentiles. It reminds me of the centuries-old, apparently unending, hostility between Catholics and Protestants in Northern Ireland. Feuds in the name of religion have a particularly evil depth of bitterness. Secondly, their prejudice made the Jews ready to jump to false conclusions. Fact—they saw Paul in the city with Trophimus. Fact—they saw Paul in the temple. Assumption—he had brought the Ephesian into a sacred area. $2 + 2 = 6$! The rumour spread, as inaccurately as rumours do, in a city crammed with pilgrims for the Feast of Pentecost. A riot followed, and the assault on Paul was stopped only by the soldiers' intervention. Will you stop for a moment and ask God what he wants to show you from these events before you read my suggestions for prayer?

A way to pray

Lord, help me to recognize and acknowledge the good things in the people I don't like. Please save me from prejudice; from jumping to false conclusions; from spreading gossip to others' detriment.

RG

Religious blinkers

'Then the Lord said to me, "Go, I will send you far away to the Gentiles." ' The crowd listened to Paul until he said this. Then they raised their voices and shouted, 'Rid the earth of him! He's not fit to live!' As they were shouting and throwing off their cloaks and flinging dust into the air, the commander ordered Paul to be taken into the barracks. He directed that he be flogged and questioned in order to find out why the people were shouting at him like this.

The mob did not mind when Paul spoke about Jesus, but *Gentiles!* The word was like a red rag to a bull. How could any Jew have dealings with the Gentiles? It was unthinkable! Isn't it sad? Here were religious people who claimed to obey the Old Testament, but they ignored passages like Isaiah 49:6. 'I will also make you a light for the Gentiles, that you may bring my salvation to the ends of the earth.' So convinced were they that the Gentiles were to be utterly shunned that they were selective in the texts they chose to obey—or to ignore.

Yet we often do the same. I look back to the time when I studied Matthew's Gospel for a school exam. There were plenty of verses I wanted to eradicate, words like 'They will throw them into the fiery furnace, where there will be weeping and gnashing of teeth' (Matthew 13:42). That did not fit with my image of a God of love, so (I thought) the Gospel must be wrong. Now I see that, while I may not always understand the Bible, I should be willing to submit to its teaching, even when I don't like it.

A prayer

Lord, please take off my blinkers of ignorance, prejudice or false assumptions, that I may see the light of your truth.

RG

An encouraging vision

There was a great uproar, and some of the teachers of the law who were Pharisees argued vigorously. 'We find nothing wrong with this man,' they said. 'What if a spirit or an angel has spoken to him?' The dispute became so violent that the commander was afraid Paul would be torn in pieces by them. He ordered the troops to go down and take him away from them by force and bring him into the barracks. The following night the Lord stood near Paul and said, 'Take courage! As you have testified about me in Jerusalem, so you must also testify in Rome.'

Paul longed to preach the gospel in Rome—but would he ever leave Jerusalem alive? Jesus gave him a special gift when he appeared in a vision, and promised 'You will reach Rome.' Paul must have thought of these reassuring words many times in the next three years of his slow and difficult progress to Rome.

I have sometimes had a similar experience with the Bible. God almost takes a pen and underlines a verse, to speak to me personally for my current situation.

I remember when, as a new Christian, I was to be a witness against my mother for her careless driving. Life was exceedingly uncomfortable while we waited six weeks for the Magistrates' court. I read how Peter told slaves who were unjustly treated by their masters to look at Jesus' example. 'When they hurled their insults at him, he did not retaliate ... Instead, he entrusted himself to him who judges justly' (1 Peter 2:23). That verse was like a rope tied round my waist to hold me tight.

To think about

Do I expect the Bible to be a living book of encouragement, example and warning?

RG

God uses ordinary people

When the son of Paul's sister heard of this plot, he went into the barracks and told Paul. Then Paul called one of the centurions and said, 'Take this young man to the commander; he has something to tell him.' So he took him to the commander. The centurion said, 'Paul, the prisoner, sent for me and asked me to bring this young man to you because he has something to tell you.' The commander took the young man by the hand, drew him aside and asked, 'What is it you want to tell me?' He said: 'The Jews have agreed to ask you to bring Paul before the Sanhedrin tomorrow in the pretext of wanting more accurate information about him. Don't give in to them, because more than forty of them are waiting in ambush for him. They have taken an oath not to eat or drink until they have killed him. They are ready now, waiting for your consent to their request.' The commander dismissed the young man and cautioned him, 'Don't tell anyone that you have reported this to me.'

The day after the uproar in the Sanhedrin forty Jews vowed to fast until they had killed Paul. (I wonder if they kept their oath when their plan failed!) Somehow Paul's nephew—probably still in his teens—heard about it. He took a simple step; he visited Paul in prison and told him the news. A simple act—with big consequences. The ambush was thwarted; Paul lived to continue his mission. It is easy to feel 'I'm not important. What can I possibly do?' But we may not know what a big difference one small deed may make. Perhaps I have a 'hunch' that I should make a phone call, pay a visit, write a letter. Is there the risk of making a mistake and appearing foolish? But there is also a risk in saying 'I'm too busy... It looks stupid... It's too difficult.' I fail God and other people by my reticence.

Pray

Lord, please help me to know that there are things you want me to do. Make me more sensitive to your nudges and more ready to obey.

RG

Doers, not hearers

Be doers of the word, and not hearers only, deceiving yourselves. For if any one is a hearer of the word and not a doer, he is like a man who observes his natural face in a mirror; for he observes himself and goes away and at once forgets what he was like. But he who looks into the perfect law, the law of liberty, and perseveres, being no hearer that forgets but a doer that acts, he shall be blessed in his doing. If any one thinks he is religious, and does not bridle his tongue but deceives his heart, this man's religion is vain. Religion that is pure and undefiled before God and the Father is this: to visit orphans and widows in their affliction, and to keep oneself unstained from the world.

As you come today to Holy Communion will you pray that the word of God will really penetrate your heart. There will be an Epistle (perhaps the reading from James out of which our passage comes) and a Gospel (perhaps Luke 17:11–19, telling of ten lepers who were physically healed and of just one who came back to say thank you and was made really whole).

How thankful are you for what God has done for you in Christ? When the bread and the wine are given to you today, and the words spoken to you: 'The body of Christ keep you in eternal life ... The blood of Christ ...', does your heart well up in thankfulness? Have you really grasped the glory of the fact that Christ died for you and that the Spirit of Christ dwells within you, and nourishes your life with his life—given through his death on the cross?

We say 'thank you' in our heart and also with our mouth. But we say other things with our mouth. Angry things and angry words. Cutting cruel words. We are fooling ourselves very dangerously if we think it doesn't matter and that God doesn't know or notice. At the confession, will you ask the Spirit of God to search your heart and show you how the things that you say affect other people?

SB

Sitting on the fence

Then Felix, who was well acquainted with the Way, adjourned the proceedings. 'When Lysias the commander comes,' he said, 'I will decide the case.' He ordered the centurion to keep Paul under guard but to give him some freedom and permit his friends to take care of his needs. Several days later Felix came with his wife Drusilla, who was a Jewess. He sent for Paul and listened to him as he spoke about faith in Jesus Christ. As Paul discoursed on righteousness, self-control and the judgment to come, Felix was afraid and said 'That's enough for now! You may leave. When I find it convenient, I will send for you.' At the same time he was hoping that Paul would offer him a bribe, so he sent for him frequently and talked with him. When two years had passed, Felix was succeeded by Porcius Festus, but because Felix wanted to grant a favour to the Jews, he left Paul in prison.

This final week of our readings from Acts sees Paul on his way to Rome at last. First he was taken to Caesarea, the Mediterranean port that was the home of the Roman governor of the province. There Felix heard the charges against Paul (causing riots and desecrating the temple) and Paul's defence of innocence. But Felix was a procrastinator. He dared not face God's standards of righteousness and he evaded any commitment to Christ. He preferred to receive a bribe or to curry favour with the Jews; he did not mind which. In the light of eternity it looks a poor choice. Most people in England have some belief in God's existence. But—unlike Felix, who was 'well acquainted with the [Christian] Way'—there is widespread ignorance about Jesus, and God is seen as irrelevant. Even for those who know something about Jesus thoughts of 'What is there in it for me?' and 'What would other people think?' are still barriers to wholehearted Christian commitment.

To think about

Am I sitting on the fence of full commitment? Do I care whether other people learn about the Way, or am I hindered by fear or apathy? How can I share my faith with others in this Decade of Evangelism?

RG

God's purposes

At this point Festus interrupted Paul's defence. 'You are out of your mind, Paul!' he shouted, 'Your great learning is driving you insane.' 'I am not insane, most excellent Festus,' Paul replied. 'What I am saying is true and reasonable. The king is familiar with these things, and I can speak freely to him. I am convinced that none of this has escaped his notice, because it was not done in a corner. King Agrippa, do you believe the prophets? I know you do.' Then Agrippa said to Paul, 'Do you think that in such a short time you can persuade me to be a Christian?' Paul replied, 'Short time or long—I pray God that not only you but all who are listening to me today may become what I am, except for these chains.' The king rose, and with him the governor and Bernice and those sitting with them. They left the room, and while talking with one another, they said: 'This man is not doing anything that deserves death or imprisonment.' Agrippa said to Festus, 'This man could have been set free if he had not appealed to Caesar.'

Once again Paul has told the story of his conversion on the Damascus road, and explained how Christ's death and resurrection fulfil the Old Testament in giving light to the world. His hearers are as reluctant as Felix to embrace the faith, but his arguments show them that he is innocent of any crime. But Paul, as a Roman citizen, had already lodged his appeal to be tried before the Emperor. Does it seem a pity that Paul could not be freed? No. God's purposes, matching Paul's deep desire, were being worked out. Remember the Lord's promise to Paul. 'As you have testified about me in Jerusalem, so you must testify in Rome.' Paul was proving the discovery that Job had made centuries earlier, also through adversity. Job said to God, 'I know that you can do all things; no plan of yours can be thwarted' (Job 42:2).

Reflect

God's purposes are often worked out through human weakness, though our limited vision finds many events hard to understand.

RG

A questionable decision

Much time had been lost, and sailing had already become dangerous because by now it was after the Fast. So Paul warned them, 'Men, I can see that our voyage is going to be disastrous and bring great loss to ship and cargo, and to our own lives also.' But the centurion, instead of listening to what Paul said, followed the advice of the pilot and of the owner of the ship. Since the harbour was unsuitable to winter in, the majority decided that we should sail on, hoping to reach Phoenix and winter there. This was a harbour in Crete, facing both southwest and northwest.

After appearing before Festus and Agrippa, Paul and some other prisoners were eventually handed over to a centurion, Julius, who was responsible for their journey to Rome. Their progress—probably in a cargo boat carrying grain—was slow, with the wind against them. 'I can see we are in for trouble,' said Paul as he looked at the weather conditions; he was also a man of prayer, and the assurance with which he spoke came from the insight God gave him.

It was a hard decision for Julius to make. He knew of the risk in sailing further in October, but it was natural for him to listen to the professionals rather than to Paul—the prisoner, landlubber and religious freak. Decisions are often difficult. We can take advice from a variety of people whom we respect, but ultimately the decision is ours. We look at the circumstances, take advice and use our minds when choices have to be made. As Christians we also submit the decision-making process (whether individual or corporate) to God and prayerfully ask him to lead us. The guidance may not come in a blinding flash, but he blesses the attitude of 'God, please show me/us your way.'

To think about

If I have made a wrong decision do I put all the blame on others—or beat my own breast and just blame myself. I can ask God to forgive me for my mistake and help me to forgive anyone else involved. Then I am free to look at the problem again, and ask, 'Lord, where do I go from here?'

RG

In the storm

After the men had gone a long time without food, Paul stood up before them and said: 'Men, you should have taken my advice not to sail from Crete; then you would have spared yourselves this damage and loss. But now I urge you to keep up your courage, because not one of you will be lost; only the ship will be destroyed. Last night an angel of the God whose I am and whom I serve stood beside me and said, 'Do not be afraid, Paul. You must stand trial before Caesar; and God has graciously given you the lives of all who sail with you.' So keep up your courage, men, for I have faith in God that it will happen just as he told me. Nevertheless, we must run aground on some island.'

'I told you so!' says Paul. Previously he had words of warning for the ship's company, but now he passes on the angel's message of encouragement. In the height of the storm he probably wondered 'Lord, did I get it right? Did you really come to me three years ago in that vision in Jerusalem and promise that I would testify to you in Rome?' So now the angel comes to restore his confidence and to encourage his fellow travellers.

Most of us would be afraid of knowing that we were to appear before the notorious emperor Nero. Not so Paul! His fear was that he would never reach that destination. God knows that we are prone to many fears. That is why we so often read in the Bible 'Fear not.' God usually says, in effect, one of two things. 'Don't be afraid because I am with you' or—as here—'Don't be afraid because I am in control.' We have a God who is sensitive to our fear and who wants us to lean on his strength.

A way to pray

First think about the things that cause you fear. Then draw a simple picture—a pin man if you like—of Jesus. Write by his feet one or two words to express each of your fears. Use this picture as an aid to pray; let him take charge of your fears.

RG

Hospitality and healing

Once safely on shore, we found out that the island was called Malta. The islanders showed us unusual kindness. They built a fire and welcomed us all because it was raining and cold. Paul gathered a pile of brushwood and, as he put it on the fire, a viper, driven out by the heat, fastened itself on his hand. When the islanders saw the snake hanging from his hand, they said to each other, 'This man must be a murderer; for though he escaped from the sea, Justice has not allowed him to live.' But Paul shook the snake off into the fire and suffered no ill effects. The people expected him to swell up or suddenly fall over dead, but after waiting a long time and seeing nothing unusual happen to him, they changed their minds and said he was a god. There was an estate nearby that belonged to Publius, the chief official of the island. He welcomed us to his home and for three days entertained us hospitably. His father was sick in bed, suffering from fever and dysentery. Paul went in to see him and, after prayer, placed his hands on him and healed him. When this had happened, the rest of the sick on the island came and were cured. They honoured us in many ways and when we were ready to sail, they furnished us with the supplies we needed.

A challenge to my hospitality. How many marks of hospitality did the pagan islanders show the shipwrecked men? I have to ask myself whether the quality of my own hospitality matches theirs.

A challenge to my faith. These verses abound with miracles of healing. First Paul himself was unaffected by the viper's normally fatal bite. Then Publius' elderly father, severely weakened by dysentery, was cured. Finally all the ill people on Malta came and were healed. I have to ask myself another question. Do I ever expect God to heal people today apart from modern medicine or beyond its normal bounds? There is evidence that sometimes he does.

A prayer

Father God, please enlarge my faith and increase the warmth of my hospitality.

RG

Rome at last!

'Therefore I want you to know that God's salvation has been sent to the Gentiles, and they will listen!' For two whole years Paul stayed there in his own rented house and welcomed all who came to see him. Boldly and without hindrance he preached the kingdom of God and taught about the Lord Jesus Christ.

Right at the beginning of Acts we read its keynote verse in 1:8. 'You will receive power when the Holy Spirit comes on you; and you will be my witnesses in Jerusalem, and in all Judea and Samaria, and to the ends of the earth.' As the book continued we saw the Spirit powerfully in action in healing and in exorcism. We saw the Christians, unfailing in their bold witness, despite persecution— mocking, flogging, stoning, mob riots, prejudice, unjust accusations, imprisonment. There were also internal doctrinal arguments that nearly tore the Church apart, especially over the rules for the Gentiles who turned to Christ.

Despite all these hindrances the gospel spread far afield. The book ends on a note of triumph. What did it matter to Paul that he was under house arrest in Rome? He welcomed to his home anyone, Jew or Gentile, who would come to hear about Jesus. Some were convinced, others disbelieved. There are always mixed reactions to the good news of the gospel. As I ask the Holy Spirit to make me a bold witness for Jesus I look at Paul's example in using his home, even in a difficult situation. Have you ever thought how you might use your home as a place where your friends could come to hear how Jesus Christ could be real for them in their lives? Are you willing to risk a cold shoulder from some for the sake of others who are ignorant about Jesus and would love to know?

Think and pray

Think back on our readings for the last three weeks, and to the parts of Acts we read earlier in the year. What has excited you most? What differences has it made in your life? **Pray** 'Father, thank you for your Spirit and for his power. Please help me to be and to do all that you want for me. Amen.'

RG

Called to life

Have you forgotten that when we were baptized into union with Christ Jesus we were baptized into his death? By baptism we were buried with him, and lay dead, in order that, as Christ was raised from the dead in the splendour of the Father, so also we might set our feet upon the new path of life.

Today, all over the world, people are being baptized. Some will be adults, and some will be children. Some will believe that baptism automatically makes the baptized person a Christian, others will see it as done in hope, others as an act of faith and witness. But whatever our view of baptism, this passage makes it clear that one important part of our baptism is that it is a call.

It is a call to live a new life through faith in Christ. Today, look back at your baptism. It doesn't matter whether you remember the event or not; what counts here is that you have been baptized. That baptism was God's call to serve him and live for him.

The imagery of death and burial in baptism is a call to take action to put to death the parts of our lives that cannot exist in the presence of Christ; the petty sins and selfishness, the worries and fears that point to our weakness of faith. These are part of the old life which in Christ we are called to leave behind.

When we take part in Holy Communion, we again stress the idea of dying. As Jesus died for us, so we share in the benefits of his death, and respond to the call of baptism by receiving God's strength to enable us to put our old selves to death.

Baptism and Communion both set us the pattern of Christian life; the pattern of dying and rising, of leaving behind the old and setting out with the new. So today, respond to the call of baptism and the grace of Communion, and offer yourself afresh to God, to live for him.

MM

The villain

Ahab the son of Omri became king of Israel in the thirty-eighth year of King Asa of Judah, and he reigned over Israel in Samaria for twenty-two years. More than any of his predecessors, he did what was wrong in the eyes of the Lord. As if it were not enough for him to follow the sinful ways of Jeroboam son of Nebat, he took as his wife Jezebel daughter of King Ethbaal of Sidon, and went and served Baal; he prostrated himself before him and erected an altar to him in the temple of Baal which he built in Samaria. He also set up a sacred pole; indeed, he did more to provoke the anger of the Lord the God of Israel than all the kings of Israel before him.

My five-year-old son is happy to listen to any story or watch any TV programme, as long as he is sure who are the goodies and the baddies. In the story of Elijah, it is clear from the outset who is the baddie. It is King Ahab, aided by his foreign queen, Jezebel! Of course, Ahab didn't see it that way. By marrying the king of Sidon's daughter, he had made a powerful alliance with a nation which was at the centre of civilization. In those days, treaties were sealed by oaths to the gods of both sides. An altar to Baal Melkart of Sidon was hardly too great a price for the hope of prosperity. And it was only fair to allow Jezebel the freedom to practise her own religion, to bring a few priests and prophets of her own god. It seemed a harmless compromise. But there were dangers. The people of Israel were always tempted to hedge their bets by acknowledging the gods of the local nations—after all, they were local gods and should be pretty effective. Also, Israel's kings were responsible to their people and to God. The surrounding kings were absolute despots, who would see Ahab's concern to please his people as weakness. Ahab would have to show greater strength if he was to remain credible.

It was a small compromise, for great benefits. Yet it carried the seeds of disaster for Israel, for it was a denial of God's demand for exclusive loyalty to him.

A question

How are you tempted to compromise between your loyalty to God and fitting in with the world around?

MM

Opposition

Elijah the Tishbite from Tishbe in Gilead said to Ahab, 'I swear by the life of the Lord the God of Israel, whose servant I am, that there will be neither dew nor rain these coming years unless I give the word.' Then the word of the Lord came to him, 'Leave this place, turn eastwards, and go into hiding in the wadi of Kerith east of the Jordan. You are to drink from the stream, and I have commanded the ravens to feed you there.' Elijah did as the Lord had told him: he went and stayed in the wadi of Kerith east of the Jordan, and the ravens brought him bread and meat morning and evening, and he drank from the stream.

Who was Elijah? We are told where he came from, but nothing more. Was he from one of the travelling bands of prophets who wandered the country-side? Had he been attached to a shrine? Who were his parents, his teachers, his friends? We don't know. He appears in the story like the mysterious stranger who rides into town, and who we know will sort out the bad guys in the end.

But we don't need to know much about Elijah. His qualifications aren't what count. What really matters is that he is God's man, and he is here when he is needed.

I remember when a new minister arrived in a church I used to attend. He turned things upside-down, and his preaching challenged and shattered what had become a cosy club. 'Who does he think he is?' someone asked. 'What authority does he have?' In fact, he had the only authority he really needed—he was faithful to God in a time and a place when faithfulness was at a premium. He became God's man for that church, and great things began to happen.

So Elijah appears on the scene and confronts Ahab. He may be a lone voice, but he is faithful to God, and God's power is with him.

A reflection

Who is God's person where you are? Who is faithful to him? Is it you? Or should it be?

MM

The nameless widow

After a while, the stream dried up, for there had been no rain in the land. Then the word of the Lord came to him: 'Go now to Zarephath, a village of Sidon, and stay there; I have commanded a widow there to feed you.' He went off to Zarephath, and when he reached the entrance to the village, he saw a widow gathering sticks.

Elijah stays with the widow of Zarephath for going on three years, yet we are never told her name. Some feminist readers might say this is because, as a woman, she is not important for the male-dominated society in which she lived, and in which the story was first told. There is some truth in that. As a single woman, her place was hardly worthy of notice. She had no man to defend her, provide for her or give her status in society. Yet God sent his prophet to her to be cared for and hidden from Ahab.

Or again, perhaps it's her social position which makes her forgettable. Without a male provider, a widow was the poorest of the poor—when Elijah arrives, she is preparing for death by starvation. She was one of the forgotten people, overlooked by family (if she had any) and neighbours. Thrown on life's scrap-heap she meant nothing to anyone. Yet God sent Elijah to her.

Perhaps, though, it's because she was a Gentile. One of the people of Jezebel's country of Sidon. Not one of the chosen of Israel, but an outsider, worshipping false gods. Hardly one of the great heroes of the Bible. Yet, again, it is to her that Elijah is sent by God.

Whatever the reason, her lack of a name in the story seems to show that she is a 'non-person', of no significance. Yet the story itself undermines that view, for she is the one God has commanded to look after Elijah. So what do we make of this insignificant person who is so significant?

Simply this: God finds her significant, no matter what other people may think. In a story that deals with the sins of kings, the wars of nations and the clash of prophets, an ordinary, insignificant person takes, for a time, the centre stage, and because of her, God's story can continue.

A prayer

Thank you Father, that I matter. Not because I am rich, or powerful or gifted, but because I matter to you.

MM

Never-ending story

He went off to Zarephath, and when he reached the entrance to the village, he saw a widow gathering sticks. He called to her, 'Please bring me a little water in a pitcher to drink.' As she went to fetch it, he called after her, 'Bring me, please, a piece of bread as well.' But she answered, 'As the Lord your God lives, I have no food baked, only a handful of flour in a jar and a little oil in a flask. I am just gathering two or three sticks to go and cook it for my son and myself before we die.' 'Have no fear,' said Elijah; 'go and do as you have said. But first make a small cake from what you have and bring it out to me, and after that make something for your son and yourself. For this is the word of the Lord the God of Israel: The jar of flour will not give out, nor the flask of oil fail, until the Lord sends rain on the land.' She went and did as Elijah had said, and there was food for him and for her and her family for a long time.

It is hard not to see an echo of the story of Jesus and the loaves and fishes which fed a multitude (or perhaps it is the other way round). And that is not strange, for all the Bible's stories are part of the one Story, the tale of salvation. From Genesis to Revelation, the story of God and his people is told, and we are in the midst of that story.

So here, and in the Gospels, and in our own lives, God takes the little we have to offer and uses it for his own purposes. With God, it is always enough.

In my own church, there is a woman who claims that she really has very little to offer for her work with the children's teaching ministry. Perhaps she is right—but she gets on very well. Because she is part of this story.

A reflection

It isn't what you have to offer to God that counts, but whether you offer it.

MM

Breath of life

Afterwards, the son of the woman, the owner of the house, fell ill and was in a very bad way, until at last his breathing stopped. The woman said to Elijah, 'What made you interfere, you man of God? You came here to bring my sins to light and cause my son's death!' 'Give me your son,' he said. He took the boy from her arms and carried him up to the roof-chamber where his lodging was, and laid him on the bed. He called out to the Lord, 'Lord my God, is this your care for the widow with whom I lodge, that you have been so cruel to her son?' Then he breathed deeply on the child three times, and called to the Lord, 'I pray, Lord my God, let the breath of life return to the body of this child.' The Lord listened to Elijah's cry, and the breath of life returned to the child's body, and he revived.

What is the key word in this story? Surely it is 'breath'. The boy doesn't simply 'die'—his breathing stops. It is his breath that Elijah uses to symbolize life, and returning breath that he prays for.

Breath is a major theme in the Bible, and all the more so when we remember that the words for breath and soul, wind and spirit are all related. In Genesis, God forms the first human from the soil, and *breathes* life into him.

Life is the gift of God, and not only physical life, but spiritual life. Elijah is a prophet, full of the Spirit/breath of God, and from that Spirit, new breath returns to the dead child.

In the Christian story, it is the Spirit of God who comes to bring new life, and by the breath of God we are born again. The new life that Jesus offers is life brought to us by the Holy Spirit who dwells in our hearts.

A way to pray

Turn your breathing into prayer. Concentrate on the flow of air into you, and make it a prayer that the Spirit of God will flow into all your life as the air brings life to every cell of your body.

MM

Up and down faith

Elijah lifted him and took him down from the roof-chamber into the house, and giving him to his mother he said, 'Look, your son is alive.' She said to Elijah, 'Now I know for certain that you are a man of God and that the word of the Lord on your lips is truth.'

Well, we might say, she ought to have got the idea from the way the flour and oil were still going strong. And of course, she did. The nameless widow knew Elijah was God's man, but as with all of us, her attitude to God swung wildly. No doubt she was thankful and awed by the miraculous supply of food. Then she was angry and guilty over her son's illness and death ('It's all my fault; God is punishing me for my sins'). Then she was overjoyed by his marvellous recovery.

In fact, what we take to be our spiritual state is more often due to our physical or emotional condition. We can probably all identify with the changes in the woman's attitude. Not long ago, I was afraid I was developing a serious illness. I prayed frantically, and rather bitterly and whiningly, but God seemed very far away. Then I was pronounced all clear (for now at least!) and I was ready to sing God's praises with all the company of heaven.

I don't really think I was any closer to God at any particular point of my ups and downs, but my normal human reactions told me otherwise. The point is that what I felt was normal and natural, as were the widow's various reactions. In our spiritual life, we need to take notice of our bodies and minds, and to be aware of the part they play in our prayer and feelings.

None of these feelings and attitudes is wrong, but they are a part of who we are, the person God created. Too often we try to separate our faith from the rest of us, and it simply can't be done.

A way to pray

Spend some time reflecting on your present situation; health, finances, family or whatever. How do they affect the way you feel? Make those feelings the basis of your prayer, as you offer them to God.

MM

Grace

You are a people holy to the Lord your God; the Lord your God chose you out of all nations on earth to be his special possession. It was not because you were more numerous than any other nation that the Lord cared for you and chose you, for you were the smallest of all nations; it was because the Lord loved you and stood by his oath to your forefathers, that he brought you out with his strong hand and redeemed you from the land of slavery, from the power of Pharaoh king of Egypt. Know then that the Lord your God is God, the faithful God . . .

One of the saddest things about many Christians is the way their faith is tinged with guilt. 'I know I ought to pray more . . .' 'I really ought to go to church more often . . .' 'I wish I was a better person . . .' Sometimes what we feel bad about is genuinely wrong. At other times it is imaginary. But whether the faults we lament are real or not, our guilt is based on a false idea of God.

In today's reading, Moses tells the Israelites that there is nothing special about them—except for the one important thing, that they belong to God. And they belong to God because he loved them and kept his promises, no matter what they were like.

We could do with remembering this. When we become aware of our faults and begin to feel guilty, we need to remember that God loves us. That is, he loves *us*—not some ideal of what we ought to be, but the real us, faults and all. He has chosen us, not because we are good, but simply out of love.

When we grasp that, our prayers and our worship are liberated from the feel-

ing that we ought to try harder to please him, and instead become a joyful celebration, not of our worth, but his gracious love. Today in your prayers, forget what you are like, and think only of what God is like—unconditionally loving.

MM

Secret hero

Time went by, and in the third year the word of the Lord came to Elijah: 'Go, appear before Ahab, and I shall send rain on the land.' So Elijah went to show himself to Ahab. At this time the famine in Samaria was at its height, and Ahab summoned Obadiah, the comptroller of his household, a devout worshipper of the Lord. When Jezebel massacred the prophets of the Lord, he had taken a hundred of them, hidden them in caves, fifty by fifty, and sustained them with food and drink. Ahab said to Obadiah, 'Let us go throughout the land to every spring and wadi; if we can find enough grass we may keep the horses and mules alive and not lose any of our animals.' They divided the land between them for their survey, Ahab himself going one way, and Obadiah another.

'The blood of the martyrs,' wrote the church Father, Irenaeus, 'is the seed of the church.' And so it is. Those whose faithfulness to God stands firm up to the point of death are a witness (*martyros* in Greek) to the Lordship of Christ and his claim to our first obedience. But martyrdom is a gift of God which is not given to everyone. In times of persecution, there are always those who stand by their faith quietly and in an unspectacular way work for God.

One such person was Obadiah. A high official in Ahab's government, he remained faithful to the Lord of Israel and was able to use his power to save the lives of many of the prophets who were threatened by the queen's zeal for her god.

Again we see a minor character in the story who yet has an important role. And he is a reminder (as God will later remind Elijah) that true faith can never be stamped out—try as they will, the forces of evil will never extinguish it. One of the most moving news items I have ever seen was a picture of a priest in Romania celebrating Mass in a city square on Christmas Eve after the end of communism. A crowd of thousands heard for the first time the meaning of Christmas.

So pray for those of your fellow Christians who hold the faith quietly and in adversity, treasuring the flame against the time when once again it will burn brightly.

MM

Unpleasant tasks

As Obadiah went on his way, Elijah suddenly confronted him. Obadiah recognized Elijah and prostrated himself before him. 'Can it really be you, my lord Elijah?' he said. 'Yes,' he replied, 'it is I. Go and tell your master that Elijah is here.' 'What wrong have I done?' protested Obadiah. 'Why should you give me into Ahab's hands? He will put me to death. As the Lord your God lives, there is no region or kingdom to which my master has not sent in search of you. If they said, "He is not here," he made that kingdom or region swear an oath that you could not be found. Yet now you say, "Go and tell your master that Elijah is here." What will happen? As soon as I leave you, the spirit of the Lord will carry you away, who knows where? I shall go and tell Ahab, and when he fails to find you he will kill me . . .' Elijah answered, 'As the Lord of Hosts lives, whose servant I am, I swear that I shall show myself to him this day.' So Obadiah went to find Ahab and gave him the message, and Ahab went to confront Elijah.

It has been said that the reward for doing a difficult task is to be set a harder one. After a life of faithful and often dangerous service, Obadiah finds himself confronted with an apparent command to commit suicide.

If we think for a few moments we can probably sympathize. Do you remember that time when you really believed that you should do something that was right, that was God's will, but it filled you with fear?

We know too, that Jesus himself faced the same fear—knowing God's will, but seeing the task as too great for human courage. Yet Jesus knew that God was to be trusted. Obadiah was to find that, too. And so must we. God doesn't set us tasks without giving us the power to see them through.

A reflection

Is there any task you face which seems too much? Is it the right thing to do? Then thank God for the strength he has ready for you, and trust him for it.

MM

Different viewpoints

As soon as Ahab saw Elijah, he said to him, 'Is it you, you troubler of Israel?' 'It is not I who have brought trouble on Israel,' Elijah replied, 'but you and your father's family, by forsaking the commandments of the Lord and following Baal. Now summon all Israel to meet me on Mount Carmel, including the four hundred and fifty prophets of Baal and the four hundred prophets of the goddess Asherah, who are attached to Jezebel's household.' So Ahab sent throughout the length and breadth of Israel and assembled the prophets on Mount Carmel.

Perhaps it's fanciful, but I feel I can detect a certain respect between Ahab and Elijah. Ahab knows (though he will not admit it) that Elijah is indeed a prophet of the God of Israel—though that God is troublesome and prone not to keep in his proper place; not at all like the more convenient gods of his neighbours. Elijah knows that Ahab is still the king of God's people, and for that reason not entirely abandoned by God.

Each sees the other as the cause of Israel's problems. The troublesome prophet of a troublesome God, interfering in politics and economics and all kinds of non-religious affairs faces the worldly-wise king, leading his people into strong alliances and economic prosperity, and away from God. Perhaps they should just agree to differ, live and let live, and let people choose their own religion and their own lifestyle?

But that won't do. Elijah knows that in the end there is no middle ground, no balancing of options. There is God or nothing.

A reflection

What do you try to balance out with God? What other things do you give equal weight to, or try to keep separate from the life of faith? How successful are you?

MM

Moment of truth

Elijah stepped forward towards all the people there and said, 'How long will you sit on the fence? If the Lord is God, follow him; but if Baal, then follow him.' Not a word did they answer. Then Elijah said, 'I am the only prophet of the Lord still left, but there are four hundred and fifty prophets of Baal. Bring two bulls for us. Let them choose one for themselves, cut it up, and lay it on the wood without setting fire to it, and I shall prepare the other and lay it on the wood without setting fire to it. Then invoke your god by name and I shall invoke the Lord by name; the god who answers by fire, he is God.' The people all shouted their approval.

Well, they would, wouldn't they? What a spectacle; and no admission fee! But how many realized what Elijah was truly saying? Today the people of Israel faced a great choice. It was the choice that Moses had put to their ancestors, and Joshua after him: 'Choose today whom you will serve.'

Like their king they were sitting on the fence. Not exactly denying God, but allowing themselves plenty of room for other options. But they had to make up their minds. There could be no half measures with God.

What Elijah was offering was not truly a once for all choice. It was a commitment to a life of choice. Each day we are faced with hundreds of choices, and in many of them God has a part to play. We choose afresh each day whether to serve God. On waking, as we commit the day to him (or not), as we meet people who annoy us and we respond in love and forgiveness (or not), as we give precious time to friends and family (or not), as we accept opportunities to do good (or not).

We often fail to make the right choice. But there is good news in our story too—God had given the choice to Israel before, but he was still willing to come back and offer it again. In the grace of God, failure is never final, as long as we are willing to make the right choice again.

A way to pray

Offer to God your choices and ask for his guidance. Offer your failures and ask him for his forgiveness.

MM

Triumph

Elijah said to the prophets of Baal, 'Choose one of the bulls and offer it first, for there are more of you; invoke your god by name, but do not set fire to the wood.' . . . and they invoked Baal by name from morning until noon, crying, 'Baal, answer us'; but there was no sound, no answer . . . At midday Elijah mocked them: 'Call louder, for he is a god. It may be he is in deep thought, or engaged, or on a journey . . .' All afternoon they raved and ranted till the time of the regular offering, but still there was no sound, no answer, no sign of attention . . . At the hour of the regular offering, the prophet Elijah came forward and prayed . . . The fire of the Lord fell, consuming the whole-offering, the wood, the stones, and the earth, and licking up the water in the trench. At the sight, the people all bowed with their faces to the ground and cried, 'The Lord is God, the Lord is God.' They [the prophets of Baal] were seized, and Elijah took them down to the Kishon and slaughtered them there in the valley.

The power of God is demonstrated without a doubt. Even soaked and surrounded with water, the sacrifice is ignited, and the people rise up and do away with the prophets of the false god. A terrible and bloody triumph, but one which is bound to restore Israel to the right path. The drought is ended, as God pours rain and blessing on his people.

It seems the perfect ending. The wicked witch is dead, the hero is victorious, and the people live happily ever after. If only life were really like that. But we know that our moments of joy and triumph are undermined by the future. The story for us goes on, and there will be sorrow and failure ahead.

Wait a bit, though. Elijah's story isn't over either. There is sorrow and failure for him too. But that can't remove the fact of this victory. Perhaps we could learn from him that moments of glory are the gift of God and should be thankfully received. We know that our moments of joy and wonder are not for ever, but don't let that detract from what we receive.

A way to pray

Think of your times of wonder and triumph, and give thanks for them.

MM

Despair

When Ahab told Jezebel all that Elijah had done and how he had put all the prophets to the sword, she sent this message to Elijah, 'The gods do the same to me and more, unless by this time tomorrow I have taken your life as you took theirs.' In fear he fled for his life, and when he reached Beersheba in Judah he left his servant there, while he himself went a day's journey into the wilderness. He came to a broom bush, and sitting under it he prayed for death: 'It is enough,' he said, 'now, Lord, take away my life, for I am no better than my fathers before me.'

It should have been so different. The people should have demanded a return to the old ways of God. Ahab, surely convinced by the miracle of Carmel, should have sent Jezebel home and broken off the alliance she represented. The great event should have sparked renewal in Israel. Instead, the queen was firmly in charge of Ahab and Israel, and out for blood. Surely evil was triumphant.

Part of the problem was no doubt the Israelites. They had had their revival meeting and seen great wonders. But now they were back on their farms and life seemed much the same as usual. Elijah too was back to earth with a bump. Religious fervour is so hard to sustain.

Perhaps we also know the feeling. God is so close, the power of his Spirit almost tangible. We can do anything. (Elijah ran for miles ahead of Ahab's chariot.) Then it all fades, and we doubt even the memory.

But as we saw yesterday, the great events are special gifts. The real business of knowing God is about everyday life. We are not made for a continual high (at least not in this life). We are made to serve God in the everyday business of his world, and the real test of faith is not the frequency of great spiritual experiences but the continual working out of our relationship with God. And when we get that right, there is joy of a different kind.

A way to pray

Look at the day ahead of you and what you know you will be doing. Offer each activity to God in advance.

MM

Uncontrollable God

God spoke, and these were his words: I am the Lord your God who brought you out of Egypt, out of the land of slavery. You shall have no other god to set against me. You shall not make a carved image for yourself nor the likeness of anything in the heavens above, or on the earth below, or in the waters under the earth.

When I was a student, an Old Testament lecturer commented that many of the prophets really didn't understand the idolatry they condemned. They laughed at other nations for worshipping gods of stone and wood, but no one really believed that the idol was the god—it was a focus for the presence of the god and an aid to worship. Looked at in that light, the commandment against idols seems a bit extreme.

But I think the prophets understood idolatry all too well. Of course the idol wasn't thought to be the god. But that isn't the point. An idol gave an idea of what the god was like, and brought it down to human scale. It gave a sense of control over the god. And the true God cannot be limited by human imagination. The commandment against idolatry is saying, 'Don't think you can control God; he alone knows what he is like.' Or as he put it to Moses, 'I am who I am.' Not what we like to think he is.

Yet in time, God did provide an image of himself. Not a model or statue, but a living human being, in whom we see God: Jesus Christ.

When we pray, we are to pray not to the God we imagine, or the God we would like to have, but to the real God. And, thank God, we have an image we can grasp, yet which still stretches our understanding, as we pray to the Father through his Son.

MM

Help on the way

[Elijah] lay down under the bush and, while he slept, an angel touched him and said, 'Rise and eat.' He looked, and there at his head was a cake baked on hot stones, and a pitcher of water. He ate and drank and lay down again. The angel of the Lord came again and touched him a second time, saying, 'Rise and eat; the journey is too much for you.' He rose and ate and drank and, sustained by this food, he went on for forty days and forty nights to Horeb, the mount of God. There he entered a cave where he spent the night.

The picture of Elijah's exhaustion (emotional and spiritual as well as physical) is as realistic as that of his despair. He slumps at the end of his tether, and rises only to take food before collapsing again. Even the marvellous provider of the food is not enough to excite a spark of interest.

Elijah's story is not one of high-flying spirituality. Like ours, it is a tale with its own share of weariness and defeat. But along the way, Elijah receives help; unexpected and miraculous—and nothing like enough.

Or at least, so it might have seemed to him. What he would have needed was surely a full return to strength, and the assurance that he would triumph in the end. But what he gets is a couple of meals and a long walk. In the end though, it turns out to be enough after all.

Time and again we discover that God is not the instant cure for all our problems. In grief or sorrow, anguish or despair, we call to him—and the final all-satisfying answer to our troubles fails to appear. What does come, however, is the strength or the courage or determination to take a few more steps through our troubles, until at last, like Elijah, we pass through them.

The simple fact is that though our road may often seem weary, it is generally the only one we can follow to reach the point that God is taking us to. Along the way we get his help. It is often not the help we could wish for, but it is always what we need.

A reflection

'My grace is sufficient for you.'

2 Corinthians 12:9 (RSV)

MM

Restoration

The word of the Lord came to him: 'Why are you here, Elijah?' 'Because of my great zeal for the Lord, the God of Hosts,' he replied. 'The people of Israel have forsaken your covenant, torn down your altars, and put your prophets to the sword. I alone am left, and they seek to take my life.' To this the answer came: 'Go and stand on the mount before the Lord.' The Lord was passing by: a great and strong wind came, rending mountains and shattering rocks before him, but the Lord was not in the wind; and after the wind there was an earthquake, but the Lord was not in the earthquake; and after the earthquake fire, but the Lord was not in the fire; and after the fire a faint murmuring sound. When Elijah heard it, he wrapped his face in his cloak and went and stood in the entrance to the cave. There came a voice: 'Why are you here, Elijah?'

Elijah can only repeat his earlier words. He is here because he has been faithful to God—and see what a mess that has got him into! It is a cry of self-pity, and a cry of doubt. If God is so great, if God has called Elijah to be his prophet, if God has shown himself able to work marvels, then why is everything coming apart?

God's answer is simple, and tomorrow we shall see it. For now, it is more important simply to see what Elijah is doing. He is complaining to God. There is a great tradition in the Bible of complaint to God, and we need to take it seriously. At the simplest level it is better to scream and shout at God than to ignore him or give up on him.

We get a flavour of this in Jesus' Gethsemane prayer, where anguish almost leads to rebellion against God's will. But the important thing is to keep the channel of communication open. As long as we do that, God will respond.

A way to pray

Bring out into the open all your doubts and fears; the thoughts that you are ashamed to admit are there, the questioning of God's love and goodness, his power and compassion. Lay them before God—but don't expect a clearer answer than Elijah (or Jesus) got.

MM

Faith

The Lord said to him, 'Go back by way of the wilderness of Damascus, enter the city, and anoint Hazael to be king of Aram; anoint also Jehu son of Nimshi to be king of Israel, and Elisha son of Shaphat of Abel-meholah to be prophet in your place. Whoever escapes the sword of Hazael Jehu will slay, and whoever escapes the sword of Jehu Elisha will slay. But I shall leave seven thousand in Israel, all who have not bowed the knee to Baal, all whose lips have not kissed him.'

Elijah has come, after a long journey, to the place where God made his covenant with the people of Israel. On the way, he has been supported by God, and here he has poured out his grief and despair. Surely, now that God has met him to his face, he will find out the answer to his fears and desperation?

At first sight, it seems not. All that happens is that he is given a list of new jobs to do. But with them comes a promise—that God is in charge, and that the new tasks will lead to a revolution in Israel which will put the nation back on God's path.

For Elijah and us there are several lessons here. Firstly, Elijah is not alone; there are seven thousand Israelites (no small number in those days) who are still faithful to God. It is Elijah's pride which has led him to think that he is alone, and that he is the only one that God can depend on.

With that news comes the further revelation that Elijah's task will not end in his lifetime. Just as we are part of the one great story, so is Elijah. His work is only a part of the whole work of God, and it will go on far beyond his death.

But by far the greatest news is that though everything has seemed pointless, God is working out his plan. He knows what will come of Elijah's work (and ours). Our part is to trust him and carry on with the job we have been given.

A prayer

Thank you, Father, that you are in charge. When things seem hopeless to me, remind me that you know what you are doing, and give me the grace to carry on with the task that is my part of the whole story.

MM

True owner

Elijah departed and found Elisha son of Shaphat ploughing; there were twelve pair of oxen ahead of him, and he himself was with the last of them. As Elijah passed, he threw his cloak over him. Elisha, leaving his oxen, ran after Elijah and said, 'Let me kiss my father and mother goodbye, and then I shall follow you.' 'Go back,' he replied, 'what have I done to prevent you?' He followed him no farther but went home, took his pair of oxen, slaughtered them, and burnt the wooden yokes to cook the flesh, which he gave to the people to eat. He then followed Elijah and became his disciple.

To anyone who has read the Gospels, there is a sense of familiarity in this story. Elijah's throwing of his cloak is more dramatic than Jesus' call of his disciples, but the overall effect is the same. Elisha leaves his home and family and sets off to be the disciple and eventual successor to Elijah.

In outward appearance, there is a world of a difference between Elisha's experience and ours. He, like the Galilean fishermen, was called to be a wandering preacher and prophet. We, for the most part, stay at home and strive to serve God in our normal lives. He sacrificed his greatest possessions to God, we are taught to keep them well as part of our Christian stewardship. At a deeper level, though, there is (or should be) a close similarity. Elisha could sacrifice his oxen and their gear because he already saw them not as his, but as God's. He was able to leave home because his first commitment was not to his farm work but to God.

You could say that the call of Elisha only confirmed what was already true of him: that God was his first love. Even though we are unlikely to be called to drop everything and head off into the wide blue yonder, it is worth asking whether we could. Are we so wedded to our present lives and possessions that God could not separate us from them? Or do we truly see them as his, held in trust and used for his service?

A reflection

All things come from you, and of your own do we give you . . .

Alternative Service Book

MM

Never too late

The word of the Lord came to Elijah the Tishbite: 'Go down at once to King Ahab of Israel, who is in Samaria; you will find him in Naboth's vineyard, where he has gone to take possession . . . Say to him, "This is the word of the Lord: Where dogs licked the blood of Naboth, there dogs will lick your blood." ' Ahab said to Elijah, 'So you have found me, my enemy.' 'Yes,' he said, 'because you have sold yourself to do what is wrong in the eyes of the Lord. I shall bring disaster on you; I shall sweep you away and destroy every mother's son of the house of Ahab in Israel, whether under the protection of the family or not . . .' When Ahab heard Elijah's words, he tore his clothes, put on sackcloth, and fasted; he lay down in his sackcloth and went about moaning. The word of the Lord came to Elijah the Tishbite: 'Have you seen how Ahab has humbled himself before me? Because he has thus humbled himself, I shall not bring disaster on his house in his own lifetime, but in that of his son.'

We often get the impression that God in the Old Testament is seen as implacably angry. But that isn't true. The prophecies of judgment so often come about not because God won't listen to repentance, but because his hearers are implacably sinful. At last, Ahab repents, and doom is averted, at least for a time.

Don't forget that the Old Testament knows almost nothing of real life after death. For Ahab, the words of God are equivalent to salvation. He has repented and God has responded with forgiveness.

First, though, he had to have his nose rubbed in his misdeeds. It is easy to fall into a habit of ignoring God, perhaps in only one area of our lives. Then we become accustomed to sin—what the Bible calls hardness of heart. God's only way to get through to us is to deal harshly with us and force us to turn back to him. It's painful, but it's grace.

A reflection

Have there been times in your life when God has dealt with you harshly? Do you have the courage to thank him for the lesson?

MM

End of an episode

Fifty of the prophets followed [Elijah and Elisha], and stood watching as the two of them stopped by the Jordan. Elijah took his cloak, rolled it up, and struck the water with it. The water divided to right and left, and both crossed over on dry ground. While they were crossing, Elijah said to Elisha, 'Tell me what I can do for you before I am taken from you.' Elisha said, 'Let me inherit a double share of your spirit.' 'You have asked a hard thing,' said Elijah. 'If you see me taken from you, your wish will be granted; if you do not, it will not be granted.' They went on, talking as they went, and suddenly there appeared a chariot of fire and horses of fire, which separated them from one another, and Elijah was carried up to heaven in a whirlwind. At the sight Elisha cried out, 'My father, my father, the chariot and the horsemen of Israel!' and he saw him no more. He clutched hold of his mantle and tore it in two. He picked up the cloak which had fallen from Elijah, and went back and stood on the bank of the Jordan. There he struck the water with Elijah's cloak, saying as he did so, 'Where is the Lord, the God of Elijah?' As he too struck the water, it divided to right and left, and he crossed over.

The double share that Elisha asks for doesn't mean that he wants to be twice the prophet Elijah was. It is simply a way of asking to inherit Elijah's business as God's prophet to Israel. And he does. As he strikes the water, and the Jordan rolls back, the watching prophets exclaim that the spirit of Elijah is still here. Indeed it is, for it is God's Spirit, and the work of God continues. The story of God has no neat ending, but goes on throughout history. With the passing of Elijah, the story does not end, but simply enters a new episode. For Christians, the story has an added meaning. Since Pentecost, the Spirit who was in Elijah is the Spirit of the Church. All of us bear the prophet's mantle. If the waters don't roll back before us, that is nothing compared to the fact that the word of God is still spoken; by him to us, and by us to others.

MM

A thank you letter

In the early Church they didn't have Bibles. They had the Old Testament Scriptures written on scrolls—and those would be read out regularly in synagogue (which the Jewish Christians still went to when they were allowed in). But the New Testament as we know it was still being written—and a lot of it consists of letters written to young churches.

For the next four weeks we are going to look at just one of these letters—Paul's letter to the Philippians. When it arrived by messenger (not in a envelope with a stamp on it delivered by a postman) the Christians in Philippi would have been called together by the elders of the church, and the letter would have been read out. Probably over and over again in the coming months and years (as well as circulated to other churches in the Middle East) and talked about and discussed.

Philippians is a thank you letter. About Paul's thankfulness and delight in the Philippians (and for the gift they had sent him, though that is almost incidental) and about his thankfulness for all that God has done and is. And he tells the Philippians to be thankful too, and to rejoice in God.

May you always be joyful in your union with the Lord. I say it again: rejoice. Don't worry about anything, but in all your prayers ask God for what you need, always asking him with a thankful heart. And God's peace, which is far beyond human understanding, will keep your hearts and minds safe in union with Christ Jesus.

Philippians 4:4–7 (GNB)

Home again

While he was yet at a distance, his father saw him and had compassion, and ran and embraced him and kissed him. And the son said to him, 'Father, I have sinned against heaven and before you; I am no longer worthy to be called your son.' But the father said to his servants, 'Bring quickly the best robe, and put it on him; and put a ring on his hand, and shoes on his feet; and bring the fatted calf and kill it, and let us eat and make merry; for this my son was dead; and is alive again; he was lost, and is found.' And they began to make merry.

When we hear again a familiar story, we can sometimes be struck by something entirely new. I have always seen the tale of the prodigal son as being about forgiveness (which it is) but today a new thought struck me. It is also about belonging.

One of Augustine's most famous sentences is the prayer, 'You have made us for yourself, O God, and our hearts are restless till they find their rest in you.' Meeting God is about coming home.

We are indeed restless in much of our lives. We are beset by worries and demands on our time, our skills and our love. But when we are with God, we should relax, for we are at home, in the bosom of the family, and have nothing to prove, no one to impress.

Today as you prepare to worship, to pray, to take Communion, think about this. In the midst of worship we are in our family, and at home, accepted for what we are.

MM

In Christ in prison

Paul and Timothy, servants of Christ Jesus, To all the saints in Christ Jesus who are at Philippi, with the bishops and deacons: Grace to you and peace from God our Father and the Lord Jesus Christ.

I thank my God in all my remembrance of you, always in every prayer of mine for you all making my prayer with joy, thankful for your partnership in the gospel from the first day until now.

Paul was sitting in a Roman prison remembering. But it wasn't a sad remembering—feeling sorry for himself as he looked back to happier days. Paul's heart was welling up within him—in immense thankfulness to God for all the people who thronged into his mind, the people to whom he was writing this letter. They were all the saints in Philippi—and for Paul that meant all the believers in Christ Jesus. Saints because they belonged to Christ, and were therefore sanctified and holy.

They weren't yet all they would be (more of that tomorrow) but they were "in Christ", and they had been partners with Paul in telling out the good news about God in Christ ever since the start of their life in Christ. They belonged to Christ—and so did Paul and Timothy. They were the slaves of Christ, and a slave belonged to his master for ever. He couldn't go off and get another job with another master. Paul gloried in the fact that he belonged utterly to his beloved God.

Paul's beloved Christians in Philippi also belonged to God—and in Christ, in his prison cell, Paul prayed for them. A stream of joy welled up in his heart and flowed out in a bubbling thankfulness. It streamed into the presence of God and took the Philippians along with it. Paul wanted them to know the grace of God and the peace of God. Grace was the Greek word of greeting and peace was the Jewish word of greeting. Paul put them together and prayed for the beauty, joy and pleasure of grace, and the total well-being of peace, in the only way those things could ever be really known. Through a relationship with God in Christ.

A way to pray

Remember the past—and the people who have been important to you in your Christian life. Remember the people to whom you have been important. And let a stream of joy and thankfulness to God well up within you.

SB

Grow, know and love

And I am sure that he who began a good work in you will bring it to completion at the day of Jesus Christ. It is right for me to feel thus about you all, because I hold you in my heart, for you are all partakers with me of grace, both in my imprisonment and in the defence and confirmation of the gospel. For God is my witness, how I yearn for you all with the affection of Christ Jesus. And it is my prayer that your love may abound more and more, with knowledge and all discernment, so that you may approve what is excellent, and may be pure and blameless for the day of Christ, filled with the fruits of righteousness which come through Jesus Christ, to the glory and praise of God.

The person who 'began a good work' in the Christians in Philippi wasn't Paul. It was God the Holy Spirit—the one who, as it says in the Church of England baptism service, 'sanctifies the people of God'. The beginning of the Spirit's work is set out in chapter 3 of the Gospel of John. It tells how Nicodemus came to Jesus by night, to find out who he really was. The Spirit had begun a good work in Nicodemus by bringing him to Jesus. But that was only the start of it. Jesus said to Nicodemus, 'Unless one is born of water and the Spirit he cannot enter the kingdom of God. That which is born of the flesh is flesh, and that which is born of the Spirit is spirit' (3:6).

Every Christian is born again as a baby in Christ—and just as a baby has to grow so do we. Our Christian life grows through our prayers, through our Bible reading, through Holy Communion and through fellowship with God and with our brothers and sisters in Christ. Just the things which the BRF was created to foster. And the Christian life of the Philippians grew as Paul prayed for them.

A way to pray

Read Paul's prayer aloud, starting at 'And it is my prayer that your love may abound . . .' Pray it for your church and for yourself.

SB

Who'd have thought it

I want you to know, brethren, that what has happened to me has really served to advance the gospel, so that it has become known throughout the whole praetorian guard and to all the rest that my imprisonment is for Christ; and most of the brethren have been made confident in the Lord because of my imprisonment, and are much more bold to speak the word of God without fear.

Just a few weeks ago I was in a prison, talking with some of the men who were in there. Some of them were in 'for life'— and most of the small group who met with me were also 'in Christ'. One of them said to me, 'It doesn't matter being in prison any more because Jesus is in here'—and he thumped his chest. I had gone to meet with them because they wanted the BRF to produce some material that would speak to the hearts of men and women in other prisons. They could say from the depth of their hearts what Paul said from the depth of his, that 'what has happened to me has really served to advance the gospel'.

In Paul's case the gospel was made known 'throughout the whole praetorian guard, and to all the rest', because every day Paul would have been chained to one of the guards. Paul couldn't escape from the guards, but neither could the guards escape from him, and with every changing of the guard Paul would have talked again about the gospel message. He also wrote about it—when he was in his prison cell and when he wasn't.

In one of the letters he wrote to the Christians in Corinth he summed up the gospel message and also his own mission and purpose in life: 'If anyone is in Christ, he is a new creation; the old has passed away, behold, the new has come. All this is from God, who through Christ reconciled us to himself and gave us the ministry of reconciliation; that is, in Christ, God was reconciling the world to himself, not counting their trespasses against them, and entrusting to us the message of reconciliation. So we are ambassadors for Christ, God making his appeal through us. We beseech you on behalf of Christ, be reconciled to God' (2 Corinthians 5:17–20).

A prayer

Pray for men and women in prison—for those who know Christ and those who don't. Think of something that has happened to you that you would never have chosen—and think how it has (or could) really serve to advance the gospel.

SB

264

Preaching and praying

Some indeed preach Christ from envy and rivalry, but others from good will. The latter do it out of love, knowing that I am put here for the defence of the gospel; the former proclaim Christ out of partisanship, not sincerely but thinking to afflict me in my imprisonment. What then? Only that in every way, whether in pretence or in truth, Christ is proclaimed; and in that I rejoice. Yes, and I shall rejoice, for I know that through your prayers and the help of the Spirit of Jesus Christ this will turn out for my deliverance, as it is my eager expectation and hope that I shall not be at all ashamed, but that with full courage now as always Christ will be honoured in my body, whether by life or by death.

Paul had an astonishingly big heart. Imagine rejoicing that someone is preaching the gospel with a double agenda: (1) To preach it. (2) To do it better than Paul and put him down. But they didn't manage to. He went on rejoicing and he went on praying. I haven't a shadow of doubt that he prayed for them as well as for all the others. And he wanted people to pray for him.

As I write these notes Terry Waite has not long been released from prison, and he told of the enormous comfort of hearing on the BBC World Service (when he was allowed a radio) that people were still remembering him. Paul wouldn't have known how many people were remembering him and praying for him. But God knew, and their prayers would have had a profound effect for Paul in his prison.

I suppose that God could have given Paul all the help he needed even if people hadn't prayed. He *could* have. But it seems that in some ways God somehow links his action with our prayers. Jesus said, "Ask, and it will be given you" (Luke 11:9) and told us to pray to the Father, "Thy will be done." So if we don't ask it won't be given, and if we don't pray then the Father's will won't be done.

A thought and a prayer

Think about who you pray for. Name some people, and some situations. Think about how you pray. Doubtfully, or rejoicingly? Then pray, confident and rejoicing in the power and the love of God.

SB

Christ—here and there

For to me to live is Christ, and to die is gain. If it is to be life in the flesh, that means fruitful labour for me. Yet which I shall choose I cannot tell. I am hard pressed between the two. My desire is to depart and be with Christ, for that is far better. But to remain in the flesh is more necessary on your account. Convinced of this, I know that I shall remain and continue with you all, for your progress and joy in the faith, so that in me you may have ample cause to glory in Christ Jesus, because of my coming to you again.

Paul knew that he was facing a death sentence. Finally it was passed, and tradition tells us that he was put to death in Rome. But Paul was certain that death would be even better than life here on earth. He could say, 'For to me to live is Christ'—and all his letters tell of his love for Christ and his delight in the richness of the relationship. He struggled to express the inexpressible: 'The life I now live is not my life, but the life which Christ lives in me,' (Galatians 2:20)—and that made Paul more fully himself, not less.

Here in this life Paul was suffering, and so were other Christians. But he could write, 'I consider that the sufferings of this present time are not worth comparing with the glory that is to be revealed in us,' (Romans 8:18) and that 'This slight momentary affliction is preparing for us an eternal weight of glory beyond all comparison.' (2 Corinthians 4:17) Life on the other side would be glorious beyond believing—so his desire was to depart from this life and be with Christ in that one. But he could say to God the Father what God the Son had

said to him when he was a man on this earth: 'Not as I will, but as you will' (Matthew 26:39). It wasn't really Paul's choice whether he lived or died. But it seemed that his Christian converts needed him. So he would remain with them—for as long as need be.

A reflection

Do you desire to depart from this life to be with Christ in that one—the eternal life in the nearer presence of God, where you will know 'an eternal weight of glory beyond all comparison'? If you do, reflect on the glory of Christ that you will know then, and on the glory that you know now. And pray for those who don't know it ...

SB

A doubtful privilege

Only let your manner of life be worthy of the gospel of Christ, so that whether I come and see you or am absent, I may hear of you that you stand firm in one spirit, with one mind striving side by side for the faith of the gospel, and not frightened in anything by your opponents. This is a clear omen to them of their destruction, but of your salvation, and that from God. For it has been granted to you that for the sake of Christ you should not only believe in him but also suffer for his sake, engaged in the same conflict which you saw and now hear to be mine.

Paul's own manner of life was 'worthy of the gospel of Christ'—and he wanted the same thing to be true for the Christians in Philippi. He was confident that through their prayers and the help of the Holy Spirit 'with full courage now as always Christ will be honoured (or glorified) in my body, whether by life or death' (1:19–20). These Christians would need the same courage, and the same Spirit, so that they could stand firm in the faith. And they would suffer in the process.

Suffering seems a fairly doubtful privilege to be granted—a privilege that most of us would prefer to do without. But suffering is at the heart of the Christian faith. In the Western world we don't seem to experience it at its worst, in the form of terrible persecutions and torture and imprisonment. But to take our faith seriously, and to obey the ten commandments, will mean that we shall experience a degree of suffering—some of it very severe. Really to keep the seventh commandment in our sex-mad world is going to cost us. To keep the eighth commandment can cost us our job, and I heard recently of a man in the City of London who lost his because he refused to go along with a common practice in his firm that was tantamount to stealing.

A prayer

Lord Jesus, if I'm honest I don't really want the privilege of suffering—even for your sake. Show me why I must—and help me to understand the privilege of it. Give me some courage. Help me to be brave, and really to keep your law and your commandments in a world that despises them.

SB

The man who saw Jesus

Entering Jericho, Jesus made his way through the city. There was a man there named Zacchaeus; he was superintendent of taxes, and very rich. He was eager to see what Jesus looked like; but, being a little man, he could not see him for the crowd. So he ran on ahead and climbed a sycamore-tree in order to see him . . . When Jesus came to the place, he looked up and said, 'Zacchaeus, be quick and come down; I must come and stay with you today.' . . . At this there was a general murmur of disapproval. 'He has gone in,' they said, 'to be the guest of a sinner.' But Zacchaeus stood there and said to the Lord, 'Here and now, sir, I give half my possessions to charity; and if I have cheated anyone, I am ready to repay him four times over.' Jesus said to him, 'Salvation has come to this house today!—for this man too is a son of Abraham, and the Son of Man has come to seek and save what is lost.'

Have you noticed that we are not actually told that Zacchaeus was dishonest? In fact, if he was in a position to repay four times over anything he may have got by cheating, even after giving away half his wealth, there can't have been much that was truly ill-gotten.

What seems more obviously to be the problem is that he was willing to accept contempt and disapproval from his neighbours for working for the Romans, for the sake of wealth.

However that may be, the coming of Jesus into his life brings about restoration to the community of the people of God; 'This man too is a son of Abraham.' Jesus has opened Zacchaeus' eyes to things more important than wealth and self. And Jesus' words proclaim to all around that Zacchaeus is restored to fellowship.

This is the idea which lies behind sharing the 'peace' in many communion services. Here in the centre of our worship we celebrate and affirm our fellowship, and have the opportunity to greet those we usually don't get on with too well. For Jesus has invited us and them to dine, and together we make up the people of God.

MM

You're great!

So if there is any encouragement in Christ, any incentive of love, any participation in the Spirit, any affection and sympathy, complete my joy by being of the same mind, having the same love, being in full accord and of one mind. Do nothing from selfishness or conceit, but in humility count others better than yourselves. Let each of you look not only to his own interests, but also to the interest of others.

Christians ought not to be selfish or conceited, but we often are. Our selfishness and conceit spoil and divide the Church, and the unbelievers look at us and laugh—not amused, but mocking and despising.

Love and unity are not automatic in the Christian life. We have to look to ourselves and to the Spirit to live out our new lives in Christ. We have to realize how much God loves us (which will mean reflecting on our faith, and knowing it, and praying it in) and then love other people with the same love.

When Paul says 'in humility count others better than yourselves,' he isn't saying, 'Pretend...' that (for example) someone is a superb administrator when they are manifestly hopeless. If you or I are good at something then we can be pleased, and deeply thankful, and give God the glory for it. And we can be aware of our infinite importance and preciousness to God. Your soul is worth more than the whole world, and so is mine. We know that because Jesus said that if a man should gain the whole world and lose his own soul (or his true self) then he wouldn't make a profit but a loss.

But then we can forget about ourselves, for the time being, and put other people in the spotlight. We can delight in what they do—and even more in what they are: beloved children of God (and our brothers and sisters) and precious to him and to us. We can affirm them and tell them these things. It's a way of expressing love.

A reflection

Reflect on what it means to count others better than yourself, in humility. Think of your own value. Then think of a person you know of whom you haven't a very high opinion. Pray for him, or for her, and spend some time thinking of that person's preciousness to God, and also what he or she is good at.

SB

The glory of God

Have this mind among yourselves, which is yours in Christ Jesus, who, though he was in the form of God, did not count equality with God a thing to be grasped, but emptied himself, taking the form of a servant, being born in the likeness of men. And being found in human form he humbled himself and became obedient unto death, even death on a cross. Therefore God has highly exalted him and bestowed on him the name which is above every name, that at the name of Jesus every knee should bow, in heaven and on earth and under the earth, and every tongue confess that Jesus Christ is Lord, to the glory of God the Father.

Today's passage is a hymn of praise to the wonder and glory of Christ—one of the greatest that has ever been written. If, as Christians, we want to know how to act in this world, we can find out by discovering how God acted in this world—and this passage tells us.

He wasn't, and isn't, a God who hangs on to his dignity and high position and refuses to let it go. Our God abandons his glory and comes down to us just where we are. The servant king, born in a stable in Bethlehem. A friend of publicans and sinners—the outcasts of society. (I wonder who he would be friendly with in our society?) Some of those outcasts were prostitutes. Others were Jews who collected taxes for the occupying Roman authorities from their brother Jews, who hated them for it. But the God who became a man and a servant (and a Jew) loved them. So much that he died for them (and for us) by hanging on a cross. The glory of God shone out of him when he was a man in our world and he said that he was the light of the world. It shone out brightest of all from the cross, where he was obedient to death—and to God.

A way to pray

Spend some time reflecting on the nature of God—made known in Jesus Christ. Think of God—our creator, our servant and our lover. Christ died for love of us— to suffer for our sins and to bring us to the Father. Think of the glory of God that shone out of Jesus and showed us what God is like. Then confess, out loud (if you believe it) that 'Jesus Christ is Lord'.

SB

God—at work in you

Therefore, my beloved, as you have always obeyed, so now, not only as in my presence but much more in my absence, work out your own salvation with fear and trembling; for God is at work in you, both to will and to work for his good pleasure.

When Paul wants people to do something he tells them the facts and sets out the relevant Christian truths. Then he says 'Therefore...' He does it in several of his letters, several times in each, and he does it here. He tells us of the glory of God shown to us in the incarnation and the death of Christ, who 'became obedient unto death, even death on a cross'. And therefore, because that happened, Paul says, you are to be obedient too. 'Work out your own salvation...' Not *for* it, mind! It is a gift of God.

The Christians in Philippi, like all Christians, were the children of God, born again of the Spirit of God. A Christian knows the forgiveness of God and can draw on the power of God and know the presence of God. All that glory is in us, in Christ. But we have to 'work it out'. The Greek word which Paul uses 'always has the idea of bringing to completion, to a full and complete and perfect accomplishment and conclusion' (Barclay). But although we have to work it out we don't have to do it on our own—and Paul says why not: 'For God is at work in you, both to will and to work for his good pleasure.'

But we have to let him do what he wants. He will do all that needs to be done—but we can stop him. We can quench the Spirit and put out the fire. The lover of our souls wants a response from us but we can refuse him—just as we can refuse a human lover, or turn away from a human friendship. We can say, 'Thus far and no farther...' The Book of Revelation tells of the redeemed worshipping God and the Lamb of God at the throne of the universe, and says that 'it is these who follow the Lamb wherever he goes' (Revelation 14:4). Total commitment—and the worship of God with all our heart, all our strength, all our soul and all our mind. That's what God's 'good pleasure' is for us—and it will give us our highest pleasure and our deepest delight.

A way to pray

Ask God what he wants to work in you—and ask him to show you how to work it out. Then spend a few moments in silence...

SB

The bent and beloved world

Do all things without grumbling or questioning, that you may be blameless and innocent, children of God without blemish in the midst of a crooked and perverse generation, among whom you shine as lights in the world, holding fast the word of life, so that in the day of Christ I may be proud that I did not run in vain or labour in vain. Even if I am to be poured as a libation upon the sacrificial offering of your faith, I am glad and rejoice with you all. Likewise you also should be glad and rejoice with me.

Some people are always grumbling and criticizing. Nothing and no one ever seems to be right—and they put themselves up by putting other people down. 'Don't be like that,' says Paul to the Philippians (and through them to us). You are the children of God (and once we know that glory we should never need to put anyone down to put ourselves up). So be what you are—the light of the world. Jesus said that he was and that we are too: 'You are the light of the world ... Let your light so shine before men that they may see your good works and give glory to your Father who is in heaven' (Matthew 5:14–16).

Paul takes up the same idea, and speaks of shining as lights in the world 'in the midst of a crooked and perverse generation'. But God still loves crooked and perverse generations and crooked and perverse people, and he wants to straighten out their crookedness and bring their perverseness into line with his loving will for them. Christians are called to be part of the healing process. To straighten out God's beloved world. To lighten its darkness. And to offer it the word of life that Christ died to speak. And Paul was happy to die, like a cup of wine poured out as a libation on the offering of the Christian's sacrificial faith.

A prayer

Lord Jesus Christ, light of the world, shine into me and out of me, with your healing light, and lead me to the people you love so that I can hold out to them the word of life.

SB

What interests Jesus

I hope in the Lord Jesus to send Timothy to you soon, so that I may be cheered by news of you. I have no one like him, who will be genuinely anxious for your welfare. They all look after their own interests, not those of Jesus Christ. But Timothy's worth you know, how as a son with a father he has served with me in the gospel. I hope therefore to send him just as soon as I see how it will go with me; and I trust in the Lord that shortly I myself shall come also.

Timothy was like a son to Paul and now he was going to send him to Philippi. That tells us how much Paul loved the Christians in that church, because it must have been an enormous comfort to him to have Timothy there in Rome, able to visit him in his prison cell and to talk with him about the Christian faith and the God whom they both worshipped and adored. But Paul was prepared to give that up. The Philippians were always in his heart, and he was always praying for them and thanking God for them. But he wanted definite news and a proper progress report. So he would send Timothy—who was always willing to be his messenger and who was as anxious as Paul for the Philippians' welfare.

Paul picks up the theme that he wrote about in 2:4: 'Let each of you look not only to his own interests but also to the interests of others.' Timothy looked after the interests of Jesus Christ—and what Jesus was (and is) interested in is the salvation of souls and the growth to maturity of Christian people. That's what he died for. To bring us to God, and to make us into the sons and daughters of God. Like Christ.

A prayer

Lord Jesus Christ, show me what you are interested in, and what you most mind about. Then show me what I am interested in, and what I most mind about. Help me to be honest, and to allow you to show me the truth about myself. Then help me to change my interests and concerns into yours.

SB

Good gamblers

I have thought it necessary to send to you Epaphroditus my brother and fellow worker and fellow soldier, and your messenger and minister to my need, for he has been longing for you all, and has been distressed because you heard that he was ill. Indeed he was ill, near to death. But God had mercy on him, and not only on him but on me also, lest I should have sorrow upon sorrow. I am the more eager to send him, therefore, that you may rejoice at seeing him again, and that I may be less anxious. So receive him in the Lord with all joy; and honour such men, for he nearly died for the work of Christ, risking his life to complete your service to me.

We saw in chapter 1 how Paul was confident that, through the prayers of the Philippians and the power of the Holy Spirit, 'with full courage now as always Christ will be honoured in my body, whether by life or death'.

Epaphroditus had need of that same high quality of courage—to turn up at the Roman prison and offer his services to a man who was awaiting trial on a charge which carried the death penalty. Epaphroditus risked his life for Paul, and for Christ. He nearly died of an illness. And his association with Paul could have got him involved in the same capital charge. So Paul decided to send him home—with the glowing testimonial to his courage, and his comforting of Paul, which is our reading for today.

Paul says that Epaphroditus 'gambled' with his life for the sake of Christ. In the early Church there was a group of men and women called the *parabulani*, the gamblers, who visited those who were sick and in prison— especially those with infectious and dangerous diseases. In AD252 plague broke out in Carthage; the heathen threw out the bodies of their dead, and fled in terror. Cyprian, the Christian bishop, gathered his congregation together and set them to burying the dead and nursing the sick in that plague-stricken city; and by so doing they saved the city, at the risk of their lives, from destruction and desolation.

Reflect

Who might Christ want us to gamble our lives for—for his sake? Your life, and my life . . .

SB

Pray... Father...

For this reason I bow my knees before the Father, from whom every family in heaven and on earth is named, that according to the riches of his glory he may grant you to be strengthened with might through his Spirit in the inner man, and that Christ may dwell in your hearts through faith: that you, being rooted and grounded in love, may have power to comprehend with all the saints what is the breadth and length and height and depth, and to know the love of Christ which surpasses knowledge, that you may be filled with all the fullness of God.

On Sundays in *Day by Day* we think about Holy Communion or prayer. Two readings (which the Alternative Service Book puts together in its lectionary) give us perfect models of how to pray. One, from the Gospels, is the Lord's prayer out of Luke 11, the instruction about prayer that Jesus gave to his disciples when one of them said, 'Lord, teach *us* to pray...' That request was made after Jesus himself had been praying—and they must have been aware of a quality of prayer beyond their own.

The key to it was the relationship with God the Father. Jesus said to them, 'Say this when you pray: "Father..."' Jesus' perfect relationship with his Father, and his total trust in him, made his prayers what they were. As our relationship with God deepens, and we trust him more and more, our prayers will get richer and our prayer life will get deeper.

The prayer from Ephesians follows the pattern of Jesus' perfect prayer. 'I bow my knees to the Father...' But all the persons of the Godhead are involved in all our prayers. The Spirit gives us inner strength; and the purpose and the will of God is that 'Christ may dwell in [our] hearts by faith'. Then we are filled with all the fulness of God, and we know the love of Christ which surpasses knowledge. Then the love of God will burn in the Church and the world like a fire—and people will be attracted to the flame and the warmth of it.

A way to pray

Pray the prayer from Ephesians for your church. Then make it personal and pray it for yourself: 'That he may grant me to be strengthened... that Christ may dwell in my heart through faith.'

SB

A cut to the heart

Finally, my brethren, rejoice in the Lord. To write the same things to you is not irksome to me, and is safe for you. Look out for the dogs, look out for the evil-workers, look out for those who mutilate the flesh. For we are the true circumcision, who worship God in spirit, and glory in Christ Jesus, and put no confidence in the flesh.

The word 'rejoice' comes eight times in this letter. Paul is full of rejoicing in his prison, and he wants the Philippians to rejoice in the Lord even in the face of persecution. Some of their persecutors were Jews. This gives the Church no excuse at all for the way it has sometimes behaved to the Jewish people throughout the centuries. But all those who belong to the Church don't belong to Christ and don't obey him. They are the tares in the wheat, and Jesus said that their final end would be destruction. And these Jewish teachers said that salvation belonged to the Jews (and in one sense it did: Jesus was a Jew) and that in order to be saved a man had to become a Jew and be circumcised. But Paul said 'No!' Christians are the 'true circumcision'.

The prophet Jeremiah had called to the men of Judah (4:4) 'Circumcise yourself to the Lord, remove the foreskin of your hearts.' Powerful imagery. God was saying, 'Remove it so that I can make it clean.' His promise through the prophet Ezekiel was 'I will sprinkle clean water upon you, and you shall be clean from all your uncleannesses, and from all your idols I will cleanse you. A new heart I will give you, and a new spirit I will put within you; and I will take out of your flesh the heart of stone and give you a heart of flesh' (36:25–26). Paul knew all the promises of the old Covenant (or Testament), and he knew Christ and the new power of the new Covenant.

A reflection

Jesus said, 'God is spirit, and those who worship him must worship in spirit and truth' (John 4:24).

What does it mean to have a circumcised heart?

What does it mean to have a new heart?

SB

All lost for Christ

Though I myself have reason for confidence in the flesh also. If any other man thinks he has reason for confidence in the flesh, I have more: circumcised on the eighth day, of the people of Israel, of the tribe of Benjamin, a Hebrew born of Hebrews; as to the law a Pharisee, as to zeal a persecutor of the church, as to righteousness under the law blameless. But whatever gain I had, I counted as loss for the sake of Christ.

Paul had been everything a Jew could ever want to be. If getting it right as a Jew was what could give a man real confidence in God then Paul had it all. He had been circumcised on the proper day—the eighth day. He was an Israelite who could trace his descent from Jacob—to whom God had given the new name of Israel after his all-night wrestling match at Jabbok. He was of the tribe of Benjamin, which was the highest of all the tribes of Israel—the aristocracy. He was born of a Hebrew mother and a Hebrew father—which meant that they (and he) actually spoke Hebrew. So his blood and his language were the best—utterly pure. He was a Pharisee—trained in the Jewish law.

Paul had kept the law, which would have meant all the endless rituals and regulations of the Jewish law—far heavier than the biblical regulations of the Old Testament (though in Romans he says that the Old Testament law finally showed him that he was a sinner: 'I should not have known what it is to covet if the law had not said, "You shall not covet" . . .', Romans 7:7). Paul knew it all—and in terms of his status as a Jew he'd got it all. But in terms of getting himself into a right relationship with God all those things were useless. They weren't a gain. They were a loss. All because of the encounter which Paul (Saul, he was, then) had with the risen Christ on the road to Damascus, when the whole of his life was turned around, and he worshipped the one whom he had persecuted.

A question

In your relationship with God, in what— or in whom—do you put your confidence? Think what it must have been like for Paul, the proud Pharisee, to abandon all his Jewish credits for the sake of Christ.

SB

That I may know him

Indeed I count everything as loss because of the surpassing worth of knowing Christ Jesus my Lord. For his sake I have suffered the loss of all things, and count them as refuse, in order that I may gain Christ and be found in him, not having a righteousness of my own, based on law, but that which is through faith in Christ, the righteousness from God that depends on faith; that I may know him and the power of his resurrection, and may share his sufferings, becoming like him in his death, that if possible I may attain the resurrection from the dead.

All the things that Paul had glorifed in before were worthless to him—because of the all-surpassing worth of 'knowing Christ Jesus my Lord'. Paul is utterly consecrated to the Christ he adores and worships, and the deepest desire of his heart is to know him better—more and more deeply. But for that to happen—for Paul and for us—there has to be suffering. We undergo a process of stripping and purging—and it hurts.

Fairly soon after the start of my own Christian life I made those words of Paul into my own prayer: 'That I may know him and the power of his resurrection, and may share his sufferings, becoming like him in his death.' I prayed the first phrase with total commitment and enthusiasm. The next two phrases I was less enthusiastic about, since suffering didn't appeal to me very much and death didn't appeal to me at all. But I so wanted to know Christ, in the deepest way that it was ever possible for me (such as I am) to know him, that I was prepared to go along with the suffering and the death. And he takes us at our word even while he sympathizes with our feelings. He can lead us through the suffering of disappointed hopes and the death of human, and quite natural, desires, in order to give us the true and the deepest desire of our heart—which when it is prised out of the confusion of our divided hearts is always for the union and communion of love, with ourselves as beloved and also lover. It is only God with whom we can know that total love—always there, and there for always. It is only God who can deal with our inner loneliness and totally satisfy the desire of our heart for love.

A prayer

Pray those words of Paul for yourself . . .

SB

Grown up

Not that I have already obtained this or am already perfect; but I press on to make it my own, because Christ Jesus has made me his own. Brethren, I do not consider that I have made it my own; but one thing I do, forgetting what lies behind and straining forward to what lies ahead, I press on toward the goal for the prize of the upward call of God in Christ Jesus. Let those of us who are mature be thus minded; and if in anything you are otherwise minded, God will reveal that also to you. Only let us hold true to what we have attained.

What Paul has not yet already obtained is the last sentence of yesterday's reading—the resurrection from the dead. He cannot be talking about the resurrection body which lies ahead for all Christians on the other side of death—when Christ will 'change our lowly body to be like his glorious body' (verse 20 of this chapter, which we shall look at on Saturday). That resurrection body is one of Paul's certainties. What he is writing about here is living out the resurrection life of Christ in *this* life, and in *this* body. It has to do with growing to Christian maturity and pressing on to 'perfection', which isn't the same as being sinless. In this life we shall never be that. The Greek word 'perfect' which Paul uses means *full-grown* in contradistinction to undeveloped; for example it is used of a full-grown man as opposed to an undeveloped youth. It is used to mean *mature in mind*, as opposed to one who is a beginner in a subject; it therefore means *one who is qualified in a subject* as opposed to a mere learner. When it is used of Christians, it often means *'baptized persons who are full members of the Church*, as opposed to those who are still under instruction and who are still not qualified to be members of the Church' (Barclay). An old hymn describes the life Paul is writing about—and says how to live it.

A prayer

'Within the Veil', thy spirit
deeply anchored,
Thou walkest calm above
a world of strife;
'Within the Veil' thy soul
with Him united
Shall live on earth His
resurrection life.

F.H. Allen

SB

Truth and love

Brethren, join in imitating me, and mark those who so live as you have an example in us. For many, of whom I have often told you and now tell you even with tears, live as enemies of the cross of Christ. Their end is destruction, their god is the belly, and they glory in their shame, with minds set on earthly things.

What Paul is telling the Philippian Christians to imitate is the lifestyle which he described in verses 8–14 (see Wednesday). 'If we are to imitate him, then we must be like him not only in our growing delight in Christ (v. 8), our reliance on Him alone for salvation (v. 9), our determination to be like Him and do His will (vv. 10–12), and our single-minded active pursuit of the prize (vv. 13,14). We must also esteem truth as he did, marry truth to love, and balance individualism with pastoral care.' (J.A. Motyer, *The Richness of Christ; Studies in the Letter to the Philippians*, IVF, 1966)

For Paul there was nothing more important than the truth (since to get it wrong was to be an enemy of the cross of Christ). But love was equally important, and Paul loved his Christian converts with a deep intensity and a great and practical pastoral concern. 'The truth must be married to love. Paul was a great weeper. He shed great tears in his yearnings for the Ephesians (Acts 20:19–31); he cried over the Corinthians when he had to issue an apostolic rebuke (2 Corinthians 2:4); and here again we find him full of tears, with the difference that here he *weeps* for those about whom he must *warn*' (Motyer). We don't know who they were, these people whom Paul was writing about. It doesn't very much matter. What does matter is that we heed Paul's solemn warning. In verse 14 he had written of 'the upward call of God in Christ Jesus'. But these enemies of the cross of Christ weren't looking up. They were looking downwards. Worshipping a false god. Satisfying all their bodily appetites. And glorying in the shame of it. What lay ahead for them was destruction. No wonder Paul wept.

A way to pray

Are you imitating Paul? Read 3:8–14 again. Reflect on what Paul says about the destruction of those who 'live as enemies of the cross of Christ'. Then pray in silence—without words—waiting on God and attentive.

SB

Citizens of heaven

But our commonwealth is in heaven, and from it we await a Saviour, the Lord Jesus Christ, who will change our lowly body to be like his glorious body, by the power which enables him even to subject all things to himself. Therefore, my brethren whom I love and long for, my joy and crown, stand firm thus in the Lord, my beloved. I entreat Euodia and I entreat Syntyche to agree in the Lord. And I ask you also, true yokefellow, help these women, for they have laboured side by side with me in the gospel together with Clement and the rest of my fellow workers, whose names are in the book of life.

Now Paul contrasts the end of the enemies of Christ with the end of the lovers of Christ.

'Our commonwealth', or 'our citizenship', is 'in heaven'. Paul was (as always) using a picture that would be absolutely plain to his readers. The Romans set up colonies all over the world that they had conquered. But they all knew that they were Romans, and to be made a full citizen of Rome was the greatest reward they could have. In their colonies they wore Roman dress, administered Roman justice, were governed by Roman magistrates, and spoke the Roman language, which was Latin. They never forgot that they were Romans, and that the city they belonged to was Rome. And Paul is saying to the Christians, 'Our citizenship is in heaven.' One day our Saviour will come again in glory from the heavenly city (the Saviour who lives in the heart of every Christian, but with a hidden glory) and then our earthly bodies will be transformed into glorious resurrection bodies. That is the great Christian hope. Christianity is about living life in all its fulness *now*—in that relationship with God which is what eternal life is. But Christianity is also about a future life, beyond the grave, when we shall be 'with Christ, which is far better'.

A way to pray

Think of the 'life in all its fulness' that Christ can give us now—and be thankful. Then think of the Christian hope of glory—when Christ will come in glory, and when we shall live with him for ever in the glory of heaven.

SB

Pray for peace

First of all, then, I urge that supplications, prayers, intercessions, and thanksgivings be made for all men, for kings and all who are in high positions, that we may lead a quiet and peaceable life, godly and respectful in every way. This is good, and it is acceptable in the sight of God our Saviour, who desires all men to be saved and to come to the knowledge of the truth. For there is one God, and there is one mediator between God and men, the man Christ Jesus, who gave himself as a ransom for all, the testimony to which was borne at the proper time. For this I was appointed a preacher and apostle (I am telling the truth, I am not lying), a teacher of the Gentiles in faith and truth.

In the Roman Empire in which this letter to Timothy was written all the kings and rulers can't have been Christians. But Christians were to pray for all of them—and to pray for peace. And for the Jew and for the Christian peace was far more than the absence of war or strife. Rather, it was the presence of all those things which make for humanity's highest good—right relationships between people and nations, social justice, and freedom to sit under your own fig tree (which was about having your own place and your own space). These things only happened when the loving will and righteousness of God was lived out in a loving social system in which everyone mattered. Peace has to do with right and loving relationships between human beings—and between them and their God. Peace would only come into being through the reconciliation that Jesus Christ came to bring—through his birth, his life, his death and his resurrection, and then the giving of his

Holy Spirit. 'Peace on earth, good will towards men . . .' through the Christ of God. So Christians were to pray for peace—and for their kings and rulers. There could be no peace on earth without the Prince of Peace—so the prayer of all Christians for all those in authority has to be that they will come to know the 'one mediator between God and man, the man Christ Jesus, who gave himself as a ransom for all'. God our Saviour wants 'all men to be saved and to come to the knowledge of the truth'. Our task is to pray for them so that they will.

SB

Rejoice!

Rejoice in the Lord always; again I will say, Rejoice. Let all men know your forbearance. The Lord is at hand. Have no anxiety about anything, but in everything by prayer and supplication with thanksgiving let your requests be made known to God.

Today we look at Paul's teaching about our relationships and our circumstances, and tomorrow at our thought life and our behaviour. Because of our relationship with God we are to rejoice. If we reflect on the wonder of it, day by day, then our hearts will be full to overflowing with praise and delight: 'Ransomed, healed, restored, forgiven, Who like me his praise should sing?' (J. Newton).

Because of that, our relationship with all people has to be characterized by a gracious gentleness. Forbearance can make us think of someone pursing their lips rather disapprovingly, to show that they are somehow managing to be patient with a person who is causing them considerable irritation.

But the real meaning of the word is someone who knows how to temper justice with mercy. A person like Jesus—who didn't apply the letter of the law to the woman taken in adultery. He didn't condone it. He said, 'Go, and sin no more' (John 8:11, AV). And perhaps, because he was merciful, she didn't—or not in that way. Perhaps she followed Jesus and had all her sins forgiven. It doesn't say and we don't know. But we do know how Christ showed forbearance—not with the pursed lips of disapproval, but with love and mercy.

Our relationship with God will make a radical difference to our circumstances. First of all we rejoice in the God who loves us and forgives us— and we think about what our God is like. That's easy—because he is like Jesus. 'He who has seen me has seen the Father...' (John 14:9). And Jesus taught us how to pray, and to say 'Our Father...' So we aren't to be anxious, and we're to pray about everything. Everything that matters to us matters to our heavenly Father. Nothing is too big and nothing is too small. So...

A way to pray

Pray about everything that makes you anxious—and everything that's in your heart. 'And the peace of God, which passes all understanding, will keep your hearts and your minds in Christ Jesus' (Philippians 4:7).

SB

Whatever you think

Finally, brethren, whatever is true, whatever is honourable, whatever is just, whatever is pure, whatever is lovely, whatever is gracious, if there is any excellence, if there is anything worthy of praise, think about these things. What you have learned and received and heard and seen in me, do; and the God of peace will be with you.

The love relationship with God our Saviour is always there, and God is always there—with us—in all our circumstances, all our thoughts, and all that we do. We might do wrong things and think wrong thoughts—but God is still with us, grieving at our sin, but still loving us, and because he loves us, wanting us to stop sinning.

Since our sin so often starts in our thought life, what we think about is crucially important. If someone has hurt us and been nasty to us, we can think nasty thoughts about them—and quite often enjoy ourselves thinking about all their unpleasant characteristics and their character weaknesses (*their* short temper, *their* tendency to criticize other people...) And since none of us is sinless we shall all think unpleasant thoughts about our friends as well as our enemies for some of the time. But the time had better be as short as possible, so that we move on to thinking about their good points, and their kindness and generosity and affection towards us. After all, no one is perfect—not even you or me!

Television can affect our thought life very powerfully, and I believe it can corrupt us. We look and listen to adultery being seen as natural behaviour and as a joke—and our thinking changes. What we see is not pure, or lovely, and it isn't even true, because it's being acted. But in the world the act of adultery is true, and it breaks up marriages and families and causes deep unhappiness. And we look at it on television and join in the laughter. We are letting 'the world round [us] squeeze [us] into its own mould' (J.B. Philips). We are thinking wrong thoughts and we aren't worshipping God with all our minds. If we do, and if we follow Paul's instructions and copy his behaviour, then he makes us a promise: 'The God of peace will be with you.'

A prayer

Lord God, help me to change my thought life so that it makes you (and me) glad and not sad.

SB

Content in all things

I rejoice in the Lord greatly that now at length you have revived your concern for me; you were indeed concerned for me, but you had no opportunity. Not that I complain of want; for I have learned, in whatever state I am, to be content. I know how to be abased, and I know how to abound; in any and all circumstances I have learned the secret of facing plenty and hunger, abundance and want. I can do all things in him who strengthens me.

Paul had to learn how to be content. It isn't a natural quality in a human being. What we say naturally is, 'I want...' and then we set about trying to get it. Paul had discovered what sin was by discovering that he coveted—but now he didn't want anything apart from Christ. Whatever his situation was he was content. That word 'content' came from the Stoics. It means self-sufficiency. But the Stoics learned it in a totally different way from Paul—and it was a totally different quality. To start with the Stoics practised by saying, 'If a cup breaks, I don't care...' Then they advanced down the ladder of not caring. 'If my pet dog dies, I don't care.' Finally a Stoic could say, 'I don't care,' as he watched his wife or his son suffering and dying. It was a religious activity, because they believed that everything which happened was the will of God. So they had better put up with it. And the best way to avoid being hurt was simply not to care. 'Love was rooted out of life and caring was forbidden. As T.R. Glove said, "The Stoics made of the heart a desert, and called it peace" ' (Barclay).

But the true nature of God is love, and God-in-Christ suffers for us and with us, and weeps over Jerusalem and at the grave of his friend Lazarus. Paul's contentment in all his suffering, and all his circumstances, was *through* that Christ—so that he could write, 'I can do all things in him who strengthens me.' Paul in Christ and Christ in Paul—loving one another and suffering with one another.

A way to pray

Spend some time reflecting on your life. If you are content, like Paul, then pray and be thankful. If you are not content, then pray and be truthful—and ask for a change of heart.

SB

A gift of love

Yet it was kind of you to share my trouble. And you Philippians yourselves know that in the beginning of the gospel, when I left Macedonia, no church entered into partnership with me in giving and receiving except you only; for even in Thessalonica you sent me help once and again.

It was because Christ was in him that Paul could handle being either rich or poor. He was totally content with either state. He didn't need anything, because of the deep delight and satisfaction that his relationship with Christ gave to him. But he was delighted that the Philippians had cared so much for his welfare and well-being that they had sent Epaphroditus to him with their gifts, and the reason for his delight and his rejoicing was that it showed him the quality of their Christian lives. It is God-like to give—and meanness and tight-fistedness can never flow from the love of God. Jesus spoke of giving a good measure that was pressed down and 'running over' (Luke 6:38)—and when someone gives to us like that, out of their love and affection for us, it warms our heart, even if we don't in the strictest sense 'need' their gift. That's how it was for Paul.

The 'fruit' that Paul longed to see growing in his converts was the fruit of the Spirit: 'Love, joy, peace, patience, kindness, goodness, faithfulness, gentleness and self control' (Galatians 5:22, 23). Every year an old apple tree in my garden bears a heavy crop of red apples, with a sweet smell and a lovely flavour, crunchy and juicy—and every time I go past the tree I can't resist picking one and eating it (and the same goes for my friends). My apple tree bears apples like that because that's the sort of tree it is—and the Christians in Philippi sent their gift to Paul out of the love of their hearts, because that's the sort of people they were. Christians with a generous heart of love, like the heart of God.

A reflection

Think of sweet, ripe apples on a tree, warm with the autumn sunshine, fragrant and juicy. Think of your own giving to your friends and your family, and to your church and to the needs of the hungry world. Think of the self-giving love of God...

SB

All needs supplied

Not that I seek the gift; but I seek the fruit which increases to your credit. I have received full payment, and more; I am filled, having received from Epaphroditus the gifts you sent, a fragrant offering, a sacrifice acceptable and pleasing to God. And my God will supply every need of yours according to his riches in glory in Christ Jesus. To our God and Father be glory for ever and ever. Amen.

Greet every saint in Christ Jesus. The brethren who are with me greet you. All the saints greet you, especially those of Caesar's household. The grace of the Lord Jesus Christ be with your spirit.

Christians have believed the promise which Paul made to the Philippians ever since he made it. The promise was that 'my God will supply every need of yours according to his riches in glory in Christ Jesus', and Paul knew the truth of that in his personal experience. It was true in the material sense and also in the realm of spiritual attainment and riches. Paul had believed once that he had gained his own righteousness in the sight of God by keeping the Jewish law. But once Christ met him on the road to Damascus Paul realized that all his law keeping and good deeds were worthless and useless rubbish. But in abandoning his confidence in them he discovered 'the surpassing worth of knowing Christ Jesus my Lord' (3:8). The Philippians had made a material sacrifice to send their gifts to Paul. But they wouldn't be the poorer for it. They would experience God meeting their material and natural needs in a supernatural way. In the Western world we don't need very much in a material sense. And most of us hardly know anything about sacrificial giving. Perhaps that is why the Church in the West is a bit short of the glory of God. He can't fill us with his glory, or meet our needs from his glory, because we are full up already. So there isn't much space for God.

A way to pray

Pray about your needs, and your church's needs—material and spiritual. Pray about your giving, and your church's giving—material and spiritual—to Christians in need and to a needy world. Give glory to God— and pray . . .

SB

God's creatures

Thou makest springs gush forth in the valleys; they flow between the hills, they give drink to every beast of the field; the wild asses quench their thirst. By them the birds of the air have their habitation; they sing among the branches. From thy lofty abode thou waterest the mountains; the earth is satisfied with the fruit of thy work. Thou dost cause the grass to grow for the cattle, and plants for man to cultivate, that he may bring forth food from the earth, and wine to gladden the heart of man, oil to make his face shine, and bread to strengthen man's heart. The trees of the Lord are watered abundantly, the cedars of Lebanon which he planted. In them the birds build their nests; the stork has her home in the fir trees. The high mountains are for the wild goats; the rocks are a refuge for the badgers.

As I write this a blackbird is singing his head off in the silver birch tree just outside my study window. Because his song is out in the open we do not realize how powerful it is. Had he perched inside the house I should have had to plug my ears. But the birdsong is meant to be heard by other birds at a distance. All this the author of Psalm 104 would say is the design of God the Creator. The birds are his and he has provided for them, and for the cattle, the wild goats and the badgers. And we are bracketed with birds and animals as far as the Creator's provision is concerned; wine to make our hearts glad and oil to polish up our faces. Well, this is not quite how we would express it! But let us not miss the point. The Bible talks about God's provision whereas we talk about Nature's provision and leave God out; or else assume that God and Nature are the same which is definitely not what the Bible teaches.

The world of Nature certainly is wonderful. Modern television programmes reveal the wonders as never before but we must not deify nature. It is God's creation and the animals are God's creatures and it is our special duty *as human beings* to praise God for his creation.

A prayer

Lord, I thank you for that blackbird and all the rich variety of nature that you have given us. Praise be to you the wonderful Creator.

DCF

More letters to young churches

The New Testament starts with the four Gospels. They are followed by the book of Acts (which we have been looking at). After that almost all of it consists of letters, and for most of this section we shall be reading some more of them.

First the shortest letter of all—Philemon—which Henry Wansbrough takes us through. Then the seven letters from the risen Christ to the seven churches in the province of Asia, written by John at the start of the Revelation given to him in a vision on the island of Patmos. Graham Dodds leads us through those letters, and they have just as much to say to our own churches as they had to say to the churches in Asia in the first century.

Six days with Douglas Cleverley Ford on the Psalms comes next—Psalms that cry for help, and that we can use ourselves when we are crying out in distress or perplexity.

The last three weeks in this section is Paul's letter to the Galatians—about the gospel of God's grace, and Christian freedom and responsibility. David Winter takes us through that letter—and shows us the way to walk in the Spirit and to live by faith.

By faith

By faith Moses, when he was born, was hid for three months by his parents, because they saw that the child was beautiful; and they were not afraid of the king's edict. By faith Moses, when he was grown up, refused to be called the son of Pharaoh's daughter, choosing rather to share ill-treatment with the people of God than to enjoy the fleeting pleasures of sin. He considered abuse suffered for the Christ greater wealth than the treasures of Egypt, for he looked to the reward. By faith he left Egypt, not being afraid of the anger of the king; for he endured as seeing him who is invisible. By faith he kept the Passover and sprinkled the blood, so that the Destroyer of the first-born might not touch them.

The whole of chapter 11 of the letter to the Hebrews is about faith. It is full of examples of faith, and it begins by saying what faith is: 'Now faith is the assurance of things hoped for the conviction of things not seen. For by it the men of old received divine approval. By faith we understand that the world was created by the word of God, so that what is seen was made out of things which do not appear' (vv. 1–2).

Faith is not just a feeling, though sometimes feelings can accompany it. Faith is putting our trust in the word and the promises of God, and acting accordingly. That is what Moses' parents did, and it is what Moses did. It is what we do when we come to Holy Communion and it has never been better put than in the words of the Book of Common Prayer at the administration: 'The Body of our Lord Jesus Christ which was given for thee, preserve thy body and soul unto everlasting life: Take and eat this in remembrance that Christ died for thee,

and feed on him in thy heart by faith with thanksgiving.'

We cannot see Christ as he gives himself to us through the bread and wine, but by faith we have the assurance that he does: and we hope that one day we shall see him. 'Beloved, we are God's children now; it does not yet appear what we shall be, but we know that when he appears we shall be like him, for we shall see him as he is' (1 John 3:2).

SB

Peace

From Paul, a prisoner of Christ Jesus and from our brother Timothy; to our dear fellow worker Philemon, our sister Apphia, our fellow soldier Archippus and the church that meets in your house. Grace and the peace of God our Father and the Lord Jesus Christ.

This letter seems to begin with an entirely conventional greeting, just like any other letter written about this time in the Greco-Roman world. First it mentions the writers of the letter, then the recipients, and then it gives a greeting, usually 'Peace', the greeting that was current then in Judaism, and still is today, 'Shalom'.

But is it entirely so conventional? The peace is not just a casual 'Shalom', but is the peace of God our Father. This is the special peace which was eagerly awaited especially from the time of Isaiah, when the wolf will live with the lamb and the panther lie down with the kid, when the natural enmities in nature will no longer hold. The Messiah was to bring this peace, a restoration of the peace and harmony of the condition of Paradise, when there was no hostility. So it is the peace 'of the Lord Jesus Christ', which his people are to spread to the world. The theme of peace runs through Paul's letters: 'you were called in peace', 'Christ is our peace', 'the fruit of the Spirit is love, joy and peace'—just as Jesus in his ministry brought peace to those tormented by disease and mental turmoil. We must search our consciences: is our Christianity truly a cause of peace or of division? Do we see it as our vocation to reconcile conflict, to be peace-makers? Am I a person of peace, with the peace of Christ at the quiet centre of my being, from which it radiates to all those I meet?

If this is a taxing vocation, it is worth remembering that 'peace' is preceded by the greeting of the 'grace of God our Father'. 'Grace' has become a meaningless word which needs to be freshened up. It really means the favour, the lavish and unmerited generosity bestowed by an all-powerful ruler on those chosen favourites to whom he has taken a fancy without any merits of their own. We don't deserve it, but we are all his favourites, basking in his smile, and should be wallowing contentedly in the sea of his generosity.

For reflection

How beautiful on the mountains are the feet of the messenger announcing peace.

Isaiah 52:7

HW

Love

I always thank my God, mentioning you in my prayers, because I hear of the love and the faith which you have for the Lord Jesus and for all God's holy people. I pray that your fellowship in faith may come to expression in full knowledge of all the good we can do for Christ. I have received much joy and encouragement by your love; you have set the hearts of God's holy people at rest.

Greco-Roman convention prescribed that the title of the letter should be followed by some good wishes, so Paul always starts with a little complimentary passage about the faith of his correspondents—always, that is, except when he is writing to the Galatians, whose Christian faith and practice he considers to be distinctly wobbly. These good wishes are not just any good wishes, but are normally related to the subject which he covers in the letter, preparing the readers for it. So here it is significant that he twice compliments Philemon on the love he shows, and prays that his fellowship, literally, his 'sharing', may be fully activated (the Greek word used could be translated 'be energetic': Paul is praying that Philemon's love may be energized).

So Philemon could be aware that he was going to be called upon to be generous. In the early Christian Church the word 'love' had a resonance which makes the ears prick up and the heart beat faster. To the Jews, love was not a gooey feeling but a practical matter of rolling up the sleeves and getting on with it. The primary place for such love was a close-knit family in which the members are alert to one other's needs; they stick by each other and bail one another out when in difficulty. Whatever sibling rivalry there may be, when the crunch comes we know where to turn. This obtains all over the family of God: God first loved us in this way, so that we may return such love. Christ showed this love in a supremely practical way by not sparing himself on the cross, for his brothers and sisters were in need.

The way Paul puts it is typical of his tact and appreciation: he does not chide Philemon for severity or selfishness or lack of love. He does not even call upon him to improve. He simply assumes Philemon's love and thanks God for it.

For reflection

The love of God has been poured into our hearts by the Holy Spirit which has been given to us.

Romans 5:5

HW

A slave and a son

Therefore, although in Christ I have no hesitations about telling you what your duty is, I am rather appealing to your love, being what I am, Paul, an old man, and now also a prisoner of Christ Jesus. I am appealing to you for a child of mine, whose father I became while wearing these chains: I mean Onesimus. He was of no use to you before, but now he is useful both to you and to me. I am sending him back to you—that is to say, sending you my own heart.

This is, perhaps, the most personal and affectionate passage of all Paul's letters. Onesimus was a slave who ran away from Philemon, came to Paul in prison and there became a Christian. Presumably he stayed to help, perhaps wait on, Paul, before Paul decided to send him back to his erstwhile master with this letter. Paul now opens himself to Philemon, stressing his own helplessness and dependence in every way, and pointing out both his need and affection for Onesimus. There is gentle humour too, for the runaway slave's name, 'Onesimus', means 'useful', and Paul makes a double play on this meaning. At the same time he stresses what a difference it made to Onesimus that he has now become a Christian: he was useless, and has now become useful. Was Onesimus really a disaster as a slave, or is Paul only using the name for a joke? Or was it perhaps that Onesimus was disaffected and the uselessness was that he ran away and was not any more available to his master? The mere fact of following Christ and being filled with Christ's Spirit should make a difference to our effectiveness, our way of acting and our value as persons. It is touching that Paul describes himself as 'a prisoner of Christ Jesus', rather than of the Roman authorities. He understands himself as the Servant of Christ. Jesus' own title of honour was to be the Servant of the Lord, close to God and empowered by God as his special agent, doing his work, and Paul sees himself as the special agent of Jesus, doing his work, close to him, empowered by him, imprisoned and suffering like him in order that he might share his glory. So Paul sees himself to be a prisoner, not because the Roman authorities have imprisoned him, but because he willingly imitates his Master: it is suffering willingly undertaken.

For reflection

The Son of man himself came not to be served but to serve, and to give his life as a ransom for many.

Mark 10:45

HW

A slave and a brother

I should have liked to keep him with me; he could have been a substitute for you, to help me while I am in the chains that the gospel has brought me. However, I did not want to do anything without your consent; it would have been forcing your act of kindness, which should be spontaneous. I suppose you have been deprived of Onesimus for a time, merely so that you could have him back for ever, no longer as a slave, but something much better than a slave, a dear brother; especially dear to me, but how much more to you, both on the natural plane and in the Lord.

To most people in the ancient world this way of writing would have seemed sheer lunacy: to call a slave 'a dear brother'! It was accepted that slaves were not to be regarded as human. They were mere sub-human investments, to be worked to the limit and then cast aside, without rights, without feelings, like a worn-out wheel-barrow. One writer contemporary to Paul patronizingly congratulates himself on pretending that his slaves have some legal rights, and unctuously compliments himself on his foolishly soft heart because he claims to be upset when they die. But of real human affection or awareness of brotherhood there is no trace. The brotherhood of the human race did not extend to slaves. This new Christian idea that a slave could really be a brother—and Paul obviously means it, for he has said that he is 'sending you my own heart'—is totally revolutionary. And Onesimus is to be not just a temporary companion or work-mate, but a brother for all eternity: their lives are intertwined for ever by belonging to the same Christian family.

At the same time Paul shows his affection for Philemon by suggesting that Onesimus would have reminded Paul of his master, and been a substitute for him at his side. The whole letter is so gracious and delicate, in marked contrast to what often passes for Christianity. The importance of theological principles can often lead Christians to act in accordance with all the principles of justice, forgetting that we are dealing with vulnerable human beings, uncertain of themselves and needing encouragement and gentleness of treatment.

For reflection

Whoever does not love the brother whom he can see cannot love God whom he has not seen.

1 John 4:20

HW

You owe me!

So if you grant me any fellowship with yourself, welcome him as you would me; if he has wronged you in any way or owes you anything, put it down to my account. I am writing this in my own hand: I, Paul, shall pay it back—I make no mention of a further debt, that you owe your very self to me!

Paul would hardly have made this comment about a further debt—and with the humorous reference to debiting his own bank-account, and signing a cheque with his own hand—unless he had a fairly shrewd idea that Onesimus had wronged Philemon in some way. Perhaps Onesimus had taken something with him when he deserted his master. Perhaps he really was a good-for-nothing, and in the name of Christian fellowship Paul is calling on Philemon to forgive him for substantial injuries.

Why does Philemon owe himself to Paul? Presumably because Paul by baptizing him brought him into fellowship with Christ, which is the only life worth living. It is firmly Paul's principle that life is Christ and to live is to live in Christ, so that life without Christ is no life at all. He often uses the figure of his begetting children in Christ. This is perhaps not without importance for godparents and pastors who have brought children, young or already adult, to Christ; this creates a permanent link, as important as that of natural fatherhood.

By invoking the concept of fellowship, Paul brings in the idea of Christian sharing and community, which was one of the strongest ideas of early Christian living. On the material level, fellowship in the earliest community meant sharing of possessions. But it goes far beyond that, for every Christian shares the life of every other, so that if one suffers, all suffer; if one sins, all are affected. This gives sin its seriousness, but also gives joy in sharing and benefiting the perseverance of others. It is because we are in fellowship with one another and with Christ that we can make up the fullness of the sufferings of Christ. All live in Christ, and so the shared life of Christ is evident in all. Benedict, in his *Rule for Monks*, teaches that in every guest Christ is received, in every sick brother Christ is served. In everyone we meet Christ is encountered.

For reflection

Christ will be glorified in my body, whether by my life or my death. Life to me, of course, is Christ.

Philippians 1:20–21

HW

Workers and witnesses

Well then, brother, I am counting on you, in the Lord; set my heart at rest, in Christ. I am writing with complete confidence in your compliance, sure that you will do even more than I ask. There is another thing: will you get a place ready for me to stay in? I am hoping through your prayers to be restored to you. Epaphras, a prisoner with me in Christ Jesus, sends his greetings; so do my fellow-workers Mark, Aristarchus, Demas and Luke. May the grace of our Lord Jesus Christ be with your spirit.

Again in his final greetings Paul's tact and encouragement show in his confidence that Philemon will respond to his request. There is nothing mean or niggling about Paul's teaching of Christianity: it is always positive and confident of Christ's strength in his followers. The participation of so many fellow-workers with Paul gives a breadth to his message which is often forgotten: Paul has sometimes been seen as the only teacher in early Christianity. Who these partners were we hardly know. Two of them may be the evangelists Mark and Luke; but Mark is one of the commonest names in the Roman world, and Luke is by no means uncommon. Aristarchus and Demas are certainly unknown. It is one of those precious indications that there is a whole lot that we do not know about the early Christian community, of which only tiny corners of knowledge emerge. The variety of people, men and women, at work for Christ; the variety of offices and vocations in the community; the variety of structures in different local communities—all these show a freedom in the Spirit which goes with Paul's confidence. The people of God, or God's holy people, was a reality and was the basis of Church structure. Not only were all these important in governing and guiding the local communities, but they were all instrumental in preserving and shaping the traditions. We do not even know who wrote many of the works of the New Testament, for the real authorship of many of the letters, and even the Gospels, is quite uncertain. The important truth is that these and subsequent generations felt them to express validly the life of the Church.

For reflection

With so many witnesses in a great cloud all around us, we too, then, should throw off everything that weighs us down and the sin that clings so closely.

Hebrews 12:1

HW

'Let thy face shine!'

Restore us, O God;
let thy face shine, that we may be saved!
O Lord God of hosts,
how long wilt thou be angry with thy people's prayers?
Thou hast fed them with the bread of tears,
and given them tears to drink in full measure.
Thou dost make us the scorn of our neighbours;
and our enemies laugh among themselves.
Restore us, O God of hosts;
let thy face shine, that we may be saved!
Thou didst bring a vine out of Egypt;
Thou didst drive out the nations and plant it.

As you come today to Holy Communion will you think about failure? About things that start with a bright shining, but then seem to fizzle out. Think of the disappointment of the one who started them. The Psalmist here is crying out of his desolation to God, and reminding him that he brought the nation of Israel out of Egypt as his special vine. But the prophet Isaiah speaks out of the desolation in the heart of God: 'What more was there to do for my vineyard, that I have not done in it? When I looked for it to yield grapes, why did it yield wild grapes?' (Isaiah 5:4).

The Psalmist cries out to God, 'Let thy face shine, that we may be saved!' Years later his prayer is answered far more gloriously than he could ever have dreamed. God himself takes human flesh so that the world may be saved, and we see his glory shining in the face of Jesus Christ. Christ the light of the world and Christ the true vine.

As you drink the cup at Communion, think of the grapes that were picked and crushed so that they could be made into wine. And think of the death of Christ.

'The blood of Christ, keep you in eternal life . . .'

' . . . May we who share Christ's body live his risen life; we who drink his cup bring life to others; we whom the Spirit lights give light to the world . . .'

(*Service of Holy Communion, Rite A, Alternative Service Book*)

SB

The vision of Jesus

I turned around to see the voice that was speaking to me. And when I turned I saw seven golden lampstands, and among the lampstands was someone 'like a son of man ', dressed in a robe reaching down to his feet and with a golden sash round his chest. His head and hair were like wool, as white as snow, and his eyes were like blazing fire. His feet were like bronze glowing in a furnace, and his voice was like the sound of rushing waters. In his right hand he held seven stars and out of his mouth came a sharp double-edged sword. His face was like the sun shining in all its brilliance.

John on the island of Patmos is far more engrossed with the Spirit than the local scenery. He is overtaken by this miraculous picture, with the risen Christ at the centre, and John sees him in strongly Old Testament imagery. Jesus is wearing the long robe of the high priest. He is the Son of Man, recalling the glory of the Most High in the book of Daniel, and in John's vision he sees the white hair, the blazing eyes penetrating the soul, and the feet of bronze, conveying the imagery of the God of Judgment. From his mouth comes the awesome voice like rushing waters, and the double-edged sword which both judges and protects.

When I was seventeen I wanted to know if there was a God or not, and I decided to write down who I wanted God to be. The first sentence read, 'If God is describable or possible I don't want it or him. My God will be both impossible and indescribable.' John proves this for me, because I sense that there is much more that he just couldn't write. It was indescribable. He does the best he can but then it's up to each of us to make it our own and see him for ourselves. I wouldn't want it any other way.

A prayer

Lord, I was made in your image
Yet I am damaged and not a true
reflection.
May your glory be revealed to me,
that your face might shine upon me
and I might be a light in your world.

GD

The risen Christ in view

When I saw him I fell at his feet as though dead. Then he placed his right hand on me and said: 'Do not be afraid. I am the First and the Last. I am the Living One; I was dead and behold I am alive for ever and ever! And I hold the keys of death and Hades. Write therefore, what you have seen, what is now and what will take place later. The mystery of the seven stars that you saw in my right hand and of the seven golden lampstands is this: The seven stars are the angels of the seven churches, and the seven lampstands are the seven churches.'

It is not very often that I am totally overwhelmed by God. But that is what happened to me one Easter Sunday at our evening service. And not just to me. It had been a meaningful service. We had sung the great Easter hymns and there had been a strong sense of God's presence. Then, at the end of the service, I moved to the back of the church with the other clergy to say goodbye. But as we stood there no one moved. Minutes went by, everyone sitting in deep prayer until one of the musicians began quietly playing one of the Graham Kendrick Easter songs. With loud, tuneful voices the whole congregation burst into song: 'You're alive, You're alive, You have risen'.

It was the vision of the risen Lord that made John fall to the ground. Like Isaiah, John collapses before so great a sight. Only the compassion and power of Jesus revives and restores him. A task is to be done. He is to share the message of Christ with the churches. As we share in the same task we too need the 'Easter Vision'. The vision that transformed the disciples from scared and tired men into zealous witnesses. The vision that turned around the persecutor Saul to become Paul, the greatest missionary. The vision that roots us to the spot, but then enlivens and sets our souls on fire to work for him, our risen Lord.

A thought

Our task as laymen is to live our personal communion with Christ with such intensity as to make it contagious.

Paul Tournier

GD

Let there be love

To the angel of the church in Ephesus write: These are the words of him who holds the seven stars in his right hand and walks among the seven golden lampstands: I know your deeds, your hard work and your perseverance. I know that you cannot tolerate wicked men, that you have tested those who claim to be apostles but are not, and have found them false. You have persevered and have endured hardships for my name, and have not grown weary. Yet I hold this against you: You have forsaken your first love.

The church in Ephesus had got bogged down. Hard work, perseverance, no tolerance of wicked men, and the testing of each and every message had become more important than the joyful expression of the faith. Of course these things are important. Without them heresy and apostasy lie just around the corner. But the Ephesians had lost their first love, their love for God and each other. They were so keen to keep out heretics and prevent them infiltrating the church that they built spiritual defences around themselves. So much so that they prevented the believers from enjoying true fellowship.

Sometimes I am better at finding fault than encouraging people. In a church I served in, the youth group leader (a friend of mine) started to lead the group away from the church. He led them into a strange, unaffiliated existence, so that they didn't belong anywhere. I spent hours of time and a lot of energy dissecting the situation and analysing it, determined to put it right. Then he was sacked from his duties. Needless to say, I was not the flavour of the month! But soon after that he became very ill. So ill that he wasn't expected to live. I went to the hospital to see him—and God dramatically humbled me. God healed my friend—and also healed our relationship. And he showed me in the process that it is more important 'to speak the truth in love' than 'to love to speak the truth'.

A thought

Our Lord does not care so much for the importance of our works as for the love with which they are done.

Teresa of Avila

GD

First love forsaken

Yet I hold this against you: You have forsaken your first love ... He who has an ear, let him hear what the Spirit says to the churches. To him who overcomes, I will give the right to eat from the tree of life, which is in the paradise of God.

Since I have been an adult Christian my love for God has matured—and I realize so much more than I did at the beginning. I remember the ecstatic prayer meetings we had in my youth group. We met in a darkened room, and expressed our emotions to God. We demonstrated our faith in him by boarding a local train. We would wait until it set off and then walk up and down the aisle preaching loudly to annoyed passengers (who were of course persecuting the Christian church when they swore at us!).

Is God really saying go back to those times? He wasn't, in Ephesus. The enthusiastic love that young Christians have can be attractive, but God had a different interest in the Ephesians. He was more concerned that they retrieved the love that went with their works. They had lost a loving motivation for their service, and were simply amassing good works. He wanted them to restore the right attitude to what they did.

It took me three years of adult faith to begin to understand what Jesus had done for me on the cross. Up to then I had been on a spiritual high, rejoicing in my new-found faith. Then the words of Jesus, 'My God, my God, why have you forsaken me?' suddenly became real. My life resonated with his as he hung there—pathetic and broken. It is his intense love, not ours, that forms the first love of our lives. Only this love restores the relationship between God and humanity, and gives us access to paradise and the tree of life. When we accept Jesus' love then we are accepted by God the Father. The tree of life transforms all our works and ensures us eternal life.

A prayer

Were the whole realm of nature mine
That were an offering far too small
Love so amazing, so divine
Demands my soul, my life, my all!

Isaac Watts

GD

Rich little poor church

To the angel of the church in Smyrna write: 'These are the words of him who is the First and the Last, who died and came to life again.'

The Christians at Smyrna were facing persecution. John encourages them by bringing to mind two dimensions of the Christian's life in Christ—eternity and the resurrection.

I hadn't been a Christian very long when I went to a praise meeting in Newcastle upon Tyne. After some introductory remarks the leader simply sat down—and the meeting was open for anyone to contribute. There was no order or control and the whole thing turned into a free-for-all (actually a free-for-some—those who had been before) to do what they wanted. I was terrified at the intense emotions shouted around the room, and I just longed for someone to come and control it all.

Happily for us, Jesus surrounds everything and all things with his order and love and self-control. To be the first and the last, or the alpha and omega, means he not only begins all things and ends all things but he is also there in the middle of it all. We can trust him because there is nothing beyond him. Not even death.

It took me three years of adult faith to start to understand the cross and another ten to begin to unravel the resurrection. We were studying Acts 17 in a staff meeting, and looking at how Paul preached to the 'men of Athens'. Sud-denly I realized that many people believe that Jesus lived and died, but the real leap of faith is to believe that he was raised. It's the centre of our faith. God offers the blessings of eternity and the glorious riches of the resurrection to all his people. Maybe we don't realize it until we really need it.

A prayer

*Lord Jesus Christ,
who, according to the will of the Father,
through the co-operation of the Holy Ghost,
hast by thy death given life to the world;
Deliver me.*

The dying prayer of St Margaret,
Queen of the Scots AD1093

GD

Getting alongside

I know your afflictions and your poverty—yet you are rich! I know the slander of those who say they are Jews and are not, but are a synagogue of Satan. Do not be afraid of what you are about to suffer. I tell you, the devil will put some of you in prison to test you, and you will suffer persecution for ten days. Be faithful, even to the point of death, and I will give you the crown of life.

Smyrna (Izmir, as it is now called) owes its roots to merchants who sailed the Mediterranean. They established it as a rich trading port, years before the Roman army occupied it. Smyrna had a strong pagan interest and loyalty to Rome from ancient times, erecting a temple to the goddess of Rome in 195BC. When Christianity took hold there, a clash of religious allegiance was inevitable.

The synagogue at Smyrna had attempted to isolate the Christians. It is likely that most of the church suffered at the hands of the Jews, and very possibly found it difficult to make much of a living in the area. Although the city was known for its riches, Christians were poor and afflicted. God therefore seeks to reassure his church.

Sympathy is as far from empathy as the east is from the west. Empathy is about getting alongside and feeling with a person. Many of us are just longing for someone to understand us but often all we get is advice. Our lives can be just so unbearable and lonely that we ache for someone who really knows us and who will always be there for us. God is precisely that someone who meets our need.

Fear, sadness, grief, joy, disgust and many other feelings need to find their way out rather than be bottled up inside. The mark of Jesus' love is that it is able to carry our emotions. He understands how we feel. When we come close to him and tell him all about it, he gives us hope even in the worst situations. In Smyrna, he showed them that the persecution would only be for ten days, even though some would be tested to the limit.

A thought

What do I need to do to empathize with others?

GD

Soil

[Jesus] said in a parable: 'A sower went out to sow his seed; and as he sowed, some fell along the path, and was trodden under foot, and the birds of the air devoured it. And some fell on the rock; and as it grew up, it withered away, because it had no moisture. And some fell among thorns; and the thorns grew with it and choked it. And some fell into good soil and grew, and yielded a hundredfold.' As he said this, he called out, 'He who has ears to hear, let him hear.'

I'm not a great gardener, though I do like messing about with bonsai trees. I do know, though, that the most important thing for any plant, in a pot or in a garden, is the soil in which it is planted.

In today's well-known story, it is the soil that counts. The seed is the same, the sower is the same, but the soil makes all the difference. And in case we don't grasp it, the story actually has an interpretation added on—the seed is the word of God, and the soil represents the various responses the word receives: from rejection, through to half-hearted and temporary acceptance, to full commitment.

It's one of those parables that church-goers find oddly comforting. It's all about those folk who won't respond to the gospel (and perhaps it provides us with some sort of excuse for ineffective evangelism too!) It needn't really concern us. But of course it does.

It is indeed about responses to the word. But it is not only the unbeliever who is challenged by God. Christians too need to grow, to bear fruit, and to flourish in their spiritual life. We need to hear God and respond. And that too depends on what sort of soil we are.

We have an advantage over those who are not interested in God: we know our need. Just as a gardener can improve soil by careful digging and feeding, we too can improve our receptivity to God by feeding ourselves.

In our prayers, we can focus on those areas of our lives that need improvement. We can pay particular attention to those aspects of Christian teaching that make us uncomfortable (and so probably point to areas of need). And as we do this we will prove more and more able to bear fruit for God.

MM

The cutting edge

To the angel of the church in Pergamum write: These are the words of him who has the sharp, double-edged sword. I know where you live—where Satan has his throne. Yet you remain true to my name. You did not renounce your faith in me, even in the days of Antipas, my faithful witness, who was put to death in your city—where Satan lives.

Pergamum was the capital of the area, and the most loyal to the Emperor of Rome. The 800-foot hill in the city was littered with temples and shrines to the gods, and crowned with an enormous altar to Zeus. There was no escape from the fact that Christians were living in a 'foreign land'. The question arises from this passage: how can Christians develop a cutting edge to their faith?

What Jesus seems to say is that the Christians must look at their society and look to God, and discover what it is that God is calling them to do. Then they will find the cutting edge of the 'sharp double-edged sword'. Jesus knows where they live, and also knows that some will be called upon to make the ultimate sacrifice as Antipas did. His thorough knowledge of them makes it all the more important that each church member should play his or her part fully. There are so many needs in the world that to find God's specific will is essential. To do that, we can ask three questions:

1. What is God saying to me through prayer? Without this there will be no real motivation in what we do, and we shan't have the courage to do it anyway.

2. What are my best skills at the moment? God always equips us to do his will but often our skills can vary depending upon how sharp we are.

3. What possibilities are presenting themselves? We need to match the blade to the material, and not try to take on the world with a hacksaw.

At the end of the day it is Jesus who is the sharp double-edged sword, and we must rely totally on him. I have discovered that, when I do, he calls me to be his witness, and that can often be a testing and incisive experience.

A prayer

Lord, may I be salt and light for you.
Someone who is not frightened to do your will,
Someone who obeys your every command.
Equip me, send me, and use me, in Jesus' name. Amen.

GD

Hold to what is true

I have a few things against you: You have people there who hold to the teaching of Balaam, who taught Balak to entice the Israelites to sin by eating food sacrificed to idols and by committing sexual immorality. Likewise you also have those who hold to the teaching of the Nicolaitans. Repent therefore! Otherwise I will soon come to you and will fight against them with the sword of my mouth. He who has an ear, let him hear what the Spirit says to the churches. To him who overcomes, I will give some of the hidden manna. I will also give him a white stone with a new name written on it, known only to him who receives it.

Balak (King of Moab) tried to get Balaam, a seer, to curse the Israelites who were encamped on his land. Although Balaam refused, he counselled Balak to entice the Israelite men to indulge in sexual immorality with the Moabite women. Likewise, the Nicolaitans led the people of God into sexual immorality and eating food offered to idols. For the average pagan of the time, using a prostitute was a trifling offence, and almost all the food would be offered to an idol somewhere on its way to the shops. Being a Christian wasn't easy. But it never has been. Difficult decisions face us all the time, especially in the work place. I have known friends lose their jobs or resign their positions because they wouldn't compromise their faith or take part in shady deals.

The reward for faithfulness is threefold. It was for the Christians at Pergamum and it is for us today. Hidden manna is given to us, reminding us of the food given to the Israelites in the wilderness. Jesus is saying, symbolically, that he will give to us the food of life. A white stone is given to us—and a white stone was given to someone acquitted after a trial. The guilty party was given a black one. Again symbolically, Jesus is saying we shall receive forgiveness for our sins. Finally, a new name will be given to us—a unique name given to each person who discovers a relationship with the risen Lord. Reward indeed!

A thought

Our world is so exceedingly rich in delusions that a truth is priceless.

Carl Jung

GD

Jesus the judge

To the angel of the church in Thyatira write: These are the words of the Son of God, whose eyes are like blazing fire and whose feet are like burnished bronze. I know your deeds, your love and faith, your service and perseverance, and that you are now doing more than you did at first. Nevertheless, I have this against you: You tolerate that woman Jezebel, who calls herself a prophetess. By her teaching she misleads my servants into sexual immorality and the eating of food sacrificed to idols. I have given her time to repent of her immorality, but she is unwilling. So I will cast her on a bed of suffering, and I will make those who commit adultery with her suffer intensely, unless they repent of her ways.

Jesus is the 'Son of God', the redeemer and saviour. He acts in full compliance with God the Father. His eyes are like blazing fire, refining, judging, and penetrating the soul. Although this church had some qualities to commend it, it had fallen to the same problems as the Christians at Pergamum. Banquets that regularly ended in orgies challenged their faith. The Nicolaitans encouraged participation. They had again spread their sinister ideas of eating unclean food and indulging in sexual misconduct. Jesus the judge, yet merciful, gives Jezebel time to repent, but when she refuses he brings immense suffering on her for her adultery. Those who are unwilling to repent cannot be tolerated in the church. Sinners are people for whom Christ died and he will bring them to eternal life, but those who refuse to accept his forgiveness, and blatantly continue to sin will no doubt suffer the same consequences as Jezebel.

Sobering thoughts for the Christians at Thyatira, and for us.

A prayer

Judge eternal throned in splendour,
Lord of lords and King of kings
With the living fire of judgment,
Purge this realm of bitter things.

Crown O Lord your own endeavour,
Cleave our darkness with your sword,
Cheer the faint and feed the hungry
With the richness of your word;
Cleanse the body of this nation
Through the glory of the Lord.

H.S. Holland

GD

The morning star

To him who overcomes and does my will to the end, I will give authority over the nations—'he will rule them with an iron sceptre; he will dash them to pieces like pottery'—just as I have received authority from my Father. I will also give him the morning star. He who has an ear, let him hear what the Spirit says to the churches.

I have been to a number of Greek islands for holidays. I love the atmosphere, the rugged hills, the parched landscape and the clear green sea. In the summer, it is so hot that it is difficult to sleep at night, but the early morning is perfect. The night gives way to the deep blue sky, which in turn slowly brightens, to reveal the day. Once, as I watched the dawn rise, a bright crystal hung in the sky as the other stars disappeared. It shone with a distinct radiance, penetrating, icy and sharp against the rolling daylight. It was the morning star.

Jesus is described twice in Revelation as the bright morning star. Even in the ordinary light of day he shines with a distinctive light. Against the backdrop of this fallen world, his works are a complete contrast. In places of evil, creation waits for release, longing for his light to destroy the darkness. When John said that Jesus is the morning star he was making a claim that people would recognize.

The morning star is Venus, and from Babylonian times Venus represented sovereignty. Roman soldiers would carry it as a symbol on their standard to claim victory and supreme control.

Those who worshipped the morning star worshipped the one who gave sovereignty. As we worship Jesus, we are reminded that he is distinctive, crystal clear, penetrating to the soul and radiant. Above all, he is our sovereign Lord.

A meditation

Come see the beauty of the Lord,
Come see the beauty of his face,
See the lamb that once was slain,
See on his palms is carv'd your name.
See how our pain has pierced his heart,
And on his brow he bears our pride:
A crown of thorns.

Graham Kendrick

GD

Wake up!

To the angel of the church in Sardis write: These are the words of him who holds the seven spirits of God and the seven stars. I know your deeds; you have a reputation of being alive but you are dead. Wake up! Strengthen what remains and is about to die, for I have not found your deeds complete in the sight of my God. Remember therefore, what you have received and heard; obey it and repent. But if you do not wake up, I will come like a thief, and you will not know at what time I will come to you.

There must have been some shocked Christians around when these letters to the churches were delivered. None more so than in Sardis. Imagine a big and thriving church. There are stimulating homegroups, much pastoral work, music, drama and dance *par excellence*. Everyone around knows it as the 'cathedral' of the area. Then it receives this letter: 'you have a reputation for being alive, but you are dead'.

Sardis was a sad place. A city of past glory with a famous reputation, but dying underneath. The church reflected the city's secret ruin. Jesus appeals to them to repent and remember what they had. If they did not wake up to his word, then they would awake to his judgment. We may be tempted to sit back and criticize a local church in the light of the passage. But the church is made up of individuals and which of us can say that we are totally alive to God?

Our car was broken into recently. What annoyed me the most was not the damage, but that if I had only remembered to put the alarm on it might have been different. Many people have this 'if only…' feeling often in life. Perhaps it can awaken us to a more important thief-like event and, unlike Sardis, spur us on to be ready.

A prayer

Jesus, help me and help my church to remember what we have received and heard. Help us to obey it, and to repent. If we are dead in your sight, show us—and make us alive again.

GD

The book of life

Yet you have a few people in Sardis who have not soiled their clothes. They will walk with me, dressed in white, for they are worthy. He who overcomes will, like them, be dressed in white. I will never erase his name from the book of life, but will acknowledge his name before my Father and his angels. He who has an ear, let him hear what the Spirit says to the churches.

When I take a wedding I always worry that something will go wrong at the signing of the registers. Most couples visibly relax at that moment. But I tense up, because I know that the signing must be accurate and precise. I probably labour the point in the rehearsal, but at the end of the day these signatures are going to remain for as long as time will allow. They are not destroyed or erased at any point.

The idea of there being a heavenly register, the 'book of life', is first found in Exodus 32:32. The names of all God's people appear in it. The book belongs to the Lord. He wrote it and, like the wedding registers, a marriage must take place before his people can be written in. The Church, as the bride of Christ, is entered, but when we consider the church at Sardis we see that the relationship is in serious trouble. The bride is not the white-clothed beautifully adorned lady. A rather soiled image, in danger of being blotted out of the register, is the condition of many in the church.

However, Jesus does say that there are a few who are worthy. These are the ones who will wear the white garments of holiness, the ones who will be acknowledged by Christ to the Father. They are assured of eternal life and an intimacy with Jesus as they walk with him. These qualities of purity, worth, reassurance and intimacy are the marks of a good relationship. Our responsibility as the Church, the bride of Christ, is to overcome the temptations of evil and remain worthy of having our names written in the book.

A question

What are the vows that have been made between ourselves and God?

GD

The body of Christ

It was not on tales artfully spun that we relied when we told you of the power of our Lord Jesus Christ and his coming; we saw him with our own eyes in majesty, when at the hands of God the Father he was invested with honour and glory, and there came to him from the sublime Presence a voice which said: 'This is my Son, my Beloved, on whom my favour rests.' This voice from heaven we ourselves heard; when it came, we were with him on the sacred mountain. All this only confirms for us the message of the prophets, to which you will do well to attend, because it is like a lamp shining in a murky place, until the day breaks and the morning star rises to illuminate your minds.

The glory of God is pretty daunting— unless he hides it. The tale that we are, reading today (a true one, the writer tells us) is of a day when the glory of God shone out of Jesus and they saw it. It isn't that the writer is boasting. He is simply saying that this is what happened, and he is telling the truth. The disciples on the mount of transfiguration heard a voice from the Presence saying just who Jesus was. It confirmed the message of the prophets for them, and if their readers will also listen to it it will be a light for them in their darkness.

Before the transfiguration the disciples saw the man Jesus. Then, in the dazzling event, they saw Elijah the prophet and Moses the lawgiver talking with Jesus. Afterwards they just saw Jesus. Perhaps as we read the Old Testament, or listen to it read in church, we can pray for the insight that connects the law and the prophets with Jesus, and with us. And when we are given the bread, in the service that is about communion be-tween God and man through Christ, perhaps we can pray to be made aware of the glory of what is given to us: 'The body of Christ...'

SB

Opening the door

To the angel of the church in Philadelphia write: These are the words of him who is holy and true, who holds the key of David. What he opens no-one can shut; and what he shuts, no-one can open. I know your deeds. See, I have placed before you an open door that no-one can shut. I know that you have little strength, yet you have kept my word and have not denied my name. I will make those who are of the synagogue of Satan, who claim to be Jews though they are not, but are liars—I will make them come and fall down at your feet and acknowledge that I have loved you.

Someone I know once batted for six an idea that I had been working on, and I was very angry. I felt like showing him up in front of others. In conversation with a friend, I worked through what would happen if I did; for him, for me and for other people. Then, still holding to my view, I let go of the problem, submitting to God's command to love. The relationship was immediately restored; and more, it was deeply enriched.

History tells us the so-called Jews in Philadelphia abused and victimized the Christians. Yet the church never took vengeance, even though they were wildly provoked. What was their secret? Jesus tells us. They kept the word of God—the Old Testament. John's reference to the key of David reminds us that Eliakim, in Isaiah 22:22, held the key and exercised complete control in the house of David. Now Jesus holds it and decides what will happen. He is the supreme authority. He even holds the keys of death and Hades. The Philadelphians obeyed God's word, and gained a perspective that enabled them to see beyond this life to eternity.

God's love can transform our revengeful attitudes into noble and gracious ones. The Philadelphians had learned this secret, and of all the Christians in Revelation they stand out as a great example of faithfulness and commitment to God.

A prayer

Lord, transform my attitudes through your love, and help me to keep your word.

GD

A pillar of the church

I am coming soon. Hold on to what you have so that no-one will take your crown. Him who overcomes I will make a pillar in the temple of my God. Never again will he leave it. I will write on him the name of my God and the name of the city of my God, the new Jerusalem, which is coming down out of heaven from my God; and I will also write on him my new name. He who has an ear, let him hear what the Spirit says to the churches.

The Philadelphians were used to things not lasting for ever. Their town suffered great destruction from earthquakes, especially the one in AD17. Some of the citizens didn't return but settled in the neighbouring districts for protection. Jesus says that he will make them a pillar in the temple, the everlasting place where God dwells. They must have felt good. At last there was some permanence in a very shaky world. In ancient times, pillars often had inscriptions on them describing members of the community who had been honoured. These 'pillars of society', soldiers, great statesmen and others, were commemorated for all to see.

Pillars in some churches are weedy-looking affairs, completely useless save for decoration. My idea of proper pillars are the ones you will see as you enter Durham Cathedral. Some must be fifteen to twenty feet in diameter. Coming from the North East, I spent many hours of my childhood admiring these magnificent, strong, sturdy, faithful, yet simply decorated supports.

Jesus commends the Philadelphians by suggesting that they will be pillars of the temple of God. They will have inscriptions written on them. The name of God, the place of God and the new name will mark them out. If we were to write these inscriptions in today's language they might read like this: You belong to me; You have a place in heaven; You are redeemed.

A thought

What does it mean to you to be a pillar in the house of your God? And what will it mean?

GD

313

Neither cold nor hot

To the angel of the church in Laodicea write: These are the words of the Amen, the faithful and true witness, the ruler of God's creation. I know your deeds, that you are neither cold nor hot. I wish you were either one or the other! So, because you are lukewarm—neither hot nor cold—I am about to spit you out of my mouth.

Imagine a hot spring. It flows steaming from its source across a plateau—winding its way, and cooling all the time. After some miles it cascades over a cliff edge into a putrid lukewarm pool. This picture would be very familiar to the Christians at Laodicea. Close to where they lived was this natural feature of landscape, and I bet it smelt awful in the town. So when Jesus says that he will spit or spew them out for their lukewarmness, they knew what he meant.

One of the worst things in the world is lukewarmness, like tepid food or coffee left standing, a bath that's gone cold or a weak handshake. What Jesus wants is for us to be on fire. God doesn't want us to remain half-hearted. He will help us to see areas of our lives that are apathetic. He will show us the reason why it is so, if we ask him. Then he will help us to reignite them. The spark of the Holy Spirit will awaken in us his new life, robust, joyful, ecstatic. As we mature the flame will burn more subtly. We will identify with him in the deeper qualities of the Spirit, responsibility, wisdom and suffering. All we are asked to do is to be open to him as he knocks at the door.

A prayer

Fire of God, Titanic Spirit,
Burn within our hearts today;
Cleanse our sin—may we exhibit
holiness in every way:
Purge the squalidness that shames us,
Soils the body, taints the soul;
And through Jesus Christ who claims us,
Purify us, make us whole.

Michael Saward

GD

I stand . . . and knock

Those whom I love I rebuke and discipline. So be earnest, and repent. Here I am! I stand at the door and knock. If anyone hears my voice and opens the door, I will go in and eat with him and he with me. To him who overcomes, I will give the right to sit with me on my throne, just as I overcame and sat down with my Father on his throne. He who has an ear, let him hear what the Spirit says to the churches.

Jesus knocks at the door when we begin the Christian life, but it doesn't stop there. St Teresa had a vision of our lives as an enormous castle with many rooms to be cleaned and sanctified. There are many doors to be opened, and some are easier to open to God than others. The easy ones lead to rooms that look quite clean and respectable, well arranged, nicely decorated and comfortable. My good works shine as examples of this kind of room. Jesus is very welcome here. But when I get down to the dungeons, things deteriorate. I'm not so keen to let others down here, especially not to that very dank and black one. The smell is appalling, and I certainly wouldn't allow Jesus to come in. Yet perhaps a better picture is not of me as host, showing Jesus around, but of me locked inside, waiting for Jesus to encourage me to unlock the door.

A meditation

O Lord your tenderness,
melting all my bitterness,
O Lord I receive your love.

O Lord your loveliness,
changing all my ugliness,
O Lord I receive your love.

Graham Kendrick

GD

To him who overcomes

To him who overcomes I will give . . . the right to eat of the tree of life . . . protection from the second death . . . some of the hidden manna . . . a white stone . . . a new name . . . authority over the nations . . . the morning star . . . a white robe . . . a name in the book of life . . . acknowledgement before my Father . . . a place in the temple as a pillar of God . . . the right to sit with me on my throne.

When I went to junior music circle as a child, I played the piano in front of the whole class. I hated doing it, but I loved the reward my parents bought me afterwards. The 'overcoming' could not have been easy in all these Revelation churches, but to those who achieved it the rewards were overwhelming.

How can we overcome? I heard a saying yesterday, 'It's easy to jump into a mud pool but it's much more difficult to get out.' Like jumping into a mud pool, different sins are tempting to some and repulsive to others. We're all different, and will be secretly tempted in different ways. This has the added bonus for the tempter of placing us in glorious isolation. The Christian finds him or herself so embarrassed about the temptation that overcoming it has to be a private endeavour.

My experience of overcoming sin tells me that it cannot be faced alone. There is something almost sacramental about getting it into the open, confessing it, debunking its power. When that occurs, the battle is half won. Sin no longer holds the pent-up energy that arms the trap. I've also found that to overcome temptation or sin means facing it head on. Asking myself questions: What will happen if I continue to do this? Why do I keep doing it? Is there a better way of living? To prevent falling, I need to get in touch with my God-given power of choice. And I don't do this alone. I need someone else who knows me, whom I can trust and who will be broad-minded enough not to judge me.

A thought

No temptation has overtaken you that is not common to man. God is faithful, and he will not let you be tempted beyond your strength, but with the temptation will also provide the way of escape, that you may be able to endure it.

1 Corinthians 10:13

GD

Listening for the Spirit

He who has an ear, let him hear what the Spirit says to the churches.

This epitaph after each letter deserves to be looked at on its own. For year after year Christians have tried faithfully to hear the Spirit's voice. Yet so often the Church has been divided and disunited over the truth. In our own day, there are constant disagreements. The ordination and role of women. What the Bible really means. Even belief in the resurrection. Where is the Spirit's voice?

I've noticed that many Christian leaders no longer issue a statement of agreement at the end of conferences. It's not possible because the entire time would be spent in drafting it. It would end up so bland that it would be worthless. Yet a new consensus of what the Spirit is saying is emerging. It happens when we work together and it's about the Bible in action rather than intellectual assent.

Christians are hopping across denominational boundaries and discovering how God is working. Contemplative prayer is helping all kinds of groups to hear the Spirit. People are 'marching for Jesus', meeting in homes to pray and study, spreading the gospel in their local area.

Jesus' prayer for his followers on the night before he died was that they should be one. John records the conversation in chapter 17 of his Gospel. In chapter 16 he outlines the work of the Spirit which is to reveal the truth and bring glory to Jesus. In the next week will you try to find time to read those two chapters? We are now learning by experience that to find out what the Spirit is saying to the churches we need to get together and listen.

A prayer

O Breath of life, come sweeping through us,
Revive your church with life and power;
O Breath of life, come cleanse, renew us
And fit your church to meet this hour.

Elizabeth Head

GD

The blood of Christ

But Christ has come, as the high priest of all the blessings which were to come. He has passed through the greater, the more perfect tent, which is better than the one made by men's hands because it is not of this created order; and he has entered the sanctuary once and for all, taking with him not the blood of goats and bull calves, but his own blood, having won an eternal redemption for us. The blood of goats and bulls and the ashes of a heifer are sprinkled on those who have incurred defilement and they restore the holiness of their outward lives; how much more effectively the blood of Christ, who offered himself as the perfect sacrifice to God through the eternal Spirit, can purify our inner self from dead actions so that we do our service to the living God.

As I write the world is in a terrible mess, with war and conflicts in a number of areas. There are only two ways to maintain peace. One is the outward way, which is to shoot, bomb or otherwise destroy those who refuse to keep the peace—and to do that is not to make peace anyway. It is simply controlling the amount of warring that takes place. The other way is the inner way. This is a peace that comes from the heart, so that a person chooses peace and in all their actions rejects destruction. It isn't a mass choice; only and always an individual choice. Like the words of Sir Cecil Spring-Rice's hymn:

And soul by soul and silently,
her shining bounds increase,
And her ways are ways of gentleness,
and all her paths are peace.

The law of Moses was written on tablets of stone, and the blood of the Old Testament sacrifices was sprinkled on the outside of people. But the law of the new covenant is written on our hearts, and the blood of Christ is sprinkled on our hearts. Within us, which is where the action always springs from.

So if you go to the Eucharist today, pray that the words will come to you in power and enter into you.

'Peace be with you . . .'

'The blood of Christ . . .'

SB

Bad people

Why make your wickedness your boast, you man of might, forging wild lies all day against God's loyal servant? Your slanderous tongue is sharp as a razor. You love evil and not good, falsehood, not speaking the truth; cruel gossip you love and slanderous talk. So may God pull you down to the ground, sweep you away, leave you ruined and homeless, uprooted from the land of the living.

Whoever wrote this Psalm felt violently. He wanted God to pull the liars and the slanderers and the gossips down to the ground, sweep them away and leave them ruined and homeless.

Does God hear that kind of prayer? If not, was the Psalmist wrong to harbour prayerful thoughts like these? This at least can be said, he was being honest, he did so feel about the wicked doers, and far better that than excusing their obnoxious deeds; and he clearly had very definite standards about right and wrong.

If to long for the downfall of anyone, however bad, is not a proper sentiment in prayer (and there are more violent ones than this in the Psalms), God knows how to sort out our prayers, hearing the good and turning a deaf ear to the bad. And if judgment is to fall on the evil men who plot and plan evil deeds (and who shall say it isn't?), God will execute it in his own good time. It is not for us to interfere.

A Prayer

Lord, I pray today for the people in prison: some of them good people— prisoners of conscience; some of them bad people—murderers, terrorists, rapists. Lord, you know these prisoners as we do not know them, you know what has made them what they are. You are a God of judgment but you are also a God of infinite mercy. Lord, I do not know what to pray but I commit them into your hands.

DCF

Catastrophes

God is our hope and strength: a very present help in trouble. Therefore will we not fear, though the earth be moved: and though the hills be carried into the midst of the sea.

What is in mind here is troubles on a *world scale*. And we cannot dodge them. This is the terror of television. It brings murder and rape and hunger and devastation from earthquake, famine and flood right into our sitting rooms at the end of the day, just when we are relaxing after the day's work. But we can't relax. It gets us 'worked up'. And people who live alone say, 'It gets you down.' And no small part of the trouble is caused by the fact that we can do very little about these world catastrophes, beyond responding possibly to an appeal for financial help from some relief fund.

We aren't wrong to be upset. We would be callous creatures if we were not; but the tragedy is that if we hear too much and too long of nothing but calamities we become insensitive to them. The human heart does not possess the capacity to take on the troubles of the world. So what should we do? Switch of the television? Stop taking a daily newspaper? This may be the right action sometimes but it is too negative to deal with our fears. We shall know all the time that the catastrophes are continuing.

We must bring God into our picture of the world. It is, after all, his world, not mine or yours. Actually I am his too and so are you. Some people will say, 'Ah! but it is because of these catastrophes that we cannot believe in God any more.' But are catastrophes new? Were there no catastrophes in the Psalmist's day when he wrote the verse we have just read? Read your Old Testament. Plenty of carnage and cruelty there. But 'God is our hope and strength . . .'

A prayer

Lord, sometimes I get 'worked up' about air pollution, about the spoilation of the environment, the terrorism, the vandalism and the burglars. I can't help it. I am made that way. Lord, let me see you in control. I want to be a strong person. You can make me strong.

DCF

Freedom from sins

Out of the depths have I called to thee, O Lord; Lord, hear my cry. Let thy ears be attentive to my plea for mercy. If thou, Lord, shouldst keep account of sins, who, O Lord, could hold up his head? But in thee is forgiveness, and therefore thou art revered. I wait for the Lord with all my soul . . . more eagerly than watchmen for the morning. Like men who watch for the morning, O Israel, look for the Lord. For in the Lord is love unfailing, and great is his power to set men free. He alone will set Israel free from all their sins.

The trouble with sins is that they turn into habits if neglected. Then they wind round and round our thoughts and actions like convolvulus in the garden. Then freedom to develop is restricted. We are not all we might be. This is obvious in extreme cases like drug-addiction, alcoholism and chain smoking. Health is undermined. But cruelty, dishonesty and greed can so gain a hold in people's lifestyle that they seem incapable of being anything else but cruel, dishonest and greedy.

So let us beware. We are all sinning one way or another—which does not mean everybody is as bad as everybody else. But we need to confess our sins and seek for God's forgiveness, which he readily gives. God alone can set us free, but we must cry to him, even from the depths.

Prayer

Almighty God, who forgives all who truly repent, have mercy upon me, pardon and deliver me from all my sins, confirm and strengthen me in all goodness, and keep me in life eternal; through Jesus Christ our Lord.

DCF

In the deep

Save me, O God: for the waters are come in, even unto my soul. I stick fast in the deep mire, where no ground is: I am come into deep waters, so that the floods run over me . . . Hear me, O God, in the multitude of thy mercy: even in the truth of thy salvation. Take me out of the mire, that I sink not: O let me be delivered from them that hate me, and out of the deep waters. Let not the water-flood drown me, neither let the deep swallow me up: and let not the pit shut her mouth upon me.

I would not recognize you as someone I could understand if you told me you had never been in the deep like the writer of the above prayer for deliverance, because that is what it is. Have you never been let down by a friend and cried your heart out? Do you know nothing of that empty feeling when you walk away from a hospital ward knowing that there can't be many more visits, for that patient's illness is incurable; it is only a matter of time? Or you are short of money. Or your job is likely to come to an end. Or you wonder how you will 'cope' when you are old. Or you have made an awful blunder and can't see how you can escape the consequence.

If you don't know life turning this kind of face towards you, ugly and menacing, then you had better tear up Psalm 69, it has nothing for you. But Jesus knew it. He sank in the deep mire where no ground is, and he prayed this Psalm. So keep it by you. You may need it some day.

A prayer

Lord, remember today the broken-hearted, the faint-hearted, and all those who have completely lost heart; Thou, Lord, unto whom all hearts are open, all desires known, Lift them up I beseech thee, and let them praise thy name.

DCF

Down at the bottom

My God, my God, why hast thou forsaken me and art so far from saving me, from heeding my groans? O my God, I cry in the day-time but thou dost not answer, in the night I cry but get no respite. And yet thou art enthroned in holiness, thou art he whose praises Israel sings. In thee our fathers put their trust; they trusted, and thou didst rescue them. Unto thee they cried and were delivered; in thee they trusted and were not put to shame. But I am a worm, not a man, abused by all men, scorned by the people.

Do we have to read these depressing verses? Can't we tear them out of the Bible leaving only the inspiring bits? Who wants to be made miserable? If, however, we did this, the Scriptures would only speak to part of our experience, because at times we are wretched like the writer of these verses. George Orwell wasn't far out when he wrote, 'Most people get a fair amount of fun out of their lives, but on balance life is suffering, and only the very young or the very foolish imagine otherwise.'

Physical pain is the trouble here, the kind of pain which for its intensity and duration scorches you. Some will know what this is like. You can't think of anything or anybody. You certainly can't pray. There is nothing but the pain. The whole world has shrunk to that one thing. You are down at the bottom.

Please God you who read this won't descend there today, but if you do, try to remember this—others have been down there before you, and among them, chiefest among them, Jesus Christ our Lord. Don't we say in the Creed, 'He descended into Hell'? But God brought him out didn't he? He does not fail nor forsake us.

Pray today

—for any known to be ill, the broken in body, some broken in mind, the blind, the deaf, the crippled: Lord, have mercy upon them, I beseech you.

DCF

Confession

Happy the man whose disobedience is forgiven, whose sin is put away! Happy is a man when the Lord lays no guilt to his account, and in his spirit there is no deceit. While I refused to speak, my body wasted away with moaning all day long. For day and night thy hand was heavy upon me, the sap in me dried up as in summer drought. Then I declared my sin, I did not conceal my guilt. I said, 'With sorrow I will confess my disobedience to the Lord'; then thou didst remit the penalty of my sin.

Here is a man who is proud, wooden and stubborn. He knows he has broken one of God's commandments but he won't admit it. Or more likely he says to himself, 'Well, everyone does it, why shouldn't I?' And if he is very sophisticated he argues along the lines that the lifestyle looked for from Christians in the New Testament does not apply in our different cultural environment. We know so much better these days how the human body and mind work. No there really is no sin to confess. But his uneasy conscience won't go away. It makes him miserable. And aspirins don't really help. Even his physical health is undermined when this inner unease drags on.

A bad case! Yes, no doubt, but even in mild cases of 'not coming clean' in God's presence, prayer becomes a farce and worship barren. The remedy, however, is at hand. 'Lord, I did wrong...'

Then the sun breaks out again through the clouds. Whoever does not know what all this means cannot ever have really faced up to himself in the presence of God.

A prayer

Dear Lord and Father of mankind,
Forgive our foolish ways!
Re-clothe us in our rightful mind,
In purer lives thy service find,
In deeper reverence praise.

J.G. *Whittier*

DCF

Those in authority

I urge, then, first of all, that requests, prayers, intercession and thanksgiving be made for everyone—for kings and all those in authority, that we may live peaceful and quiet lives in all godliness and holiness. This is good, and pleases God our Saviour, who wants all men to be saved and to come to a knowledge of the truth. For there is one God and one mediator between God and men, the man Christ Jesus, who gave himself as a ransom for all men—the testimony given in its proper time. And for this purpose I was appointed a herald and an apostle—I am telling the truth, I am not lying—and a teacher of the true faith to the Gentiles.

The Epistle for today picks up the theme of 'those in authority'. The writer tells Timothy, a relatively young (thirty-year-old!) church leader, that prayers should be said 'first of all' for 'kings and those in authority'. When we think that the 'kings' he must have had in mind would have included the Roman Emperor and all those other local monarchs we read about in Acts (Agrippa, Festus and so on), we can appreciate that it is not necessary to approve of them in order to pray for them.

All authority comes from God—that's Paul's argument in Romans 13:1. God is on the side of law and order. He wants us to lead 'peaceful and quiet lives' (v. 2). The opposite of order is anarchy and lawlessness, and that contradicts the divine pattern of human life. We should pray for those who have authority because it is a fearful responsibility and because, in so far as they are maintaining an ordered and lawful society, they are doing God's work.

Of course that doesn't mean that we have to collude with evil, or that Christians can never oppose anyone in authority. John the Baptist opposed Herod. The apostles refused to obey a legal order to desist from preaching the gospel (Acts 4:19–20). But it does mean that we recognize the value of lawful authority and only oppose it when we are sure it is setting itself up against the will of God. And, all the while, we pray.

A prayer

Lord God, you have called us to live in peace with one another. Bless the peacemakers and give wisdom to all those in authority, that they may seek your will and honour your way. For Jesus Christ's sake. Amen.

DW

An apostolic torpedo

Paul, an apostle—sent not from men nor by man, but by Jesus Christ and God the Father, who raised him from the dead—and all the brothers with me, To the churches in Galatia: Grace and peace to you from God our Father and the Lord Jesus Christ.

St Paul usually begins his letters to the churches with a greeting... 'Dear Galatians'... and some friendly and encouraging things about them. This letter is very different. His opening is abrupt ('Paul, an apostle') and his good wishes are simply 'grace and peace'. It's as though he's angry and upset and can't wait to get to the point! As the letter was read out to the Christians in Galatia, I expect they guessed what was coming. They were about to be struck amidships by an apostolic torpedo!

It's never easy to write an unpleasant letter, much less an angry one—even when, as here, we believe it's absolutely essential. Paul could not stand by and watch the church at Galatia, which he had helped to found, drifting off into error. And he wasn't going to pull his punches in warning them. You may feel, as you read on in this letter, that he was a bit too aggressive and angry. But from what we can gather the church did take note of his warnings and acted on them.

What can't be denied is the passion with which Paul wrote. It really mattered to him that these new Christians were being led away from the simple, liberating truth of 'grace' and 'peace' through Jesus Christ.

For him, grace and peace always went together. Both were gifts of God. They couldn't be earned by fulfilling ritual or observing religious rules. They could only be received. It really worried him that the Galatians might miss out on God's priceless gifts.

Perhaps the lesson for us is that it's sometimes better to be angry in the cause of peace than peaceful just for the sake of avoiding anger!

A prayer

Dear Lord, Help me to care about those whose faith is under attack and even to be angry, if necessary, when I see people being misled. But help me to temper my anger with the gifts of grace and peace. Amen.

DW

It's all about grace

I am astonished that you are so quickly deserting the one who called you by the grace of Christ and are turning to a different gospel—which is really no gospel at all. Evidently some people are throwing you into confusion and are trying to pervert the gospel of Christ. But even if we or an angel from heaven should preach a gospel other than the one we preached to you, let him be eternally condemned . . . Am I now trying to win the approval of men, or of God? Or am I trying to please men? If I were still trying to please men, I would not be a servant of Christ.

It doesn't take Paul long to get into his main theme: 'I am astonished that you are so quickly deserting the one who called you by the grace of Christ and are turning to a different gospel'. That's his point—what you are now accepting is a completely different message from the one that originally brought you to Christ. It's not even a different gospel, really—it's no 'gospel' at all, because it isn't 'good news' but bad. It isn't a gospel of 'grace' (that word again—v. 6) and so it cannot be the gospel of Christ.

Paul always saw the issue in very stark terms. For him, as a Jew, it was crystal clear. Either we are justified before God on the grounds of what we have done or on the grounds of what God has done—what he polarized as 'Law' versus 'Grace'. There was no middle ground, because if we could save ourselves (by keeping God's law and living moral and upright lives) then there was no need of Jesus Christ and the cross.

In some ways, this really is the central issue in religion. Many people would welcome a religion that said, 'Here are the rules, there are the rituals, these are the requirements: keep the rules, observe the rituals, fulfil the requirements—and God will be satisfied'. It would also satisfy human pride (Look, I did it!) and it would seem just and fair, even if we failed. So it is rather difficult sometimes to accept that the Christian faith simply isn't like that at all. There are no rules, no rituals and no requirements beyond the sovereign law of love. It is a religion of gift. It is all about grace.

A prayer

Heavenly Father, help me to please you not because I have kept the rules but because I love you. Amen.

DW

The journey to faith

I want you to know, brothers, that the gospel I preached is not something that man made up. I did not receive it from any man, nor was I taught it; rather, I received it by revelation from Jesus Christ. For you have heard of my previous way of life in Judaism, how intensely I persecuted the church of God and tried to destroy it . . . But when God, who set me apart from birth and called me by his grace, was pleased to reveal his Son in me so that I might preach him among the Gentiles, I did not consult any man . . . I went immediately into Arabia and later returned to Damascus. Then, after three years, I went up to Jerusalem to get acquainted with Peter . . . Later I went to Syria and Cilicia. I was personally unknown to the churches of Judea that are in Christ. They only heard the report: 'The man who formerly persecuted us is now preaching the faith he once tried to destroy.' And they praised God because of me.

Paul relates (not for the first time) his 'faith journey', what people sometimes call their 'testimony'. He does it for a particular reason—to make it clear that the message of the gospel which he originally brought to them was not 'something that man made up' (v. 11), but something that God revealed to him through Jesus Christ (vv. 12 and 15–16). His journey to faith followed a familiar path: call, revelation, response. For most of us it is less dramatic than Paul's journey, but time and again people say that they felt that God was 'speaking' to them and that as they responded to that revelation so God drew them to Jesus Christ . . . gradually, perhaps, but firmly. At any rate, most of us will agree that the process was ninety per cent God and only ten per cent ourselves. Paul was 'extremely zealous' for his former religion (v. 14) but it was

not until God spoke to him ('revealed his Son in me') that he took the decisive step of faith.

I think that's why for Paul the gospel itself is so vitally important. Left to himself—to human logic and reason—he would have remained in a religion of law, desperately trying to fulfil its demands. God had shown him a better way. Now why on earth would the Galatians want to go back on that?

A prayer

Heavenly Father, thank you for the truth you have revealed in Jesus. Help me to accept it, and the freedom that it brings. Amen.

DW

It's not 'DIY'

Fourteen years later I went up again to Jerusalem, this time with Barnabas. I took Titus along also . . . Yet not even Titus, who was with me, was compelled to be circumcised, even though he was a Greek. This matter arose because some false brothers had infiltrated our ranks to spy on the freedom we have in Christ Jesus and to make us slaves. We did not give in to them for a moment, so that the truth of the gospel might remain with you.

Here Paul describes an occasion fourteen years or more after his conversion, when he went to Jerusalem a second time in order to meet the church leaders there, including James, Peter and John. What a gathering—and how fascinating it would be to have a video of it!

Paul went because he wanted to be sure that the message he was preaching was the one Christ gave originally. He had received it by a 'revelation', as we know, but the other apostles had had the privilege of sitting at the feet of Jesus and sharing in his words and actions. Well, Paul was pleased to find that his message received their approval.

Not only that, but Titus, who also accompanied Paul, and who was not a Jew, was not required to be circumcised. So the leaders in Jerusalem, Paul felt, had implicitly accepted his position that Christians did not need to submit to the ritual requirements of Jewish law. This had become an issue, because the Church had been infiltrated by some 'false brothers' (v. 4) who resented the freedom Christians had—freedom, that is, from the law—and wanted to bring them back into slavery to its demands.

Paul saw that this was a direct challenge to the 'truth of the gospel' (v. 5), because, as we have already seen, it isn't possible to believe that Christ died to bring us to God and that we can get to God through our own actions, however zealous we are or commendable our religious observance. If we could save ourselves, then why did God need to send his Son to save us? It's a question that each of us needs to ask ourselves whenever we begin to think, in our human pride, that we can 'do it ourselves'.

A prayer

Heavenly Father, help me to live today in the freedom that the gospel offers— freedom from guilt about the past, freedom from fear about the future, freedom from anxiety that 'I haven't done enough'. I thank you for the completeness of what you did for us in sending Jesus to be our Saviour, and I put my trust wholly in that. Amen.

DW

Recognizing God's grace

As for those who seemed to be important . . . those men added nothing to my message. On the contrary, they saw that I had been entrusted with the task of preaching the gospel to the Gentiles, just as Peter had been to the Jews. For God, who was at work in the ministry of Peter as an apostle to the Jews, was also at work in my ministry as an apostle to the Gentiles. James, Peter and John, those reputed to be pillars, gave me and Barnabas the right hand of fellowship when they recognised the grace given to me. They agreed that we should go to the Gentiles, and they to the Jews. All they asked was that we should continue to remember the poor, the very thing I was eager to do.

What a meeting this must have been! Place—Jerusalem. Date—perhaps AD47. Participants—the apostles Peter, James, John and Paul. The topic—Paul's ministry among the Gentiles.

On the evidence of the New Testament, you have four quite powerful characters there, not given to mincing words. And we know that there had been questions about Paul's approach to Gentiles (that is, non-Jews), with some of the Jewish Christians wishing that he gave more weight to their scruples about food, fasting and feasts. These issues were to be thrashed out, and settled, at the Council of Jerusalem in AD49 (Acts 15).

Anyway, on this momentous occasion, the three leading apostles gave Paul 'the right hand of fellowship' and 'added nothing' to his message . . . in other words, they gave their approval to his approach. As Paul says, 'They recognised the grace given to me'.

Sometimes it's very difficult for us to do that—to recognize that another Christian, with a quite different approach from ours, and perhaps not doing things exactly the way we should like to see them done, is nevertheless doing God's work. Sometimes in our church life it is necessary for us to 'recognize' the 'grace of God' at work in others, including those from whom we differ. These great apostles did it, and in doing it set us an example. They listened to what Paul had to say. They recognized God's hand in it. And they offered him their 'fellowship'—the word means 'partnership'—in what he was doing. And, incidentally, Paul also 'recognized' the quite different work that Peter was doing among the Jews (v. 7).

A Prayer

God of love and peace, help us to recognize your grace at work in others, especially those whose approach is very different from our own. Amen.

DW

The peril of hypocrisy

When Peter came to Antioch, I opposed him to his face, because he was clearly in the wrong. Before certain men came from James, he used to eat with the Gentiles. But when they arrived, he began to draw back and separate himself from the Gentiles... When I saw that they were not acting in line with the truth of the gospel, I said to Peter in front of them all, 'You are a Jew, yet you live like a Gentile and not like a Jew. How is it, then, that you force Gentiles to follow Jewish customs? We who are Jews by birth and not "Gentile sinners" know that a man is not justified by observing the law, but by faith in Jesus Christ. So we, too, have put our faith in Christ Jesus that we may be justified by faith in Christ and not by observing the law... For through the law I died to the law so that I might live for God. I have been crucified with Christ and I no longer live, but Christ lives in me. The life I live in the body, I live by faith in the Son of God, who loved me and gave himself for me.'

In yesterday's reading we saw Paul and Peter agreeing over their respective ministries. Here, on a later occasion, in Antioch, we see them in sharp disagreement. Peter had been quite happy to eat with Gentile Christians—until a party of strict Jewish Christians arrived. Then, realizing that they were likely to be offended by this 'liberalism', he and then some of the other Jewish Christians (including Barnabas), decided they would not eat with Gentiles any longer.

Paul was obviously furious at what he calls their 'hypocrisy' (v. 13), and he 'opposed Peter to his face'—in front of all the others (v. 14). He felt that Peter should have realized that what he was doing was casting doubt on the sufficiency of the faith of the Gentile Christians—'that we are justified by faith in Christ and not by observing the law'

(v. 15). Of course Peter knew this, but it is one thing to know it in our heads and quite another to live by it. In the memorable words of Paul in verse 20, the Christian now lives 'by faith in the Son of God, who loved me and gave himself for me'. Because, as he goes on to argue (v. 21), 'if righteousness could be gained through the law, Christ died for nothing'.

A Prayer

Father, help me to know the truth of the gospel—and, even more important—help me to live by it. Amen.

DW

Welcoming the rejected

There was a rich man who was dressed in purple and fine linen and lived in luxury every day. At his gate was laid a beggar named Lazarus, covered with sores and longing to eat what fell from the rich man's table. Even the dogs came and licked his sores. The time came when the beggar died and the angels carried him to Abraham's side. The rich man also died and was buried. In Hades, where he was in torment, he looked up and saw Abraham far away, with Lazarus by his side. So he called to him, 'Father Abraham, have pity on me and send Lazarus to dip the tip of his finger in water and cool my tongue, because I am in agony in this fire.' But Abraham replied, 'Son, remember that in your lifetime you received your good things, while Lazarus received bad things, but now he is comforted here and you are in agony.'

The Bible tells us to 'love our neighbour' and that may seem easy when our neighbour is very much like us—a decent, respectable, deserving kind of person. But supposing the neighbour is a beggar covered in sores? That was the challenge which the rich man in this story failed to accept.

It isn't, of course, a parable about being kind to beggars. Its central thrust is that what we do during this life determines where we are in the next one. But, by choosing two such contrasting characters as a naked beggar and a well-dressed rich man, Jesus was undoubtedly inviting his hearers to consider how they would have acted in the same circumstances.

As we join in worship in church today, and especially as we come to Communion, we are reminded of the beggar who longed 'to eat what fell from the rich man's table'. Every Sunday we say that we are not worthy 'so much as to gather up the crumbs' from the Lord's Table—but it is not easy to put ourselves in the position of beggars. Perhaps we shall never really value our neighbour until we have seen ourselves as the poor man at the gate, rather than as the rich man living it up inside.

A prayer

Heavenly Father, you invite us to your table as we are. Help us to welcome those whom the world rejects, seeing them through your eyes. For Jesus Christ's sake. Amen.

DW

Grace, from first to last

You foolish Galatians! Who has bewitched you? Before your very eyes Jesus Christ was clearly portrayed as crucified. I would like to learn just one thing from you. Did you receive the Spirit by observing the law, or by believing what you heard? Are you so foolish? After beginning with the Spirit, are you now trying to attain your goal by human effort? . . . Consider Abraham: 'He believed God, and it was credited to him as righteousness.' Understand, then, that those who believe are children of Abraham.

This passage begins with a cry of frustration: 'You foolish Galatians!' The word Paul used means 'unintelligent, lacking understanding'—he simply couldn't understand how sensible people who had believed the gospel and received the Spirit could now exchange that for the slavery of the law. 'After beginning with the Spirit, are you now trying to attain your goal by human effort?'

It's a mistake easily made. As beginners in the Christian life we are usually very aware that all we can bring to our salvation (as Archbishop Coggan once said) 'is the sin from which we wish to be redeemed'. We know we don't deserve God's forgiveness or his gifts of new life and love, but we thankfully receive them. But later on, perhaps, as we 'progress' in the Christian life, we may begin to feel that we have reached a stage where it is now 'up to us'—that having been saved by grace we are now meant to go on by 'works'. Paul is adamant. From first to last the Christian life is built upon, rooted and grounded in the grace of God. From first to last it is his gift.

He calls in Abraham as evidence—as James does, incidentally, to make a rather different point about grace and works (James 2:20–24). For Paul, Abraham's obedience was a matter of faith—he 'believed God and it was credited to him as righteousness' (v. 6). This is to be a model for the Gentiles in later ages, because they, too, obeyed God as they received the gospel—and they too were thereby 'justified'; 'credited as righteous'. And, of course, that means it's a model for us.

A prayer

Heavenly Father, help us to continue in the Christian faith in the way in which we began it, trusting you completely for everything and not relying on our own strength, but on yours. For Jesus Christ's sake. Amen.

DW

Avoiding the dead end

All who rely on observing the law are under a curse, for it is written: 'Cursed is everyone who does not continue to do everything written in the Book of the Law.' Clearly no-one is justified before God by the law, because, 'The righteous will live by faith.' The law is not based on faith; on the contrary, 'The man who does these things will live by them.' Christ redeemed us from the curse of the law by becoming a curse for us, for it is written: 'Cursed is everyone who is hung on a tree.' He redeemed us in order that the blessing given to Abraham might come to the Gentiles through Christ Jesus, so that by faith we might receive the promise of the Spirit.

This is a difficult passage for the modern reader! Paul goes back to a statement in Deuteronomy: 'Cursed is everyone who does not continue to do everything written in the Book of the Law'. So if anyone relies on keeping the law (that is, the Law of Moses—moral and ritual), and fails to keep any tiny part of it, he is accursed. It's not the sort of language we are used to, and it's not the sort of idea we find acceptable.

But Paul's point is that the 'circumcision party', as he calls them (2:13), are turning back to the law as a way of pleasing God and that means, by the terms of that very same law, that they are putting themselves under a 'curse'. He's quoting the law they admire so much to prove that trying to use it as a way of salvation is a dead loss: you try, but you end up under a curse!

This rather tortuous argument ends, however, in a magnificent statement about the cross. Again quoting Deuteronomy, Paul reminds them that anyone who is 'hung on a tree' is 'cursed'. So when Jesus died by being hung on a tree he 'became a curse for us'. That's to say, he bore the curse of human sin, all our failure to 'do everything written in the Law'. Redemption from the curse enables us to receive the blessing promised to Abraham (yes, that man again!). So Jesus met the demands of the Law and satisfied them on our behalf. How wrong, then, to seek justification by the Law. It's literally a 'dead end'.

A prayer

God our Father, thank you for Jesus, who endured the cross in order to redeem us from the curse of the Law. Help me to live by faith and in the strength of the Holy Spirit, according to your promises.
Amen.

DW

Covenant of blessing

Brothers, let me take an example from everyday life. Just as no-one can set aside or add to a human covenant that has been established, so it is in this case. The promises were spoken to Abraham and his seed. The Scripture does not say 'and to seeds', meaning many people, but 'and to your seed', meaning one person, who is Christ . . . The law, introduced 430 years later, does not set aside the covenant previously established by God and thus do away with the promise . . . You are all sons of God through faith in Christ Jesus, for all of you who were baptised into Christ have clothed yourselves with Christ. There is neither Jew nor Greek, slave nor free, male nor female, for you are all one in Christ Jesus. If you belong to Christ, then you are Abraham's seed, and heirs according to the promise.

Paul uses a word here that is quite familiar to modern people, but not in this context. It's 'covenant'.

A 'covenant' is an agreement between two parties, in which one party promises to do something provided certain conditions are fulfilled by the other party. A tax covenant is an example. You promise to pay a certain sum annually to a charity and the Inland Revenue promises to give the charity the tax you have paid on it.

God made a covenant with Abraham, that through his 'seed' all the nations of the earth would be blessed. This covenant pre-dated the Law of Moses, so—Paul argues—the Law can't set it aside, it still applies. So, 'What was the purpose of the Law?' (v. 19). It was an interim measure, he says, to cope with 'transgressions'—breakings of the Law—until the promised 'Seed', the Messiah, should come. But in every respect the Covenant is better.

And it has better results, making us children of God (v. 26) without distinction of race, social status or gender (v. 28). The Letter to the Galatians would be worth reading just for that one magnificent statement!

A prayer

Thank you Lord for your promise that in Christ all our earthly distinctions are abolished and we are made your adopted children by your gift of grace. Help us to live like your children. Amen.

DW

Then—and now

As long as the heir is a child, he is no different from a slave, although he owns the whole estate. He is subject to guardians and trustees until the time set by his father. So also, when we were children, we were in slavery under the basic principles of the world. But when the time had fully come, God sent his Son, born of a woman, born under law, to redeem those under law, that we might receive the full rights of sons. Because you are sons, God sent the Spirit of his Son into our hearts, the Spirit who calls out *'Abba*, Father.' So you are no longer a slave, but a son; and since you are a son, God has made you also an heir. Formerly, when you did not know God, you were slaves to those who by nature are not gods. But now that you know God—or rather are known by God—how is it that you are turning back to those weak and miserable principles? Do you wish to be enslaved by them all over again? You are observing special days and months and seasons and years! I fear for you, that somehow I have wasted my efforts on you.

This is a passage about 'then' and 'now'—and the difference between then and now is the coming of Jesus. 'Then' we were like children, under the strict supervision of guardians and trustees (the Law, of course!), until the time when we should inherit our father's 'estate' (vv. 1–4). 'Then' we were like slaves, dominated by 'weak and miserable principles' (v. 9), shackled by rules and rituals. 'Now', since the coming of Christ, born as a Jew, 'under the law', Christians are set free ('redeemed', v. 5) and have received the 'full rights of sons'. Now they are no longer slaves, but 'sons' and 'heirs' of God—and they can call him *Abba*.

Abba is the Aramaic word for 'daddy'. It was the mother tongue of Jesus, and it's the way he would have addressed Joseph. Now, all of us who are redeemed by Christ can call our heavenly Father 'Daddy'.

And yet, says Paul to the Galatians, even in the face of this, you still want to go back to the old ways, the era of slavery and fear? No wonder he remarks, 'I fear for you, that somehow I have wasted my efforts on you.'

A prayer

Abba, Father, help me to come to you day by day with the simple trust of a child—not in fear, as a slave, but in confidence as your child and heir. For Jesus' sake. Amen.

DW

A zeal for what is right

I plead with you, brothers, become like me, for I became like you . . . As you know, it was because of an illness that I first preached the gospel to you. Even though my illness was a trial to you, you did not treat me with contempt or scorn. Instead, you welcomed me as if I were an angel of God, as if I were Jesus Christ himself. What has happened to all your joy? I can testify that, if you could have done so, you would have torn out your eyes and given them to me . . . Those people are zealous to win you over . . . to alienate you from us . . . It is fine to be zealous, provided the purpose is good . . . My dear children, for whom I am again in the pains of childbirth until Christ is formed in you, how I wish I could be with you now and change my tone, because I am perplexed about you!

At last, Paul tries a change of tone! Up till now his letter has been angry and intense ('you foolish Galatians!'), but now he tries a gentler approach. He reminds them of his first visit to them, when he was ill and they treated him with great kindness—'you would have torn out your eyes and given them to me'. I wonder if his illness was to do with his eye-sight?

Yet the warning note is still there. 'These people'—the 'circumcision party'—are zealous, there's no doubt about that. But their zeal is mis-directed. 'It is fine to be zealous', Paul remarks, 'provided the purpose is good.'

Religion does tend to produce 'zeal'. People have strong beliefs, which they want to promote strongly. And sometimes that leads to bigotry and intolerance. It's a good thing to be totally committed; but our commitment should not blind us to the feelings of others, even those with whom we dis-

agree. It is a God-given grace to believe strongly but be able to respect those whose faith is 'weak'.

And we need to ensure that the 'purpose' of our zeal is good. Paul could tell the Galatians that he was 'zealous' that 'Christ should be formed in you' (v. 19). Is our zeal as well directed as that?

A prayer

Help me, Lord, to be committed without being bigoted. And may my 'zeal' have the purpose of sharing your blessing with others, whoever they may be. Amen.

DW

The slavery that sets us free

Tell me, you who want to be under the law, are you not aware of what the law says? For it is written that Abraham had two sons, one by the slave woman and the other by the free woman. His son by the slave woman was born in the ordinary way; but his son by the free woman was born as the result of a promise. These things may be taken figuratively, for the women represent two covenants. One covenant is from Mount Sinai and bears children who are to be slaves: This is Hagar. Now Hagar stands for Mount Sinai in Arabia and corresponds to the present city of Jerusalem, because she is in slavery with her children. But the Jerusalem that is above is free, and she is our mother.

Well, Paul seems to be saying, you want to be 'proper' Jews… then let's talk about a proper Jew, Abraham. He had two sons, one by the slave woman, Hagar, and one by the free woman, his wife Sarah. The first was born 'in the ordinary way', but the second came as a direct result of a promise by God.

Now, he argues, think of this as a picture of the two covenants. The Law of Moses, given on Sinai, represents our past slavery to the Law—a slavery still perpetuated in the temple in Jerusalem. That is one covenant. But there was another, made with Abraham and connected with the birth of a free-born son. That covenant (a covenant based on faith) sets us free—and that covenant is celebrated in the 'new' Jerusalem, the kingdom of heaven.

It's a fairly obscure argument to the modern reader, perhaps. But it illustrates a truth which is absolutely central to Christianity. We do not live under a covenant of rules and regulations, of taboos and obligatory rituals, but within the new covenant, based on faith in Jesus and secured by the promise of God.

A prayer

Heavenly Father, set me free from a religion of slavery to rules and bring me into a freely accepted 'slavery' to Jesus Christ, so that by my own choice, and your strength, I may live life as you want it to be. Amen.

DW

The proof of faith

When Jesus had finished saying all this in the hearing of the people, he entered Capernaum. There a centurion's servant, whom his master valued highly, was sick and about to die. The centurion heard of Jesus and sent some elders of the Jews to him, asking him to come and heal his servant. When they came to Jesus, they pleaded earnestly with him. 'This man deserves to have you do this, because he loves our nation and has built our synagogue.' So Jesus went with them. He was not far from the house when the centurion sent friends to say to him: 'Lord, don't trouble yourself, for I do not deserve to have you come under my roof. That is why I did not even consider myself worthy to come to you. But say the word, and my servant will be healed. For I myself am a man under authority, with soldiers under me. I tell this one, "Go", and he goes; and that one "Come", and he comes. I say to my servant, "Do this", and he does it.' When Jesus heard this, he was amazed at him, and turning to the crowd following him, he said, 'I tell you, I have not found such great faith even in Israel.' Then the men who had been sent returned to the house and found the servant well.

Today's theme is 'The proof of faith' and this story offers the most telling proof possible. The centurion—not even a Jew—has no doubt that Jesus can heal his servant. Indeed, he utters one of the great statements of faith in the Gospels: 'Say the word, and my servant will be healed'. He knows what it is to exercise authority (v. 8) and he recognizes in Jesus an authority greater than anything he has encountered before. His faith is uncomplicated by theology or tradition. His servant needed a miracle, and here was the one who could provide it.

In one sense the 'proof' of faith in this story is the miracle, of course. But its real proof, as Luke relates the event, is in the centurion's words—they were what provoked Jesus to say, 'I have not found such great faith even in Israel.'

The 'proof', the 'test' of faith is within the believer. Faith recognizes who Jesus is and whose authority he has.

A Prayer

Dear Lord, give me the gift of faith, so that I may trust where I cannot see and believe where I cannot know, for Jesus Christ's sake. Amen.

DW

Set free

Now you, brothers, like Isaac, are children of promise. At that time the son born in the ordinary way persecuted the son born by the power of the Spirit. It is the same now. But what does the Scripture say? 'Get rid of the slave woman and her son, for the slave woman's son will never share in the inheritance with the free woman's son.' Therefore, brothers, we are not children of the slave woman but of the free woman. It is for freedom that Christ has set us free. Stand firm, then, and do not let yourselves be burdened again by a yoke of slavery.

This passage includes a real clarion call! 'It is for freedom that Christ has set us free. Stand firm, then, and do not let ourselves be burdened again by a yoke of slavery'.

Many people think of Christianity as a kind of 'slavery'—it requires this and that of us, demands time and money, imposes disciplines and rules that they would find irksome. It's amazing how often those outside the Church speak in those terms about what it means to be a Christian. They make it sound like a life sentence to hard labour.

Sadly, quite a few Christians experience religion in that way, too—perhaps most of us do at times. That's to say, what should be a matter of freedom and joy and peace with God becomes tension, struggle and duty. Whenever we feel a touch of the slaveries coming on, this is the verse to turn to!

The order of the words as Paul wrote them is important. 'Freedom' is the goal for which Christ set us free, it is the object of the exercise. The second half of the verse gives the negative of this—don't allow yourselves to be shackled again with the 'yoke of bondage'. That's daring language, because the Jews of Paul's time spoke of the 'yoke of the Law' with reverence. But for Paul it is a yoke of slavery. He preferred the 'yoke' Jesus spoke of (Matthew 11:30)—'my yoke is easy'. Why reject the 'easy yoke' of the Saviour and submit yourself to the heavy yoke of the Law? The question is as relevant for burdened Christians today as it was for those of first-century Galatia.

A prayer

Lord Jesus, whose yoke is easy and whose burden is light, deliver me from all the self-imposed yokes of struggle, tension and duty that I take upon myself. Set me free to enjoy your freedom. Amen.

DW

Faith expressed through love

Mark my words! I, Paul, tell you that if you let yourselves be circumcised, Christ will be of no value to you at all. Again I declare to every man who lets himself be circumcised that he is required to obey the whole law. You who are trying to be justified by law have been alienated from Christ; you have fallen away from grace. But by faith we eagerly await through the Spirit the righteousness for which we hope. For in Christ neither circumcision nor uncircumcision has any value. The only thing that counts is faith expressing itself through love.

The freedom Christ gives us is not a licence to 'do what we like'. That's the thought behind verse 5—we 'eagerly await through the Spirit the righteousness for which we hope'.

It's an important point to make, because Paul's rejection of the Law as a way to righteousness can easily be misread as a rejection of law as a standard of behaviour (what is called 'antinomianism'). No one who knows Paul's letters could think for a moment that he regarded right living as optional! His point, reinforced in verses 4 and 6, is that the Law simply cannot bring about righteousness. Rules aren't the way to it. Right living, living in the way God intended, is only possible through 'grace' (v. 4) and 'faith expressed in love' (v. 6). Such things as whether or not a person has been circumcised are totally irrelevant (v. 6)—outward rites and imposed rules can't change human nature. Only God's Holy Spirit can do that, and the gift of righteousness is just that, a gift—grace, in other words.

'Faith expressed through love' is a marvellous phrase. It tells us what the motive and dynamic of faith is—love: God's love for us, and our love for him in response. This kind of faith is not a dry recital of a creed but a warm, committed response to love. It is from soil like that that the flowers of holiness may grow.

A prayer

Heavenly Father, help me to live by love and faith, the one flowing from the other—and living in that way, to begin to see your righteousness growing in me. Amen.

DW

Pushed off track

You were running a good race. Who cut in on you and kept you from obeying the truth? That kind of persuasion does not come from the one who calls you. 'A little yeast works through the whole batch of dough.' I am confident in the Lord that you will take no other view. The one who is throwing you into confusion will pay the penalty, whoever he may be. Brothers, if I am still preaching circumcision, why am I still being persecuted? In that case the offence of the cross has been abolished. As for those agitators, I wish they would go the whole way and emasculate themselves! You, my brothers, were called to be free. But do not use your freedom to indulge the sinful nature; rather, serve one another in love. The entire law is summed up in a single command: 'Love your neighbour as yourself.' If you keep on biting and devouring each other, watch out or you will be destroyed by each other.

Athletics in ancient Greece was a very popular spectator sport, of course, but as running involved nudity—and often tributes to pagan gods—Jews were forbidden from taking part or attending. Which makes it strange that St Paul is so fond of taking illustrations from the athletics arena. Here, he tells the Galatians that they were running a 'good race', but someone has 'cut in on them', pushing them off the track. That 'someone' ('whoever he may be') was probably known to Paul, but declining to name him is a way of showing his contempt for the man's actions. The contempt is expressed in even stronger—some would say crude—terms in verse 12!

Verses 13–15 return to the warnings already given, that the freedom Christ gives is not a freedom to sin: 'Do not use your freedom to indulge the sinful nat-ure'. People do sometimes get the idea that Christians can 'do what they like' so long as they later confess it and receive absolution. Such an idea would have horrified Paul. The freedom we have in Christ is the freedom not to sin!

But most of all it is, as we've already seen, a freedom to love—the whole law can be summarized, says Paul, in one command: 'Love your neighbour as yourself.'

A prayer

Lord, set me free, not to indulge myself, but to show your love to others. Amen.

DW

The two natures

So I say, live by the Spirit, and you will not gratify the desires of the sinful nature. For the sinful nature desires what is contrary to the Spirit, and the Spirit what is contrary to the sinful nature. They are in conflict with each other, so that you do not do what you want. But if you are led by the Spirit, you are not under law. The acts of the sinful nature are obvious: sexual immorality, impurity and debauchery; idolatry and witchcraft; hatred, discord, jealousy, fits of rage, selfish ambition, dissensions, factions and envy; drunkenness, orgies and the like. I warn you, as I did before, that those who live like this will not inherit the kingdom of God. But the fruit of the Spirit is love, joy, peace, patience, kindness, goodness, faithfulness, gentleness and self-control. Against such things there is no law. Those who belong to Christ Jesus have crucified the sinful nature with its passions and desires.

Here is Paul's picture of our two 'natures'—'flesh', as he calls it, and Spirit. 'Flesh' stands for everything that ties us to our fallen condition—we might say it is the lower side of human nature. His list (vv. 19–21) gives a vivid enough picture of what that nature produces. Looking at human history, and reading today's newspaper, confirm that humankind has a lower nature, and that it is contagious and destructive.

But it is possible for us, through Christ, to have a new nature, one which is 'led by the Spirit' (v. 16). Law, in the sense of imposed rules, cannot produce this nature—it is the 'fruit' of the Spirit (v. 22). And Paul's second list shows the qualities which flow from a life which lives by the Spirit and 'keeps in step with the Spirit' (v. 25). The world would be a better place, and the news a lot less depressing, if these qualities were to predominate. Again, the law which can't stop evil can't produce good— you can't order people to be good! But those who 'belong to Christ Jesus' have accepted a death sentence on their old nature (v. 24) and set out on a new life with a new dynamic.

A prayer

Heavenly Father, by your Holy Spirit create in me a new heart, new motives, new goals . . . and enable me to live the new life. For Jesus Christ's sake. Amen.

DW

Burdens and loads

Brothers, if someone is caught in a sin, you who are spiritual should restore him gently. But watch yourself, or you also may be tempted. Carry each other's burdens, and in this way you will fulfil the law of Christ. If anyone thinks he is something when he is nothing, he deceives himself. Each one should test his own actions. Then he can take pride in himself, without comparing himself to somebody else, for each one should carry his own load . . .

Do not be deceived: God cannot be mocked. A man reaps what he sows. The one who sows to please his sinful nature, from that nature will reap destruction; the one who sows to please the Spirit, from the Spirit will reap eternal life. Let us not become weary in doing good, for at the proper time we will reap a harvest if we do not give up. Therefore, as we have opportunity, let us do good to all people, especially to those who belong to the family of believers.

At first glance, there's a contradiction here. In verse 2 we are told to 'carry each other's burdens' and in verse 5 'each one should carry his own load'. The clue is the difference between 'burden' and 'load'. The 'load' was the personal pack carried by a Roman soldier—we should take responsibility for our own actions: a point hammered home in verse 7. But we should also carry each other's 'burdens'—those extra weights that all of us experience from time to time: bereavement, suffering, loneliness and even, in this context, temptation and failure. So, as Paul says, 'let us do good to all people', sharing their burdens (v. 10).

Undoubtedly the key verse is verse 7: 'What you sow, you reap.' A famous fraudster of a past era was visited in prison by a friend. He saw that he was working on some mail bags and said, 'Ah, Bottomley, I see you're sewing.' 'No,' he replied curtly, 'Reaping.' That is really the practical consequence of 'carrying our own load'. We answer for our choices, good or bad. We are responsible for what we do.

A prayer

Dear Lord, help me to take responsibility for my own actions, but also to share the burdens of those who have to carry more than I do. Amen.

DW

Real value

See what large letters I use as I write to you with my own hand! Those who want to make a good impression outwardly are trying to compel you to be circumcised. The only reason they do this is to avoid being persecuted for the cross of Christ. Not even those who are circumcised obey the law, yet they want you to be circumcised that they may boast about your flesh. May I never boast except in the cross of our Lord Jesus Christ, through which the world has been crucified to me, and I to the world. Neither circumcision nor uncircumcision means anything; what counts is a new creation. Peace and mercy to all who follow this rule, even to the Israel of God. Finally, let no-one cause me trouble, for I bear on my body the marks of Jesus. The grace of our Lord Jesus Christ be with your spirit, brothers. Amen.

Just in case anyone in the church in Galatia doubted the authenticity of this letter, St Paul adds a few words in his own, apparently rather clumsy, handwriting. He wanted them to be in no doubt that this was his personal message to them. It's an emotional conclusion to an emotional appeal.

His opponents, he says, want to boast about their conquests—how they have persuaded the Galatian Christians to undergo circumcision, or whatever (v. 13). He, on the other hand, has nothing to boast about except 'the cross of our Lord Jesus Christ', through which 'the world has been crucified to me, and I to the world' (v. 14).

The Greek word used here for 'world' is *cosmos*—human society organized as though God didn't exist. Its values were no longer his values. And he finds his value not in what the world thinks of him—his reputation, as we say—but in

the fact that God gave his Son to death on the cross for him. That, in the end, is the only worthwhile measure of our value to God and of his love for us. 'Peace and mercy' (v. 16) flow from it.

A prayer

Heavenly Father, may I find my true value in the cross of Jesus, rather than in the opinions of other people. For his sake, Amen.

DW

The God who comes to us

We start this section with six Psalms of sorrow for sin—because in many churches the weeks that lead up to Christmas are traditionally a time for penitence and for getting ready for Christmas and the coming of Christ into our world. He came as a baby on the first Christmas Day—and he obviously doesn't come again in that way, even though we talk as if he does, and of the way we can prepare for his coming. Yet to remember all the events of the Christian story day by day all through the year is a way of realizing what they mean to us in our own Christian lives, and to find ourselves renewed and restored.

Christmas is about Emmanuel, which means God with us. So in this section Joyce Huggett helps us to reflect on the practice of the presence of God. That is the subject of Brother Lawrence's little book, which has been a great blessing to the people of God all through the years since he wrote it in the seventeenth century. Then we go through Christmas with Gerard Hughes—and know that the events that happened two thousand years ago are about now just as much as then.

O holy Child of Bethlehem,
Descend to us, we pray;
Cast out our sin, and enter in:
Be born in us today.
We hear the Christmas angels
The great glad tidings tell:
O come to us, abide with us,
Our Lord Emmanuel.

Bishop Phillips Brooks

Strong weakness

I know a man in Christ who, fourteen years ago, was caught up—whether still in the body or out of the body, I do not know; God knows—right into the third heaven . . . In view of the extraordinary nature of these revelations, to stop me from getting too proud I was given a thorn in the flesh, an angel of Satan to beat me and stop me from getting too proud! About this thing, I have pleaded with the Lord three times for it to leave me, but he has said, 'My grace is enough for you: my power is at its best in weakness'. So I shall be very happy to make my weaknesses my special boast so that the power of Christ may stay over me, and that is why I am quite content with my weaknesses, and with insults, hardships, persecutions, and the agonies I go through for Christ's sake. For it is when I am weak that I am strong.

We don't know what Paul's thorn in the flesh was—a sickness, a troublesome person or a moral failing. It could have been any of these things, but whatever it was it could be described as a messenger of the devil. Yet it played an important role in his life, for it removed the much worse temptation to believe that the success of his missionary work was due to his great abilities.

I find this passage very helpful, for I know I have many weaknesses—some of them no doubt very bad in a clergyman. But still God doesn't abandon me, and I know that when I turn to him in my weakness I receive help; not with the removal of the weakness, but I am given the strength to serve God as I otherwise could not.

Probably, if truth be told, many of us are like that. We soldier on, and get through literally by the grace of God, rather than our own physical, emotional or moral strength. That's why I get so angry when people trumpet the sins and indiscretions of important people, and perhaps especially of prominent Christians. What do they expect? What do we expect? Perfection is found only in heaven and on earth we are beset by thorns in the flesh. But we also have the grace of God. So pray for all who minister in weakness, but in the strength of God.

MM

Out of focus

Turn to me and show me thy favour, for I am lonely and oppressed. Relieve the sorrows of my heart and bring me out of my distress. Look at my misery and my trouble and forgive me every sin. Look at my enemies, see how many they are and how violent their hatred for me. Defend me and deliver me, do not put me to shame when I take refuge in thee.

It is easy to be depressed in November. Then life gets out of focus. That fool we made of ourselves the other day. We harp on it. That sarcastic remark we were meant to overhear; we start thinking everyone is against us—'Look at my enemies, see how many they are'.

BRF members may never be charged with telling thumping great lies, or profiting by 'inside information' on the Stock Exchange. If seasons like Advent and Lent only relate to sinners of this stamp, then their theme of penitence has nothing to do with us. We can skip them. But what if it is wrong to be depressed? I don't mean an occasional 'down in the dumps', but more often than not. Then we ought to seek God's deliverance and his forgiveness. We are not trusting God the heavenly Father. Now re-read the Psalm.

A prayer

Lord, I am not boasting—but I really haven't 'done the dirty' on anyone as far as I know; but if I have, I am sorry, Lord, I admit I have been a bit grumpy sometimes, well, more than a bit, quite sharp, in fact, critical, if not a trifle unjust, at home, at the office, among my friends. I am sorry, Lord. And I admit I have felt sorry for myself, I have let my life get out of focus, I have forgotten all you have given me, and worried about the future. I am sorry, Lord. Lift me up, Lord, deliver me from my depression, and forgive me my sins. I trust you, Lord, I really do.

DCF

A bad lapse

Be gracious to me, O God, in thy true love; in the fullness of thy mercy blot out my misdeeds. Wash away all my guilt and cleanse me from my sin. For well I know my misdeeds, and my sins confront me all the day long. Against thee, thee only, I have sinned and done what displeases thee, so that thou mayest be proved right in thy charge and just in passing sentence.

Something has gone badly wrong here. Traditionally this penitential Psalm has been thought to come from the pen of King David after his lapse into an adulterous relationship with Bathsheba, the wife of Uriah the Hittite—not a pretty story! It contains the usual 'cover-ups' which accompany this kind of sin—for a sin the doer of it accounted it to be. That is something. It is a great deal. If sin is not acknowledged there can be no forgiveness. But where there is acknowledgement we can be sure the sinner is not rotten right through.

So don't write any man or woman off for one bad lapse.

Read the Psalm again. The words that stand out are: 'Against thee only have I sinned'. Well, what about the woman? Hasn't he pulled *her* down?—even if she did have a hand in pulling *him* down! And what about the woman's husband? Hasn't he been sinned against? But David—if it was David—sees his adultery as a sin *against God*. All of which must mean that he was a man very conscious of the presence of God in and around his life. It was God he had offended in the first place in taking another man's wife into his bed. And God judges rightly. Read the last line again.

Remember before God

—those who have made shipwreck of their marriage, children from broken homes, parents anxious about teenage sons and daughters, leaders of public life who mould opinions, the Church's witness to what God requires.

DCF

Cleansing

In iniquity I was brought to birth and my mother conceived me in sin; yet, though thou hast hidden the truth in darkness, through this mystery thou does teach me wisdom. Take hyssop and sprinkle me, that I may be clean; wash me, that I may become whiter than snow; let me hear the sounds of joy and gladness, let the bones dance which thou hast broken. Turn away thy face from my sins and blot out all my guilt.

Please bear with a little explanation in respect of these verses. Taken simply as they stand the words 'my mother conceived me in sin' could look like a sweeping condemnation of all sexual relationships, not least within secure marriage. It is as if David were saying, 'Don't blame me for my adultery—didn't we all come into the world that way?' But sex is not counted a dirty thing in the Bible. It is a God-given instinct. We cannot, however, fool around with it or we are in trouble.

Nor is David excusing his simple act by a reference to original sin, as much as to say, 'I can't help being a sinner, everyone of us is caught in a network of sin by reason of heredity, the whole tree of humanity is defective.' No, there are no excuses here, quite the reverse. He is saying 'Yes, I have committed a sin against God, but if only you knew, I am worse than you think, I've been like that ever since I was born.'

Prayer

Lord, I give up.
I give up trying to justify myself,
even though I know I am no scoundrel.
But I admit that all along,
ever since I was born,
I keep on falling below
what I would like to be,
and want to be,
but somehow I can't be.
Cleanse me, Lord.
Clean up my mind
my waking mind
my half-waking mind.
Give me a new start
I know you will
if I trust you.

DCF

A pure heart

Create a pure heart in me, O God, and give me a new and steadfast spirit; do not drive me from thy presence or take thy holy spirit from me; revive in me the joy of thy deliverance and grant me a willing spirit to uphold me. I will teach transgressors the ways that lead to thee, and sinners shall return to thee again.

Whoever it was (David?) who wrote this Psalm, or this part of it, had gone badly 'off the rails', as we say. Sometimes even the best of people 'come a cropper'. Then the way back—and there certainly is a way back to a right standing with God—is via repentance (which isn't the same as remorse or owning up to having been a fool) *and* receiving the forgiveness of God. Humbling? Of course! but it is the way. This writer, however, looked further ahead. He had no wish to 'come a cropper' again. He had had enough of the consequences, namely a sort of sickness inside, almost physical. He reckoned what he needed was *a pure heart*. So he prayed God for it.

What is 'a pure heart'? We know what it is to be hard-hearted, heartless, heart-felt and hearty. We can understand 'a broken heart', but what is a pure heart? I can only suggest, a heart which 'suffereth long and is kind' ... that 'beareth all things, believeth all things, hopeth all things, endureth all things.' Such is a Christlike heart. And we can't work it up. We can only pray for it and keep our Lord in view.

Prayer

Lord, I don't want to fall down again, You know I don't. Please regard my heart's wishes and not my achievements. I know you do not look on the outward appearance, you look upon the heart. But I confess, I am afraid, because I do not always hold to the right path. Create a pure heart in me, O God and give me a new and steadfast spirit: in the name of Jesus Christ our Lord.

DCF

A wounded heart

O Lord God, my deliverer, save me from bloodshed, and I will sing the praises of thy justice. Open my lips, O Lord, that my mouth may proclaim thy praise. Thou hast no delight in sacrifice; if I brought thee an offering, thou wouldst not accept it. My sacrifice, O God, is a broken spirit; a wounded heart, O God, thou wilt not despise. Let it be thy pleasure to do good to Zion, to build anew the walls of Jerusalem. Then only shalt thou delight in the appointed sacrifices; then shall young bulls be offered on thy altar.

We come to God through our wounds or we don't come at all. Our sins make wounds. And sometimes God has to rub salt into them to cleanse them before he can heal them. The worst situation is to have untreated wounds, wounds left to fester. And it isn't only sins that make wounds, a 'let down' can do it, a lost love, or a failure. And if the almost inevitable wound called bitterness isn't treated, troubles will be set up. God heals wounds. And when we have offered him, as a sacrifice, our wounded heart and broken spirit, our other offerings will be acceptable. This is what our reading today says. We shall of course have to *decodify* the bit about offering young bulls upon God's altar! But this is often necessary in dealing with poetry.

Prayer

Open my lips, O Lord,
that my mouth may proclaim thy praise.
I don't want to labour my sins,
my weaknesses or even my wounds.
I want to be a joyful Christian,
someone with a light in the eye,
and a song in the heart;
and to make lights and songs in other
people's hearts.
With thanksgiving and praise therefore,
O Lord,
I accept your forgiveness.
I can scarcely believe it,
but I do.
I see the price you paid at Calvary.
What can I do but accept?

DCF

Blunders

O Lord, I call to thee, come quickly to my aid; listen to my cry when I call to thee. Let my prayer be like incense duly set before thee and my raised hands like the evening sacrifice. Set a guard, O Lord, over my mouth; keep watch at the door of my lips. Turn not my heart to sinful thoughts nor to any pursuit of evil courses. The evil-doers appal me; not for me the delights of their table. I would rather be buffeted by the righteous and reproved by good men. My head shall not be anointed with the oil of wicked men, for that would make me a party to their crimes.

If you never 'go out and about', but pass all your life among saintly men and women, if you never find yourself in the company of people who 'swear like troopers', and tell smutty stories, if you never have to sit through entertainment which tacitly denies all the moral standards you believe in—then don't bother with this Psalm, it has nothing for you.

Imagine yourself at an office party. How will you react? If by constant protest, you'll be written off as a crank. Perhaps by silence; and if you have not hidden the fact that you are a churchgoer and a Christian, then your silence will be eloquent.

Prayer

Lord, I don't want to be a pious prig. I don't want to be stuffy, self-righteous and smug. And I know that all that is vulgar is not wicked, but just vulgar, and tastes differ. But I want to side with all that is best in life, and I haven't always; sometimes through fear, sometimes kidding myself that I was so broadminded, so charitable, so wise. Forgive me, Lord, for my blunders. I am sorry.

DCF

Total turnaround

You, Yahweh, are our Father, 'Our Redeemer' is your name from of old. Why, Yahweh, do you let us wander from your ways and let our hearts grow too hard to fear you? Return for the sake of your servants, the tribes of your heritage.

Advent is the time of new beginnings, when we turn away from the tired old year—those endless Sundays of the Year—and begin seriously to think about Christmas and the coming of Christ. So it is a time of preparation, a much better time for good resolutions than the pagan New Year on 1 January. Traditionally the two Sundays at the turn from the old year to Advent concentrate on the Last Judgment, promising reward or threatening punishment for our past conduct. But, without the carrot-and-stick approach, it is a good opportunity to turn back to the Lord. Before moving on to the repentance of the New Testament, the community formed ready for the Messiah by John the Baptist, we are first reminded of the repentance of the age-old People of God.

Pray. Lord, I constantly need a jolt and a reason to turn back to you, to examine whether I am your faithful servant or not. But the story of your own chosen people is a story of desertion and repentance, monotonously repeated. It is not without reason that you put the story of Adam at its head, the story of a fall from a trusted and privileged position, where Adam is surrounded by almost every care, but still manages to find a way of turning away from you. Yet even there you promised that evil would not triumph, that Adam's child would eventually crush the serpent's head. You proclaimed yourself our Father, correcting us with the gentleness of a loving Father. You called yourself our 'Redeemer', the closest member of our own family, who was bound to intervene to pull us out of trouble. This is the rescue I am celebrating at Christmas, and I need to get myself ready, to renew my openness to being swept up into your family with renewed closeness, as your Son is born to be one of my brothers.

HW

Do everything for God

'I really feel I could do without Christmas this year. I'd just like life to return to some kind of normality instead of being faced with cards to write and all those presents to wrap up and food to buy and prepare.'

The person who said that to me one Christmas was a young mum with a lively toddler and a newborn baby.

'What would Brother Lawrence have said to her?' I wondered, as I thought about the overwhelming sense of pressure she seemed to be under.

I turned once more to *The Practice of the Presence of God* and this is what I read: 'Do everything for the love of God.'

This advice reminded me of Mother Teresa of Calcutta and her helpers. When they rescue the sick and the suffering, the diseased and dying, they do it for a Person: God. They see God in the person they are helping.

Jesus encourages us to do this in the parable he told to describe what will happen when he returns to the world as Judge. On that day he will sit on his throne in heavenly glory with all the nations gathered before him and he will separate the people as a shepherd separates his sheep from his goats. He will put the sheep on his right and the goats on his left.

He will say to those on his right:

'Come, you who are blessed by my Father; take your inheritance, the kingdom prepared for you since the creation of the world. For I was hungry and you gave me something to eat, I was thirsty and you gave me something to drink, I was a stranger and you invited me in, I needed clothes and you clothed me, I was sick and you looked after me, I was in prison and you came to visit me.'

JH

Meet God in creation

How can we keep Christ central to Christmas? How can we train ourselves to acknowledge his presence and tune into his enfolding, ever-present love in the middle of the busy-ness? Those are the questions we shall examine for the next two weeks. And, as we search for an answer, we shall look at the Bible's teaching and the advice given by the seventeenth-century monk, Brother Lawrence.

When Brother Lawrence was eighteen years old, a certain tree 'spoke' to him so eloquently that its message changed the direction of his life. The tree convinced the eighteen-year-old of the existence and power, the goodness and faithfulness of God. All Brother Lawrence saw with his physical eyes was a tree stripped of its leaves, but with the eyes of his imagination he saw the same tree re-clothed first with leaves, then with flowers, finally with fruit. As he marvelled at the mystery of it all he found himself drawn into the deeper mystery of the One who had conceived such perennial miracles.

This testimony reminds us that one way of reminding ourselves of the presence of God is to observe nature. Jesus seems to expect us to do this: 'Look at the birds of the air ... See how the lilies of the field grow ...' (Matthew 6:26, 28).

In other words, contemplate created things. Hear their message. For just as a book bears the hallmark of the author, so nature bears the imprint of its Creator and speaks an international language which people of every generation, tribe and nation can understand.

As the Psalmist describes it:

The *heavens* declare the glory of God; the *skies* proclaim the work of his hands. Day after day they pour forth speech, night after night they display knowledge ... Their voice goes out into all the earth, their words to the end of the world.

Look carefully at the sky or a Christmas cactus or some other piece of God's creation today. Ask yourself: What is God saying through the work of his hands? Then, what is he saying *to me*? Make your own response to the message which seems to be coming to you. Thank God for making his presence known.

Open my eyes, Lord, that with the Psalmist I might be able to pray: 'I praise you ... because your works are wonderful' (Psalm 139:14).

JH

Talk to God frequently

Nature is shot through with messages from God. One way of being continually aware of God's presence is to learn to listen to this language. Another way is to recognize that, because God is everywhere and because he has promised, 'Never will I leave you; never will I forsake you,' (Hebrews 13:5) we can punctuate our day with mini-conversations with him, no matter where we are or what we are doing.

Brother Lawrence persuaded those who wanted to master the art of practising the presence of God that this was a vital discipline. Using military language he reminds us that, even when we are on a march with our sword in our hand, short prayers are very acceptable to God. Such arrow prayers fortify us for the task in hand.

Had Brother Lawrence been writing today, he might have said: 'Even with a hoover or a duster in your hand, while sitting at your computer, nursing a patient or loved one, engaged in DIY or washing the car, short arrow prayers are acceptable to God.'

But he would have emphasized that the aim of these prayers is not primarily to ask for God's help but rather to maintain and deepen our relationship with him. 'A little lifting up the heart' suffices, he says, 'a little remembrance of God'. Like the quick telephone calls we make to friends or loved ones, such prayers are for no other reason than to keep in touch.

Jesus and his Father seem to have kept in touch in precisely this way. At Jesus' baptism, we hear the Father saying: 'You are my Son, whom I love; with you I am well pleased' (Luke 3:22). And during the Last Supper, Jesus converses with his Father as though he was physically present: 'Father... glorify your Son, that your Son may glorify you...' (see John 17:1ff).

·

A project and a prayer

Today, try to remember that God is the invisible passenger in your car, the unseen guest in your home, the companion who accompanies you in the supermarket queue, to the shops, at work. Talk to him frequently using short prayers such as the ones Brother Lawrence prayed:
'My God, I am wholly Yours.'
'O God of Love, I love You with all my heart.'
'Lord, make me more like You.'

JH

Ask for God's help

Let God speak to you through scarlet holly berries or the leaves of variegated ivy which you see in the garden, the hedgerows or on Christmas cards. Pepper your day with snatched conversations with God. These are ways of ensuring that you remain in touch with him even when you are busy. According to Brother Lawrence, there is another way also. Ask for God's help with even mundane tasks. Jesus also seems to encourage this:

**'Ask and it will be given to you . . .
For everyone who asks receives.'**

Jesus goes on to show that such asking is not pointless because we pray to a good and generous Father:

'Which of you, if his son asks for bread, will give him a stone? Or if he asks for a fish, will give him a snake? If you then, though you are evil, know how to give good gifts to your children, how much more will your Father in heaven give good gifts to those who ask him!'

Although this prayer practice sounds so obvious, it does not come naturally to most of us. It therefore goes against the grain to seek his help. Even Brother Lawrence admitted that, at first, he found the practice difficult and often forgot to request God's help. But after a while, having confessed his failure, the practice became as natural to him as breathing.

Other spiritual giants such as George Muller encourage Christians to lay all their transactions before God, to seek his help, to look for answers to prayer and to keep a record of the ways in which God responds to these prayers of the heart.

A prayer

Take a piece of paper or your prayer journal and a pen or pencil. Look ahead to the coming twenty-four hours. Anticipate your needs, as far as you are able. In a column on the left-hand side of your paper, make a note of those occasions when you know you will need God's strength to carry you through the busy-ness. Tomorrow, take another look at this list, record how God has responded to each request. This method of prayer can be a real faith-booster.

A resolve

*I weave into my life this day
The Presence of God upon my way,
I weave into my life this hour
The mighty God and all his power . . .
I weave into each deed done
Joy and hope of the Risen Son.*

David Adam, The Weaver Tides and Seasons: Modern prayers in the Celtic tradition, *Triangle, 1989*

JH

Be still...

Last Christmas my mother-in-law and my son joined my husband and me for Christmas. As Christmas Day approached, we looked forward to the family reunion because times to relax together are rare. Because I wanted to spend time with the family, I began to prepare early—making and freezing mince pies, baking and icing the Christmas cake, cooking the Christmas pudding. That way I felt I could enjoy being with my guests.

God is the heavenly guest who indwells us throughout the year. Some of us are so busy serving him that we have not time to be with him. But that is not what he wants. Through the Psalmist, he begs us to create pockets of stillness when we can just be with him: 'Be still,' he invites, 'know that I am God' (Psalm 46:10).

God is not inviting us to be still simply that we might learn *about* him. He invites us to quieten ourselves so that we might meet him and so deepen our relationship with him. This is implied by the use of the verb 'to know'—a verb which is also used to describe the intimacy between a husband and wife. It means oneness. Jesus evidently enjoyed this kind of closeness with his Father. He gave silence an obvious and costly priority. He would frequently leave the crowds who thronged him and slip away to a still place where he could 'just be'. And he taught his disciples to do the same because he realized that they could not cope without it.

As the author of *Poustinia* puts it:

'If we are to witness to Christ in today's market places, where there are constant demands on our whole person, we need silence. If we are to be always available, not only physically, but by empathy, sympathy, friendship, understanding and boundless *caritas*, we need silence. To be able to give joyous, unflagging hospitality, not only of house and food, but of mind, heart, body and soul, we need silence.'

Brother Lawrence would do the same. There were times each day which were earmarked for silence when he would simply soak up the love of God. It was from this silence that he would emerge to take up his duties in the kitchen and it was to this silence that he would return at various stages of the day. Stillness punctuated busy-ness.

A meditation

Re-read that quotation from Poustinia *and resolve to create some 'Kingdom moments' this Christmas when you can be still with God.*

JH

Believe in God's presence

Christmas cards can keep alive friendships we value but have little time to foster. One such card I received last year came with the words EMMANUEL—GOD WITH US on the front. It reminded me that God also wants to be remembered. He wants us to benefit from the good news Matthew spells out:

'The virgin will be with child and will give birth to a son, and they will call him Immanuel—which means, "God with us"' (Matthew 1:23).

'God with us.' This means that, whatever happens to us, God is there; that whatever comes next to us comes with God.

Brother Lawrence was so constantly aware of this that he could claim that not only was his prayer nothing but a sense of the presence of God but, even when he was working, he was still conscious of little else than the divine love which enfolds us. So he spent his time praising and blessing God.

Many Christians today testify to a similar sense of the presence of God—as they travel, as they work, as they lie in hospital ... They, too, spend their time praising God through the words of choruses, hymns or the haunting chants which have come to us from the Taizé community. But, as C S. Lewis reminds us, we need not worry when this awareness of the presence of God evaporates: 'The presence of God is not the same as the *sense* of the presence of God ... the *sense* of the presence is a super-added gift for which we give thanks when it comes.'

C. S. Lewis is right. Jesus has promised: 'Never will I leave you; never will I forsake you' (Hebrews 13:5). 'I am with you always, to the very end of the age' (Matthew 28:20). Belief in these promises enables us to live the whole of our lives in the presence of God even when we do not feel him near.

A prayer

Jesus, these eyes have never seen
that radiant form of Thine:
The veil of sense hangs dark between
Thy blessed face and mine.
I see Thee not, I hear Thee not,
Yet art Thou oft with me:
And earth hath ne'er so dear a spot
As where I meet with Thee.
Yet, though I have not seen, and still
Must rest in faith alone,
I love Thee, dearest Lord, and will,
Unseen but not unknown.

Ray Palmer (1801–1887)

JH

Get ready for Christ

In due course John the Baptist appeared; he proclaimed this message in the desert of Judaea, 'Repent, for the kingdom of Heaven is close at hand.' This was the man spoken of by the prophet Isaiah when he said: 'A voice of one that cries in the desert, "Prepare a way for the Lord, make his paths straight."'

On this second Sunday of Advent each year the Baptist calls the People of Israel to repent. He is preparing a way for the Lord, preparing a new community which will be ready to receive the Lord when he comes. He stands at the ford of the River Jordan where the great road from the East to the Mediterranean crosses, a ford at which all kinds of people would pass, soldiers, officials, merchants, business people and farmers. Each of these he challenges to put aside the compromises and bad habits which have become ingrained over the years. His message is uncompromising, yet all he demands for entrance to the community of the Messiah is that they should lay aside excess and return to the way of life due to their profession.

Pray. Lord, as we prepare for the coming of Christ at Christmas, your first demand on us is integrity. Surrounded as we are by the commercial flutter and hype of the pre-Christmas shopping, it is hard to remember the real purpose of this season. You do not demand that we cut ourselves off from the world, that we become self-righteous kill-joys, but only that we prepare to make it a true feast of love. We too want to be your people, preparing to receive you into our lives with new intensity. Help us to remember at least two aspects of this preparation.

As we prepare the parties and the presents, help us to prepare your way by remembering in a practical way those we know who are cut off from this joy and merry-making. Help us to bring joy to just one or two individuals in our circle who are bereaved, or lonely, or cut off by illness or immobility, who are down on their luck, or even who are incompetent, or even who deserve to be unloved.

Help us also to make his paths straight by reviving the vision of beauty of the Christian community, so that the way to you may be straight and that those who seek you, even without knowing it, may find their way to you. May they see the life of Christ in the Christian community. Let peace and generosity be our watchwords, not excess and selfishness.

HW

Never wilfully forget God

On Saturday we placed the spotlight on one of God's names: Emmanuel—God with us. Brother Lawrence was aware that God is not only with us, he resides in us. Taking up the language of Paul he writes: 'We must make of our heart a temple of the Holy Spirit.' Paul put that same sentiment this way: 'Don't you know that you yourselves are God's temple and that God's Spirit lives in you?' (1 Corinthians 3:16). God reminds us through Ezekiel that we are indwelt by the Spirit: 'I will put my Spirit in you . . . you will be my people, and I will be your God' (36:27). Through Jesus, he goes further, promising that he, himself and the Son will take up residence in those who obey him (John 14:23–24).

Because Brother Lawrence was so acutely aware that the King of Kings and Lord of Lords had taken up residence within him, he concluded that he must never wilfully forget or neglect his royal guest. When others asked how they could practise the presence of God he advised them never to allow their minds to wander far from God and never wilfully to neglect him.

This sounds so obvious—even easy—but many Christians discover that the theory is easier than the practice. Within each of us runs an ingrained seam of selfishness which persuades us to choose our own way rather than God's. This selfish streak persuades us,

from time to time, to ignore Paul's advice to the Philippians: 'Whatever is true . . . noble . . . right . . . pure . . . lovely . . . admirable . . . praiseworthy—think about such things' (4:18); to use our senses to watch and listen to and say things which are impure, untrue, unlovely. We then wonder why God seems so far away, forgetting that he hasn't moved but we have distanced him by our behaviour.

Archbishop Anthony Bloom has stated the ideal succinctly and persuasively: 'We must learn to behave in the presence of the invisible Lord as we would in the presence of the Lord made visible to us. This implies primarily an attitude of mind and then its reflection upon the body. If Christ was here, before us, and we stood completely transparent to his gaze, in mind as well as in body, we would feel reverence, the fear of God, adoration or else perhaps terror but we should not be so easy in our behaviour as we are.'

A prayer

O come to us, abide with us
Our Lord, Emmanuel.

Phillips Brooks (1835–1893)

JH

Do nothing which could displease God

Yesterday we saw how Brother Lawrence claimed that he did everything for the love of God—even mundane things like turning the omelette in the pan or like picking up a piece of straw. This attitude was one of the factors which contributed to the unbroken enjoyment of God's presence which characterized his life.

But there was another factor which he was quick to point out to those who asked how they, like him, might learn to tune into the presence of God even when they were busy. He expressed the secret in this way: 'Do nothing, say nothing, and think nothing which may displease Him.'

Isaiah explains why this is so important:

Surely the arm of the Lord is not too
short to save,
nor his ear too dull to hear,
But your iniquities have separated
you from your God;
your sins have hidden his face
    from you,
so that he will not hear.
For your hands are stained with
    blood,
your fingers with guilt.
Your lips have spoken lies,
and your tongue mutters wicked
    things.

Brother Lawrence would be the first to admit that, like us, he failed. His failures erected a barrier between himself and God. But so keen was his awareness of the goodness and love of God that, whenever he became aware of personal failure, he sought reconciliation by confessing and receiving God's freely-offered forgiveness.

At this time of year, the word Saviour is constantly heard through Bible readings and Christmas carols. That word reminds us that we have no need to grovel when our sins separate us from God. All we have to do is to recognize our failure, allow this awareness to point to our need for a Saviour, then turn to the Saviour and ask him to rescue us from the power of our own guilt and waywardness.

A meditation

*You are to give him the name
Jesus because he will save
his people from their sins.*

Luke 1:21

363

Trust God in suffering

Last Advent, a friend telephoned me to tell me that his wife had left him. I ached for them both and wondered how they would cope with the tinsel and trimmings of Christmas when they were hurting so badly inside. And it made me realize that, somehow, we believe that everyone has a right to be happy at Christmas—to be free from emotional or physical pain.

But something my friend said on the phone reminded me of some letters Brother Lawrence had written to someone who appears to have been in intense physical pain. My friend admitted that he and his wife had turned their back on God of late; that the crisis had prompted him to turn back to God. This confession seemed to support Brother Lawrence's claim that 'God has many ways of drawing us to him'. Sometimes he seems to conceal himself from us, 'but the simple faith which will not fail us in time of need must be our support and the foundation of our trust which must be all in God.'

He suggests that we therefore use the crises of life to tune into the ever-present, ever-enveloping love of the heavenly Father and he suggests four ways of doing this.

The first is, 'Worship [God] in your infirmities,' and the second, 'In your worst pain ask him humbly and lovingly, like a child his good father' for the ability to accept his will in the situation and, at the same time, ask for strength and courage to cope. Thirdly, he suggests that, at such times, we surrender ourselves afresh to the ever-faithful God who loves us enough to purify us through suffering. Fourthly, 'console yourself in ... the father of the afflicted, for he is always ready to help us.'

As I thought about my friend's troubles and Brother Lawrence's fourth suggestion, my mind went to Psalm 46:1,11:

God is our refuge and strength,
an ever-present help in
trouble ...
The Lord Almighty is with us;
the God of Jacob is our fortress.

I prayed that in that safe place my friend might find peace in the middle of the storm.

A prayer

As Christmas approaches, pray for those who dread it—the bereaved, families locked in conflict, the homeless, the destitute, those spending Christmas alone.

JH

Believe that God is love

As Christmas draws ever closer, we find ourselves contemplating the mystery which John summarizes in his Gospel: 'God so loved the world that he gave his one and only Son...' (3:16) and those words which come in his epistle: 'God is love' (1 John 4:16).

When national tragedies hit the headlines at this time of year or when personal tragedy strikes, it is easy to doubt John's claims; to forget that love is what God is. But, according to Brother Lawrence, if we are to practise the presence of God, whatever befalls us, we must stake our lives on the fact of God's never-ending love: 'If we knew how much he loves us, we should be ever ready to receive equally at his hand the sweet and the bitter.'

Brother Lawrence wrote that from the experience of having suffered intense physical pain: 'I have been on numerous occasions near to dying... I have... never asked for relief, but I have asked for the strength to suffer with courage, humility and love... It is sweet to suffer with God, great though the sufferings be. Take them with love. It is a Paradise to suffer with him.'

In a letter to a fellow worker in India, Mother Teresa recently wrote something similar: 'Thank you for praying for the healing of my chest—but I am happy to accept whatever He gives and give whatever He takes with a big Smile.'

People for whom the word 'God' conjures up not a picture of love personified but rather a tyrant or a spoil-sport need Christians to bring the light and love of God to them when they are in any kind of need. That is why one of the things God may ask us to do this Christmas is to take his love to someone who is suffering in some way—by buying 'charity' Christmas cards, visiting someone who is housebound or in hospital, supporting those who work for any of the relief agencies or inviting into our homes those for whom Christmas would otherwise be cheerless.

A prayer

Jesus,
shine with hope into the hearts
of those in despair;
warm with love the hearts of those
who have been hurt;
kindle afresh in our hearts
the flame of compassion
that we may take your love to others
this Christmas time.

JH

Surrender yourself

'Be born in us today.' That is a prayer many of us will sing many times between now and Christmas, because it appears in the carol 'O Little Town of Bethlehem'.

Since God was literally born in Mary, the mother of Jesus, we can best understand what that little prayer means by placing the spotlight on this girl who was hand-picked by God to be the mother of his Son.

This teenager from Nazareth whom her aunt described as 'the most blessed of all women' has set every Christian an example of her willingness to place everything she had and everything she was at the disposal of God:

God sent the angel Gabriel to Nazareth ... 'Very soon now, you will become pregnant and have a baby boy, and you are to name him "Jesus". He shall be very great and shall be called the Son of God ...' Mary asked the angel, 'But how can I have a baby? I am a virgin.' The angel replied, 'The Holy Spirit shall come upon you, and the power of God shall overshadow you; so the baby born to you will be utterly holy—the Son of God ...' Mary said, 'I am the Lord's servant, and I am willing to do whatever he wants. May everything you said come true.'

What Mary was doing when she said this momentous 'yes' to God was placing at God's disposal absolutely everything: her home, her possessions, her energy, her ability to give and receive love, her sexuality, her reputation, her body, her emotions, her will, her present, her future.

Such self-abandonment to the will of God, is, according to Brother Lawrence, one of the ways of ensuring that we remain in tune with his enfolding love at every stage of our life: 'We should give ourselves utterly to God in pure abandonment, in temporal and spiritual matters alike, and find contentment in the doing of his will, whether he takes us through sufferings or consolations.'

A prayer

When the Bible uses the word 'heart' it includes: the intellect, the will, the emotions, the imagination, the ability to love.

What can I give him
Poor as I am?
If I were a shepherd,
I would bring a lamb;
If I were a wise man,
I would do my part;
Yet what I can I give Him—
Give my heart.

Christina Rossetti
(1830–1894)

JH

Recall God's goodness

Yesterday we reminded ourselves of Mary's selfless surrender to God. When she became 'the selfless space where God became man', she seemed to be thinking of one person only: God. But God is no man's debtor. He made available to her his own vast resources and took responsibility for her. So when Joseph, her fiancé, threatened to break off the relationship, God broke into his confusion and convinced him that Mary was speaking the truth when she said that the Father of her baby was God:

An angel of the Lord appeared to [Joseph] in a dream and said, 'Joseph, son of David, do not be afraid to take Mary home as your wife, because what is conceived in her is from the Holy Spirit . . .' When Joseph woke up, he did what the angel of the Lord commanded him and took Mary home as his wife.

If Joseph had refused to marry Mary, she and her family would have been publicly disgraced so the divine intervention must have filled them all with joy. Like Mary, Brother Lawrence found himself on the receiving end of God's generosity and faithfulness. So much so that he once wrote: 'We have a God infinitely good, and who knows what we need ... He will come in his good time, and when you least expect him. Hope in him more than ever. Thank him for the favours that he shows you, particularly for the strength and the patience he is giving you ... an evident sign of the care he has for you.'

He goes on to claim that one of the rewards of learning to practise the presence of God is that for the Christian who masters this form of prayer faith becomes more alive. Because, 'by a simple act of the memory', they see and feel that God is ever-present in all situations, it becomes natural to talk to him 'easily and meaningfully' so that, eventually, they can almost claim: 'I no longer believe, I see and I experience.'

A prayer

Think back over occasions when you have experienced God taking responsibility for you or intervening on your behalf in some way and pray Mary's prayer:

*My soul glorifies the Lord
and my spirit rejoices
in God my Saviour . . .
for the Mighty One has done
great things for me—
holy is his name.*

Luke 1:46, 49

JH

Creating the kingdom

He is the one of whom scripture says, 'Look, I am going to send my messenger in front of you to prepare your way before you.' In truth I tell you, of all the children born to women, there has never been anyone greater than John the Baptist; yet the least in the kingdom of Heaven is greater than he.

In the preparation for Christmas, this third Sunday of Advent is the second Sunday of the Baptist. Last week the Baptist was preparing a community into which the Messiah might come, a nest ready to receive him. This Sunday is the moment when John actually points him out as the Lamb of God. But here is a passage which gives us the reverse, not the Baptist's introduction to Jesus, but Jesus' own view of the Baptist.

Pray. Lord Jesus, you paid tribute to the Baptist who pointed you out as God's final messenger. But, more than this, you must have meant that with your coming creation reached its climax. Evolution had gone on over the long centuries since the universe became recognizably a universe. It still continues, with thousands of creatures coming into being each day and thousands going out of existence. But we who are your followers see the process not as a continuous line, or series of lines, or even a loop or circle, but as a picture brought into focus and given meaning by your appearing. Were it not for the kingdom of God, the picture would consist of random strokes and meaningless dots and dashes. Your kingdom at least reveals its sense and purpose.

The daunting and joyful element for us in your statement about John is that the kingdom consists of people. Our dignity as members of your kingdom is immense, our privilege unfathomable, chosen out of all possible beings. This is a cause of gratitude and praise to you. But you give us this privilege not simply so that we can congratulate or cuddle ourselves. With the gift, you give us responsibility as members of your kingdom to spread your kingdom of love, peace and justice. Even the least in the kingdom of God must be a cell reproducing itself, a focus of life, flowering and broadening to those on every side.

HW

Expect to fall

At this very busy time of year there are many reasons why we might fail in our attempt to follow Brother Lawrence's example—to practise the presence of God. In addition to our normal routine, there are presents to buy and wrap, cards to choose and send, carol services and parties to attend and family reunions to look forward to or dread. All this can become quite overwhelming.

Brother Lawrence not only expects us to fail in our attempt to tune into the presence of God, he urges us not to allow ourselves to grow discouraged:

'Be not disheartened at your many falls; truly this habit [of practising the presence of God] can only be formed with difficulty.' It requires time and great patience but it is worth persevering because when the habit of practising the presence of God has been made 'it can give great joy'.

One reason why Brother Lawrence persuades us not to despair when we allow busy-ness or tiredness to elbow out the sense of God's presence is that he himself had found it difficult to master this form of prayer but God had so honoured his struggles that the day came when he could claim: 'For me the time of action does not differ from the time of prayer, and in the noise and clatter of my kitchen, while several persons are together calling for as many different things, I possess God in as great tranquillity as when upon my knees at the Blessed Sacrament.'

Another reason is that he believed fervently that God's love for us does not run dry when we cease to recognize his presence. His love never gives up. As God expresses it through Hosea:

**How can I give you up . . .?
How can I hand you over . . .?
For I am God, and not man—
the Holy One among you.**

A prayer of Brother Lawrence

*O Lord,
enlarge the chambers of my heart
that I may find room for Thy love.*

A prayer

*Thou didst leave Thy throne
And Thy kingly crown
When Thou camest to earth for me;
But in Bethlehem's home
Was there found no room
For Thy holy nativity:
O come to my heart, Lord Jesus;
There is room in my heart for Thee.*

Emily E. Steele Elliott (1836–1897)

JH

Love for the world

The angel Gabriel was sent by God to a town in Galilee called Nazareth, to a virgin betrothed to a man named Joseph, of the House of David; and the virgin's name was Mary. He went in and said to her, 'Rejoice, you who enjoy God's favour! . . . Look! You are to conceive in your womb and bear a son, and you must name him Jesus.'

In the week before Christmas our thoughts go to Mary as she waits for her son to be born. She had received the divine message which enabled her to appreciate the meaning of the mysterious conception of her child. Following the conventions of the time the divine message is represented as brought by a messenger. The terms in which the message is expressed are those of fulfilment of all the promises made to God's People; God's favour was guaranteed to the line of David, and this guarantee comes to its completion in the renewal of the world. Every mother reflects, during those long nine months as the baby signals its growth ever more insistently, on the destiny of the child to be born. Mary no doubt turned over in her mind the words of God's promises, seeking to see how they would be completed in her beloved child. How would he renew the world? How would he bring God's kingdom to be?

Pray. As Christmas is finally upon us, we reflect, Lord, on the meaning of those promises for us.

Who is Jesus for me?

Where is he to be found? In the church and the prayer at the bedside, or in the sick and marginalized, in those I meet as I go about my business of engaging in the delights and the chores of life?

Help me to see your son in everyone.

How does he affect my destiny? As a jack-in-the-box to be kept fastened up except when I choose to open the box on Sundays, or as a continual presence at least in the background of my life? Is Christ's presence as real to me as it was to Mary?

Enable me to keep your son at my side.

What is this renewal of the world? Help me at Christmas to renew the world, to bring your kingdom more to completion in some way, to further your will and liberate your love just that little fraction more effectively.

HW

Incarnation in you

'I am the handmaid of the Lord' said Mary, 'let what you have said be done to me.' And the angel left her.

When we read the Scriptures, we are not just reading of events of two or three thousand years ago: we are reading about our own lives. The God of Abraham, Isaac and Jacob, the Father of Our Lord Jesus Christ, is the God who now holds you and me in existence. In today's reading, Mary is told she is to become the mother of a child, 'who will be great and will be called Son of the Most High'. As Christians we believe that child grew up, died and rose again. He lives now in you and me. 'The Spirit of him who raised Jesus from the dead is living in you' (Romans 8:11). St Paul prays for the Ephesians that through the Spirit their inner self will grow strong, 'so that Christ may live in your hearts through faith' (Ephesians 3:17).

St Paul also wrote, 'For to me, to live is Christ' (Philippians 1:21, RSV). The poet Gerard Manley Hopkins writes of Mary that she:

> *This one work has to do—*
> *Let all God's glory through.*

So the meaning of our life is to let Christ be in us in our circumstances, in our family, with our temperament, abilities and disabilities.

When Mary first hears the news, her first reaction is to be deeply disturbed. Even when reassured by the angel with, 'Do not be afraid you have won God's favour', she is still not satisfied and asks, 'But how can this be?'

When we realize God is inviting us to change our ways, to let Christ be in us, to forgive instead of nursing resentment, to treat others as we would have them treat us, to love our enemies, it is disturbing. We ask ourselves, as Mary did, How can this be? I am too weak, my friends will think me stupid, I shall be laughed at.

In imagination, talk to Mary about your fears and listen to her saying to the angel, 'Let what you have said be done to me.'

A prayer

God, may Mary's words, 'Let what you have said be done to me', be the words of my heart, so that my whole being may become a channel of your peace.

GWH

Where God is, joy is there, too

Why should I be honoured with a visit from the mother of my Lord? For the moment your greeting reached my ears, the child in my womb leapt for joy.

St Thomas Aquinas, the great theologian, was forever asking himself questions. One question was, 'Why did God create the world?' His answer was, 'Because goodness is, of its nature, expansive.' When we receive good news, most of us have an irresistible urge to communicate it and have a celebration. Goodness is not only expansive, it grows in the spreading. Think of those scenes of delight on TV when the Berlin wall came down.

Mary, in her delight, rushes over the hills to share the good news with Elizabeth, so intensifying the delight of both that the baby dances in Elizabeth's womb and Mary speaks her exultant poem, 'My soul magnifies the Lord'.

'A sad saint is a sad kind of saint.' Committed Christians are more noted for their extreme earnestness than for their exuberant joy. Joy, when manifest in Christian gatherings, often appears dutiful, and so ends with the religious service.

We need to pray to know in our hearts the joy of God's goodness. That is why the Psalmist keeps praying, 'Show me your face.' To know the goodness of

God is to divert attention from me, my preoccupations, anxieties, failings and fears, and to centre them on my true self, my Christ-self, rooted in God, my rock and my refuge. The delight I experience, I shall want to communicate, and from this new perspective I shall be able to laugh at my own self-importance. Hear God say to you, calling you by name, 'Before the world was, I chose you, chose you in Christ, to live through love in my presence' (Ephesians 1:4). Be still, and let those words sink through your mind into your heart. Those words are life-giving, and you will have to communicate your joy.

A prayer

Lord, speak to my heart and show me your attractiveness, so that surrendering my personal kingdom, I may enter yours.

GWH

His power in our weakness

My soul proclaims the greatness of the Lord and my spirit exults in God, my saviour.

A very useful exercise is to take a piece of paper, divide it into two columns, one headed 'events which enliven me', the other 'events which deaden me', then scribble down whatever thoughts come to you, without trying to analyse or judge what you write. 'Events' can include anything or anyone. Once you have started, you can keep adding to both columns later. Many people discover that the first things which come to mind are external events and other people, but later discover that they are writing about their own attitudes, the way they think and react to these external events. If, for example, I only come to life when I succeed in some achievement, or prove myself better than someone else, then failure will always deaden me, and I am doomed to failure in the end.

Mary's delight, expressed in the Magnificat, has nothing to do with her sense of personal achievement. Her delight is in God's greatness. He, not she, pulls down princes from their thrones and exalts the lowly, fills the hungry with good things and sends the rich empty away. It is precisely because she recognizes her own littleness that she can delight in God's greatness.

We can now do some analysis on our own lists. To what extent has my list of events which enliven nothing to do with my achievements, my superiority over others? If you do find that your list has everything to do with your personal achievements and successes, don't be dispirited. You can learn something very valuable from this discovery, namely that the secret of peace and happiness is to move the centre of your consciousness from the narrow limits of your own kingdom, and set it instead in his kingdom of justice, mercy and compassion for all creation.

A prayer

O God, enlighten my mind and set it free from my imprisoning self, so that I may delight in your wisdom and goodness and become its willing servant.

GWH

373

Deeper into God

Yahweh, make your ways known to me, teach me your paths. Set me in the way of your truth, and teach me, for you are the God who saves me . . . All Yahweh's paths are love and truth.

Literally, 'Advent' means 'The Coming'. In fact, God neither comes, nor goes: He is. But we need to use such terms to help us understand the reality in which we are living. God is always present to us and in us. We have to come to consciousness of his presence within us and amongst us, that he is the reality in which we are living.

The Psalmist is aware of this truth, so keeps on praying 'Make me know your ways, teach me your paths.' The same awareness is deep in Christian consciousness and that is why the Church, from earliest times, has been called the 'Pilgrim Church'. Individually and corporately, we are on a journey, engaged in an Advent, a coming to God, but the journey is an inner journey of our minds and hearts, a journey of our consciousness through the labyrinthine ways of our minds, through the barriers of our conditioning, of our fears, anxieties and false assumptions, to the truth of our being, that we are called to be at one with God, in Christ. The pathway is the path of truth, for God is truth. In struggling to be true, to be as we show ourselves and to show ourselves as we are, we are approaching God. We can only come to him through the everyday events of our lives: there is no other way. As we approach him along the path of truth, his faithfulness and love will become ours, so that our thoughts and fears will no longer centre on 'me'. We shall gradually be liberated from our self-preoccupations and become more free to enter the mind and heart of God, who loves all his creation and whose living Spirit is in all.

A prayer

Be with us in Advent, guiding our steps along the paths of truth, of faithfulness and love.

GWH

God with us——our lover

You are to be a crown of splendour in the hand of Yahweh... no longer are you to be named, 'Forsaken'... but you shall be called 'My Delight', and your land, 'The Wedded'... Like a young man marrying a virgin, so will the one who built you wed you, and as the bridegroom rejoices in his bride, so will your God rejoice in you.

These words of Isaiah are addressed to Israel, exiled in Babylon, forsaken and abandoned. The passage compares God's relationship to Israel to a marriage, re-echoing the promise of Isaiah 54, 'For now your creator will be your husband, his name, Yahweh Sabaoth... He is called the God of the whole earth.'

The Christian Church sees the fulfilment of these words in the birth of Jesus, the at-one-ment, for in him, heaven and earth have met.

Christmas Eve in Britain is a day of frantic last-minute shopping and preparation for those who have money to spend, family and friends to celebrate with: for others, without money, or family, or friends, it can be a day of acute pain and grief at their own loss. Whether engaged in exhausting activity, or caught up in the pain of loss, give yourself a few minutes to ask, 'Why the rush, why the pain?' Make these few minutes your Christmas present to yourself, so that you can begin to recognize the gift you have been given, beyond price, which no one can take from you and which grows more precious with every Christmas. The gift is your life.

With our conscious minds we can only grasp a fraction of the reality in which we live. The reality is 'Emmanuel', that God is with us, whether we are rich or poor, surrounded by family and friends, or bereft of both. Let God into your mind and heart, to delight with you, or weep with you. If we let him into our delight, he will increase it, for his delight is in giving. He prompts us to be generous and saves us from destructive self-indulgence. If we let him into our pain, he becomes a light to our darkness. The shepherds, poor men and homeless, were the first to see the child.

A prayer

God, still our minds and hearts, so that we may recognize your loving presence in every experience of our lives.

GWH

This is our God . . .

Now at this time Caesar Augustus issued a decree for a census of the whole world to be taken...So Joseph set out from the town of Nazareth in Galilee and travelled up... to the town of David called Bethlehem, since he was of David's House and line, in order to be registered together with Mary, his betrothed, who was with child. While they were there the time came for her to have her child, and she gave birth to a son, her first-born. She wrapped him in swaddling clothes, and laid him in a manger because there was no room for them at the inn.

As we listen to the Christmas story we shall worship and wonder at the fact of the incarnation. But we also need to ask 'What does it mean?' for us now (as the Hebrews would have done). We ask the story to put us in touch with our present reality, so that we can better understand it. Pondering Luke's sentence, 'She wrapped him in swaddling clothes' can put us in touch with the reality of God now.

There is a story in the earliest Greek historian, Herodotus, of a Greek tyrant who heard that a child was to be born who would usurp his throne. The tyrant discovered the parents and sent seven policemen to the house with instructions to ask to see the child, hold it, then dash it to the ground. The unsuspecting mother handed the child over to policeman No. 1. He raised it up to dash it to the ground, but as he did so, the child smiled at him, so he passed it on to policeman No. 2, to whom the same thing happened. The smiling child overwhelmed all seven, so they warned the mother of the tyrant's plot and advised her to keep the child hidden. He was thereafter named 'Cypselos', the hidden one, and eventually usurped the tyrant.

We can be infected with terrifying images of God: God the avenger, God the punisher, God whose one interest is in our sins. Ponder the child lying in the manger. See him smile on you. He is the image of the unseen God. He entrusts himself to us, is restricted as we are, enters into our pain and sinfulness, into our death, and is risen again.

God comes to us in gentleness. Christ is constantly being born in you and me. When we are prompted to act justly, to love tenderly, to walk humbly before God, those are the stirrings of the Christ-self coming to birth within us.

A prayer

God, by our communion with God made man, may we become more like him, in whom our lives are made one with yours.

GWH

The Spirit within us

As they were stoning him, Stephen said in invocation, 'Lord Jesus, receive my spirit'. Then he knelt down and said aloud, 'Lord, do not hold this sin against them'; and with these words he fell asleep.

At first, it seems odd that the Church should celebrate the feast of St Stephen on 26 December, instead of continuing to reflect on Jesus' birth and infancy, but on reflection we can see how right it is, because Christmas is also celebrating the meaning of our own lives.

Today's reading describes the Spirit of the living Christ at work in the infant Church. The Book of Acts says of Stephen that when members of the Sanhedrin began to dispute with him they were defeated by his wisdom, because it was the Spirit that prompted what he said. This infuriated his opponents, who rushed at him and stoned him. Dying, the Spirit of Christ prayed in Stephen 'receive my spirit', echoing Jesus' cry on the cross, 'Into thy hands I commend my spirit'. Finally, he prays, 'Lord, do not hold this sin against them', echoing Jesus' 'Father, forgive them.'

The Christ who lived in Stephen lives in you and me. For a child, Christmas is a magical time, a time of delight, of gifts and surprises. For most of us, sadly, sooner or later, the magic diappears, and for some, Christmas becomes the most painful season of the year, for it forces us to face our own disillusionment, broken dreams, torn relationships, losses and failures. We should pray to God to restore to us that childlike sense of wonder, not at the external trappings of Christmas, but at the truth it celebrates, namely that the gift of God to us is the gift of life, which is a share in his own life. This gift is continuously being offered, no matter what damage may have been done to us, or damage we have done.

A prayer

God, you sent the Holy Spirit, who lived in Jesus and raised him from the dead, into Stephen, who died praying for his enemies. Deepen our faith in the presence of your Spirit within us, so that we, too, may bear witness to you in our lives and in our death.

GWH

The wedding of God with us

Something that has existed from the beginning, that we have heard, and we have seen with our own eyes ... this is our subject ... What we have seen and heard we are telling you so that you too may be in union with us, as we are in union with the Father and with his Son Jesus Christ.

John the Evangelist is also called St John the Divine, because his Gospel emphasizes the divinity of Christ.

The first miracle in John's Gospel is the marriage feast of Cana, when Jesus turns the water into wine. John ends his description of the miracle with, 'This was the first of the signs given by Jesus.'

The Cana wedding is a symbol of the real wedding between God and humanity in the person of Jesus. The symbolism is emphasized by the miracle, in which water, representing our humanity, is transformed into wine, representing divinity. The Roman Missal has a prayer 'Grant that by mixing this water and wine, we may share in his Divinity, who humbled himself to share our humanity.'

At Christmas, we celebrate Jesus' birth in order to help us understand the gift of our own lives. We can identify ourselves in all kinds of ways: in economic terms as a high earner, a low earner, or on the dole; in social terms, as upper, middle, lower, or under-class. We can identify ourselves in terms of religious affiliation, political leanings, in ethnic terms. We can also identify ourselves in spiritual and moral terms as no good, hopeless, sinful, doomed to failure, or virtuous, law-abiding, godly, upright.

Whoever we are, and however high or low on the success ladder's rung we may think ourselves to be, Christmas is reminding us that these comparisons are an irrelevance. Our real value does not rest in any of these things, but in the truth that our existence is an invitation to let God be God in us and touch us. 'For now your creator will be your husband ... He is called the God of the whole earth' (Isaiah 54:5).

A prayer

God, help us to recognize that you are calling us in all the messiness, disappointments and failures of our lives, and transforming us into the image of your Son.

GWH

Give me your fears

Get up, take the child and his mother with you, and escape into Egypt, and stay there until I tell you, because Herod intends to search for the child and do away with him.

This story keeps recurring in history. The individual, or group, in power will go to any lengths, including the murder of the innocent, to retain their power.

It is said that the most powerful are also the most insecure, a saying which, at first sight, seems very improbable. Whatever else we may say of Genghis Khan, Stalin and Hitler—or even Sir Winston Churchill or Lady Thatcher—it is not immediately obvious that they are lacking in confidence!

Fear is one of our most powerful emotions. In the grip of fear, we can surprise and surpass ourselves. If chased by a bull, we can discover a surprising speed and agility.

Pondering our existence can be very frightening. What does the future hold for us in this life? After death, does it all end, or are we bound for heaven and eternal bliss, or hell and eternal agony? Most of us opt for not thinking: some can do so with ease, others must engage in frenetic activity to dull the fear. As children, we whistle in the dark to reassure ourselves: as adults, we make use of less innocent means, controlling and exercising power over others. The greater our capacity to experience fear, the more power and control we need to reassure ourselves and keep our fears at bay. Our instinct for self-preservation, our most primitive and strongest instinct, becomes perverted into the desire to control, whatever the cost, even if it is the death and destruction of others. Herod, no doubt, justified his action to himself and to others by declaring that his action was in the interests of national security. We do the same today.

We need to look at our own fear, then look at the child in the manger. God is saying to us, 'Don't be afraid. You are bound neither for oblivion, nor for hellfire. Give me your fears, and then you will live, and living, bring life to others.'

A prayer

God, grant us the grace to face our fears, so that in them we may recognize you beckoning us to let go our own desire to control. Show yourself to be our rock, our refuge, our only security.

GWH

The condition of happiness

When the parents brought in the child Jesus to do for him what the law required, [Simeon] took him into his arms and blessed God; and he said, 'Now, Master, you can let your servant go in peace, just as you promised; because my eyes have seen the salvation which you have prepared for all the nations to see, a light to enlighten the pagans and the glory of your people Israel.'

The Gospel gives little detail about Simeon except that he was an upright man, who had been told that he would not die until his eyes had seen the promised Messiah. When he recognizes the fulfilment of the promise in this child being presented in the temple, he tells God that he is now ready to die in peace. He sees the child as a bond of unity for all peoples, and as a light to dispel the world's darkness. In effecting this unity and understanding, he prophesies that the child will meet with opposition, be rejected, and that his fate will pierce his mother's heart. But in that opposition, masks will drop and the truth of our hearts will be revealed.

As the old year dies, we are reminded of the certainty of our own death, a certainty which we normally keep hidden away in an insulated part of our minds, lest it infect our consciousness with gloom and foreboding. Simeon has no such fear. He has longed for the unity of all peoples, for light in our darkness, for God's presence to be manifest in Israel, and now he believes he has seen the answer to his longing, so he is ready to let go of life.

This story of Simeon raises useful questions for us. What is the ultimate longing of my life? With that longing satisfied, would I face death with peace, or with dread? If the longing of my life is my own glorification, then I must face 'that strange and uttermost collapse of all that makes me man', with dread. If the longing of my life is 'Glory to God and peace on earth', that Christ should live in me, then I shall see death, not as annihilation, but as another stage on my journey into God, in whom all created things have their being.

A prayer

God, grant us the courage so to face the fact of our death—that we may live fully in Christ, and meet our death in peace.

GWH

'God, who is, who was, and who is to come...'

The Word was made flesh, he lived among us, and we saw his glory, the glory that is his as the only Son of the Father, full of grace and truth ... from his fulness we have, all of us, received—yes, grace in return for grace.

Today, the media will be full of reviews of the year. It is good for us to do our own personal review of the year. Take time to relax, then ask yourself, 'What have I found good this year?' Even if it has been the blackest year of your life, start by looking at what has been positive for you. Don't rush over this exercise—take time to relish the good memories. God is the source of all that is good, so thank him for his gifts. Avoid any self-judgment, approval or disapproval. 'From his fulness we have, all of us, received—yes, grace in return for grace.' He gives us these gifts, not because we deserve them, or have earned them, but because it is of the nature of God to give life and love.

Then pray for enlightenment. In everything that has happened during the past year, God has been drawing you to himself. Now look at the pain and darkness of the past year, your losses, failures, anxieties, fears. Show them to God and beg for light. God does not inflict pain on us. Part of our pain is self-inflicted. We can cling to things and to people as though they were our ultimate good. When they are taken from us, we suffer, but the suffering can teach us to realize that our ultimate good is not in them. Or we may feel pain on behalf of others, sharing their grief, their losses. This is the pain of compassion. God, the God of compassion, shares that pain with us.

Pray to know God's presence in all the joys and sorrows of the coming year.

A prayer

God, keep our minds and hearts directed to your goodness in the coming year, so that, knowing your forgiveness for all our failings, we may become channels of your forgiveness and peace to all whom we meet in the coming year.

GWH

Notes from BRF

If you have enjoyed reading and using *Day by Day* volume 2 you may wish to know that similar material is available from BRF in a regular series of Bible reading notes, *New Daylight*, which is published three times a year (in January, May and September) and contains printed Bible passages, brief comments, and prayers.

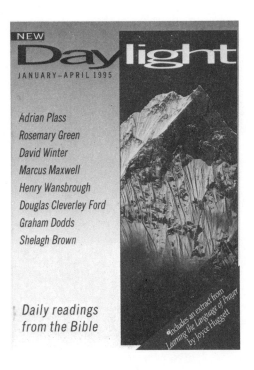

For further information, contact your local Christian bookshop or, in case of difficulty, The Bible Reading Fellowship, Peter's Way, Sandy Lane West, Oxford, OX4 5HG.

Anthologies from BRF

Two thoughtful and wide-ranging resource books of quotations, Biblical and other, which contain insights into 2000 years of Christian and religious experience, covering a broad range of subjects. For personal use, for sermons and talks, and for reflection groups, with advice about how to use the material with groups. An ideal gift for adult confirmation, ordination, birthdays or Christmas.

Visions of Hope
0 7459 2591 X

Visions of Love
0 7459 2522 7

Price: £9.99 each